CHINA'S
BITTER
THE WAR
WITH JAPAN
1937–1945
VICTORY

CHINA'S BITTER VICTORY

THE WAR WITH JAPAN 1937–1945

Edited by
JAMES C. HSIUNG & STEVEN I. LEVINE

An East Gate Book
M.E. Sharpe, Inc.
Armonk, New York
London, England

An East Gate Book

Copyright © 1992 by M. E. Sharpe, Inc.

All rights reserved. No part of this book may be reproduced in any
form without written permission from the publisher, M. E. Sharpe, Inc.,
80 Business Park Drive, Armonk, New York 10504.

Library of Congress Cataloging-in-Publication Data

China's bitter victory : the war with Japan, 1937–1945 / [edited] by
James C. Hsiung & Steven I. Levine
p.   cm. (Studies on modern China)
Includes bibliographical references and index.
ISBN 0-87332-708-X(cloth)   ISBN 1-56324-246-X (pbk.)
1. Sino-Japanese Conflict, 1937–1945. I. Hsiung, James Chieh,
1935– . II. Levine, Steven I. III. Series.
DS777.53.C525   1991
940.53—dc20
91-6961
CIP

Printed in the United States of America

The paper used in this publication meets the minimum requirements
of American National Standard for Information Sciences—
Permanence of Paper for Printed Library Materials, ANSI Z39.48-1984.
♾
MV (c)   10   9   8   7   6   5   4   3   2
MV (p)   10   9   8   7   6   5   4   3   2   1

To the countless victims, many of them nameless,
of what was in effect an Asian Holocaust,
probably on an even grander scale

CONTENTS

PREFACE

James C. Hsiung

MORE THAN forty-five years have passed since the guns fell silent, signaling the end of the bloody Sino-Japanese War of 1937–45. During those eight terrible years, the Chinese people endured what was probably the most brutal war ever fought in the Pacific region, but the story of how they survived has not yet been fully told. Meanwhile, of course, much has been written about the experience of other countries and peoples during World War II. The gap relating to China in the literature of World War II is extremely unfortunate, to say the least.

The attitudes of the principal Chinese parties in this tragic conflict obviously have had a great deal to do with the perpetuation of this lacuna. Due to their long-standing mutual enmity, neither the Kuomintang authorities in Taipei nor the Chinese Communist rulers in Peking can agree on who should get credit for the victory that finally came in 1945.[1] Neither party has yet provided very much detailed and comprehensive information in a form that presents a composite picture of China's eight-year War of Resistance. Instead, there have been piece-meal releases of information about particular military campaigns and the publication of memoirs by a few remaining veteran military leaders.

In contrast, voluminous accounts have appeared in Japan of the glorious exploits of the Imperial Army during the Pacific War. The Japanese, however, have no compelling reasons to tell the whole truth about an event that many among them now much prefer to gloss over or forget. In its controversial textbook revisions of the 1980s, Tokyo sought to play down the aggressive war launched by the Japanese militarists of the 1930s as a mere "forward advance" in China.[2] In early 1988, a member of the Japanese cabinet unabashedly proclaimed that the Japanese invasion of China five decades earlier was not an act of aggression. Although he subsequently resigned under fire from the opposition, he was forced to do so for his undiplomatic behavior rather than for his historical inaccuracy.[3] Indeed, in that episode, a group of forty-one politicians in the ruling Liberal Democratic party rushed to his defense, and a significant number of Japanese were also reported to agree with him.[4] It is an indisputable fact that more innocent Chinese were massacred by Japanese soldiers in the December 1937 Rape of Nanking than Japanese were killed by the atomic bomb dropped on Hiroshima in 1945, yet present-day Japanese youths are asking whether Nanking was really raped.[5]

It is not surprising that historians, lacking uninhibited access to archives that the principal parties still jealously guard from impartial scrutiny, have not yet been able to produce authoritative assessments of the Sino-Japanese War. In undertaking this book, our collective purpose has been the modest objective of making a start at reviewing the tragedy of the Sino-Japanese War within its overall historical context. For that purpose, the co-editors assembled a team of scholars, all of whom are well-established authorities in their fields. Each of these scholars enjoys a well-deserved reputation for independent and unbiased work. Together they address a cross-section of important topics relating to wartime China during 1937–45.

What we have produced is not a rehashed short history of the war that merely chronicles the military conflict.[6] Rather, ours is a book about China itself—the political, diplomatic, military, economic, and cultural dimensions of an eight-year struggle that China did not seek in the first place and that it was initially not prepared to fight. While other accounts cover only certain aspects of the war, such as military battles or the human suffering, our volume takes a holistic approach to the question of how the country responded to the impact of war. Other books focus only on certain subperiods, but ours covers the war in its entirety. As such, to the best of our knowledge, there is no other volume like ours.

A bit of the inside history of this project may be in order. At the outset of our endeavor, in my capacity as co-editor, I negotiated in earnest with authorities in Taipei to secure unprecedented access for the book's contributors to the archives in the holdings of the Kuomintang Party History Commission (Tang Shih Hui), the government's National Archives Agency (Kuo Shih Kuan) and the Military History Bureau (Shih Cheng Chu) of the Ministry of National Defense. After initial approval had been granted, one of the principal negotiators in Taipei, who happened to be the key "gatekeeper" to the archives, unexpectedly took objection to the makeup of our team of scholars. In particular, he demanded the removal of two contributors who, in his opinion, were too "uncontrollable" (meaning not pro-KMT). We categorically rejected this unacceptable demand, preferring to sacrifice the privilege of archival access rather than to compromise the academic independence and integrity of our team. This stance eventually cost us our privilege of access to the Taiwan archives. Our co-authors, therefore, had to resort largely to their personal research files and to sources available in the West, plus additional archival materials in the PRC made available, on a case-by-case basis, through the Chinese Academy of Social Sciences (CASS) in Peking, under a special agreement negotiated on behalf of the project.

Thus, if critics should take us to task for not having availed ourselves in all cases of the wealth of archival sources in Taipei, or for having relied too heavily on Western and Chinese Communist sources, our response—contrary to the convention observed in most scholarly works—is that the fault lies not with us but somewhere else. This is why we feel constrained to share the above information with the reader. We tried our best, but failed in our bid for access simply because we refused to surrender our intellectual honesty and integrity.

Despite this disappointment, we believe that we have accomplished what we set out to achieve—a one-volume account of China during the war years of 1937–45 that provides the reader with a concise but comprehensive and informative account of the Chinese holocaust. Our only remaining regret is that the pressure of other obligations led to the voluntary withdrawal of one of our original contributors and thus deprived us of a chapter on wartime social conditions that he had originally intended to write. This missing chapter was supposed to have provided us with an analysis, among other things, of the sweat and tears of ordinary Chinese people, of the bloodshed, sorrows, and tribulations that the war had inflicted upon the Chinese people as a whole.[7]

It remains to be said that our ultimate purpose in presenting this broad review of a too often forgotten tragedy is not to contribute to a spirit of retribution for the historical misdeeds of the past. It is, rather, to offer hope that we can all gain some wisdom from a careful scrutiny of history, and that through such an effort the tragedy of the Sino-Japanese War, no less than that of World War II in its entirety, shall never be repeated.

In addition to the co-authors whose names appear in these pages, a number of other persons have been helpful in giving us advice and encouragement in the preparation of this book. Space permits us only to mention briefly the following persons: Professors Samuel Chu of Ohio State University, Winberg Chai of the University of Wyoming, Shao-chuan Leng of the University of Virginia, T. K. Tong of the City College of New York, and C. Martin Wilbur of Columbia University. During the early stages of the book project, the co-editors were ably assisted by Yang-shan Chou and Patricia Lane. A grant from the Contemporary U.S.-Asia Research Institute helped to defray all incidental expenses, including those for a planning conference held in late 1985 in New York, during which the research strategy for the book and the division of labor among its co-authors were discussed and decided.

A word about romanization is in order. Because the time frame of the book predates the introduction of the pinyin system, we have chosen to use the Wade-Giles system of romanizing Chinese words with only two modifications: (a) Well-known post-office place names like Chungking or Canton are used in their familiar spellings; (b) Where idiosyncratic spellings for certain personal names, such as T. V. Soong and Chiang Kai-shek, were in use at the time, we use these spellings instead of their proper Wade-Giles transliterations. One problem is presented by Chinese Communist names in publications from the PRC subsequent to January 1, 1979. In these instances, we use the pinyin spelling followed in parentheses by its Wade-Giles equivalent the first time the name appears, e.g., "Zhu De (Chu Te)." For the convenience of readers, a separate Wade-Giles–pinyin conversion table is provided.

Notes

1. For recent Taiwan criticisms of Chinese Communist "distortions" of the history of China's War of Resistance against Japan, see Ting Chao-ch'iang, "History Cannot Be Distorted [by the Chinese Communists]—Rectification of Some Important Historical Facts Regarding the War of Resistance," *Chung-yang jih-pao* (Central daily news), December 14, 1988; also Mei Ch'ing, "On the Chinese Communist Obstruction During the War of Resistance and Deliberate Distortion of the War's History," *Chung-kuo ta-lu yen-chiu* (Chinese mainland studies) 28, 3 (September 1985):51–57. The Chinese Communist party (CCP) has changed its position since 1985 on the question of which party actually bore the brunt of the war effort and brought victory to China. In the summer of 1985, an exhibit was mounted in Peking of historical records and artifacts celebrating the fortieth anniversary of the end of the War of Resistance. This exhibit, which I happened to visit, contained a huge display outlining the background and progression of the war. It stated that the "regular armed forces at the command of the National Government, led by the Kuomintang, fought this the most crucial of wars confronting the life or death of the Chinese nation." The irregular troops commanded by the CCP, the huge poster added, carried on their share of the war effort "behind enemy lines." This was the first indication that the CCP's official interpretation of the war had changed from its previous claim that the KMT forces were not fighting the Japanese and that only the CCP was actively engaged in battle. For the CCP's previous position, see PLA Military Academy, *Di erci shijie dazhan* (Ti-erh-tz'u shih-chieh ta-chan) (The Second World War) (Beijing: World Knowledge Press, 1984). For the revised CCP position, see "Reassessing the War in China," *Beijing Review*, August 12, 1985, pp. 13–32.

2. For more detailed discussion of the textbook issue, see Allen S. Whiting, *China Eyes Japan* (Berkeley: University of California Press, 1989), pp. 46–51, 55–60.

3. *Japan Times* (Tokyo), May 12 and 13, 1988. See also Ami Miyazaki, "Japan's Role in World War II? Take Your Pick of History," *Japan Times Weekly*, June 11, 1988.

4. Urban C. Lehner, "More Japanese Deny Nation Was Aggressor," *Wall Street Journal*, September 8, 1988.

5. Ibid. On the history of the 1937 Nanking massacre, see Mi Chu Wiens, "Historical Archival Data on the Rape of Nanking," in *K'ang-chan sheng-li ti tai-chia* (The costs of China's victory in the War of Resistance), ed. Hsu Cho-yun et al. (Taipei: Lien-ching Press, 1986), pp. 73–78; "Nanjing Massacre: A Dark Page in History," *Beijing Review*, September 2, 1985, pp. 15–21.

6. One recent volume on the course of the actual military battles is Dick Wilson, *When Tigers Fight: The Story of the Sino-Japanese War, 1937–1945* (New York: Penguin Books, 1983).

7. To make up for the gap, readers may consult Ernest M. Wampler, *China Suffers* (Elgin, IL: Brethren Publishing, 1945); also Lin Yutang, *Vigil of a Nation* (London: Heinemann, 1946).

CONTRIBUTORS

Robert E. Bedeski is professor of political science at the University of Victoria in Victoria, Canada. He received his Ph.D. degree from the University of California at Berkeley. Among his major publications are *State-Building in Modern China: The Kuomintang in the Pre-war Period*; *The Fragile Entente: The 1978 Japan-China Peace Treaty in a Global Context*; and *The People's Republic of China—Relations in Asia: The Strategic Implications*. He has contributed to many major scholarly journals.

Hsi-sheng Ch'i is professor of political science and director of the East Asian Studies Curriculum at the University of North Carolina at Chapel Hill. He was educated at Tunghai University in Taiwan and received his Ph.D. degree from the University of Chicago. He is the author of *Warlord Politics in China, 1916–1928* and *Nationalist China at War: Military Defeats and Political Collapse, 1937–1945*. His most recent book is *Politics of Disillusionment: The Chinese Communist Party under Deng Xiaoping, 1978–1989*.

John W. Garver, associate professor of political science at the Georgia Institute of Technology, received his B.A. degree from Oklahoma State University and his Ph.D. degree from the University of Colorado. He is the author of *China's Decision for Rapprochement with the United States, 1968–1971* and *Chinese-Soviet Relations, 1937–1945: The Diplomacy of Chinese Nationalism*, and has contributed numerous articles to leading scholarly journals. At present he is completing a book-length study of the foreign relations of the People's Republic of China.

Steven M. Goldstein is professor of government and chair of the Department of Government at Smith College. He received his B.A. degree from Tufts and his Ph.D. degree from Columbia. He is the co-editor of *Single Sparks: China's Rural Revolutions* and has published widely on both Chinese foreign and domestic policy, with a particular interest in Sino-Soviet relations.

Edward Gunn is professor of Chinese literature at Cornell University. He earned his doctorate at Columbia University. Dr. Gunn has published several studies relating to the war period, among them *Unwelcome Muse: Chinese Liter-*

ature in Shanghai and Peking, 1937–45 and *Twentieth-Century Chinese Drama: An Anthology.*

Tao-tai Hsia is currently chief of the Far Eastern Law Division of the Law Library of Congress. He is also an adjunct professor of Chinese law at The George Washington University National Law Center. Dr. Hsia earned his LL.M. and J.S.D. degrees from Yale Law School and an M.S. degree from Columbia University. He is a former editor-in-chief of *China Law Reporter*, a law journal on China published by the American Bar Association. He has written numerous reports for Congress and law journal articles on various aspects of Chinese law.

James C. Hsiung is professor of politics at New York University, where he teaches international and comparative politics. He received his Ph.D. degree from Columbia University. Among his many works are *Ideology and Practice: The Evolution of Chinese Communism*; *Law and Policy in China's Foreign Relations*; *The Logic of Maoism*; *China in the Global Community* (co-edited with Samuel S. Kim); *Asia and U.S. Foreign Policy* (co-edited with Winberg Chai); *U.S.-Asian Relations: The National Security Paradox*; *Beyond China's Independent Foreign Policy: Challenge to the U.S. and Its Allies*; and *Human Rights in East Asia: A Cultural Perspective.* He is director of the Contemporary U.S.-Asia Research Institute in New York and chairs the Executive Editorial Committee of *Asian Affairs: An American Review.* He is currently working on a book, *Paradoxes in International Relations.*

William C. Kirby has been dean of University College, director of Asian studies, and professor of history at Washington University, St. Louis. In 1992 he joins the faculty of Harvard University as professor of history. He was educated at Dartmouth College and Harvard University. A historian of modern China, he is the author of *Germany and Republican China.* His present research on the development of modern China's economic bureaucracy will be published as *The International Development of China's Economy: Nationalist Industrial Policy and Its Heirs.*

Steven I. Levine, scholar in residence at the Asian/Pacific Studies Institute of Duke University, has taught political science at American University, Columbia University, Duke University, and the University of North Carolina at Chapel Hill. He received his B.A. degree from Brandeis and his Ph.D. degree from Harvard. The author of *Anvil of Victory: The Communist Revolution in Manchuria, 1945–1948*, he has published widely on various aspects of Chinese foreign policy.

James Reardon-Anderson is director of the Committee on Scholarly Communications with the People's Republic of China, on leave from the School of Foreign Service at Georgetown University. He is the author of *Yenan and*

Great Powers and *The Study of Change: Chemistry in Modern China, 1860–1949*, as well as numerous journal articles. He is currently working on a study of the relationship between environment and society in China's grasslands.

Marvin Williamsen is chairperson of the Department of Interdisciplinary Studies at Appalachian State University where he teaches Chinese history and military history. After service as an infantry lieutenant in the U.S. Army, he studied and worked in Taipei and Shenyang. He received his Ph.D. degree from Duke University. Dr. Williamsen is currently working on a book about U.S. military attachés in China.

T'ien-wei Wu is professor of Asian history at Southern Illinois University. He studied at Nanjing [Nanking] University and received his Ph.D. degree from the University of Maryland. Among his numerous works on modern Chinese history are *The Sian Incident: A Pivotal Point in Modern Chinese History* and *Lin Biao and the Gang of Four: Contra-Confucianism in Intellectual and Historical Perspective*.

Wendy Zeldin is a legal research analyst in the Far Eastern Law Division of the Law Library of Congress. She assists in the preparation of in-depth research reports on Chinese legal issues for members of Congress. Dr. Zeldin received her Ph.D. degree from the Department of East Asian Languages and Civilizations of Harvard University.

INTRODUCTION

Steven I. Levine

OUR CENTURY has been so rich in wars, it is little wonder that memories of the Sino-Japanese War of 1937–45 have long since faded from the consciousness of all but the two peoples directly involved in the conflict. Yet at that time, even a world scourged by the plagues of economic depression, totalitarianism, and militarism could not but react to the widespread horrors of this war. Such outrages as Japanese aerial attacks against defenseless Chinese civilians and the unbelievable atrocities of the Rape of Nanking in December 1937 shocked a world that was not yet inured to the routine obscenities of twentieth-century warfare.

In Western historical literature on the Second World War, China's War of Resistance against Japan, which lasted twice as long as the Soviet-German and the American-Japanese conflicts, unfortunately has been overshadowed by the wars in the European and Pacific theaters. Among the spate of World War II books published on the fiftieth anniversary of the outbreak of war in Europe, scant attention is accorded the Sino-Japanese War even by those scholars who acknowledge that World War II began in Asia in 1937, not in Europe in 1939.[1] A significant exception is H. P. Willmot's *The Great Crusade*, which explicitly integrates a succinct discussion of the Sino-Japanese War into its account of the Second World War.[2] Moreover, Willmot accurately notes that Japan's fateful "decision to challenge the greatest industrial power in the world [the United States] stemmed directly from her inability to bring her war in China to a successful conclusion."[3] His comment suggests a point of fundamental importance: namely, that China's War of Resistance may well have been the key to the outcome of the Pacific War. The eight years of sacrifice and suffering endured by the Chinese people during their resistance struggle were no less a factor in the Allied victory than American airpower or atomic weaponry. Had China been unwilling or unable to sustain its resistance during the fifty-three months (July 1937 to December 1941) when it faced Japan alone, the subsequent course of Asian and world history might well have been very different.

Viewed in terms of the postwar consequences for China, the significance of the Sino-Japanese War of 1937–45 can scarcely be exaggerated. If not for the Sino-Japanese War, it is doubtful whether the Chinese Communist party would ever have. come to power. The war provided an ideal environment for exponential growth enabling the Chinese Communist movement to become for the first time in its history a serious contender for national power. At the same time, the war fatally sapped the energies of the Chinese Nationalist government, whose defeat in the civil war of 1946–49 cannot be explained without reference to the antecedent experience of the Sino-Japanese War.[4] And if this were not enough, as James C. Hsiung spells out in the concluding chapter of this volume, the war itself and its aftermath facilitated a major transformation of the international system in ways that continue to affect us all.

This introductory chapter has several purposes. First, it provides some background information in order to place the Sino-Japanese War in its historical context. The focus of this volume is deliberately on China, not Japan, but a brief discussion of Japanese interests and policies may nevertheless be in order. Second, it relates the Sino-Japanese War to the broader context of World War II of which it is indeed an important part. Most of the issues arising in China during the course of the Sino-Japanese War find their analogues in the experience of other nations during World War II. The experience of the war provides a rich and as yet scarcely tapped vein of material for comparative historical studies. Third, this chapter introduces some of the major issues that the rest of the chapters explore in detail, and it explains the organization of the volume as a whole.

There is abundant evidence for the proposition that the Sino-Japanese War was a major turning point in the history of modern China. But what were the major trends in China on the eve of the outbreak of war in mid-1937? Which were disrupted and which were accelerated by the war? Without the need to confront Japanese aggression, would the Nationalist government have been able to consolidate and expand its political control and to guide the process of development? Or would deep-seated socioeconomic problems, particularly in the countryside, eventually have swept the Chinese Communists, or some other revolutionary force, into power?

Needless to say, no scholarly consensus exists concerning any of these questions, particularly those of the historical "what might have been" variety. It is worth noting, however, that over the last decade or two our understanding of Republican China, including in particular the Nanking decade of 1927–37, has gradually deepened. The post–World War II experience of numerous Third World countries suggests that the problems that the Nationalist government grappled with were by no means unique to China. They differed in particulars and scale rather than in kind from those faced by many other developing states. Second, seen in comparative perspective, the record of the Nationalist government looks better in retrospect than it did at the time and for many years afterward. The view held by many liberal Western scholars, who were inclined to dismiss the Nationalists as ineffectual, dictatorial, and repressive, doubtless captured some of the reality of the Nationalist regime, but there was more to it than that.

Two trends in particular deserve to be emphasized. First, the process of state-building that Robert Bedeski discusses (chapter 2) was gradually reducing the political fragmentation of China that attended the end of the dynastic system in 1912. This trend toward recentralizing power and rebuilding the bases of political authority had only partly succeeded by 1937. In fact, piecemeal Japanese aggression beginning in 1931 presented new challenges to Chiang Kai-shek's government even as it struggled on various internal fronts to expand its power. Despite the complexities of Kuomintang intraparty politics and the challenge represented by disaffected allies, regional militarists, and the Communists, there is reason to suppose that in the absence of Japanese aggression, the trend toward internal reunification under Nationalist control would have continued.

Second, recent scholarship has challenged an older view of the Nationalist period as an era of economic stagnation in which the central government and numerous regional militarists ("warlords") stymied development by draining the economy in order to indulge in internecine warfare and to enrich themselves. In his recent study, *Economic Growth in Prewar China*, Thomas G. Rawski convincingly demonstrates that on the eve of the Sino-Japanese War, Nationalist China was a successfully developing state with growth patterns very similar to those of such postwar successful developers as Japan, Taiwan, and South Korea.[5] Contrary to the myth of a rapacious state, all levels of government succeeded in appropriating less than 10 percent of the Gross Domestic Product—a very low figure when viewed comparatively. Military expenditures had little impact on the economy. The state sector was only a small, if growing, part of an economy dominated by the private sector, in which the market was an effective engine of development achieving an annual growth rate of approximately 2 percent over a twenty-year period from World War I until the outbreak of the Sino-Japanese War.[6] This was a not inconsiderable achievement in the face of numerous adverse internal and external conditions.

In China, as elsewhere, preparation for war and the management of a wartime economy vastly increased the state's economic role, a development that in many cases persisted into the postwar period.[7] In his chapter, William Kirby discusses this phenomenon in China and links it to postwar developments. In economics as in politics, incidentally, a web of connections ties together the prewar, wartime, and postwar periods. Paradoxically, a period marked by discontinuities and historical turning points also manifests significant continuities with the past as well as links to the future.

China's successes in political and economic development under the Nationalist government—partial and uneven as they were—served only to increase the danger presented by Japanese imperialism. From the first Sino-Japanese War of 1894–95 until its defeat a half-century later in World War II, Japan was the mortal enemy of Chinese nationalism. Emboldened by their nation's leap to the status of a world-class industrial and military power, the Meiji-era (1868–1912) oligarchs and their successors embarked on a course of imperial expansion focused on continental Asia. This was the root cause of the Sino-Japanese War of 1937–45.[8]

In the first few decades of the twentieth century, Japanese leaders tended to view China as a moribund and effete civilization incapable of responding on its own to the Darwinian challenges of the modern world. As success pricked their own ambitions, many Japanese leaders saw China as the primary arena in which to strive for a Japanese version of Manifest Destiny. Like other imperialist nations, the Japanese believed they were different from their international competitors. They laid claim to a "special relationship" with China based on race and culture, but this myth scarcely concealed a contempt for the Chinese that was given free rein in the course of the war.[9]

Japan's stake in China grew rapidly in the first three decades of the twentieth century. By 1930, Japanese outnumbered all other foreigners resident in China, and Japan had become the main foreign economic power in China with significant interests in manufacturing, commerce, transportation, banking, and so forth. For these reasons, most Japanese leaders resisted the piecemeal erosion of the privileged imperialist order in China that the United States, Great Britain, and France grudgingly accepted in the 1920s in response to the rise of Chinese nationalism.[10] Believing that their economic interests in China were vital to Japan's prosperity, and concerned as well with continental threats to their security, by the late 1920s Japanese military and civilian leaders increasingly perceived the rising tide of Chinese nationalism as a menace that only military force could suppress.

The ease with which Japan conquered Northeast China (Manchuria) in 1931–32 and expanded its military and political presence in North China over the next several years appeared to confirm the opinion of Japanese leaders that they faced no significant obstacles in China. The force of Chinese nationalism seemed no more substantial a barrier in their path than the ephemeral shield of international opinion had been in the way of their conquest of Manchuria. Thus, Chiang Kai-shek's decision for war in July 1937 came as an unpleasant surprise. China's determination to resist further Japanese aggression raised the awkward question in Tokyo of just what Japan's goals actually were in China. If these goals could be specified, how best might they be pursued? As so often happens in wartime, the destruction of Chinese resistance became Japan's primary goal in and of itself, largely substituting for any coherent vision of China's place in the new Asian international order that Japan was haphazardly constructing. By 1941, as the goal of subduing China continued to elude its grasp, Japan attacked European and American possessions in Southeast Asia and the Pacific, hoping to take advantage of the German victories in Europe. The sequence of events that these attacks set in motion culminated in the linking together of the European and Asian components of what now truly became the Second World War, a war that Japan could not win.

If, as the chapters that follow suggest, China was ill-prepared for its War of

Resistance against Japan, Japan itself was no less ill-prepared for a major war against the United States and its allies. Japan produced too little coal, too little steel, and too few modern weapons to sustain full-scale war against the United States and Great Britain.[11] Compared to China, Japan was an advanced industrial giant with an awesome war machine. Compared to the United States and Great Britain, Japan was a second-rate, technologically backward, semi-industrialized society, more like an Asian Italy than an Asian Germany.[12] Only a total mobilization of the Japanese economy, and the full utilization of the considerable organizational capacity of Japanese society, enabled Japanese leaders to persist as long as they did in a war that ultimately cost Japan some three million dead, or 5 percent of its population.[13]

The Sino-Japanese War of 1937–45 was itself part of a global war of unprecedented scope and intensity. In John Campbell's words: "By whatever measurement we use—geographic extent, the scale of military and economic mobilization, . . . the toll of casualties among both combatants and noncombatants, the disruption of civilian lives or the dislocation of the world economy—the war of 1937–45 affected more people around the world more directly than any other war before, or since."[14] It was, moreover, in the words of another recent student, "a savage, insensate affair, barely conceivable to the well-conducted imagination."[15] Certainly the disciplined savagery of Japanese forces in China confirms this point.

It was also a war that produced profound social and cultural as well as political and economic changes in every country that it touched. Mass internal and transnational population movements, the experience of foreign occupation, the organization of resistance forces or the decision to collaborate with the enemy, the need to mobilize female labor for wartime production, the urgency of scientific and technological innovation, and many other factors greatly accelerated the pace of social change.

Curiously, the traumas of war engendered excessive hopes for the future, perhaps to compensate for the despair of the present. A staple of wartime propaganda and a conceit of politicians was the notion that out of the ashes of war a better world would emerge. The American folk bard Woody Guthrie expressed what was perhaps a universal hope when he sang, "There's a Better World a Coming." Allied statesmen gave this hope institutional expression in creating the United Nations organization.

In sum, the experience of global war was a profoundly complex phenomenon that challenges our understanding at every juncture. On a somewhat smaller, if still enormous, scale, the experience of the Sino-Japanese War of 1937–45 is no less complex a phenomenon. The chapters in this book represent an effort to grapple with many of the key issues in the war from an interdisciplinary perspective. At the present stage of our knowledge, we believe that only a collective and collaborative effort of the sort we have attempted can begin to address the many disparate aspects of wartime China.

There is a corollary point as well. From the recruitment of contributors to the final editing of the manuscript, we have made no attempt to impose any sort of interpretive orthodoxy upon the various chapters. Controversy is the lifeblood of history, and much remains to be learned about this period in particular. In the interest of readability, however, the editors have attempted to reduce the stylistic dissonance that sometimes mars collectively authored works of this kind; we have strived for at least a modicum of uniformity in all of the chapters without in any way altering the substance or distorting the voice of each contributor.

As already noted, the fundamental premise of this volume is that the Sino-Japanese War can best be understood through a holistic approach. Several core questions that crop up time and again in various contexts throughout the chapters help to inform this approach. These questions are as follows:

1. What are the temporal boundaries of the wartime experience?
2. How did the role of the state change during the course of the war?
3. How did the state manage its foreign relations during wartime?
4. What was the impact of the war on society?
5. What legacies did the war bequeath to the postwar era?

It may be helpful to expand briefly upon each of these questions.

The issue of temporal boundaries suggests that, broadly conceived, wartime is not simply limited to the period of active combat operations but encompasses a period of preparation as well as a period of aftermath. At what point did China begin to prepare for war? What factors entered into the decision to resist Japan, and how was this decision arrived at? Was China ready for war when the decision to resist Japan was taken?

What was the capacity of the Chinese state to mobilize human and material resources for the war? How well did the state cope with the multiple tasks of managing a wartime economy, maintaining military resistance, conducting wartime diplomacy, sustaining public morale, and so forth? Did the capacity of the state to manage these tasks increase during the course of the war?

Given the disproportion in strength between China and Japan, external assistance from friendly or allied countries was essential to China's strategy of resistance. How did the Chinese state attempt to secure the support it required? To what extent was China able to coordinate its military strategy with its allies? In a broader sense, what effect, if any, did the war have in fostering an internationalist consciousness in China in cultural as well as political terms?

What kinds of changes did the war promote in Chinese society? What was the impact of the war on various social groups? Did some groups benefit from the war while others lost out? Did the social dislocation and wartime mobilization promote a greater sense of national unity in China? Or did the political divisions among the Nationalist, Communist, and occupied areas of China act as a barrier to unity?

How did the war alter the course of Chinese history? In what ways did the wartime experience contribute to the outcome of the postwar struggle for power? What legacies of the war can be discerned in the areas of the economy, literature and art, science, judicial affairs, and so on?

Some of this veritable barrage of questions are directly engaged by the chapters that follow. Others are not. Each question is further complicated by the tripartite division of wartime China into Nationalist, Communist, and occupied territories. Obviously, there are no simple answers to these and many similar questions, which together represent a research agenda for the future. Moreover, the same questions can be posed for each of the other participants in World War II. Among the many commonalities that China shared with other nations in World War II, we may list the experiences of physical devastation, economic privation, social dislocation, partial or complete occupation, resistance and accommodation, internal political cleavages, alliance politics, and so forth. How these factors combined in the Chinese case, and how China's experience compares with that of other nations in wartime, are likewise questions for further research.

This book begins with a broad-gauged essay by John W. Garver on China's wartime diplomacy that skillfully analyzes the complicated maneuvers of Chiang Kai-shek's efforts to secure foreign support for China's resistance to Japan. Only such a multilateral approach can do justice to the complexity of the issues involved. Robert E. Bedeski's chapter on China's wartime state demonstrates from a political science perspective how far Nationalist China had already gone in creating a modern state structure by the time war came. He sketches the state structure that further developed during the war and was later bequeathed to the Chinese Communist party after 1949. The first of two chapters by historian T'ien-wei Wu guides us through the political thickets of politics in Nationalist China as well as in the Japanese-occupied areas of China where Wang Ching-wei established a collaborationist regime. The second of his chapters analyzes the politics of the Chinese Communist movement, and the struggle of Mao Tse-tung to establish his hegemony over intraparty rivals. Steven M. Goldstein's chapter on the CCP's foreign policy of opposition meticulously analyzes the shifting ways in which the Communist party used the arena of foreign policy to advance its pursuit of power.

The chapters on the military dimensions of the Sino-Japanese War by Marvin Williamsen and Hsi-sheng Ch'i not only chart the major campaigns of the war but also discuss the technological, organizational, and leadership problems that hindered China's effective prosecution of the war. The two authors differ somewhat in their final assessment of China's military effort, with Williamsen emphasizing the performance deficiencies while Ch'i concludes that China's military effort, for all its obvious weaknesses, was nevertheless "a very impressive accomplishment."

William C. Kirby's chapter on the Chinese war economy demonstrates that in economic terms China was not yet ready for war in 1937. He focuses on the government's effort to gain control of the economy via the creation of a national planning mechanism whose influence extended well into the postwar period. James Reardon-Anderson's discussion of science in wartime China emphasizes the conflict between state and party bureaucrats who wished to harness science to the cart of wartime production and scientists who even in wartime insisted that science had an educational mission that transcended the demands of the moment. This tension prefigured the post-1949 conflict between the CCP and scientists in mainland China. Edward Gunn's chapter on the literature and art of the war period reminds us that similar conflicts existed in the cultural realm as writers and artists responded to the patriotic summons of the war while struggling to maintain their artistic integrity and individuality. Tao-tai Hsia and Wendy Zeldin summarize the process of legal reform in the Nationalist and Communist areas of China, and the legacy of these reforms for the postwar legal systems. Finally, James C. Hsiung's reflections on the historical significance of the Sino-Japanese War extend our vision well beyond the horizon of 1945 when the war formally ended. He informs us of the role that historical memories of the war play in contemporary Sino-Japanese relations, and he analyzes the way in which changing concepts of power have transformed the postwar international order in the several decades since the Sino-Japanese War of 1937–45 became part of history.

Notes

1. See John Campbell, ed. *The Experience of World War II* (New York: Oxford University Press, 1989); John Keegan, *The Second World War* (New York: Viking, 1989).

2. (London: Michael Joseph, 1989).

3. Ibid., p. 159.

4. See Hsi-sheng Ch'i, *Nationalist China at War: Military Defeats and Political Collapse, 1937–1945* (Ann Arbor: University of Michigan Press, 1982); also Lloyd Eastman, *Seeds of Destruction: Nationalist China in War and Revolution* (Stanford: Stanford University Press, 1984).

5. Thomas G. Rawski, *Economic Growth in Prewar China* (Berkeley: University of California Press, 1989), pp. xix–xxiii.

6. Ibid., pp. 63–64, 332.

7. For example, Herrick Chapman identifies World War II as the turning point in the emergence of the twentieth-century interventionist state in France. "The French State in the Era of the Second World War: A Look at Recent Scholarship," New School for Social Research, Working Papers Series, no. 63, August 1985, p. 1. Thomas R. H. Havens notes that government spending increased twentyfold in wartime Japan. *Valley of Darkness: The Japanese People and World War II* (New York: W. W. Norton, 1978), pp. 94ff.

8. For an excellent collection of studies on this theme, see Peter Duus, Ramon Myers, and Mark R. Peattie, eds. *The Japanese Informal Empire in China, 1895–1937* (Princeton: Princeton University Press, 1989).

9. Ibid., pp. xiii, xxiv.

10. See Akira Iriye, *After Imperialism* (Cambridge: Harvard University Press, 1965).

11. Alan S. Milward notes that "Japan's share of total world output in 1938 was under 4 percent. . . . Greater Japan in the same year still only produced 4.2 percent of world coal output and 6 percent of world steel output." *War, Economy, and Society, 1939–1945* (Berkeley: University of California Press, 1977), p. 34. The comparable figures for Germany were 13.2, 15.5, and 20.7 percent respectively. Ibid.

12. Ibid., p. 175.

13. Havens, *Valley of Darkness.*

14. Campbell, *The Experience of World War II*, p. 12.

15. Paul Fussell, *Wartime: Understanding and Behavior in the Second World War* (New York: Oxford University Press, 1989), p. 132.

CHINA'S BITTER VICTORY

THE WAR WITH JAPAN 1937–1945

1

CHINA'S WARTIME DIPLOMACY

John W. Garver

MODERN Chinese nationalism arose from a sense of shame, born of the humiliation that the West and Japan inflicted upon China in the nineteenth and early twentieth centuries. Not content merely with defending China against further foreign aggression, patriotic Chinese wished to restore their country to a position of international prominence that they believed it deserved. This was the ultimate objective of China's 1937–45 war against Japan, and, in particular, it was the goal of Nationalist China's dominant leader, Chiang Kai-shek. Since the various powers in the 1930s saw Chiang Kai-shek as the ultimate authoritative representative of China, my analysis shall likewise focus on Chiang while making reference, as necessary, to others in the Nationalist hierarchy.[1]

Chinese Nationalism and the Powers

Of all the foreign powers with which he dealt, Chiang's images of Japan and of the Soviet Union were the clearest. Deeply impressed by Japan's emergence as a major military power, Chiang was also well informed about the numerous factions within Japan's elite, and he hoped that those groups and individuals favoring an accommodation with the Republic of China (ROC) would ultimately take control in Japan. Even though China might have to make certain concessions in the process of reaching an accommodation with Japan, if Japan was prepared to respect China's sovereignty, China would then be able to strengthen itself through partnership with its eastern neighbor. Chiang had not abandoned this hope when he led China into war in July 1937. Indeed, the decision for war and much of Chiang's early wartime diplomacy must be seen as an effort to compel Japan to accept a reasonable accommodation with China. Much of Chiang's diplomacy during the first year of the war sought to exploit Japanese intra-elite differences, but unfortunately the increasing sway of the militarists over the moderates defeated Chiang's efforts at accommodation.[2]

Chiang was also quite impressed by the rapid growth of Soviet power, and convinced that Nationalist China should emulate the Leninist model of an amalgamated party, army, and government. However, his experience with Soviet and Comintern advisers in China during the 1920s made him extremely apprehensive of Soviet objectives in China. Believing that the Chinese Communists were agents of Soviet imperialism, Chiang saw the CCP's efforts to make revolution as nothing less than a Soviet attempt to take over China. Moreover, as a traditionalist, Chiang was appalled by the Soviet-derived anti-Confucian doctrine of the CCP.[3]

To Chiang, Soviet Russia, like Japan, was an imperialist power that had carved out a sphere of influence in Sinkiang and Outer Mongolia. Yet because Moscow faced simultaneous threats from Japan and Germany, Chiang believed that the USSR was the best candidate for joining China in war against Japan or, short of that, for providing China with large-scale military and financial assistance. The perennial enmity between Russia and Japan had been exacerbated by Japan's occupation of Manchuria in 1931, which triggered major increases in Soviet defense spending and a quadrupling of Soviet deployments in the Far East within a few years. To avoid conflict with Japan, in 1935 Moscow sold off its interests in the Manchurian railways. The conclusion in November 1936 of the German-Japanese anti-Comintern pact, however, which contained a secret codicil embodying a military alliance against the Soviet Union, turned Moscow toward China in search of a counterweight to Japan.

Shortly after Japan's seizure of Manchuria, Nanking began improving relations with the Soviet Union, a movement that culminated in the December 1932 restoration of diplomatic ties. While Chiang's envoys explored Soviet intentions during the mid-1930s, he remained extremely cautious about expanding relations any further, fearing that closer ties with Moscow might provoke rather than restrain Japan, and also alienate the Anglo-American powers while lending credence to Japan's "anti-Communist" justifications of its China policies. Alignment with the Soviet Union would be an effective wartime measure, but as long as Chiang hoped to work out a peaceful accommodation with Japan, he kept the Soviet Union at arm's length.

Several prominent KMT politicians did not share Chiang's skepticism about Soviet motives. Sun Yat-sen's widow, Soong Ch'ing-ling, and son, Sun Fo, party veteran Hsiao Li-tze, and ex-warlord Feng Yü-hsiang were among those who took a more sanguine view of Soviet intentions and of Sino-Soviet cooperation. Once war began, Chiang frequently turned to Sun Fo and Hsiao Li-tze to handle relations with Moscow.

Chiang had less firsthand experience with Britain and the United States. Britain had long been the nemesis of Chinese nationalism because of its imperialist past, and there was still little love lost between the British and the Chinese Nationalists. While the Nationalist elite included men such as Kuo Tai-ch'i, the ambassador to London, Foreign Minister Wang Chung-hui, and Ambassador V. K. Wellington Koo, who inclined toward Anglophilia, most Nationalist leaders suspected that Britain wished to keep China weak and divided. Both before and after July 1937, China's leaders worried a lot about the possibility that London might strike a deal with Tokyo at China's expense, and they sought means of preventing this. One reason why the Nationalists eagerly sought American action against Japan was that an activist U.S. policy was seen as a means to block the pro-Japan group in London.[4]

The Nationalists also realized that with one billion dollars invested in China—60 percent of all Western investment there—Britain had the most to lose by the establishment of Japanese hegemony over China. Consequently, China looked to Britain for support against mounting Japanese pressure. London did provide some support for China's currency reform in 1935 and, after the Sino-Japanese War began, spearheaded the League of Nation's condemnation of Japanese actions in China. Following the American lead, Britain granted financial assistance to China on half a dozen occasions between December 1938 and April 1941. But with its financial position precarious and its military power badly deteriorated, Britain's global power was severely overextended. Germany's growing power in Europe presented a more immediate threat to Britain than did Japanese actions in the Far East, so London had little stomach for confronting Tokyo.

The United States, too, was very wary of provoking a confrontation with Japan. U.S. military forces were extremely weak, while antimilitary sentiment in the country was very strong. U.S. trade with and loans to Japan far exceeded those to China. Although China looked to the United States for support, there was considerable uncertainty as to how substantive that support would be. Throughout the 1930s, the United States had limited itself to verbal condemnation of Japanese actions.[5]

At the time the war began, Chiang had had little experience with official Washington. Throughout the war, he relied heavily on his wife Soong Mei-ling and his brother-in-law T. V. Soong for advice regarding the United States. Both Soongs were Christians, had been educated in the United States, spoke fluent English, and understood American customs and thinking. Both also believed that the United States was the best partner for China.

Germany also figured prominently in China's wartime diplomacy. After his break with the Soviets in 1927, Chiang had turned to Germany, still a pariah nation, for advice and support, which was eagerly extended. Germany's inflation in the 1920s facilitated Sino-German ties by reducing the cost of German goods and education. Once the Nazis came to power, they imputed a new strategic significance to Germany's links with China and supported the ROC as a link in a chain of anti-Communist states on the periphery of the USSR.

An ideological link with the New Germany also was forged. Many KMT leaders were impressed by the speed and effectiveness with which the Nazi regime reestablished Germany as a major power and believed that New China had much to learn from the "New Germany." Such leaders included Minister of War Ho Ying-ch'in, secret service chief Tai Li, and the head of the central political training office, Ho Chung-huan. Others, such as Chu Chiu-hua and Ch'eng Tien-fong, were less enamored of National Socialist ideology but still admired the New Germany and saw it as a good economic partner.

The German role in China expanded rapidly in the 1930s. New factories were built with modern German machinery while Berlin also helped Nanking build up a small but significant munitions industry and modern army. By 1937 Chiang's Central Army had an elite core of eighty thousand German-trained and German-armed men. Several hundred German advisers, including several top-level staff officers, served with Chiang's forces. The most prominent of these advisers was General Alexander von Falkenhausen, whom Chiang trusted and respected.

Chiang's Decision for War

Sometime early in 1937 Chiang Kai-shek decided that when the next major provocation occurred, China would not yield before Japanese pressure as it had done repeatedly since 1931. On the basis of past Japanese behavior, Chiang considered it highly likely that Tokyo and its aggressive and loosely leashed armies in China would respond to Chinese firmness by attempting to compel Chinese submission. A decision not to back down was a decision for war.

Chiang made this decision with the greatest reluctance, for he realized the extreme risks that war entailed both for China and for his own regime. Despite its progress in national defense, China's military and industrial strength fell far short of Japan's, and China needed more time before it could realistically hope to defeat Japanese forces. Confronting Japan prematurely in 1937 meant that China's hopes for victory would depend ultimately not on its own efforts but on other powers. This was a risky business that put a premium on skillful Chinese diplomacy toward Germany, the United States, Britain, and the Soviet Union. If the other powers remained neutral, China might well be defeated.

A second major danger that made Chiang reluctant to go to war with Japan was his fear that the Soviet and Chinese Communists would seize the opportunity to communize China. From his experience during the first KMT-CCP united front in the 1920s, Chiang was profoundly skeptical of Communist intentions and pledges of unity. He suspected that the CCP was so enthusiastic about a war with Japan because they anticipated that such a war would create favorable conditions for the expansion of Communist power. Preoccupied with fighting Japan, the Nationalists would be less able to check the CCP. Moreover, the burdens imposed on the Chinese people were certain to be heavy, especially in a war of attrition. Chinese defeats in the initial stages were almost certain. Chiang feared that the Chinese Communists would seize on these circumstances to subvert his regime and to expand their own influence.

If the dangers were so great, why did Chiang finally opt for war? There were two linked reasons. First was the mounting force of nationalist passions within China. The Japanese advance into North China in the early 1930s challenged the Nationalist government's legitimacy, deriving as it did from its claim to represent the "redemption" of China from the depths of "national humiliation." By

1936–37, the Nationalist policy of yielding before Japanese pressure had become extremely unpopular, as manifested by the December 9 movement of 1935, the Sian Incident one year later, the anti-Japanese incidents that proliferated across China during the first half of 1937, and the increasing popularity of the CCP's line of national unity against Japan. Chiang was well aware that these swelling patriotic sentiments undercut his policy of continuing to retreat before superior Japanese force.

Second, by late 1936, the growing power of the militarist faction in Japan and the failure of Chinese diplomats to achieve a "fundamental adjustment" in Sino-Japanese relations induced Chiang to abandon his earlier hope that more moderate forces might prevail in Tokyo. He came to believe that only when Japan realized it lacked the strength to force China into a status of dependency would Japanese leaders be willing to respect Chinese sovereignty. Only after Japan suffered a military rebuff at the hands of China and its allies would it come to its senses.

Regarding the Communist danger, Chiang *may* have believed that the severe setback suffered by the CCP with the loss of its Kiangsi-Hunan bases would critically hobble the Reds for some time. Chiang also hoped to use Moscow and the Comintern to rein in the CCP. Chinese Communist docility was to be part of the price Chiang demanded of Moscow for aligning China with the Soviet Union against Japan. Bowing to Chiang's demand, Stalin tried to curb the CCP's revolutionism, but Mao Tse-tung outfoxed both Chiang and Stalin.

Chiang saw the domestic and international factors as closely linked. Like all wars, the war against Japan was a gamble, but if Chiang threw the dice and won, then China's status as well as Chiang's own domestic political position would be immensely strengthened. His German adviser, Falkenhausen, pointed out to him that war and national unification might be closely linked in China as they had been in Germany. If Chiang led China to its first victorious international war in over a century, he would enjoy a much stronger hand against the regional warlords, opposition factions within the KMT, and the rebellious Communists. It could be a major step toward national unity. War with Japan was thus a high-risk, high-payoff game.

Chiang's Strategy for Victory

Chiang went to war with both best-case and worst-case scenarios in mind. The best case was premised on the staying power of the German-trained units of the Central Army and on the willingness of Great Britain and the United States to intervene to protect their interests in China. It was commonly believed in China at this time that Japan's economic vulnerabilities made it impossible for Tokyo to wage war for more than six months or perhaps a year. By then its meager reserves of gold and foreign currency would be exhausted, its markets in China disrupted by war and patriotic boycotts, and its access to British and American bank loans restricted. London and Washington, concerned about the negative impact of war upon their economic interests in China, would intervene to force a settlement on terms acceptable to China. Anglo-American military action would not be necessary; the mere threat to Japan's trade with these powers and financial embargoes would soon bring Japan to its knees.

To reach this point, China's best military units would have to be committed early in the fighting in order to demonstrate that this was a major war, and to raise the costs for both Japan and the other powers. With luck, the Central Army might even win a local victory over Japanese forces. But military defeat had its uses too. It might precipitate Anglo-American intervention to stave off such undesirable outcomes from the perspective of London and Washington as Chinese capitulation, Chinese alignment with the Soviet Union, or even Chinese entry into the Japanese-German anti-Comintern bloc.

Chiang's worst-case scenario envisioned a protracted war of attrition. If the Anglo-American powers or the Soviet Union did not intervene, and if the Central Army's crack units were overwhelmed by Japanese forces, the national government and its army would withdraw to the interior. China's vast area, huge population, and relatively self-sufficient economy made it virtually impossible for Japan to defeat China. The deeper Japan intruded into China, the more patriotic resistance within China would grow and international opposition develop. As Japan's economic situation deteriorated, one could expect the growth of opposition within Japan. The militarists might be ousted, and there might even be a full-scale revolution in Japan.

Chiang publicly outlined his strategy of attrition in December 1937, after the loss of the capital, Nanking, and the failure of the Anglo-American powers to intervene.

> Appraising the outcome of hostilities, we are convinced that the present situation is favorable to China. The basis of China's future success in prolonged resistance is not found in Nanking, nor in the big cities, but in villages all over China and in the fixed determination of the people. The time must come when Japan's military strength will be completely exhausted, thus giving us ultimate victory.[6]

Chiang did not conceive of "victory" as meaning Japanese surrender, at least not until after Pearl Harbor. For the first four years of the war, "victory" for China meant that Tokyo acknowledged its inability to defeat China and agreed to respect China's sovereignty, independence, and territorial integrity. Exactly what this meant in practice varied with the two countries' fortunes of war.

What terms were acceptable to Chiang Kai-shek? In February 1938, Tung Tao-ning, head of the Japan desk of the Foreign Ministry and a member of Wang Ching-wei's peace faction, secretly traveled to Tokyo with a proposal that would have restored the July 7, 1937, status quo ante and turned Manchuria into a Japanese "concession" (i.e., technically still a part of China). China would not pay indemnity and would itself be responsible for anti-Communist duties. In July 1938 Finance Minister H. H. Kung's private secretary, Chao Fu-san, presented another proposal to Japanese representatives that went considerably further. According to this proposal, China and Japan would jointly develop the resources of North China and would also discuss specific Japanese proposals regarding the establishment of a demilitarized zone there. Inner Mongolia would be granted autonomy, and China would "consider" signing an anti-Communist agreement with Japan. It was also willing, but simply unable, to pay an indemnity. Finally, China would sign a treaty with Japan *and Manchukuo*, thereby recognizing the existence of the Japanese puppet state in Manchuria.

In 1940 during secret talks conducted in Hong Kong by representatives dispatched by Tai Li, Chiang went several steps further. Japan could now station troops in Inner Mongolia and at several points in North China. Japan was to be granted extensive economic and political privileges throughout China, and China would sign an anti-Soviet agreement with Japan. On the question of Manchuria, however, Chiang took a slightly firmer position. No longer would China sign a treaty with Manchukuo. Instead, Tai Li's proposal merely agreed that China would "not contest" its loss of Manchuria.[7]

It is at present impossible to determine the exact nature of Chiang's involvement in, and attitude toward, these various peace terms, or to ascertain whether Chiang was actually prepared to accept any of them. Because Chiang's opponents, especially the CCP, used leaked information about these peace talks to undermine Chiang's nationalist credentials, the KMT has been extremely reluctant to declassify information about this aspect of China's wartime diplomacy. There is no doubt, however, that strong arguments could be made in favor of even a harsh peace that would allow the Nationalists to strengthen their own position while mobilizing to defeat their domestic opponents. After the Lukouch'iao Incident, Chinese journals no longer openly spoke of such things since public advocacy of defeatism was taboo, but the arguments lost none of their force.

By mid-1938 it was clear that the CCP was rapidly expanding its infrastructure in the vast areas behind Japanese lines. The powers had not intervened. Japan's armies had successfully seized each of their objectives, inflicting a huge amount of suffering on the Chinese people. How could China win? Would not continuation of the war only benefit the Communists? On the other hand, accepting a harsh peace with Japan would enable the government to check the growth of Communist power, rebuild its military and economic strength, and liberate many Chinese from the burden of Japanese rule. Such defeatist ideas were widespread by 1940, growing in proportion to the decline of China's military fortunes, and even such prominent personages as Minister of War Ho Ying-ch'in may have shared them.

Chiang Kai-shek seems to have been less influenced than most of his colleagues by such defeatist views, perhaps because he realized that a Carthaginian peace, whatever its presumed benefits for the Nationalist regime, would almost certainly doom his own political career. It may be, too, that his own identity was completely wrapped up in the recovery of China's national sovereignty. Whatever the reason, during the dark days of 1940 Chiang's tenacity as a wartime leader emerged most clearly. Whatever his flaws, one cannot help but admire Chiang's determination to continue with the resistance and to rally the Chinese people to persevere in their struggle even through the apparently hopeless days of 1940.

Chiang's various peace bids to Tokyo may also be partly or wholly explained in terms of the utility of the threat of Chinese surrender in influencing the behavior of the United States, the Soviet Union, and Great Britain. One of Chiang's basic tactics for dealing with the powers was to threaten Chinese "collapse" (a euphemism for surrender) unless more support from them was forthcoming.

After Japan's attack on various Anglo-American positions in December 1941, Chiang's war aims and his definition of what constituted victory changed considerably. With major allies and Japan's ultimate defeat now virtually assured, Chiang advanced a five-part set of objectives designed to restore China's national grandeur. First, Japan was to be militarily defeated and expelled from the Asian mainland. Second, territories lost by China during its century of "humiliation," including Manchuria, Taiwan, Hong Kong, and Outer Mongolia, were to be returned. Third, the unequal treaties of the nineteenth century were to be terminated and new, equal treaties negotiated in their stead. Fourth, the great powers would formally recognize China as one of their equals. Fifth, the powers would agree to support China's internal unification and economic development under the Nationalist government.

China's Diplomacy Toward the Powers

When the Sino-Japanese War began, Chiang hoped to build a broad coalition of the powers in support of China. If Germany could be persuaded to continue its assistance, Britain and the United States to adopt economic sanctions against Japan, and the Soviet Union to step up military pressure, such international support, combined with China's own determined military resistance, might suffice to bring Japan to its senses.

Germany was initially China's major foreign supplier of modern weapons. German advisers served with China's crack units, often accompanying them into battle against Japan. Moreover, as a friend of both China and Japan, Germany was in an excellent position to mediate the conflict or even nudge Tokyo toward a generous settlement with China. There was an obvious contradiction, however, between Germany's support for China and its anti-Comintern treaty of November 1936 with Japan. With the onset of war, Berlin initially tried to finesse the contradiction by declaring neutrality and attempting to mediate a Sino-Japanese settlement, but German neutrality had a distinctly pro-Chinese cast inasmuch as Berlin refused Tokyo's demands that it recall its advisers and cancel existing arms sales contracts. Japanese pressure on Berlin mounted over the ensuing months.

Chiang did everything possible to retain German support. He dispatched Finance Minister H. H. Kung to Germany in September–October 1937 to flatter the Nazi leaders and dispense promises of future Chinese concessions and gratitude if Germany stood by China. He also endorsed Austria's Anschluss with Germany in March 1938 and issued ringing endorsements of Germany's reemergence as a great power. But these efforts were to no avail. In April 1938 Hitler, judging that Japan was too valuable an ally to risk alienating, capitulated to Tokyo's demands by withdrawing German advisers and suspending munitions sales to China.[8]

Until then, however, Chiang tried to use the German factor to persuade the Soviet Union, Great Britain, and the United States to step up support for China. Chiang made sure that news of German mediation efforts in December 1937, and of the terms proposed, reached Moscow, Washington, and London. The message was that unless these powers increased their assistance to China, he would be compelled to accept the German-mediated proposals, and the other powers would be confronted by Chinese entry into the German-Japanese bloc. This threat proved effective in persuading Moscow to increase its support for China, but it was less effective with the United States. During the first year of the war, Washington showed little interest in aiding China. Ambassador Wang Cheng-t'ing and his successor Hu Shih generated lots of publicity and lobbied officials, including President Roosevelt himself, seeking U.S. assistance to China, but they elicited nothing more than lofty statements condemning Japanese actions.[9]

China did all that it could to encourage U.S. and British intervention. As noted earlier, Chiang's decision to commit the bulk of his modern forces in the battle of Shanghai in 1937 was influenced by the realization that Anglo-American interests were centered in Shanghai. (Shanghai's trade fell from $31 million in June 1937 to $6.7 million in October.) His decision to withdraw up the Yangtze River to Wuhan, and then to Chungking, rather than to China's northwest or distant southwest, was also influenced by the knowledge that this great transport artery bore most of Anglo-American commerce into China's interior. A desire to involve the Anglo-American powers was not the only or the most important consideration in these decisions, but it was a significant factor.

China's early hopes for Anglo-American intervention focused on the convocation of a conference of the nine powers signatory to the Washington Treaty of 1922 that purported to guarantee China's continued unity and independence. When the United States, the initiator of the Washington Conference, refused to undertake the responsibility of convening another Nine Power Conference, Belgium finally agreed to serve as host. The United States agreed to attend the conference, which was held outside the framework of the League of Nations to allow American participation. The official purpose of the Brussels Conference of

November 1937 was to seek a mediated settlement to the Sino-Japanese conflict. Chiang and his advisers believed, however, that prior to the adoption of economic sanctions against Japan, the search for a mediated solution was doomed to failure. What they sought was the adoption of effective sanctions. Chiang's hopes that the United States might support such a move were disappointed. Like the other powers, Washington did not want to risk confrontation with Japan.[10]

While China's representative at the League of Nations, V. K. Wellington Koo, invoked the principles of civilized international conduct against Japan's rapacious barbarism, Chinese representatives in the United States also worked assiduously to win public opinion to China's side. Hu Shih, a fluent English-speaking intellectual with liberal political inclinations, proved to be an especially able spokesman for China's cause in the United States. Chinese representatives provided authentic information about Japanese atrocities in China to Western news agencies and concerned political groups. So overwhelming was the brutality depicted in the movie footage and photos of the bloody massacres of Chinese civilians in Nanking—most of it taken by participating Japanese soldiers as mementos of the carnage—that the newsreel actually had to be edited and toned down to make it credible to American audiences. Such Chinese propaganda activities were important in shifting U.S. public opinion to China's side. Chinese representatives also encouraged and assisted campaigns to boycott Japanese goods or to collect funds for refugee relief in China. After the organization in January 1939 of the American Committee for Non-Participation in Japanese Aggression, Chinese representatives did everything they could to assist its activities.

Perhaps the most effective way in which China won U.S. support was by portraying Japanese actions as part of a drive for hegemony in East Asia. Japan's war against China was said to be nothing less than an attempt to overturn the 1922 Nine Power Washington Treaty and to establish full Japanese preeminence over China. The next step, the Chinese suggested, would be to exclude Anglo-American economic interests, that is, to close the Open Door, and to establish Japanese hegemony in the Western Pacific.[11]

In several ways, China's warnings about Japan took on a self-fulfilling quality. China's refusal to surrender caused Japan to adopt ever more forceful measures in an attempt to compel Chiang Kai-shek to capitulate. Like the United States in Vietnam thirty years later, an elusive victory led to further escalation. Despite Tokyo's efforts to avoid provoking the Western powers, Japan's escalation of the war increasingly restricted Western activities in China, leading to louder Anglo-American protests and a public opinion that was more and more hostile toward Japan.

By mid-1938, U.S. policy was beginning to change. Some officials, notably Treasury Secretary Henry Morgenthau, came around to the point of view that Chinese representatives had been arguing since the previous year, namely, that the United States should help sustain China in order to prevent Japanese domination of China, which would threaten American interests. In December 1938 Morgenthau and Chinese financier Ch'en Kuang-fu concluded an agreement providing a $25 million loan by the U.S. Export-Import Bank to be repaid by shipments of Chinese tung oil. The loan was strictly commercial and went to a private company set up by the Chinese as a front. Tung oil was also a strategic material used as a drying agent for paints and for waterproofing cloth. By these means, adverse Japanese and U.S. congressional reaction to the loan was minimized. This was the first U.S. wartime assistance to China. Concluded shortly after the fall of Wuhan and Canton, and after Wang Ching-wei's defection, the U.S. "tung oil loan" helped sustain Nationalist morale.

Meanwhile, Japan's desire to isolate Nationalist China drew Japanese forces southward. Canton was seized in October 1938, Hainan Island in February 1939, and the Spratley Islands in March as steps in an ongoing effort to seal China's coast and prevent supplies from reaching Nationalist armies. The farther south Japan moved, the more suspicious Washington became that Tokyo's ultimate aim was the oil-rich Dutch East Indies and hegemony over all of Southeast Asia.[12] The more apprehensive American leaders became of Japan's aims in China and in Southeast Asia, the more willing they became to check Japan's advance. In April 1940 the United States extended an additional $45 million loan to China. In July and September 1940, Washington embargoed aviation fuel and exports of scrap iron and steel to Japan, and announced a new loan to China. Chinese representatives worked assiduously to ensure that Americans drew the correct conclusions from each expansionist Japanese move.

While the United States eventually forged an alliance with wartime China, it was the Soviet Union to whom Chiang Kai-shek initially looked for substantial military assistance against Japan. After July 7, 1937, Chiang set aside his reservations about Soviet intentions and moved quickly to align with the USSR. Chiang initially sought a mutual security treaty such as Soviet Ambassador Dimitrii Bogomolov had proposed as recently as June 1937, only to be told that this offer no longer stood. Chiang then settled for his second-best option. The treaty of mutual nonaggression, signed in August 1937, was perhaps the greatest success of Chiang's initial wartime diplomacy as it provided the basis for multifaceted Sino-Soviet cooperation against Japan through 1939.

The foreign policies of the ROC and the USSR were broadly parallel during the first two years of the Sino-Japanese War. While building up its own military strength in the Far East and rebuffing Japanese encroachments along the Soviet and Outer Mongolian borders, Moscow also supported China's War of Resistance in order to tie down Japanese troops and reduce the likelihood of a Japanese attack against the Soviet Union itself. Chiang Kai-shek understood Stalin's calculations very well, and Chinese Ambassador Yang Chieh and Chiang's special representative to Stalin, Sun Fo, bargained hard to extract as much Soviet assistance as possible in exchange for China's role in helping to guarantee Soviet security. Chiang's diplomatic arsenal included the threat to make peace with Japan, a threat given apparent substance by the German mediation effort of late 1937 and the peace talks with Japan in 1938.

Substantial Soviet military assistance to China during the first two years of the war was extremely important to China's war effort. Several thousand Soviet advisers, including some of the Red Army's best officers, spent tours of duty in China and were instrumental in improving the combat ability of China's armies. Large amounts of equipment and munitions were supplied to China, including several hundred of the Red Army's most advanced warplanes. Soviet pilots flew many of these aircraft and engaged in aerial combat operations. The armies of the world were just then entering the era of combined air-ground operations, and Soviet aviation support to China gave its armies an important edge. China, like Spain, served as a testing ground for new weapons and tactics and a training ground for officers.

From Chiang's perspective this was not enough. He wanted not only material support, but also direct Soviet participation in the war. Repeatedly, through direct and indirect means, Chiang sought to secure Soviet entry into the war, arguing to Stalin and Soviet diplomats that the best way for Moscow to avert an eventual combined German-Japanese attack was to strike a timely Soviet blow against Japan right away. Chiang urged that the Soviet Union, together with China, should defeat Japan before Germany was prepared for war in the West. He seized on the "stabilization" of the European situation produced by the Munich settlement of September 1938 to suggest that the Soviet Union could now safely deliver a swift knock-out blow against Japan. Stalin had no intention of attacking Japan, yet in order not to undermine Chinese resistance, he occasionally hinted that he might enter the war. By the fall of 1938, Chiang realized that short of a direct Japanese attack on the Soviet Union or Outer Mongolia, Moscow would not go to war with Japan.

A critical factor constraining Moscow's approach to Japan was the unwillingness of the Western democracies, especially the United States, to enter into any kind of "collective security" agreements against Japan despite repeated Chinese and Soviet efforts to get them to do so. Had Washington and London been willing to cooperate against Japan, that probably would have been good enough for Moscow even though its primary concern was Germany not Japan. Chinese and Soviet diplomats worked tirelessly to secure cooperation from the Western democracies on joint measures ranging from diplomatic protests against various Japanese actions, to economic sanctions, to Anglo-American naval demonstrations in the Western Pacific timed to coincide with Chinese offensives against Japanese forces and Soviet maneuvers on the Manchurian borders. All these efforts failed. U.S. opinion was strongly antiwar, and Britain was preoccupied with Germany. More than anything else, it was such Western hesitancy that led to the collapse of the ROC-USSR alignment.

The ROC and Soviet-German Alignment

A diplomatic upheaval producing a profound impact on Chinese diplomacy occurred in August–September 1939 when Moscow and Berlin concluded a nonaggression pact and Britain and France went to war with Germany following the
Danzig crisis. To the extent of his limited influence, Chiang Kai-shek had sought
peace in Europe because he thought a European war would make the powers less
likely to intervene against Japan. Yet sensing certain opportunities in the European war, V. K. Wellington Koo quickly proposed to Chiang that China formally
ally itself with Britain and France in order to counter their tendency to appease
Japan. As it had done during World War I, China could supply Chinese manpower and materials to the common war effort.

Chiang supported Koo's proposal and ordered his diplomats to explore the
attitudes of the various powers. As it turned out, given the Soviet Union's new
alignment with Germany, Moscow strongly objected to China's proposed affilia-
tion with the Allies. These objections torpedoed the project since Chiang ar-
dently desired to retain Soviet support against Japan.

As this episode indicates, the Soviet-German nonaggression treaty had a profound impact on the global structure of power.[13] In the first place, it led to the
temporary rupture of the German-Japanese bond. Tokyo, outraged by the Mos-
cow-Berlin pact, felt betrayed by its putative German ally just at the time that
mounting Soviet-Japanese tension had erupted into large-scale fighting at
Nomonhan near the trijuncture of the Soviet, Outer Mongolian, and Manchurian
borders.[14] The advent to power in Tokyo of a more pro-Western government
intent on improving relations with the United States and Britain revived China's
fear of Anglo-American conciliation with Japan. Chiang had hoped to block such
a dangerous development by allying China with Britain and France in September
1939.

Even more significant, for the purposes of this study, was the impact of the
Hitler-Stalin pact on China's relations with the Soviet Union. Soviet cooperation
with Germany soon extended across a whole range of political, military, and
economic issues, and was closely followed by the beginning of better Soviet-
Japanese relations. Soviet defeat of a large Japanese army at Nomonhan, combined with the collapse of Japan's anti-Soviet relationship with Germany, caused
Tokyo to reevaluate its belligerent approach toward the USSR. Moscow responded in kind, and Japanese-Soviet relations gradually improved, a process
that culminated in the Soviet-Japanese neutrality agreement of April 1941.

Seeking desperately to retain Soviet support, Chiang Kai-shek faced a difficult dilemma. The United States was finally becoming apprehensive of Japan's
expansionism and increasingly ready to support China. Britain, hoping for American support in Europe, was willing to follow the American lead in the Far East.
But now that the Soviet Union was aligned with Germany, Moscow would be
alienated if China aligned with the Anglo-Americans.

China's dilemma came to a head during the Russo-Finnish Winter War of 1939–40. The British and French governments viewed the Soviet attack on Finland as tantamount to Soviet entry into the European war on Germany's side.[15] Moreover, the Soviet attack outraged Western public opinion. Thus, London and Paris supported a Latin American resolution to expel the Soviet Union from the League of Nations. According to the League Covenant, expulsion required a unanimous vote of the League Council. As one of the members of the council, this requirement put China on the spot. The quandary could have been resolved by resigning from the council, but that seat had proved very useful in China's effort to appeal to Western public opinion. Thus, Chiang, and more particularly Wellington Koo, was loathe to give it up, and Koo abstained on the critical vote. China failed to exercise its veto power to block the expulsion of the Soviet Union. Moscow was outraged.

The strategic objective of Chiang's diplomacy during the period of Soviet-German alignment remained unchanged from the 1937–38 period: Soviet-Anglo-American-Chinese cooperation against Japan. The Chinese leader still hoped that although the Soviet Union and the Western democracies were aligned on opposite sides of the European conflict, they could find a way to cooperate against Japan in the Far East. Chiang and his diplomats continued their attempts to persuade Moscow, Washington, and London of the wisdom of such a course.

China's stance during the Winter War led to a deterioration in Sino-Soviet relations. Moscow not only protested China's lack of support, but also suspended the shipment of military aid. Chiang Kai-shek was convinced that the vote at Geneva was merely a pretext; Moscow's real purpose, he believed, was to improve relations with Japan inasmuch as one of Tokyo's key demands in the Soviet-Japanese negotiations taking place at this time was precisely that Moscow cut off its aid to China. Moscow, in fact, may have acquiesced to Japan's demands—at least for a while.

The key argument Chiang addressed to Moscow at this juncture was that a Soviet effort at rapprochement with Japan would backfire and lead to a Japanese-American bloc against the USSR. The United States, Chiang and his representatives told Stalin, was just beginning to implement economic sanctions against Japan, which the USSR and China had long urged it to do. If Washington saw that Soviet-Japanese relations were improving, it would conclude that Japan could substitute Soviet for American goods. Realizing that U.S. sanctions would simply drive Moscow and Tokyo closer together, Washington would refrain from implementing such sanctions and would outbid Moscow for Tokyo's favor. Chiang warned Stalin that Japan and the United States could accommodate each other's interests, but since Tokyo saw the USSR as its prime enemy, no such accommodation was possible between Japan and the Soviet Union. It would be wise, Chiang concluded, for the Soviet Union to continue its "traditional" policy and work with China to draw the United States into an anti-Japanese front.

Chiang also employed positive and negative inducements in his effort to

retain Soviet support. The positive inducements involved diplomatically phrased proposals of military bases, rail and troop transport rights, and economic concessions in China. In April 1940 Chiang's special representative in Moscow, Ho Yao-tsu, proposed to Soviet Foreign Minister Molotov that the Soviets enter the war against Japan in exchange for certain privileges in China after Japan's defeat. Ho's cryptic proposal read: "At this time the Chinese government is prepared to conclude immediately an agreement with the Soviet Union regarding all problems related to the road to eternal peace in the Far East, to economic and provisional measures as well as permanent constructions, and to assume responsibility for a portion of the honor."[16]

The phrase "provisional measures" implied transit rights for Soviet forces across Chinese territory during wartime such as were eventually secured from China in August 1945. The reference to "the road to eternal peace in the Far East" implied Soviet military bases in China after the defeat of Japan. From the Soviet perspective, and perhaps from the Chinese as well, "eternal peace" could only be guaranteed by strengthening the Soviet position vis-à-vis Japan. The phrase "permanent constructions" hinted at railway rights across Manchuria such as those that Moscow had sold to Tokyo in 1935 when it disposed of the Chinese Eastern Railroad, and which it was to reacquire in 1945, and to naval bases such as that at Port Arthur relinquished by Imperial Russia in 1905 and reacquired by Moscow in 1945. There is no record, as far as I know, of whether Ho Yao-tsu or other Chinese diplomats elaborated orally on the precise meaning of these diplomatic phrases, but even if they did not, Stalin and Molotov would have understood. These diplomatic seeds would bear fruit in the 1945 Yalta agreement.

As discussed earlier, Chiang's negative inducements involved subtle threats to make peace with Japan, thereby freeing Japanese armies for use elsewhere, and taking China into a Japanese-led anti-Communist bloc.

Stalin was unmoved by Chiang's arguments, offers, and threats. Because China's bid was too low to counter the gains Moscow could achieve through cooperation with Tokyo, Stalin unceremoniously dropped China. Soviet-Japanese cooperation at China's expense peaked with the conclusion of the Neutrality Agreement of April 1941, which nullified the 1937 Sino-Soviet non-aggression treaty and involved the cross-recognition by Tokyo and Moscow of each other's sphere of influence in Manchukuo and Outer Mongolia.

Up to this point, the outcome of the great power maneuvering was almost exactly the opposite of what Chiang Kai-shek had sought. Instead of Soviet noninvolvement in the European war and Soviet-American cooperation in the Far East, the Soviet Union remained neutral in the Far East until quite literally the last days of that war, while cooperating with the United States in Europe.

The first half of 1940 was China's diplomatic nadir. Tokyo was unwilling to come to terms with Chiang despite the collapse of its hopes for a short war, and the adverse effects the Sino-Japanese War was having on Japanese-American relations. China's major ally, the Soviet Union, had defected to Japan. Britain and France, preoccupied with European affairs, were increasingly vulnerable to Japanese pressure. In June 1940, after the defeat of France, Paris acceded to Japanese occupation of Annam, and the very next month London agreed to close the Burma Road. China's last remaining international supply routes—the Haiphong-Kunming and the Rangoon-Myitkina railways—were thus closed. Together with the suspension of Soviet aid, this meant that China lacked even a single supply route to the outside world.

The United States now became China's only hope. Although the United States was beginning to rearm and Washington was shaking off its diplomatic lethargy, U.S. policy remained equivocal. Like London and Paris, Washington gave priority to the German threat and wished, if at all possible, to avoid adding Japan to its list of enemies.

Chiang's peace talks with Japan in 1940, mentioned earlier, were partly an attempt to solidify U.S. support for China. He understood the utility of the implied threat to surrender in influencing the United States. Another component of Chiang's "peace diplomacy" involved an opening to the Third Reich. In August 1940, meetings between China's new military attaché in Berlin, General Kuei Yung-ching, and Reichsmarshall Herman Goring led to the reactivation of German mediation efforts for the first time since early 1938. In early November Foreign Minister von Ribbentrop sent a message to Chiang Kai-shek noting the German domination of Europe and pointing out the futility of China's hopes for American or British help under such circumstances. Europe would soon be united under German leadership, he said. If China reached a compromise settlement with Japan as soon as possible and joined in the just concluded Tripartite Treaty, Germany would be prepared to guarantee Japan's fulfillment of any mutually agreed upon peace terms. Whatever Chiang's private thoughts may have been, there is no doubt that Washington was the immediate object of this "peace diplomacy." Shortly after receiving Berlin's note, Chiang ordered its contents conveyed to U.S. Ambassador Nelson T. Johnson.

The Formation of China's Alliance with the United States

Only if one understands the dire threat confronting the United States in 1940 can one appreciate the ardent desire of the U.S. government to keep China in the war against Japan. Germany's domination of Europe, challenged only by Great Britain, facilitated the rise to power in Tokyo of the most extreme militarists who decided to join with Germany in destroying the old British, French, and Dutch colonial empires. Tokyo's immediate objective was the oil fields of the Dutch East Indies, whose capture might free Japan from American economic coercion. As Japan's drive south gained momentum, Tokyo and Berlin formed a military alliance against the United States. In the fall of 1940 Moscow and Berlin began discussing Soviet adherence to the Axis bloc, and in April 1941 Moscow guaranteed Japan's northern flank, enabling it to strike south.[17] In these circumstances, peace between China and Japan, possibly leading to Chinese entry into the Axis bloc, would have further isolated the United States. As the influential geopolitician Nicholas Spykman was then pointing out, the United States faced the very real possibility of confronting a hostile "world island" combination embracing all of Europe, Asia, and Africa. Britain and China were the only two countries offering hope to the United States.

Aware of Axis military strength and its own military weakness, Washington wished to avoid a simultaneous war with both Germany and Japan but was unwilling to suspend aid to China as the price for Japan's dissociation from Germany. That would have been like relinquishing one's shield to a powerful enemy in exchange for a promise that he would not strike. Washington was ready during 1941, however, to conclude a provisional agreement with Japan restoring a degree of U.S.-Japanese commerce if Tokyo took specific steps to dissociate itself from Germany's offensive against the Western powers. Learning of the U.S.-Japan talks from Hu Shih, his ambassador in Washington, Chiang Kai-shek cabled Hu in reply:

> If the United States relaxes or changes any aspect of its economic embargo of Japan prior to a basic resolution of the problem of Japanese aggressor troops in China, China's war of resistance will obviously collapse forthwith. Even if the United States afterwards gives China aid, it will be pointless. China cannot again hope for assistance from its ally and henceforth international trust and human morality will be worthless.[18]

Chiang also directed T. V. Soong, appointed in mid-1940 as his personal representative to the United States, to inform the U.S. military chiefs that any relaxation of the U.S. economic embargo of Japan would seriously shake Chinese military morale. He cabled a similar message to Prime Minister Churchill.

Most likely Chiang was bluffing. Only the month before he had confided to his diary:

> If by chance America reaches an accommodation with the Japs and uses the China problem as a concession in exchange for the Japs withdrawing from the Axis alliance, although this would be injurious to our country's international situation and a great psychological blow, we will continue our war of resistance, await changes in the international situation, and await the time when England and America are attacked by Japan.[19]

Chiang's bluff worked. One factor preventing a last-minute compromise between Japan and the United States was the American fear that it would lead to the collapse of Chinese resistance. Chiang did not have long to wait. On November 26, a Japanese carrier task force, which had assembled in the Kurile Islands, put out to sea headed for the American naval base at Pearl Harbor.

As soon as the United States and Great Britain were immersed in a world war, China's bargaining position was greatly strengthened. Now the Anglo-American powers needed China at least as much as China needed them. If the more than one million Japanese soldiers stationed in China (not counting additional Japanese forces in Manchuria facing the Soviet Union) were released for redeployment elsewhere, whether by a formal Japanese-Chinese peace agreement or, more likely, by some sort of de facto cease-fire agreement, the burden placed upon Anglo-American forces would increase proportionately.

Understanding this very clearly, Chinese and American leaders struck a bargain whereby China would continue to fight Japan in exchange for an appropriate quid pro quo. Throughout the war there was continual bargaining about the terms of this deal. How much fighting would Chinese forces do? What was the appropriate quid pro quo for China's continued resistance? Chiang was a hard bargainer and used continual threats of peace with Japan to pressure U.S. acceptance of his demands.[20] What was essentially an instrumental deal was complicated by suspicions and mistrust on both sides. The Chinese feared that they might again be betrayed by their allies, as had happened so many times before. Thus, Chiang approached his alliance with the United States and Great Britain deeply suspicious that those powers, and especially Britain, might be willing to sacrifice China's interests whenever it suited them.

Unfortunately, the first major attempt at Chinese-U.S.-British cooperation during the war, the defense of Burma in early 1942, only deepened Chiang's suspicions. Burma was a vital corridor through which U.S. Lend-Lease materials (authorized for China by Executive Order in May 1941) might be transported to China, and after Japan's occupation of Tonkin, Rangoon harbor, the Rangoon-Myitkina railway, and the Myitkina-Kunming road provided China's only remaining overland supply link with the Western powers. Defense of this route was extremely important to China, so as early as mid-1941 Chiang's generals favored deploying strong Chinese forces in Burma. This would enable them to prepare strong defensive positions in the rugged terrain along the Thailand-Burma border where the Japanese advance might be ground down and halted. British authorities, however, confident that British Indian Army forces could defend Burma unassisted, rejected the Chinese government's plan. Chinese leaders suspected London's real concern was that Chinese participation in the defense of Burma might ultimately weaken Britain's hold over Burma. China also had an old territorial claim in northern Burma. In any case, Britain did not allow Chinese forces to enter Burma in significant numbers until February 1942 when the Allied position in Burma was already critical.[21]

To defend Burma in 1942, Chiang placed two of his best-trained and equipped armies, led by General Tu Yu-ming, under the overall command of American General Joseph Stilwell. But ever suspicious of British motives and of British influence on the United States, Chiang feared that his forces might be sacrificed merely to cover a British withdrawal into India, which he suspected was the real British objective. Britain would not be averse to seeing China further weakened and isolated, Chiang believed, since a weak China would be less of an obstacle to British imperial interests in the postwar era. Seeking to ensure that his forces were not sacrificed simply to serve British purposes, Chiang retained ultimate command over them, but to no avail. General Stilwell simply ignored Chiang's orders.

The 1942 campaign confirmed Chiang's worst suspicions. The British abandoned Rangoon harbor without a fight and refused to commit their air power to Burma. Not only did Stilwell ignore Chiang's orders, but his tactics led to the encirclement of the Chinese forces under his command, which disintegrated under Japanese assaults. Abandoning what remained of his army, Stilwell fled on foot to India with a small headquarters force. When he got there he blamed his defeat on Chinese incompetence and interference.

Chiang was outraged by both the conduct and the outcome of the Burma campaign. Stilwell's self-serving public criticisms of Chinese forces, which had already fought Japan for four and a half years, were an affront to Chiang's pride. More important, the loss of Burma severely limited the amount of aid China could expect to receive from its American ally by placing the entire burden for transporting foreign materials to China on the air ferry over the mountains between Assam and the Yunnan plateau (a region known during the war as "the Hump").

A second major irritant in the Sino-American alliance was the Europe First strategy that Washington and London agreed upon in August 1941. According to this strategy, the war against Japan, and more especially the China theater, was ranked at the bottom of the priority list. Quite naturally, Chiang perceived Japan as a more dangerous enemy than Germany. Moreover, he was keenly aware that the Europe First strategy meant less equipment for his armies and a diminished role for China both during the war and at a peace settlement. Thus, he resisted that strategy at every opportunity. This frequently took the form of demands for major increases both in the number of American aircraft assigned to the Hump ferry and in the total tonnage of cargo supplied by that operation. Cognizant of Chinese bitterness and extremely concerned that China might leave the war in the aftermath of the Burma catastrophe, U.S. leaders agreed to Chiang's demands for increased Hump tonnage and more supplies for China's forces.

To make good on these promises, Washington committed itself to the reconquest of Burma. The idea was to combine American technology and training with Chinese manpower to create large, powerful, Americanized Chinese armies capable of driving Japan's forces into the sea. Stilwell's plan for the reconquest of Burma envisioned a three-pronged coordinated offensive by Chinese forces in Assam and Yunnan and by an Anglo-Indian force along the Bay of Bengal. Enthusiastic, but at the same time skeptical of his allies' true intentions, Chiang believed that if the purpose of a second Burma campaign was really to reopen a supply route to China, its objective had to be the early seizure of Rangoon harbor and the Rangoon-Myitkina railway. Moreover, to provide a safe margin of victory, the Anglo-Americans should commit adequate forces to the campaign, including air and naval forces to establish supremacy over the Bay of Bengal, and an amphibious landing in southern Burma. A second Chinese defeat in Burma, Chiang feared, might lead the Japanese to seize Kunming and shut down the Hump ferry. Moreover, Chinese public opinion would criticize Chiang for sacrificing Chinese armies in foreign lands to serve Anglo-American purposes.

After months of diplomatic effort, at the Cairo summit in November 1943 the Chinese finally persuaded Roosevelt to agree to an amphibious invasion of southern Burma. But immediately thereafter, Stalin's pledge at Teheran to enter the war against Japan after Germany's defeat meant that China's assistance was no longer essential to defeat Japanese forces on the Asian continent. The Anglo-American leaders promptly scrapped the southern, amphibious component of the Burma operation and informed Chiang Kai-shek of their decision.[22]

Again Chiang felt betrayed, this time on a matter of critical interest to China. Roosevelt's abrupt and unilateral cancellation of an agreement that had just been concluded caused Chiang a great loss of face among those of his subordinates whom he had already informed. Chiang responded by demanding a $1 billion gold "loan" and a substantial increase in Hump tonnage. Unless these demands were met, he threatened Chinese resistance might "collapse." To lend substance to these threats, Chiang opened contacts with Japan's China Expeditionary Army.

The scrapping of the amphibious component ended China's obligation to participate in the Burma campaign as far as Chiang was concerned since he had all along made clear that China's participation was predicated on the amphibious operations. Stilwell, with different ideas, launched an offensive into Burma, with the Assam-based army of Chinese whom he commanded. He correctly calculated that this move would force Chiang to commit his Yunnan troops to the operation. Confronted by repeated and direct requests from Washington, and increasingly blunt threats to cut off U.S. aid, Minister of War Ho Ying-ch'in finally ordered the Yunnan force into Burma in April 1944. Fortunately, the Chinese armies fought well, and there was no repetition of the 1942 catastrophe.

The Stilwell Incident

Until 1944 the prevailing image of China in the United States—an image that China's representatives carefully cultivated—was of a heroic ally struggling for freedom and democracy under the leadership of enlightened, Christian men and women. There was a striking discrepancy between this public image and the deepening resentment that Chinese and American leaders already felt toward each other. By 1944 Chiang was increasingly embittered by what he felt was the high-handed and arrogant way the Americans were treating him and China. For their part, U.S. officials increasingly saw Chiang and his fellow Nationalists as venal and craven, interested only in American dollars and unwilling to fight the Japanese.

These private sentiments, which had largely remained out of public view, broke through the veneer of congeniality and fraternity in 1944 when the most powerful Japanese offensive since 1938 overwhelmed Nationalist resistance and precipitated a fundamental clash between Chinese and American interests. As China's defenses crumbled, Washington demanded that Stilwell be given effective command over all Chinese armies, both Nationalist and Communist. From the American perspective, such a move would facilitate the rational reorganization and redeployment of Chinese forces in a way that would maximize their effectiveness vis-à-vis Japan. Stilwell firmly believed that the whole purpose of U.S. aid to China had been to fight Japan, and he considered Chiang's refusal to intensify the war against Japan as sheer betrayal and perhaps even cowardice.[23]

Chiang viewed as extremely presumptuous the demand that a foreigner be given command of China's armies. Neither his earlier German nor Soviet partners had ever made such a demand. Moreover, he considered Washington's failure to provide China with adequate supplies and its insistence that China deploy its best Yunnan armies in Burma as partly responsible for the Japanese successes in 1944. Washington had repeatedly slighted China. It was also insensitive to the complex structure of personal and regional loyalties on which Chiang's power was based. If Stilwell was allowed to reorganize China's military forces in accordance with Western notions of impersonal efficiency and rationality, he might undermine Chiang's power base.

The Chinese leader also failed to see any advantage to China in providing Chinese Communist forces with U.S. weapons and training, or in redeploying and reorganizing Nationalist forces without regard either to their loyalty to his regime or to their role in the containment of the CCP. The two Burma campaigns convinced Chiang that the sole U.S. objective was simply to have China's armies kill as many Japanese as possible, regardless of whether these operations accorded with China's own interests. Might not the Americans' short-sighted sense of military expediency now cause them to give the Communists critical advantages?

Preparing for an inevitable postwar showdown with the CCP, Chiang sought to conserve Nationalist strength while carefully containing the Communists. Having borne the burden of fighting Japan for so many years, Chiang was disinclined to sacrifice his political interests simply to reduce U.S. casualties in its Pacific campaigns against Japan. Chiang also believed that American military and diplomatic officers in China tended to have a very naïve understanding of Communist aims and strategy. They took CCP professions of moderation at face value and seemed to think that only a lack of goodwill stood in the way of Communist-Nationalist cooperation.

As he pondered Roosevelt's final ultimatum demanding Stilwell's appointment, Chiang also began to suspect more sinister motives. If naïveté and military expedience did not fully explain the American demand, there were two other seemingly plausible, rational explanations of U.S. policy. One was that the U.S. government had been infiltrated by Communist agents who were deliberately facilitating the expansion of Communist power in China. The second was that Roosevelt had struck a spheres of influence deal with Stalin and was now seeking to turn North China into a Soviet sphere of influence. Chiang mulled over both of these possibilities as he rejected Roosevelt's demand to appoint Stilwell his chief-of-staff.

Roosevelt capitulated to Chiang's demand for Stilwell's recall because he feared that to do otherwise might lead to China's withdrawal from the war against Japan, and because he viewed Sino-American amity as an essential condition for postwar international stability. This was a major victory for Chiang Kai-shek, but also a very costly one. The Stilwell incident was the single most important factor in shifting the popular U.S. image of Chiang from that of a courageous, patriotic, and upright leader to that of a corrupt and reactionary dictator.

China's Payoff

Early in the war the United States found itself in something of a quandary. Aware of China's vital role in tying down Japanese troops, Washington was extremely anxious to prevent any slackening of China's war effort, but the loss of Burma and the Europe First strategy severely limited the amount of military goods that could be supplied to China. Chiang and his close associates repeatedly threatened that unless China's demands were met, the morale of the Chinese people and army might collapse, and further resistance to Japan would become impossible. American leaders took these threats very seriously. In August 1943, for example, the U.S. Chiefs of Staff concluded, "Although a formal separate peace [between Chungking and Tokyo] is highly improbable, it is possible that if China's condition is not effectively relieved an 'undeclared peace' may eventually result."[24] How, then, could the United States induce China to remain effectively in the war?

One solution to this dilemma was the provision of large loans, paying highly inflated Chinese government fees for goods and services procured by the U.S. military in China, and turning a blind eye to the diversion of huge amounts of U.S. funds and goods into the private pockets of various Nationalist officials. By 1943–44 corruption among Nationalist military and civilian officials had become a serious problem in U.S.-China relations.[25]

Another form of U.S. payoff to China for remaining in the war was diplomatic support for China's emergence as a great power. On her trip to Washington in early 1943, Madame Chiang presented China's territorial demands, including Manchuria, Taiwan, Hong Kong, and the Ryukyu Islands. At Cairo in

November, Chiang himself pressed his demand for Outer Mongolia and secured U.S. consent to the return of Manchuria and Taiwan. Later in 1945 Chiang had to drop his claim to Outer Mongolia, grant the Soviet Union certain special rights in Manchuria, and drop his demand for the return of Hong Kong. He succeeded, however, in reacquiring Taiwan and Manchuria—overwhelmingly Han Chinese areas that had been parts of China for many centuries before being seized by Japan in 1895 and 1931 respectively.

Washington was initially quite ready to grant China symbolic great power status. The first step in this direction came with China's signature of the United Nations declaration of January 1942 as one of the "Big Four" powers. The cancellation of the nineteenth-century unequal treaties was the next step. After the Burma fiasco in spring 1942, the United States took the initiative in discussing this matter with Britain, and negotiations with the Chinese resulted in the signing of new treaties in January 1943. At the end of that year Chiang met with Roosevelt and Churchill at Cairo, symbolizing China's status as one of the great powers.

The United States was reluctant, however, to grant more substantive great power status to China, for example, by allowing Chinese participation in the joint allied staff conferences at which basic decisions were made and war plans drafted. U.S. leaders feared that such participation might interfere with the vigorous prosecution of the war since China disagreed with such fundamental Allied priorities as the Europe First strategy. Moreover, they believed that China could not be trusted to maintain military secrets.

Nonetheless, Chinese pressure, backed by threats to leave the war, was partially successful in overcoming this reluctance. After repeated protests and threats, Chinese Foreign Minister T. V. Soong and military attaché Chu Shih-ming were allowed pro forma participation in a joint staff conference in Washington in May 1943. Then, at the joint staff conference at Quebec in August 1943, Soong met with Roosevelt and Churchill for the first time. This was China's first entry into the great power club, and although its participation was largely symbolic, it laid the foundation for later, more substantive gains.

A major diplomatic victory for Chiang was securing U.S. support in overcoming British and Soviet opposition to China's confirmation as a great power. Believing that China lacked the economic and military attributes of a great power, British leaders were concerned about their commercial interests in China, intent on holding on to Hong Kong, skeptical of Chinese aims in Tibet, and fearful that a strong, self-confident China might help undermine British power in India. Yet U.S. pressure succeeded in overcoming British resistance. Churchill saw China as a secondary issue and finally accepted Washington's view of China's supposed importance for the sake of Anglo-American amity.

For its part, the Soviet Union was downright hostile to China during the midwar period. Chiang Kai-shek had availed himself of the German invasion of the Soviet Union to oust the Soviets from Sinkiang. Since maintaining Japanese neutrality was the paramount Soviet Far Eastern concern until 1944, Stalin was irked by Chiang's repeated efforts, continuing until mid-1943, to undermine Soviet-Japanese neutrality and bring the Soviet Union into the war against Japan. Differing Chinese Nationalist and Soviet interests in Manchuria and toward the CCP also harbored the possibility of conflict.

Such considerations translated into Soviet opposition to China's designation as a great power. Stalin saw no reason to reward Chiang Kai-shek for diligently working at cross purposes to Soviet interests. But again U.S. pressure was successful in overcoming this opposition. The pivotal point occurred at the Moscow foreign ministers conference in October 1943 when Secretary of State Cordell Hull persuaded Stalin and Molotov to allow Chinese Ambassador Fu Ping-chang to sign the official declaration. The principle thus set, of treating China as one of the Big Four, was institutionalized with China's acquisition of one of four permanent Security Council seats in the new United Nations organization established a year later at Dumbarton Oaks. These impressive diplomatic victories, demonstrating the utility of the U.S.-ROC alliance, were further consolidated during the last six months of the war when the United States again played a key role in facilitating a Sino-Soviet accommodation.

During Vice-President Henry Wallace's June 1944 visit to China, Chiang requested American help in easing strained Sino-Soviet relations. Vowing that he desired "good neighbor" relations with Moscow, Chiang said he would be willing to listen to any proposals that Roosevelt might have in this regard.[26] Wallace returned to Washington with a letter to Roosevelt from Madame Chiang saying that Chiang Kai-shek was "in full accord" with Roosevelt's desire for "closer cooperation and real collaboration" between China and the Soviet Union and was "willing to do everything in his power to help bring it about."[27] The United States agreed to intercede and worked out the general terms of future Sino-Soviet relations during discussions between U.S. and Soviet leaders at Yalta in February, in Moscow in May, and in Potsdam in July 1945. Washington's own key objectives were to secure Soviet entry into the war against Japan, and to work out an accommodation between China and the Soviet Union that would serve as a basis for postwar cooperation among the Big Four.[28]

The final terms of the U.S.-sponsored ROC-USSR accommodation were embodied in the August 1945 Sino-Soviet Treaty of Friendship and Alliance. In it, Moscow guaranteed to respect Chinese sovereignty in Sinkiang and Manchuria, and not to support the Chinese Communists. China's quid pro quo was a pledge not to conclude any alliance or take part in any coalition directed against the Soviet Union—in plain words, not to ally with the United States against Russia. China also granted rail rights and harbors in Manchuria to the Soviet Union and had to recognize Outer Mongolian independence.[29] All in all, despite the Chinese concessions, it was by no means a bad deal for the Nationalists.

These concessions, however, particularly the cession of Outer Mongolia, were damaging to Chiang's nationalist reputation. Following the KMT's loss of the mainland, Chiang blamed the United States for forcing the terms of the Sino-Soviet agreement upon him, claiming that he had had no recourse but to accept those terms. This "myth of Yalta" was domestically useful to him but did not fully accord with the facts. Chiang had solicited U.S. mediation and had also discussed in general terms the issue of Soviet ports in Manchuria (though not of railroad rights) with Roosevelt at Cairo. Roosevelt had informed Ambassador Wei Tao-ming in January 1944 that at Teheran Stalin had indicated a desire for railroad rights, and Chinese representatives subsequently raised no objections to the United States on this matter.[30] Moreover, Chiang's Manchurian concessions to Moscow in 1945 could be traced back to Chiang's April 1940 offer to Stalin. Only on the issue of Outer Mongolia did Chiang have legitimate grounds for surprise and outrage at what his American allies had agreed to.

Conclusion

The list of China's wartime diplomatic accomplishments is quite impressive. Manchuria, Sinkiang, and Taiwan were recovered. The onerous unequal treaties, which two generations of nationalists had struggled against, were finally abolished. China was recognized as a great power and received a permanent United Nation Security Council seat. Perhaps most important, China's ability to confront and defeat a first-rank world power was universally acknowledged, a recognition symbolized when China's representative was the second of the Allies (after Douglas MacArthur) to sign Japan's formal surrender aboard the battleship *Missouri* in Tokyo Bay. This was an impressive legacy that was passed on to the People's Republic of China.

Given the manifold weaknesses of China and of the Nationalist regime at the time, the appropriate question to consider is how China was able to accomplish so much. Undoubtedly, these diplomatic gains were due ultimately to the courage and tenacity of millions of ordinary Chinese who enabled China to sustain a bitter eight-year war. But to what extent should Chiang Kai-shek be credited with these successes? Did China secure these gains because of, or in spite of, Chiang Kai-shek?

Most of Chiang's efforts to influence alignments among the powers failed. He failed to prevent Germany's defection from its special relation with China in 1938. He failed to secure American or British intervention in 1937–38. He did secure Soviet assistance during 1937–39, but at a level short of what he desired and China needed. Chiang's efforts to prevent Soviet rapprochement with Japan in 1939–41 failed, as did his efforts to undermine Soviet-Japanese neutrality after 1941. Perhaps most significant of all, Chiang failed to persuade Japan to grant China a relatively lenient peace between 1937 and 1940.

The notable exception to this record of failure to influence relations among the great powers involves U.S. policy toward Japan. Here Chiang's efforts were ultimately successful. To be sure, it took the United States longer to confront

Japan than Chiang and his diplomats had hoped, but finally Washington moved in the desired direction.

To what extent was this due to Chinese efforts? This question has not been adequately researched, and answers can only be tentative. Were Chinese representatives among the first to suggest to Washington that Japanese actions represented a grave threat to U.S. interests in the Far East, and even to the United States itself? How much influence did such Chinese arguments have upon U.S. leaders? Were American analysts making the same arguments at this same time or even earlier? I do not know. Undoubtedly, it was Japan's own actions, above all its push into Southeast Asia, that finally convinced Washington of the need to check Japan. But, as has been seen, Japan's fatal choice to move south was closely tied to Japan's inability to end its war with China. Chiang Kai-shek understood very well that China's perseverance in the War of Resistance against Japan would ultimately bring about significant changes in the international situation.

Chiang was also extremely shrewd in grasping whatever opportunities were presented to him by great power alignments. Moscow paid substantially for China's role in tying down Japanese troops. Washington, too, paid in good coin for the same service. No passive recipient of the generosity of his Soviet or American allies, Chiang actively pressured them into giving him much of what he wanted. His most effective threat was to end China's role in tying down Japanese forces.

It is wrong to view wartime China as a passive beneficiary of U.S. generosity, or to understand China's rise to great power status as a gift bestowed by Washington. No doubt U.S. support was vital, but to a considerable degree that support was squeezed out of the United States by Nationalist pressure. There should be no doubt that Chiang Kai-shek was a hard and effective bargainer on China's behalf.

Chiang's career as a world statesman presents something of a paradox. By persevering in the difficult course of resistance to Japan, he ultimately succeeded in establishing China as a great power. Yet Chiang's steadfast refusal to capitulate to Japan allowed his Communist rivals to expand their infrastructure, creating the basis for their subsequent victory over the Nationalists in the civil war. Had Chiang made a peace settlement with Japan in 1940 or 1941, the prospects for the Nationalist government, if not necessarily for his own personal power, might have been much better. China's standing in the world, however, would have been considerably less. In a sense, then, the tragic paradox of Chiang Kai-shek was that he won by failing, and he failed by winning.

Notes

1. The best sources regarding Chiang Kai-shek's views on world events are *Chiang tsung-t'ung mi-lu* (The secret diary of President Chiang) (Taipei: Chung-yang jih-pao

chu-pan-she, 1978), and *Tsung-t'ung Chiang-kung ta-shih ch'ang-pien ch'u-kao* (Preliminary extensive chronology of President Chiang), (Taipei: Chung-kuo kuo-min-tang chung-yang wei-yuan-hui tang-shih wei-yuan hui, 1978). Volumes 3–6 cover the 1934 to 1945 period. Both of these documents contain extensive quotations from Chiang Kaishek's diaries, which have not themselves yet been declassified. The best synthetic statement of Chiang's broad objectives is *Chung-kuo chih ming-yun* (China's destiny), (Chungking: Cheng Chung shu-chu, 1943). Subsequent English translations of the latter work are quite different from the original Chinese version.

2. Regarding Sino-Japanese relations see Chang Chun, "Yu Jih-pen chieh-hsia-le pu chieh chih lu" (Record of the rupture of relations with Japan), *Chuan-chi wen-hsueh* (Biographical literature) 31, 31 (July 1977): 53. Chang Chun, "Jen wai-chiao-pu-chang ti hui-i" (Memoir of service as foreign minister), *Chuan-chi wen-hsueh*, part 1, 31, 6 (December 1977); part 2, 32, 1 (January 1978). Chiang Tso-pin, *Chiang Tso-pin hui-i-lu* (Memoir of Chiang Tso-pin) (Taipei: Chuan-chi wen-hsueh ts'ung-shu, no. 19, September 1967). Wu Hsiang-hsiang, "Jih-pen t'ung Wang Peng-sheng" (Japan expert Wang Peng-sheng), *Chuan-chi wen-hsueh* 8, 5 (May 1966): 30.

3. Primary sources for Sino-Soviet relations include: Tsiang Ting-fu memoir, Chinese Oral History Project, Rare Books and Manuscripts Library, Columbia University; Hsiao Li-tze, "Chu-shih Su-lien ti hui-i" (Memoir of ambassadorship to the Soviet Union), *Wen-shih tzu-liao hsuan-chi* (Selection of literary and historical materials) (Peking, national ed., vol. 60 [This series carries no date of publication, but Hsiao's memoir was written before 1966]); Allen S. Whiting and Sheng Shih-ts'ai , *Sinkiang: Pawn or Pivot?* (East Lansing: Michigan State University Press, 1958). There is also Chiang Kai-shek, *Soviet Russia in China: A Summing Up at Seventy* (Taipei: China Publishing Company, 1969). From the Soviet side, two useful memoirs are: Ya. Ts'ui Ko Fu (Vasilii Chuikov), *Tsai Hua shih-ming* (Mission to China) (Peking: Hsin-hua ch'u-pan-she, 1983); Aleksandr Ya. Kalyagin, *Along Alien Roads*, trans. Steven I. Levine (New York: East Asian Institute, Columbia University, 1983).

For secondary sources, consult John W. Garver, *Chinese-Soviet Relations, 1937–1945: The Diplomacy of Chinese Nationalism* (New York: Oxford University Press, 1988), and the bibliography therein.

4. Bradford Lee, *Britain and the Sino-Japanese War, 1937–1939* (Stanford: Stanford University Press, 1972); Nicholas R. Clifford, *Retreat from China: British Policy in the Far East, 1937–1941* (London: Longmans, Green, 1957); Peter Lowe, *Great Britain and the Origins of the Pacific War* (London: Clarendon Press, 1977).

5. Regarding U.S. policy prior to the 1937 war, see Richard N. Current, "The Hoover Doctrine and the Stimson Doctrine," *The American Historical Review* 59, 3 (April 1954):512–42; Henry L. Stimson, *The Far Eastern Crisis: Recollections and Observations* (New York: Harper & Brothers, 1936); Dorothy Borg, *The United States and the Far Eastern Crisis of 1933–1938* (Cambridge: Harvard University Press, 1964).

6. Cited in Werner Levi, *Modern China's Foreign Policy* (Minneapolis: University of Minnesota Press, 1953), p. 222.

7. Regarding these various peace negotiations, see *Chiang tsung-t'ung mi-lu*, 11:172–73; John Hunter Boyle, *China and Japan at War 1937–1945: The Politics of Collaboration* (Stanford: Stanford University Press, 1972), pp. 182–87; Chang Po-fung, "Kuan-yu k'ang-Jih chan-cheng shih-ch'i Chiang Chieh-shih fan-tung chi-t'uan ti chi-tz'u t'ou-hsiang huo-tung" (Regarding several instances of the capitulationist activities of the reactionary Chiang Kai-shek clique during the War of Resistance against Japan), *Chin-tai shih yen-chiu* (Research on modern history), no. 2 (1979):216. *Chung-kuo chin-tai tui-wai kuan-hsi shih tzu-liao hsuan-chi, 1840–1949* (Selection of materials on China's modern foreign relations, 1840–1949), vol. 2, book 2 (Shanghai: Ch'in-men ch'u-pan-she, 1977), pp. 60–66.

8. Regarding Sino-German relations, see Ch'eng Tien-fong, "Shih Te hui-i-lu (Memoir of ambassadorship to Germany), *Chuan-chi wen-hsueh* (Biographical literature) 4, 6 (June 1964); 5, 1 (July 1964); 5, 2 (August 1964); 5, 3 (September 1964); 6, 3 (March 1965); 7, 1 (July 1965). The captured German diplomatic documents are also useful: United States Department of State, *Documents on German Foreign Policy, 1918–1945: From the Archives of the German Foreign Ministry, Series D,* 9 vols., (Washington DC: Government Printing Office, 1949–56). Good secondary studies of Sino-German relations include: Thomas L. Lauer, "German Attempts at Mediation of the Sino-Japanese War, 1937–1938," Ph.D. dissertation, Stanford University, 1973; William C. Kirby, *Germany and Republican China* (Stanford: Stanford University Press, 1984); Hsi-huen Liang, *The Sino-German Connection, Alexander von Falkenhausen between China and Germany, 1900–1941* (Amsterdam: Van Gorum, 1978).

9. Primary sources regarding Sino-American relations include: *Hu Shih lai-wang shu-hsin hsuan* (Selected correspondence of Hu Shi), 2 vols. (Peking: Chung-kuo she-hui k'o-hsueh-yuan chin-tai-shih yen-chiu-so, 1979); Hu Shih, *Hu Shih jen chu Mei ta-shih chi-chien wang-lai tien-kao* (Hu Shih's cable correspondence during his period as ambassador to the United States), Chung-hua min-kuo-shih tzu-liao ts'ung-kao, ch'uan-t'i tzu-liao hsuan-chi (Peking: Chung-kuo she-hui k'o-hsueh-yuan chin-tai-shih yen-chiu-so, 1978); *Map Room Messages of President Roosevelt, 1939–1945* (Lanham, MD: University Publications of America, 1981). Reel 8 contains communications between Roosevelt and Chiang Kai-shek from December 29, 1941, to January 26, 1945, and communications between Roosevelt and W. Averell Harriman, U.S. ambassador to Moscow, from January 4, 1943, to April 12, 1945. The *Foreign Relations of the United States* annual and special volumes are invaluable.

10. See Tsien Tai, *China and the Nine-Power Conference at Brussels in 1937* (New York: St. John's University Press, 1964); William Tung, *V. K. Wellington Koo and China's Wartime Diplomacy* (New York: St. John's University Press, 1977). Regarding the theory of China's vulnerability to economic sanctions, see the report presented by the Chinese delegation to the Nine Power Conference in 1937: *Japan's Dependence on Foreign Supplies of War Materials,* China Reference Series, 1, 3 (December 15, 1937), Trans-Pacific News Service.

11. The course of Japanese policy after 1940 did conform to these predictions, but in 1937–39 Japan's policy was considerably more muddled and less coherent than Chiang and his envoys would have had Anglo-American leaders believe.

12. James W. Morley, ed., *The China Quagmire: Japan's Expansion on the Asian Continent, 1933–1941* (New York: Columbia University Press, 1983); James W. Morley, ed. *The Fateful Choice: Japan's Advance into Southeast Asia, 1939–1941* (New York: Columbia University Press, 1980); Herbert Feis, *The Road to Pearl Harbor* (Princeton: Princeton University Press, 1950).

13. See A. Rossi, *The Russo-German Alliance, August 1939–June 1941* (Boston: Beacon Press, 1951); Frank Y. Ikle, *German-Japanese Relations, 1936–1940: A Study in Totalitarian Diplomacy* (New York: Bookman Associates, 1956).

14. Regarding Soviet-Japanese-German interactions, see James W. Morley, ed., *Deterrent Diplomacy: Japan, Germany, and the USSR, 1935–1940* (New York: Columbia University Press, 1976).

15. The attack was carried out with German support and in accordance with the sphere-of-influences provision of the Hitler-Stalin pact.

16. *Chung-hua min-kuo chung-yao shih-liao chu-pien—tui Jih k'ang-chan shih-ch'i, ti san pien, chan-shih wai-chiao* (Preliminary compilation of important historical materials of the Republic of China, the period of the War of Resistance against Japan, vol. 3, wartime diplomacy), book 3 (Taipei: Kuo-min-tang tang-shih wei-yuan-hui, 1981), pp.

237–374. These are Chiang Kai-shek's archives and contain much information on China's relations with all the powers.

17. Regarding the April 1941 Neutrality Agreement, see George A. Lensen, *Strange Neutrality: Soviet-Japanese Relations during the Second World War, 1941–1945* (Tallahassee: Diplomatic Press, 1972).

18. *Chiang tsung-t'ung mi-lu*, 12:185–86.

19. Diary, September 12, 1941, ibid., p. 172.

20. In her best-selling and highly influential work *Stilwell and the American Experience in China, 1911–1945* (New York: Bantam, 1972), Barbara Tuchman waxed indignant at Chiang's efforts in this regard, implying that such behavior was selfish and venal. Such indignation seems inappropriate to me. After all, in effect the Americans were trying to persuade Chiang to accept higher Chinese casualties in order to lower U.S. casualties.

21. Regarding the Burma campaigns, see Charles F. Romanus and Riley Sunderland, *Time Runs Out in CBI* (Washington, DC: Office of the Chief of Military History, U.S. Army, 1959); and Raymond Callahan, *Burma, 1942–1945* (Newark: University of Delaware Press, 1978). The memoir of the Chinese commander in 1941 is Tu Yu-ming, "Chung-kuo yuan-cheng-chun chu Mian tui Jih tso-chan shu-lueh" (General description of the entry into Burma and war against Japan of China's expeditionary army), *Wen-shih tzu-liao hsuan-chi*, national ed., no date, 8:1.

22. See Chang Chi-yun, *Record of the Cairo Conference* (Taipei: China Culture Publishing Foundation, 1953); U.S. Department of State, *The Conferences at Cairo and Teheran, 1943* (Washington, DC: Government Printing Office, 1961).

23. Regarding the Stilwell incident, see Tuchman, *Stilwell and the American Experience*; also, Joseph W. Stilwell, *The Stilwell Papers*, ed. Theodore H. White (New York: W. Sloane Associates, 1948); Charles Romanus and Riley Sunderland, *Stilwell's Mission to China* (Washington, DC: Department of the Army, Office of the Chief of Military History, 1953); Charles Romanus and Riley Sunderland, *Stilwell's Command Problems* (Washington, DC: Department of the Army, Office of the Chief of Military History, 1956).

24. U.S. Department of State, *The Conferences at Washington and Quebec, 1943* (Washington, DC: Government Printing Office, 1970), p. 420.

25. Regarding the problem of corruption, see Sterling Seagrave, *The Soong Dynasty* (New York: Harper and Row, 1985); Ross Y. Koen, *The China Lobby in American Politics* (New York: Macmillan, 1960).

26. *Chung-kuo wai-chiao-shih tzu-liao hsuan-pien ti san tze (1937–1941)*. (Selection of materials on China's diplomatic history, vol. 3, 1937–1945) (Peking: Wai-chiao hsueh-yuan, 1958), pp. 211–12.

27. *Foreign Relations of the United States, 1944*, 6:234.

28. The reader should be warned that "Yalta" remains a very controversial issue. The interpretation presented here of "Yalta"—as essentially a Sino-Soviet accommodation mediated, at China's request, by the United States—differs from the standard interpretation, which sees it as a U.S. sacrifice of Chinese interests to satisfy Russia for the sake of Soviet-American cooperation. For the full evidence for the view presented here, see my *Chinese-Soviet Relations, 1937–1945*. Peter M. Kuhfus reaches similar conclusions in "Die Risiken der Freundschaft: China und der Jalta-Mythos," *Bochumer Jahrbuch zur Ostasienforschung*, no. 7 (1984). This interpretation is also similar to the views, or at least the publicly expressed views, of "Yalta" held by the Americans who themselves negotiated that set of agreements. See Robert Sherwood, *Roosevelt and Hopkins: An Intimate History* (New York: Harper and Row, 1948).

29. The documentation for the Yalta conference itself is *The Conferences at Malta and Yalta, 1945* (Washington, DC: Government Printing Office, 1955). See also U.S. Department of State, *United States Relations with China with Special Reference to the Period 1944–1949* (Washington, DC: Department of State, 1949).

30. *Conferences at Cairo and Teheran, 1943*, p. 869.

2

CHINA'S WARTIME STATE

Robert E. Bedeski

THE CYCLICAL interpretation of the historical Chinese state is too imprecise to withstand intensive scrutiny by modern social science methods. Nevertheless, the metaphor of the dynastic cycle does provide a point of departure in understanding the enormous changes that have taken place in twentieth-century China. The decline and fall of the Ch'ing (Qing) system, coupled with the intrusion of the Western state pattern, has produced several assumptions among participants and observers.

First, despite its considerable flaws, the imperial system had long provided an effective means for governing an extensive agrarian territory. Nevertheless, even before the debacle of Yuan Shih-k'ai's post-1911 attempt to continue the imperial system, it had become evident that monarchy was no longer appropriate for the needs of a modern state.

Second, a modern nation-state was the only feasible form for Chinese development. The strength and vigor of the Western state, and the rapid and successful adaptation by the Japanese of such a state, provided China with examples of how its own modernization should proceed.[1]

Third, democracy, or at least a constitutional republic, would have to replace the monarchy. The absence of democratic development in China exacerbated the problem of institution-building, with a state apparatus virtually divorced from society.

Fourth, the problem of building a new Chinese state was intrinsically difficult, especially given the strength of centrifugal regionalism since the time of the T'ai-p'ing Rebellion. This was manifested in the phenomenon of warlordism that plagued the country throughout the Republican period. These domestic problems were severely aggravated by Japanese and Western limitations on Chinese sovereignty and the proclivity of these powers to intervene in local and national politics.

From the end of the Ch'ing period until the establishment of the Chinese Communist regime in 1949, the country suffered from weak sovereignty. Since sovereignty refers to both unified government and the legal competence of a government to resist interference from outside, Republican China was obviously weak in both respects. From the collapse of the Ch'ing dynasty in 1911 until the establishment of the Nationalist government in 1927, a succession of Peking-based regimes was unable either to control the country outside the capital or to prevent foreign powers from interfering in China's vital interests.

If the sovereignty of the Peking republic (1911–27) was weak and merely nominal, it is equally obvious that the sovereignty of the current Communist regime (1949–present) is strong and real. How did this important and fundamental change come about? State sovereignty cannot be created overnight. The Communist Party of China (CCP) can no more be credited with creating sovereignty from scratch in Peking in 1949 than it can be with winning the war against Japan in 1945. For an answer to the question of how this fundamental change occurred, one must look to the period of Nationalist rule (1927–49). Indeed, the major achievement of the Kuomintang—an accomplishment that is almost universally overlooked—was the establishment of the modern sovereign Chinese state.

This chapter examines the political system introduced by the Kuomintang following the Northern Expedition. In contemporary political science terms, one would call it a "soft authoritarian" system.[2] The system established by the Kuomintang in its capital at Nanking broke with the Peking republic in form and content and absorbed lessons from a number of contemporary political movements—including Italian nationalism, the Soviet party dictatorship, and Japanese militarism. Unlike these systems, however, the Kuomintang ideology was committed to ultimate constitutional democracy.

During the first decade of Kuomintang power, the foundations of the modern sovereign state were established. In the second decade, some of these foundations were tested, strengthened, and refined, while others were abandoned. In 1927 the Kuomintang took over a state that was fundamentally lacking in the attributes of power. It succeeded in strengthening this state to the point where it was able to fight the vastly superior industrial power that was Japan and to survive. At the same time, the Nationalists continued to confront a fragmented society, provincial militarists, and an expanding Communist movement. In the face of these obstacles, it is not surprising that demoralization set in and that the revolutionary élan of the movement was undermined. This loss of momentum has been extensively documented by Lloyd Eastman and others.[3] What has barely been examined are the state-building efforts of the Kuomintang during its second decade in power, against insurmountable odds. The objective in examining the wartime political system of China is not to find out what went wrong. Others have already done this, often with political axes to grind. The purpose, rather, is to understand the evolution of the modern Chinese state. From the vantage point of over four decades later, one should be able to provide an objective assessment of that vital period in Chinese state evolution.

The legacy of the Kuomintang period—both prewar and wartime—was to establish the basic parameters of the modern Chinese state. Without the tenacity of the Kuomintang (and more specifically of Chiang Kai-shek himself), the sovereign institutions of the People's Republic of China (PRC) would not have been created so quickly or so easily. The Kuomintang and the Communist party, then, have been uncooperative but nonetheless indispensable partners in creating modern China.

Toward a Theory of the Modern Chinese State

Although Anglo-American political science generally abandoned the notion of the state after 1945 in favor of the concept of the political system, in recent years the literature has again focused on the "state." The older notions of the legal-constitutional state were too restrictive in providing much guidance to analysis of contemporary political phenomena. Modern writings on the state have absorbed some of the contributions from the political system approach and address a broader range of institutions than in the past—including party, bureaucracy, military, and pressure groups.

One way of thinking about the Chinese state is to see it as an evolutionary process, commencing with the fragmented warlord society in the period of the Peking republic, passing through a period of military unification under the Kuomintang, aiming toward a constitutional democracy during the period of Political Tutelage, and in recent years witnessing a significant softening of the party dictatorship in Taiwan. Focusing on the Kuomintang branch of this evolutionary process, one can see a clear movement from subsystem territorial fragments to the state-as-force and finally to the state-as-legal-authority.[4] A parallel, but slower, movement is evident on the mainland as well. The ongoing state-building project remains anchored in the Kuomintang foundations.

The Kuomintang State: Prewar Period

The political system that governed China during the period of the anti-Japanese War had been established following the Northern Expedition. The central framework of the Nanking state was the 1928 Organic Law. Since this was to be a party dictatorship during the period of Political Tutelage, the party became the supreme arbiter of political power and the ultimate locus of sovereignty.

The Kuomintang had been reorganized in 1924 as a Leninist party. The National People's Congress was the supreme organ of the party, while the Central Executive Committee (CEC) exercised its power between meetings of the congress. Under authority of a 1929 party resolution, the CEC exercised authority over the Central Political Council (CPC), which governed the State Council of the central government.

While the CPC was the theoretical vehicle of party dominance over the national government, central and local party departments frequently interfered in governmental administration. The CEC met weekly to discuss state affairs and sent its resolutions to the State Council, which referred decisions to the proper government organ or yuan.

The 1928 Organic Law established the five-yuan system, which had been formulated in Sun Yat-sen's *Three Principles of the People*. The State Council acted as the link between the party and the government and appointed the presidents of the five yuan. The Executive Yuan was the highest executive organ of the national government and operated similar to a cabinet in a parliamentary government. The Legislative Yuan began with forty-nine appointed members in late 1928. Under Article 25 of the Organic Law, it could decide on legislation, budgets, declarations of war, and other international matters. The official term for members was two years, but continued incumbency was not uncommon.

The Judicial Yuan was established to introduce a modern court system as well as to perform other functions of a civilized judiciary. It lacked the power to review legislation, however. The Examination Yuan was instituted to provide a mechanism for seeking the best officials for administration, but in practice only a small proportion of public officials was selected by examination. The Supervision Yuan was designed to perform censorial functions of the imperial period, but its full potential was never realized.

In practice, there was little balancing of power. The yuan presidents and vice-presidents participated in the State Council and thus played a role in formulating coordinated national policy. State Council resolutions had the force of law and therefore preempted the power of the Legislative Yuan. The national government under party control was the nucleus of the new Chinese state and provided a civilian core for the transition to constitutional government. It was also intended to construct the framework for legal sovereignty.

At the provincial level, governments consisting of seven to nine members were appointed by the national government, and one was designated as chairman. Active military officers were legally barred from membership in the provincial government, which consisted of a secretariat and four departments.

The Ministry of the Interior managed relations between the central government and *hsien*, which were designated as the future starting points of local self-government. Local elections were organized in a limited fashion, and hsien magistrates were to be given appointments after examinations. Provinces set up schools to train the local officials. The ministry also demarcated new provinces, bringing the total to twenty-eight, and set up seven special municipalities at the level of provinces. This latter proviso recognized the unique problems of urban areas.

Toward Constitutional Government

The Nanking regime faced multiple pressures to fulfill its promise to move from Political Tutelage to Constitutional Government—especially from intellectuals and the left-wing of the party. The Organic Law of 1928 supplied only one dimension of a constitution. It provided for the structure of government powers and administrative jurisdiction but contained no provisions for civil rights, elections, or constitutional amendments. Moreover, with ultimate sovereignty in the hands of a nonelected party, democracy remained unimplemented.

More conservative elements in the Kuomintang argued against a democratic constitution on the grounds that the nation was not ready. Government control did not extend to more distant provinces, nor down to the hsien level in many areas. Political unification, they contended, had to precede democratization, or else a premature constitution would be stillborn like the previous documents that tried to introduce parliamentary institutions and popular sovereignty. Experience with constitutions between 1911 and 1926 had demonstrated that even noble and well-designed constitutions without fundamental unity of state and society served no useful purpose. To the contrary, they eroded the credibility of constitutional government as a viable future goal. In addition, popular participation in government would allow opponents of Kuomintang Tutelage, such as the Communists, to undermine implementation of Sun's programs.

According to William L. Tung, the five-yuan government was concerned only with maintaining the power of the party. Unnecessary and divisive conflict would result if both party supremacy and popular participation (via representative institutions) were accommodated in the political system.[5]

The "Provisional" Constitution

The liberal intellectual Hu Shih criticized the Kuomintang's reluctance to push ahead to constitutional democracy. He argued that practice in democracy was the best school for democratic government, and that Political Tutelage without a constitution was a form of absolutism.[6] To hasten the advent of constitutional government, Wang Ching-wei and his supporters held an "Enlarged Party Conference" in Peiping, as the former capital was now called. After Nationalist armies captured the city, the conference was forced to move to Taiyuan where it produced a draft constitution on October 27, 1930. This "Taiyuan Draft Constitution" included protection for individual rights, allowed for popular election of members of the Legislative and Supervisory yuans, and established representative organs at the provincial and county levels. While the document was never implemented, it did outline the type of constitution that party liberals favored.

Chiang Kai-shek proposed a provisional constitution (*yueh fa*) to the CEC in 1931, in part to secure consensus with the Wang Ching-wei wing of the party.[7] This was opposed by Hu Han-min, who claimed that the writings of Sun Yat-sen provided the equivalent of a Provisional Constitution, and that it was premature, at this stage of Political Tutelage, to introduce a constitution. Chiang prevailed, and by May 5, 1931, a draft constitution was ready for consideration by the National People's Congress. The congress delegates were elected and adopted the draft of the provisional constitution. It was promulgated on June 1, 1931, as a transitional document during the period of Political Tutelage. When a majority of provinces had reached a certain stage of constitutional development, the central government would summon a National Assembly to adopt and promulgate a permanent constitution.

From 1931 to 1937 the Organic Law was retained and amended as the organizational law of the national government, and it had the effect of reducing the role of the party. Pressure for a permanent constitution (*hsien fa*) continued, and in 1934, the party drafted one containing ten chapters, based on the Organic Law and the 1931 Provisional Constitution. The Legislative Yuan passed and promulgated a revised version on May 5, 1936, and anticipated its adoption by a National People's Congress, which was scheduled for November of that year. Continued disorder in many parts of the country and increasing Japanese military pressure in the north precluded elections, and prevented calling the National People's Congress.

These state developments provided the basis of the wartime political system. A modicum of political order had been established, and Nanking had asserted its hegemony over the country to a degree much greater than had any government since the Ch'ing. The Kuomintang lurched toward fulfilling its promise of constitutional democracy, restrained by conservatives who wanted full implementation of Sun Yat-sen's program of national reconstruction, and pushed by liberals and leftists who wanted access to the reins of power.

Standing in the middle was Chiang Kai-shek, who controlled the only stabilizing force in the emerging state—the military. Through his actions on several occasions, Chiang established his indispensability to both the party and the state. He gradually acquired a charismatic authority as the crucial center of party, army, and government. He guided the Nationalist state through the troubles of the Northern Expedition, civil wars and militarist revolts, the Japanese invasion of Manchuria, Communist rebellions, and social disorder. His critics charged one-man dictatorship, but they offered no viable alternative to his leadership.

The Kuomintang and the Provinces—The Territorial Bases of the State

The primary goal of the Nanking government was to expand and strengthen state sovereignty, which had been established in 1928. In pursuing this objective, extending control over the provinces was vital. Three military forces opposed the central government in its quest—the regional warlords, the Communists, and the Japanese. Without consolidation of the provinces, the Nationalist republic would remain a hollow shell. Democracy at the national or local levels could have little significance unless a single state order were first established. Modern state institutions have meaning and authority only in a sovereign state.

Although the Kuomintang held nominal sovereignty over the country from

1928 through the loss of Manchuria to Japan in 1931, its actual control remained restricted to the lower Yangtze basin. Even jurisdiction over Kwangtung Province was tenuous at best. Local officials and provincial militarists had grown accustomed to relatively autonomous power and opposed any extension of central government authority into their domains. Chiang Kai-shek made alliances with some of the militarists who acknowledged the formal sovereignty of Nanking, but it generally required superior military force to impose central jurisdiction on the localities. Thus Nanking undertook a series of military efforts against its enemies designed to extend its own authority and undermine that of its rivals.

A series of encirclement campaigns to eradicate the Communists culminated in October 1933 when Nanking launched its fifth campaign. In early 1934, the Communists broke out and started on what came to be known as the Long March. In pursuing the Communist remnants, the forces of the central government entered provinces where Nanking's authority was weak and initiated a process well described by Lawrence Rosinger:

> First the Communists approached or entered a province, threatening the existing local and national authority. Central troops were then dispatched in reply. After a period of preparation by Nanking representatives, Chiang Kai-shek would go to the provincial capital by plane and announce his intention to improve local conditions. The work of provincial reorganization would now begin in earnest, the degree of change depending upon whether the local authorities were strong or weak. The Central objectives were: control of the provincial armed forces, reorganization of the military and civilian personnel of the provincial government, and the extension of Central economic influence. While this process was going on, the Communists would probably have left the province, but the central troops remained.[8]

In the continuing struggle to consolidate central government authority, Chiang Kai-shek often turned adversity into advantage, as his suppression of the Kwangsi rebellion in 1936 demonstrates. The Cantonese militarist, Ch'en Chitang, criticized Nanking for not resisting Japan with sufficient vigor. In May 1936, he joined his Kwangsi allies, Pai Ch'ung-hsi and Li Tsung-jen, in issuing a manifesto urging increased resistance to Japan.They even planned to send their forces north to attack the invaders.[9] This display of patriotism was not driven solely by nationalism. The southwestern militarists saw themselves increasingly isolated by the expansion of central government control in their neighboring provinces.

The Kuomintang quickly called a special meeting of the CEC and dismissed Ch'en Chi-tang, while confirming the Kwangsi leaders in their positions. This finalized the split between the two powerful groups in the southwest. The meeting also rejected the proposal that an anti-Japanese expedition be launched.[10] Not only had a civil war been avoided, and a source of trouble in Kwangtung removed, but the more progressive Kwangsi leaders were now more closely linked to the Nationalist cause. The two generals provided important support for the Nationalist War of Resistance, but they were also considered to be serious rivals to Chiang Kai-shek.

The Nanking political system that emerged after 1928 was a mélange of formal constitutional institutions, ad hoc party arrangements, personal factions, and military alignments. As long as the central government had to compete for authority with regional and provincial powers who had military forces to back them up, military priorities remained supreme in the formation of the Chinese state.

During the war, Chiang Kai-shek attempted to coopt some of his adversaries by awarding state and party positions to a number of regional military figures. Ch'en Chi-tang, for example, was brought into the State Council in 1938, and he served as minister of agriculture and forestry (1940–42). The National Military Council consisted of some of the very same militarists Chiang Kai-shek had fought against in earlier civil wars—Feng Yü-hsiang, Yen Hsi-shan, and Li Tsung-jen. However, these men remained outside the inner circle of power.

The move of the capital to Nanking in 1927 was not only a rejection of the old imperial city of Peking and its pretensions, but also a strategic statement that the Yangtze valley was to be the axis of the new political system. In the north, the east-west Lunghai railway demarcated the extent of effective Kuomintang military control. Szechwan, which became the wartime base of the Nationalists, was integrated into the system only partially. By ejecting the Communists from their Kiangsi bases, the Nationalists could consolidate a greater degree of control there. Chekiang, Anhwei, and Kiangsu were solidly under Nanking authority, as was Fukien after the defeat of the rebellion there. Kwangsi and Kwangtung were nominally under the Kuomintang, but local militarists exercised considerable power, even through the war.

Kuomintang Organization

Supreme authority in the Kuomintang remained vested in the National Congress, which was supposed to meet every two years. Meetings were actually held in 1924, 1926, 1929, 1931, and 1935. An "Extraordinary National Congress" was held in Hankow from March 29 to April 2, 1938, and conferred the title of *tsung-ts'ai* (director-general) on Chiang Kai-shek. Through the war, party power was exercised by the CEC and CSC since it was impossible to elect delegates to a Sixth Congress.

Through the end of 1942, the CEC held ten plenary sessions. The second session curtailed Kwangtung's autonomy in July 1936. The fifth created the Supreme National Defense Council, which was given control of all party organs of the CEC, the five yuan of the national government, and the other organs of the National Military Council. The sixth (November 1939) appointed Chiang Kai-shek president of the Executive Yuan and directed him to hold a people's congress in a year to adopt a permanent constitution. Wartime exigencies required postponement of this congress. Other plenary sessions decided on a wide range of measures, including finances, conscription, administrative reform, price control, education, disaster relief, social welfare, and relations with other parties.[11] One of the effects of the war was to concentrate political power into the Kuomintang and to shift the gravity from the party congress to the CEC. The beginnings of intraparty democracy had emerged in the 1928–37 period but were severely circumscribed thereafter.

While the formal powers of the CEC appeared formidable, it is likely that an even smaller membership controlled the party and state. Hsi-sheng Ch'i notes the growth of the body from 24 in 1924 to 119 in 1935 to 223 in 1945. As it grew in size, powers were exercised by the Standing Committee of the CEC and later by the Political Council.[12] After 1939, CEC membership included top officials in government. In effect, party oversight of government became meaningless, with interlocking membership in party and government. With the 1938 introduction of the *tsung-ts'ai* system, most crucial decisions were made by Chiang Kai-shek, with or without consultation with close advisers, or after negotiation with political rivals.[13]

As state priorities shifted from expanding its sovereignty to preserving it, a more absolutist model emerged with Chiang Kai-shek at the center. This also represented a major alteration in the nature of the political regime. The prewar political system had consisted of an unstable triumvirate—Chiang Kai-shek, Wang Ching-wei, and Hu Han-min, with the former occupying the ideological center. The death of Hu in 1936, and the defection of Wang in 1939, left Chiang alone at the center of power.

Even after Hu and Wang left the scene, however, Chiang Kai-shek was never able to exercise full dictatorial powers in the manner that critics and enemies often ascribed to him. Factions and regional groups in particular severely circumscribed his ability to mobilize society. Indeed, Hsi-sheng Ch'i suggests that during the war period the limitations on Chiang's control over society and the government were so great that ultimately his regime was "reduced to almost total reliance on his secret service."[14]

The People's Political Council

Chiang and his party associates realized the importance of mobilizing elite opinion and creating institutions that could contribute to successful prosecution of the war effort. To meet these objectives, the People's Political Council (PPC) was authorized by the Kuomintang CEC Hankow meeting in the spring of 1938, and it met in July of the same year. It was established as a forum of public opinion since the government was unable to convoke the National People's Congress (NPC) to adopt the draft constitution.[15] The PPC, which Wang Ching-wei presided over, was composed of 220 members of various sectors of society from the twenty-eight provinces of China. A majority of the members were from the Kuomintang, but the Communists had eight delegates.

The People's Political Council had little power. For example, in its session of February 13–21, 1939, it heard government reports on political, military, financial, foreign, educational, and economic affairs, and it passed six resolutions relating to such matters as strengthening air raid defenses, organizing ethnic minorities, and arranging remittance facilities under the postal administration. According to a recent history, "It could propose policies and criticize, but it could not enforce its decisions. Its powers were merely advisory. But as long as the spirit of cooperation pervaded the council, until about 1939, it was an influential organ of government."[16]

The function of this body was to supervise government policy, submit proposals to the government, and assist government in other areas, including reconstruction and resistance. The council established a number of committees to draft proposals to the government and decided to establish provincial- and municipal-level councils. These councils were intended to bring the central and provincial levels of government into closer cooperation, and especially to assist the central government in prosecuting the war.

The first PPC held five sessions between July 1938 and April 1940, although it was supposed to have a tenure of only one year. The second PPC met in Chungking on March 1, 1941. Its authorized membership of 240 included seven Communists who, however, did not attend. Members were not directly selected by the Kuomintang, and 90 delegates were elected by provincial and municipal assemblies.[17] The Presidium of the first meeting consisted of Chiang Kai-shek; Chang Po-ling, president of Nankai University; Carson Chang, leader of the National Socialist party of China; Tso Shun-sheng, leader of the China Youth party; and Wu Yi-fang, a college president.[18] At the meetings, Chiang Kai-shek, the presidents of the various yuan, and cabinet ministers all made extensive confidential reports.

Five committees were established to discuss subjects such as foreign affairs, military affairs, finance, industry, education, and agriculture. After the committees met, they gave specific recommendations to the government on matters including opium suppression, war relief, local self-government, the necessity for a people's congress, Mongolian and Tibetan affairs, foreign relations, military affairs, finances, communications, agriculture and forestry, education, and social affairs. In sum, their purview covered a very broad spectrum of issues and concerns. After issuing a manifesto, the second PPC adjourned on March 10, 1941.

The second PPC had been given the additional power to conduct investigations, and it held two sessions. Women members were increased from ten to fifteen. In all cases, the final selection had to be passed by the Supreme National Defense Council. It was intended that the PPC meet for ten days every six months, although it did not in fact meet with such regularity. Between sessions, a standing committee was to examine execution of the PPC resolutions, receive reports from officials, and make suggestions to the government. The third PPC convened in October 1942, with 164 elected delegates out of 240.

The Organic Law of the PPC specified that there were four categories of councillors: Group A, with 164 members who were chosen by provincial and municipal councils and allocated roughly according to population; groups B and C, consisting of 16 councillors representing Mongolia, Tibet, and overseas Chinese; and Group D, with the remaining 60 councillors who were selected by the CEC from among 120 names submitted by the Supreme National Defense Council.[19]

The PPC was not intended to be nor did it function as a substitute for the Legislative Yuan. It had only consultative powers. Nevertheless, Kuomintang factions maneuvered for dominant positions in committees, and in so doing they alienated minority parties to the point that these latter wound up boycotting the PPC.[20] The notion of a consultative body with no powers was incorporated into the political system of the People's Republic of China via the Chinese People's Political Consultative Conference.

Local Government

The organization of provincial governments was based on the *Revised Organic Law of the Provincial Government* (March 23, 1931). Administration of provinces was to be in accordance with the *Fundamentals of National Reconstruction*, which served as a provisional constitution until the end of the period of Political Tutelage. The provincial government had the power to issue ordinances and regulations for administration, as long as they did not conflict with central government laws.[21] Provincial governments consisted of seven to nine appointees of the central government, who formed the provincial commission, with one of the appointees serving as chairman.

The provincial government consisted of several departments, including Civil Affairs, Finances, Education, and Reconstruction as well as a Secretariat. The departments were headed by a commissioner, who was selected from among the members of the provincial government and approved by the Executive Yuan of the national government. In theory, the central government had considerable power over the provinces, but wartime exigencies added to the territorial aggrandizement of regional militarists who, in the period after the fall of the imperial dynasty, had consolidated what amounted to provincial sovereignty. This was further complicated by poor communications, the large size of the provinces themselves, and local particularism.

To facilitate administration, the national government established the Office of the Special Administrative Inspector in March 1936. The Executive Yuan appointed a special administrative inspector at the behest of the provincial government. Regulations empowered the special administrative inspector to investigate, direct, and supervise hsien governments under provincial government guidance. He could also suggest reforms to the provincial government and was concurrently commander of the police and peace preservation corps in the area.[22] The special administrative inspector had several hsien under his control, and he was authorized to convene administrative conferences to improve local government. If his area fell to the Japanese, he was responsible for carrying out resistance activities within it. The special administrative inspector system was designed to provide a government presence even in areas behind Japanese lines.

Municipalities were either special (under direct Executive Yuan control), or ordinary. The seven special municipalities included the national capital, cities with a population of over one million, and cities that possess "special political, economic, and cultural importance."[23] These included Nanking, Shanghai, Peiping, Tientsin, Tsingtao, Chungking, and Sian. Ordinary municipalities were under the jurisdiction of the provincial government, and consisted of provincial capitals, cities with a population over 200,000, and those having special importance and a population over 100,000.

Municipalities of both types were divided into *chu* (districts). Each chu was subdivided into 10–20 *pao*. A pao consisted of 10–30 *chia*, and one chia contained 10–30 households. Certified residents had the right to attend the residents' general meetings and exercise electoral rights.

The municipal governments had jurisdiction over matters such as census-taking, famine relief, labor administration, educational and cultural activities, public safety and health, and land administration. Revenue sources included taxes on land, housing, and business as well as income from public property and enterprises. Municipal governments were headed by mayors who were appointed by the Executive Yuan. Their functional offices included bureaus of Social Affairs, Police, Finance, and Public Works. When necessary, additional bureaus could be organized, such as Education, Public Health, Land, Public Utilities, and Harbor. According to law, there was a municipal affairs council composed of the mayor, counsellors, and directors of the various bureaus. In some cities where municipal representative councils had been formed, three to five delegates could be elected to attend municipal affairs council meetings.

For most of the Chinese population, the hsien was the level of government with which they had primary contact. A 1939 Law (*Organic Outline of Various Graded Units in the Hsien*) stipulated the organization of the county. The law mandated three to six classes of hsien, depending on area, population, economic conditions, cultural status, and communications facilities. The hsien was divided into *hsiang* (townships) in rural areas and into *chen* (wards) in urban areas. The rural hsiang was divided into pao and the chen into chia.

The hsien was administered by the local magistrate under the authority of the provincial government. The government was divided into functional sections (civil affairs, finance, education, reconstruction, military affairs, land administration, and social welfare). The hsien affairs council met every two weeks to discuss and decide on hsien affairs as well as resolutions passed by the hsien representative council. This council consisted of delegates elected by hsiang councils. In cases where a county was very large, it could be divided into chu or districts. By the end of 1941, there were a total of 1,469 hsien in China. Of these, 1,053 had been adjusted according to the new system of 1939.[24]

To deal with hsien that were cut off from the provincial government because of the war, the office of the special administrative inspector in the area was authorized to direct affairs there. If totally cut off from higher levels of supervision, the local magistrate could exercise discretionary powers. To simplify the administration, he could also dissolve or merge organs not directly related to the prosecution of the war. Men with military experience and hsien administrative experience were to be sought for these kinds of positions. By January 1942, the Executive Yuan provided the following figures on hsien administration: administration intact, 459; magistrate remains, hsien partially occupied, 33; hsien occupied, magistrate remains in rural areas, 324; magistrate attends to duties in neighboring hsien, 49; hsien under Japanese control, 59; total, 924.

Conclusion—State-Building Efforts of the Nationalist Government

The state structure of the wartime Nanking regime was the product of a considerable number of elements that interacted under the pressure of war. Not all of these elements mixed together easily. The structure of the regime and the politics of wartime China reflected the sometimes conflicting objectives that Nanking pursued. The Nationalists' first priority was to mobilize all human and material resources for the war effort against the Japanese invaders. Second was to expand the authority of the central government down to the provincial and local levels, and to establish a rational administrative system to meet the needs of an impoverished and fragmented society. The Nationalist state sought to achieve a degree of consensus among the various political factions and regional militarists in order to fight the war more effectively. Particularly with respect to the Communists, the Nationalists tried to find some way to use them against the Japanese without allowing them to expand their bases and territory. Kuomintang leaders attempted to create viable institutions of government that would resemble other modern states and to carry out the functions of a modern state. In so doing, the Nationalists wanted to implement the programs of Sun Yat-sen as faithfully as possible, even though he could not possibly have foreseen the political developments that followed his death. Finally, the common masses had to be brought into the state via forms of political participation that would not upset the delicate power arrangements on which the stability of the system depended. All these priorities can be summarized under the concept of modern sovereignty—a goal that the Ch'ing court had seen slip out of its grasp, and which the successor Peking republics had been unable to achieve.

Whatever flaws of design or execution the Kuomintang state evidenced, it is vital to judge it from the standpoint of the extremely harsh environment it faced. The prewar situation for the Kuomintang was already enormously difficult and challenging. James E. Sheridan concludes that the war magnified the weaknesses of the government, and that the move to western China made the Kuomintang heavily dependent on the conservative Szechwan landlords. He suggests that "The government also felt threatened because it was in warlord territory, surrounded by militarists who felt but little loyalty to Chiang Kai-shek or his party. Partly for these reasons, the government became increasingly dictatorial and repressive."[25]

Critics of the Kuomintang often use the developed modern democratic state as their standard of measure and fail to recognize the formidable obstacles to state-building. Lloyd Eastman nominated Chiang Kai-shek as the villain responsible for China's weakness:

> Chiang Kai-shek's political strategy was what has been called a balance of weakness. That is, he worked to maintain himself and his government in a position of authority by keeping all other political forces weak. He denied arms to the provincial armies; he repressed intellectuals whose ideas seemed to him dangerous; he kept even his supporters weak by balancing them one against the other. For a time this strategy worked in the sense that it kept Chiang in power. In a fundamental sense, however, it failed, *for by keeping all these elements weak, Chiang prevented the nation from becoming strong.*[26]

Eastman may be confusing centrifugalism with pluralism; he claims that Chiang should have provided "his potential supporters—such as the nation's intellectuals, or peasants, or bourgeoisie—access to the political process."[27] Eastman's simplistic suggestion that expanding elite or popular participation would have been a more viable solution ignores the complexity of establishing political order even under the most favorable conditions. Vivienne Shue, for example, suggests that in the early 1950s, when the Communists exercised a degree of control far beyond the wildest expectations of the Kuomintang, the very extension of bureaucratic control into the rural periphery augmented local ability to resist the center.[28] How much more difficult it was to achieve national integration during the wartime environment of military fragmentation, amid the loss of crucial cities and territories, the demoralization of the party, economic disasters, and political factionalism.[29]

The program of Political Tutelage was an explicit set of transitional policies to establish state institutions. The international depression added an additional obstacle to modernization, while the loss of Manchuria and the tenuous hold on North China were further distractions to orderly state-building. Add to this the Communist revolts and the existence of semisovereign militarists, and one can begin to understand what tremendous odds were faced in the efforts to create a viable political system.

The point about the handicaps Nationalist China faced is well made by Maria Hsia Chang:

> Being a "late-comer" to modernization, China did not have the luxury of the natural and gradual evolution of democratic preconditions that the West enjoyed. As a country that aspired to a delayed but rapid industrialization, it was necessary that the modernization of China's economy and polity come under the aegis of the state. State building, then, became a necessary priority. Furthermore, as a transitional system in which traditional political institutions and sources of legitimacy were no longer viable while the new institutions of a modern polity were yet unborn, state building became the responsibility of the revolutionary party.[30]

Conventional wisdom, as represented by Eastman and shared by other critics of the Kuomintang, is that the wartime political system was a personal dictatorship of Chiang Kai-shek that became entrenched in conservatism and reaction, and finally collapsed because of rampant corruption and ineptness in the face of a disciplined, united and populist Communist party in 1949. Such a hypothesis, however, does not take us much beyond the simple notion of "old regime—bad; new regime—good" (or at least effective). It recites Kuomintang failures and explains some of the rise of the Communists, but not much else.

The approach taken by Shue and others at least allows for the possibility that some positive state-building occurred during the Republican period. The process of state-building occurs at two general levels—that of national and local politics. Most scholarship has focused on the local level of state-building where Kuomintang success was notably lacking, and where the Communists were most successful. To be sure, the Kuomintang record at the national level of the political system was not particularly brilliant, but given the nature of the environment, it may have been the best possible under the circumstances.

Specifically, what were the accomplishments of the Kuomintang prewar and wartime regime? As just suggested, these were manifest more at the national and international levels than at the local. First, the territorial fragments of the Republic were significantly, but not totally, integrated into a unified state system. This simplified the task of the Communists in the civil war of the late 1940s. For the most part, the Communist victory was a matter of defeating a single government and its army rather than overcoming a series of entrenched regional militarists.

Second, the Kuomintang established the institutions and priorities of the modern Chinese state which the Communists subsequently adapted to their own purposes rather than eliminated. The united front organization, the Chinese People's Political Consultative Conference, which became the provisional government in 1949, was the direct heir of the People's Political Council—minus the Kuomintang, of course, except for its splinter Kuomintang Revolutionary Committee, which cooperated with the Communists. The ideas of Sun Yat-sen were among the important antecedents of Mao's program of New Democracy.[31] The

Leninist model of the party dictatorship, which the Kuomintang adopted in the 1920s, tugged the CCP in two different directions. The Soviet form of this model was one in which a permanent elite exercised power in the name of the proletariat until the eventual withering away of the state. The Kuomintang's form of this model was a tutelary state in which a transitional party dictatorship pointed the way toward an eventual constitutional democracy with multiple competing parties.

Far more than the Peking regimes that preceded it, the Nationalist government was able to expand the territorial integrity of the Chinese state until the Japanese invasion of Manchuria in 1931. With the Chinese armies as yet unprepared to fight a superior foe, Chiang Kai-shek was reluctant to stand up against the Japanese armies, knowing that they would easily take over the remaining Nationalist territory.

Finally, the Nationalists were able to increase the international stature of China and to secure the removal of most of the unequal treaties. Chiang Kai-shek participated in several important wartime conferences and personified China's stubborn resistance to Japanese aggression. The image of a united China—even though it was more norm than reality—was very useful in carrying out negotiations for the postwar settlement and in representing China's vital interests.

When the Communists won the civil war with the Kuomintang in 1949 they inherited an agenda for state-building that the Nationalists had already drawn up and partially implemented. This suggests the need to reexamine the dominant paradigm in Western analysis of modern China that has classified the Kuomintang political system as the last one in a series of ineffective, old regime republics.[32] An alternative hypothesis, which deserves to be further explored, is that the Nationalist regime was the transition to, or even the beginning of, a new and sovereign Chinese state system.

Notes

1. On the role of legal change in Chinese and Japanese modernization, see Gerrit W. Gong, *The Standard of "Civilization" in International Society* (Oxford: Clarendon Press, 1984).

2. See Han Soong-joo, "Political Institutionalization in South Korea, 1961–1984," in *Asian Political Institutionalization*, ed. Robert A. Scalapino, Seizaburo Sato, and Jusuf Wanandi (Berkeley: University of California, Institute of East Asian Studies, 1986).

3. Lloyd E. Eastman, *Seeds of Destruction* (Stanford: Stanford University Press, 1984).

4. Alexander Passerin d'Entreves, *The Notion of the State* (London: Oxford University Press, 1967).

5. William Tung, *The Political Institutions of Modern China* (The Hague: M. Nijhoff, 1964), pp. 122–23.

6. *North China Herald*, September 7, 1929, p. 357.

7. Robert E. Bedeski, *State-Building in Modern China: The Kuomintang in the Prewar Period* (Berkeley: University of California, Institute of East Asian Studies, 1981), p. 88.

8. Lawrence K. Rosinger, *China's Wartime Politics, 1937–1944* (Princeton: Princeton University Press, 1944), pp. 12–13.

9. Ibid., p. 18.

10. Ibid., p. 19

11. Chinese Ministry of Information, *China Handbook, 1937–1943* (New York: Macmillan, 1943), p. 42.

12. Hsi-sheng Ch'i, *Nationalist China at War: Military Defeats and Political Collapse* (Ann Arbor: University of Michigan Press, 1982), p. 215.

13. Ibid., p. 216.

14. Ibid., p. 225.

15. U.S. Department of State, *Foreign Relations of the United States*, 893.00/14744 (Despatch from Chungking, May 21, 1941), p. 2.

16. John K. Fairbank and Albert Feuerwerker, eds., *The Cambridge History of China*, vol. 13, "Republican China. 1912–1949," part 2 (Cambridge: Cambridge University Press, 1986), p. 561.

17. *China Handbook, 1937–1943*, p. 109.

18. *Foreign Relations of the United States*, 893.00/14744 (Chungking, May 21, 1941), p. 3.

19. *China Handbook, 1937–1943*, pp. 110–12.

20. Ch'i, *Nationalist China at War*, p. 212.

21. *China Handbook, 1937–1943*, p. 99.

22. Ibid., p. 100.

23. Ibid., pp. 101–3.

24. Ibid., pp. 106–8.

25. James E. Sheridan, *China in Disintegration: The Republican Era in Chinese History* (New York: The Free Press, 1975), p. 259.

26. Eastman, *Seeds of Destruction*, p. 42 (emphasis added).

27. Ibid, p. 43.

28. Vivienne Shue, *The Reach of the State: Sketches of the Chinese Body Politic* (Stanford: Stanford University Press, 1988), p. 46.

29. Ibid., p. 104.

30. Maria Hsia Chang, *The Chinese Blue Shirt Society: Fascism and National Development* (Berkeley: University of California, Institute of East Asian Studies, 1985), p. 135.

31. Robert E. Bedeski, "The Concept of the State: Sun Yat-sen and Mao Tse-tung," *The China Quarterly*, no. 70 (June 1977):338–54.

32. Eastman, *Seeds of Destruction*.

3

CONTENDING POLITICAL FORCES DURING THE WAR OF RESISTANCE

T'ien-wei Wu

BARELY one week after the Lukouch'iao Incident, Chiang Kai-shek declared that "one minute before the last hope is lost, we still hope for peace." When peace did not come, however, most Chinese had no regrets. United to face a common enemy, the whole country rallied behind the national government and Chiang Kai-shek. For the first time in the history of the Republic of China, regional militarists responded to the call of the central government. All of the political parties unanimously declared their full support and cooperation with the national government of Chiang Kai-shek in the War of Resistance against Japan. Men such as Pai Ch'ung-hsi, leader of the Kwangsi Clique, and Kuo Mo-jo, the ex-Communist, buried the hatchet and began to work together with a common spirit. The slogan "Let those who have money contribute money and those who have labor contribute labor" reverberated throughout the war.

Despite the vicissitudes of war and domestic politics, support for the War of Resistance remained at a high pitch among educated and young Chinese. When the last great Japanese offensive (Ichigo) was launched in the fall of 1944, 100,000 students joined the armed forces in response to the call of the Chungking government.

Behind the facade of unity, however, conflict and trouble flourished, sometimes openly and sometimes out of view, not only between the Kuomintang and the CCP, but also between the central government at Chungking and regional forces. Moreover, the Kuomintang itself was torn by dissension and fragmentation. Outside the territory of Free China, early in the war separate puppet governments emerged first at Peiping and then at Nanking before merging finally into Wang Ching-wei's Nanking regime. Even earlier, the Japanese had restored the Manchus to power by establishing a puppet regime in Manchuria in 1932.

This chapter focuses first on the political forces in Free China, except for the Communists who are discussed fully in the next chapter. Primary attention is given to the Kuomintang as the prerequisite for understanding KMT relations with the other political forces that challenged the Nationalists and Chiang Kai-shek's leadership. Second, I shall examine the puppet regimes, particularly Wang

Ching-wei's government at Nanking, which tried to displace the Nationalist government at Chungking.

Factions within the Kuomintang

Western Hills Group

In the closing years of Sun Yat-sen's life, an opposition group arose within the KMT and disputed Sun's policy of a Moscow-Canton entente, under which Chinese Communists had been admitted to the Kuomintang.[1] In the fall of 1925, after Sun had passed away, this opposition, inspired by the rightist ideology of Tai Chi-t'ao, assumed the title of the Western Hills Group and thereafter formed the core of the Kuomintang right.[2]

The Reorganizationalists

At the opposite end of the spectrum was the leftist faction personified by Wang Ching-wei at the Second National Congress of the Kuomintang in January 1926, which expelled most members of the Western Hills Group from the party. Wang's faction dominated the Wuhan leftist government in the spring of 1927, but not long after Wang parted company with the Communists at Wuhan, he lost his power base and again went off into European exile in early 1928.[3]

Shortly after the May 3 Incident in 1928, Wang's followers, notably Ku Meng-yu, Wang Leh-p'ing, Ch'en Kung-po, Wang Fa-ch'in, and Chu Chi-ch'ing, organized the Society for Kuomintang Reorganization. Bearing no animus toward Chiang Kai-shek, the Reorganizationalists aimed at bringing about cooperation between Wang and Chiang. Their basic platform included: (1) restoring the KMT to the spirit of the First and Second National Congresses; (2) opposing evil and corrupt forces and supporting democratic forces; (3) promoting national unification and opposing separatism and regionalism; and (4) implementing nationwide disarmament now that national unification had been achieved by the Northern Expedition.[4] Before long, however, the Reorganizationalists joined forces with various anti-Chiang elements, but their efforts ended in failure and hastened the demise of the Reorganizationalists as a quasi-political party.[5]

The September 18 Incident of 1931 aroused the greatest patriotic movement since the May Fourth Movement and ushered in a period of cooperation between Wang and Chiang that lasted until Wang was wounded by an assassin's bullet at the Fifth National Congress of the Kuomintang in November 1935. Wang went off to Europe to recuperate, but he returned home in January 1937 after the Sian Incident and adopted a firm anti-Communist stance.[6]

In the early days of the war, and during the entire Wuhan period, Wang outwardly gave wholehearted support to Chiang's war efforts. At the same time, various persons, including the Italian ambassador to China and several Japanese emissaries, made peace overtures to Wang, but he not only rejected these overtures, but also faithfully kept Chiang Kai-shek informed. Wang never failed to preach the policy of "scorched earth," which had been a slogan from the very beginning of the war. In this respect Wang was not alone, as some leading intellectuals, including Hu Shih, Tao Hsi-sheng, and Chou Fu-hai, who questioned the wisdom of fighting to the death in the War of Resistance, formed a self-styled "low-key club" to moderate the hysterical zeal for war. The low-key club turned out to be the only influential group engaged in the peace movement with Japan.[7]

Wang had other reasons for being disappointed. He was not restored to the presidency of the Executive Yuan, which he had lost after the attempt on his life. Although he served as chairman of the Supreme Council for National Defense, he had to be content with playing second fiddle to Chiang in the KMT hierarchy, a position that his boisterous wife Ch'en Pi-chun must have found hard to accept.

The low-key club may have had its counterpart in Japan. Despite Prime Minister Konoe's January 16, 1938, declaration that Japan would not deal with Chiang Kai-shek, some high-ranking officers in the General Staff wanted to see the peace channel between Japan and China remain open. Kao Tsung-wu made a secret trip to Japan where he negotiated with Col. Kagesa Sadaaki, Lt. Col. Imai Takeo, and Inukai Ken, all of whom were involved in Chinese affairs. Soon after Konoe spelled out his new policy toward China on November 3, 1938, peace negotiations commenced in Shanghai between Wang Ching-wei's representatives, Kao Tsung-wu and Mei Ssu-p'ing, and the Japanese, the outcome of which was Wang's flight from the wartime capital of Chungking in mid-December 1938.[8] Most of Wang's protégés followed him to join the puppet government at Nanking.

The CC Clique

The Ch'en brothers—Kuo-fu and Li-fu, nephews of Ch'en Ch'i-mei (1877–1916), mentor of Chiang Kai-shek in his early military career—from whom the CC Clique derived its name, had been Chiang's confidants even before his rise to power. Kuo-fu (1892–1951), ten years older than Li-fu, had been very close to Chiang ever since his uncle's death.[9] Li-fu, after studying metallurgy at Pittsburgh, returned to China and served as Chiang's secretary at the Huang-p'u [Whampoa] Military Academy on the eve of Chiang's March 20 coup d'etat in 1926, which brought him to power. Although Chiang seized the party leadership and served as chief of the organization department with Kuo-fu as his deputy, he did not really succeed in establishing control over the KMT apparatus until the Third National Congress at Nanking in March 1929.

After the September 18 Incident in 1931, Chiang increasingly leaned toward fascism in order to solidify his rule. In early 1933, the Ch'en brothers inaugurated a secret organization among high-ranking cadres called the Ch'ing-pai (blue and white) group. Later it changed its name to Society of Faithful Comrades of the KMT. Chiang was the chairman, while other important members in addition to the Ch'en brothers were Yu Ching-t'ang, Chang Li-sheng, Yeh Hsiu-feng, Hsu En-ch'eng, Chang Tao-fan, Chang Ch'ung, Wu Kai-hsien, and P'an Kung-chan. In April 1933, the CC Clique developed satellite organizations among youth, particularly in major cities like Peiping and Shanghai.

During the war years, Kuo-fu was responsible for high-level personnel assignments in the party and the state while Li-fu served as minister of education. As a result, their influence was felt not only throughout the KMT apparatus, but also in every branch of the central government. The Central School of Politics (later university) was the training ground for the CC Clique. In the political arena, the CC Clique competed with the Political Study faction. Through their control of the Central Peasants Bank and the Cooperative Monetary Treasury, they posed a threat in the economic and financial field to the nepotistic faction of H. H. Kung and T. V. Soong.

Even in the area of special services and intelligence, long before the notorious Tai Li (1897–1946) entered this field, the Ch'en brothers had been active. Li-fu had been in charge of intelligence work for Chiang. In early 1937, military and civilian intelligence were merged into the Investigation and Statistics Bureau under the Military Council of the National Government. Li-fu was the bureau chief and Tai Li headed one of the bureau's three branches. The reorganization of the bureau in 1938 marked the permanent separation between Military Intelligence (chun-t'ung) headed by Tai Li and Central Intelligence (chung-t'ung) under the KMT. In time, Tai Li's chun-t'ung developed into a mammoth, Gestapo-like operation that was so powerful and independent that even Chiang himself had a hard time controlling it.[10] Chiang's "divide-and-rule" politics was applied not merely to his warlord enemies but to his own men and inevitably contributed to factionalism in the KMT. After their separation, the CC Clique and Tai Li's chun-t'ung had little to do with each other, and the CC Clique came into conflict largely with the Huang-p'u cadets faction.

The Li-Hsing Society

The Japanese invasion of Manchuria had aroused a high tide of patriotism in China that forced the two rival KMT governments in Nanking and Canton to reach a temporary accommodation. Consequently, Hu Han-min, leader of the KMT Canton faction, who had been placed under house arrest by Chiang in March 1931, was released and Chiang himself went into temporary retirement in early November.

Shortly before Chiang's retirement, two separate developments occurred that had important consequences for the rise of fascism in China. Ten leading members of the Huang-p'u cadets—Ho Chung-han, Kuei Yung-ch'ing, Hsiao Tsan-yu, Chou Fu, T'eng Chieh, Cheng Chieh-min, Ch'iu K'ai-chi, Tai Li, K'ang Tse, and Teng Wen-i—met with Chiang on several occasions to discuss how to rejuvenate the KMT and increase morale in the military and bureaucracy. Not under discussion but implicit in Chiang's pessimistic talks during these gatherings was the question of how to save Chiang's own power. While Chiang was in retirement at Fenghua, the above ten Huang-p'u graduates, joined by five others, met in Nanking in December to plan the formation of a Huang-p'u cadets group with the aim of promoting unity.[11]

Around the same time, in November 1931, Liu Chien-ch'un and Hsuan Chieh-hsi jointly drafted a "Plan for the Blue Shirts' Revival of Revolution," which they intended but were unable to present to Chiang Kai-shek. In February 1932, Liu published a pamphlet, "Some Opinions Contributed to the Readjustment of the Party," which embodied some of the earlier plan.[12] When Chiang returned from retirement in late January 1932, organizational work for a society of Huang-p'u graduates resumed as Chiang convened three preparatory meetings of graduates from the first through sixth classes. At the second preparatory meeting, Kuei Yung-ch'ing recommended Liu Chien-ch'un to Chiang and the others present, and Chiang shortly appointed Liu to head the political training division under the Military Council (of which Chiang himself was the chief, assuming the title of Generalissimo), the political training department of the Central Military Academy (its predecessor was the Huang-p'u Military Academy), and the political training institute, thereby becoming the leader of the quasi-fascist movement.

On March 28, 1932, the San-min-chu-i Li-hsing She (Society for Vigorously Carrying out the Three Principles of the People, or Li-Hsing She for short) was established with Chiang himself as the president and twenty-eight founding members. Under the Li-Hsing She were two subordinate organizations. One was the Ko-ming Ch'ing-nien T'ung-chih Hui (Society of Revolutionary Youth Comrades), whose work was directed at high school and college students, and the other was the Ko-ming Chun-jen T'ung-chih Hui (Society of Revolutionary Military Comrades), directed toward students in military schools.[13]

In July 1933, the third and lowest level of the Li-Hsingshe, called the Fu-Hsing She (Society for Revival), was created and rapidly grew to an enormous size. The entire national revival movement was imbued with fascist ideology and practice at that time, and its vestiges survived long after it was formally dissolved during the war. When Marshal Chang Hsueh-liang, impressed during his European tour with Mussolini's and Hitler's leadership and national revival movements, returned to China, he advocated supporting Chiang as the leader of China's own revival. Certainly, Chiang never achieved the dictatorial role in China that Mussolini and Hitler enjoyed, nor was Chiang drawn to the underlying ideology, but he believed in the notion that China, like Italy and Germany, required an all-powerful leader to achieve national revival.[14]

Even before the war broke out, the Li-Hsing She had already suffered from decline due to internal dissension and factionalism within the KMT. The "grand union" of all political and military forces and the great loss of Chiang's troops in the early stages of the war rendered the Li-Hsingshe both ineffective and unnecessary. It was abolished in June 1938, and its mission and personnel were turned over to the newly created San-Min-Chu-I Ch'ing-nien T'uan (Three Principles of the People Youth Corps).

The San Min Chu I Ch'ing-nien T'uan

Shortly after the outbreak of the war, Chiang began to consider the idea of uniting all political parties into one national party. He commenced by unifying the CC Clique, the Li-Hsing She, and the Reorganizationalists. In January 1938, after the fall of Nanking, Chiang put his project into gear, and soon Tseng Ch'i of the China Youth party, Chang Chun-mai (Carsun Chang) of the National Socialist party, and Ch'en Ming-shu of the Social Democratic party announced the subordination of their respective parties under the supreme leadership of the national government and the KMT in return for Chiang's recognition of the existence of these parties.[15] The larger scheme failed, however, because of the CCP's refusal to join except as an independent ally of the KMT.[16]

Although Chiang's hopes for "one faith, one party, and one leader" seemed to vanish as a result of the CCP's attitude, he went ahead to organize the San-Min-Chu-I Ch'ing-nien T'uan (SMCICNT), which was officially approved by the KMT Extraordinary National Congress attended by delegates from the KMT Fifth National Congress on March 29, 1938. The same congress adopted the "Programs for the War of Resistance and National Reconstruction" and elected Chiang as the KMT president and Wang Ching-wei as vice-president. The SMCICNT, not the namesake of the KMT youth corps, was intended to embrace all parties and factions, but it turned out to be almost entirely a KMT organization, with the Fu-Hsing She as its core and K'ang Tse as its prime mover. It never achieved the unity Chiang desired, and from the outset it became an arena of the KMT intraparty struggle, particularly under Ch'en Ch'eng who served as secretary general until Chiang removed him in late 1938.[17]

As noted, the CCP refused to join the KMT unless allowed to preserve its independent Communist organizations as in the first united front of 1923–27. The CCP was, however, willing to join the SMCICNT, but Chiang refused because he feared the CCP might thereby attempt to infiltrate the KMT. The CCP unsuccessfully repeated its overture at its Sixth Plenum in October 1938.[18] As for the other minor parties, whose membership numbered only in the hundreds, they played no significant role until late in the war when KMT-CCP negotiations became a focus of national attention.

The Youth Corps, which even among youth did not play a major role during the war, greatly disappointed Chiang's expectations, but by 1945 its membership had swelled to one million, including a majority of high school and college students in the areas under the control of the national government. While the corps did not generate much enthusiasm among university students, it apparently had a greater impact upon youth near and behind the war zone, as evidenced by its intensive activities and the large number of its members who were killed.[19] During Japan's Ichigo offensive in the fall of 1944, the Youth Corps contributed a great deal to the formation of the 100,000-strong Youth Army in response to Chiang's call.[20]

The dilemma confronting the Youth Corps was its delicate relations with the KMT, unforeseen by its chief designer, namely, Chiang himself. Since the Third National Congress of the KMT in 1929, the Ch'en brothers had run the party. Now the CC Clique was supposed to merge with other KMT factions in the newly created Youth Corps, but not in the KMT, which it continued to dominate. This ambiguity in the relationship between the KMT and the Youth Corps existed from the outset, and competition for power between the two plagued the effectiveness of the corps until it was absorbed into the KMT in September 1947.[21]

The Political Study Clique and the Kung-Soong Factions

A narrative of KMT politics would be incomplete without consideration of three powerful political alignments that, by earning Chiang Kai-shek's trust, were able to dominate Chiang's government longer than any other faction with the exception of the CC Clique, even though they lacked institutional power bases.

The Cheng-hsueh Hui (Political Study Society) had its origins in KMT parliamentary maneuvering in 1916 during the era of the Peiyang warlords, and it led an intermittent existence until its dissolution in 1925 when its members returned to the fold of the KMT.[22] Eight years later, Yang Yung-t'ai, a leading member of the Cheng-hsueh Hui, gained prominence in Chiang's entourage. Yang found an ally in Hsiung Shih-hui, then the governor of Kiangsi Province and also one of Chiang's confidants, and the two men soon formed a trio with the addition of Chang Ch'un, a sworn brother and classmate of Chiang's at both the Paoting Military Academy and the Shimbu Gakko.

Thereafter, many former members of the Cheng-hsueh Hui beat a path to Nanchang, the headquarters of Chiang's "suppression and encirclement" campaigns against the Communists in Kiangsi, where they found positions under Yang Yung-t'ai. In 1935, a few leading intellectuals and prominent politicians joined the group, notably Weng Wen-hao, Wu Ting-ch'ang, Chang Kia-ngau, Chiang T'ing-fu, Ho Lien, Ch'en I, Wei Tao-ming, and Shen Hung-chieh. After the assassination of Yang Yung-t'ai in October 1936, the leadership centered around Chang Ch'un and Hsiung Shih-hui. Most likely, at no time did the group encompass more than forty to fifty persons, but among those Chang Ch'un and Weng Wen-hao became prime ministers while all the others served as ministers or governors. The group continued to be influential until the national government withdrew to Taiwan.[23]

Similar to the Political Study Clique in that its power derived solely from its connection with Chiang, but different in that nepotism was the soil in which they flourished, were the Kung and Soong Cliques. The students who returned from the United States and England filled a large portion of higher-echelon positions in the government bureaucracy and dominated the financial and banking fields. After the founding of the national government at Nanking, H. H. Kung and T. V. Soong virtually dominated the portfolio of the Ministry of Finance until the end of the war. Furthermore, Kung was prime minister or acting prime minister from 1935 until mid-1945 when he was succeeded by Soong.

Unlike other factions, the Kung and Soong Cliques were not involved in military or KMT party affairs. They were closely associated, however, with the Kiangsu-Chekiang financial world centering on Shanghai.[24] Both Soong, a Harvard graduate, and Kung, a graduate of Oberlin, were well-trained and competent, and they contributed to improving the efficiency of the Chinese bureaucracy. Together with Mme. Chiang Kai-shek, they also served to liberalize or democratize Chiang's regime and at the same time to draw it closer to Washington. Despite the fact that they both profited enormously from the war, it is fair to say that they nevertheless played some constructive and useful role in the war economy.

Kung and Soong were sooner rivals than partners in the government, and so were their respective sets of followers. For most of the war, Kung was in power while Soong served as liaison between Chungking and Washington and later took charge of foreign affairs. Because of his long tenure in office, Kung alienated other factions within the KMT, particularly the CC Clique. In early 1945, Kung was forced to resign after allegations that he embezzled funds from the issuance of U.S. bonds, and the CC Clique soon claimed as their victim Kung's confidant, Kao Ping-fang, chief of the National Tax Bureau, who was incarcerated for life.[25]

During the war, there were so many competing factions under the umbrella of the Kuomintang that only the authority and prestige of Chiang Kai-shek himself—the holder of the umbrella—kept the undercurrents of conflict from bursting into the open. Had Chiang supported one faction consistently, the KMT might have conducted itself more effectively, or had he encouraged the factions to compete openly for supremacy in a democratic fashion, the energy and vitality within the KMT might have been enhanced with benefit to the war effort. In actuality, all of the KMT factions had Chiang as their head and looked toward him as the ultimate authority. Chiang apparently never consistently favored one faction for very long, except for Tai Li's secret service. If one judges that this was due to his conscious efforts rather than to his narcissism or paranoia, it means that Chiang must be credited with being a master of political finesse. In any case, besides the KMT, Chiang had other political forces to contend with that caused him no end of trouble during the war.

Provincial and Political Forces

For the sake of national salvation, minor warlords from Szechwan, Yunnan, Shansi, and Kwangsi all temporarily put aside their quarrels with Nanking and came to the aid of the central government under Chiang. Some of them, like the Kwangsi Clique headed by Li Tsung-jen and Pai Ch'ung-hsi, stayed the course; others, like Yen Hsi-shan, only halfheartedly supported the war effort and managed to survive as semi-independent entities; still others, such as Lung Yun of Yunnan and Liu Wen-hui of Sikang, reluctantly participated in the war but remained recalcitrant and necessitated constant surveillance from Chungking. In this category, Szechwan demanded the greatest attention once the War of Resistance began because it was the only possible base for a protracted war.

Szechwan as a War Base

Prior to the outbreak of war, Liu Hsiang had achieved the position of *primus inter pares* among a dozen or so competing Szechwan warlords. He had further strengthened his position by nominally subordinating himself to Nanking, receiving appointment in February 1935 as governor of Szechwan and pacification commissioner of Szechwan and Sikang. Chiang Kai-shek, however, had never ceased to maneuver and conspire to effect Liu's downfall so as to bring Szechwan under his own control.

The outbreak of the War of Resistance temporarily forced a truce in this maneuvering. A 200,000-man Szechwan Army departed for the eastern front, half of it personally led by Liu Hsiang, who was appointed commander of the Seventh War Zone. But upon reaching Nanking, Liu was prostrated by his inveterate ulcer and had to be shipped back to Wuhan where he died on January 21, 1938. There seems no truth to the rumor that Liu had been poisoned by Chiang. Liu's Szechwan Army, commanded by T'ang Shih-tsun and P'an Wen-hua, did take part in the defense of Nanking.[26]

The fall of Nanking convinced Chiang that Szechwan must be secured as a strategic and logistical base for carrying on the War of Resistance. Following Liu's death, Chiang quickly appointed Chang Ch'un as governor, and later Chiang himself served concurrently in that position.[27] With Chang Ch'un's assumption of the governorship, the authority of the national government invariably prevailed in Szechwan.

During Chang Ch'un's five years in office as governor, Szechwan bore the brunt of the war burden. Each year, the peasants of Szechwan contributed to the central government 1,170,000 piculs (1 picul or shih = 133.5 lbs.) of grain, representing about one-fifth of its total grain collection in 1944 but almost half of its 1945 collection. In these five years, the people of Szechwan sent over five million of their sons to the army, to say nothing of the other human and physical resources they contributed.

The adjacent province of Sikang could not be separated from Szechwan either geographically or politically. It had been controlled by Liu Wen-hui and his Twenty-fourth Army ever since his defeat at the hands of his nephew Liu Hsiang in the 1933 "uncle-nephew" war in Szechwan, but with the younger Liu's death, Liu Wen-hui again became a factor in Szechwan politics. Because Sikang itself was so remote from the center of the war, Liu Wen-hui and his ill-equipped Twenty-fourth Army were left alone, apart from an aborted attempt in 1942 to employ them to suppress an outbreak of Tibetan separatism, abetted by the British.[28] A six-hundred-mile Sikang–K'an-ting highway that Chiang succeeded in having built by the end of the war was never opened to traffic.[29] Although Chiang's troops did not move into Sikang, he did have a stronghold at Hsi-ch'ang as his field headquarters east of the mountain barrier throughout the war. In terms of manpower and grain, Sikang's contribution to the war effort was minimal, but its vast territory gave the people a sense of security as part of China's great rear area.

Lung Yun—The Last Great Warlord

Yunnan's crucial role in the War of Resistance derived above all from its status as the only area under the national government directly accessible to the outside world. Like Szechwan, Yunnan functioned as part of the great rear area of China, remote from the front, its soil undefiled by the enemy.

Lung Yun, known as the "king of Yunnan," had come to power in 1927, and, loosely allied with Chiang, he ruled the province for the next eighteen years. At the beginning of the war, Lung Yun actively supported the War of Resistance by dispatching to the front one of his two armies—the 35,000-strong Sixtieth Army—under the command of his close relative Lu Han. This army participated in the great Chinese victory of Taierhchuang.[30] Lu Han's army returned to Yunnan in 1940 to garrison its southern border against Vietnam until the end of the war when the bulk of the Yunnan Army was dispatched to northern Vietnam to accept the Japanese surrender.

Like most former warlords, Lung was willing to fight the Japanese, but he zealously guarded his own interests against KMT penetration. As early as mid-July 1937 when Chiang summoned Lung Yun for the Supreme National Defense Conference, Lung met with Chinese Communist leaders Chou En-lai, Chu Teh, and Yeh Chien-ying to exchange a secret telegram code for future communication in case of need. Owing to their geographical separation, however, no direct contact between Yenan and Kunming was possible, so nothing came out of their initial contact. Because of the fear, hatred, and suspicion he harbored toward Chiang, Lung was extremely cautious in dealing with Chiang, and he maintained close contact with neighboring warlords, particularly the Kwangsi Clique. Following Liu Hsiang's death in January 1938, Lung signed a cooperation agreement with the Sikang and Szechwan warlords, and it was widely reported that he also reached a secret agreement with the Kwangsi Clique.

Once the national government moved to Chungking, evidence of serious friction between Lung and Chiang began to accumulate. The first instance concerned Lung's receptivity to Wang Ching-wei's peace movement and his help in facilitating the flight of Wang and his followers from Kunming to Hanoi. Lung was quoted as saying that "politically Mr. Wang is more far-sighted than Mr. Chiang. Before Mr. Wang went to Nanking, we had a long talk and I approved his views."[31] Chiang neither forgot nor forgave Lung Yun's support of Wang.

Second, with the closing of the Kunming-Hanoi road and rail links in 1940, Britain and China signed an agreement to protect the Yunnan-Burma road. In the winter of 1939, Lu Han's Yunnan Sixtieth Army was sent back to its home province, and Lu was allowed to build another army, the Ninety-third. In the meantime, however, Chiang's Fifty-second Army under Kuan Li-cheng marched into Yunnan to protect its southern border, and in the fall of 1941 Tu Yu-ming led the Fifth Army into Yunnan to take over garrison duties in Kunming itself. Shortly after Pearl Harbor, large numbers of American personnel and central government troops poured into Kunming with the establishment of the Burma-India Expedition Headquarters. The Burma-Yunnan road remained closed, however, and its replacement—the Stilwell road—was not completed until early 1945. There can be no question that for three and a half years, the American airlift of men and supplies over the "Himalayan Hump"—a massive influx of people and materials unprecedented in the history of Yunnan—produced a great impact upon Yunnan socially and politically.

Third, Kunming became the hotbed of anti-Chiang sentiment in part because of the Americans' presence but mostly because it was the site of China's most prestigious wartime university—Southwest Associated University (Lien-ta), combining Peking, Tsinghua, and Nankai universities. Far-removed from Chungking and enjoying Lung Yun's protection, the professors and students of Lien-ta provided much of the leadership of the democratic movement through anti-Chiang and anti-Chungking activities promoted by the Democratic League.[32]

Finally, probably the greatest spur to Lung's resistance of greater national government control was his concern over money. He refused to cede the sales tax to Chungking, and he appropriated to his own use part of the massive American aid flow, which he used to build up fourteen regiments without receiving any subsidies for them from Chungking. He countered the economic penetration of four central government banks by establishing seven or eight banks of his own, and he defied Chungking's orders that his Yunnan Provincial Bank cease issuing its own notes. Also contrary to Chungking's policies, he set up his own trading company to control local industries and foreign trade.[33]

Considering Lung's defiance, Chiang manifested considerable tolerance toward him, not from any feelings of goodwill, but because of considerations relating to U.S. policy toward Yunnan, public opinion, and the position of other provincial militarists. Finally, in April 1945 Chiang decided to put an end to Lung's game. Even then he tried to use persuasion to get Lung to leave, and only when that failed did he order Tu Yu-ming to seize him by force at the end of September. Lung was afforded the dignity of an appointment as president of the Military Consultation Yuan.[34]

The Kwangsi Clique and the War

Kwangsi continued its semi-independent ways on the eve of the war. In 1933 Li Tsung-jen and Pai Ch'ung-hsi had organized a secret organization called the Society of Comrades for the Three People's Principles, which aimed at the realization of the Three Principles of Sun Yat-sen, the reconstruction of Kwangsi, and the revival of China via the practice of self-defense, self-government, and self-sufficiency. (In July 1938 the Society of Comrades was merged into the Three People's Principles Youth Corps.) Self-defense would be achieved by building up a people's militia, training an educated officers' corps, and carrying out universal conscription. A militia cadre school was established that graduated about one thousand students each year, all of whom were sent to work in county, subcounty, and township governments. People's assemblies established on the township and village levels were given responsibility for local security and public works.

The slogan of "tenanted-land rent at 25 percent" was raised to ameliorate the life of peasants. Efforts were made to promote private investment and develop new industries, as well as expand foreign trade. Except for military industry to equip an enormous army, no progress in economic development had been made when the war began. Unfortunately, opium and gambling continued to be a major source of revenue. On the other hand, because of its long preparation for war, Kwangsi contributed more trained troops than any other province in the initial stage of the War of Resistance.[35]

For most of the war, Li Tsung-jen was at the front where he earned the reputation of a great general, while Pai Ch'ung-hsi remained in Kwangsi to take charge of the Kweilin Headquarters of Generalissimo Chiang. Nicknamed "little Chu Ko" after the famous Chinese strategist of the Three Kingdoms period, Pai metamorphosed from an enemy into a friend of Chiang's during the war era. In addition to his military skills, Pai was a Moslem and as such helped rally the Moslem population in support of the war.[36]

Li and Pai were no friends to the Communists, yet during the war Kweilin even more than Kunming gave a measure of freedom to the Communists led by Li K'o-nung. Kweilin was also the place where many of Chiang's former enemies, such as Li Chi-shen and Chang Fa-k'uei, congregated. During the Japanese Ichigo offensive, Li Chi-shen was in close contact both with General Stilwell and other high-ranking U.S. officers in Kweilin and with his former subordinates,

Chang Fa-k'uei in Kwangsi, Yu Han-mou in Kwangtung, and Hsueh Yueh in Hunan. Li's scheme of organizing a people's militia equipped with U.S. arms came to nothing with Stilwell's recall. It should be noted that an American report from Chungking that Li formally established an autonomous, democratic regime in early November 1944 is groundless.[37] Ever since 1929, Li had ceaselessly conspired against Chiang, and during the war years he did work closely with some leaders of the democratic movement, particularly Liang Shu-ming. At the same time, he tried to support the war effort without the equivocations of most other ex-warlords.

Yen Hsi-shan—Veteran Warlord

After the Sian Incident, Yen Hsi-shan, who controlled Shansi almost without interruption from 1911 until 1949, began to proclaim the slogan "Welcome the Communists in resisting Japan." With the help of many college and high school students he had recruited from Peiping and Tientsin, Yen established the League of Sacrifice for National Salvation led by Po I-po. When the war broke out, the league expanded rapidly to consist of over twenty "dare-to-die youth regiments" on a par with Yen's regular army, which had been reduced to less than half of its original strength after the battle of Hsinkow and the loss of Taiyuan. The new forces turned out to be much more effective fighters and were instrumental in stabilizing the military situation in Shansi. Yen's attempt to merge his old and new forces led to a revolt in which the new army joined forces with the Eighth Route Army, a blow from which the Shansi Army never recovered.[38]

Despite waging war against Japan, Yen had never severed his connection with the Japanese through his subordinates Su Ti-min and Liang Shang-chun. Dissatisfied with the current state of his fortunes, Yen began to toy with the idea of getting help from the Japanese to restore his diminished glory. The outcome of his parleys with the Japanese was the well-publicized Fenyang agreement of August 1941, according to whose terms Japan was to provide Yen with weapons, financial support, and fully equipped soldiers in return for Yen's agreement to sever his ties with Chungking and eventually declare his adherence to Wang Ching-wei's Nanking government.[39] Little came out of this agreement as Yen delayed and temporized. Eventually Japan abandoned the attempt to win Yen as a collaborator, which probably saved him from becoming a traitor. Throughout the war, Yen never went to Chungking; he did not get involved in provincial politics, nor did he lend his support to the anti-Chiang movement.[40]

Party Politics and the Democratic League

In the first two years of the war, China made great headway toward democracy as barriers of regionalism, provincialism, and even class distinction buckled under the pressures of the patriotic upsurge and the waves of refugees, soldiers, government workers, and ordinary people who followed the government upriver to Wuhan and then further inland. At Wuhan and other major Chinese cities, the prevalence of freedom of speech, assembly, association, and movement reenergized the patriotic and democratic movements and in particular reawakened long-dormant political parties, which had barely been heard from since the early years of the republic. Among these were the China Youth party, National Socialist (Democratic Socialist) party, Third party, Alliance of Comrades for Three Principles of the People, National Salvation Association, and the Trotskyite faction (Fourth International). Apart from the KMT and the CCP, all the other parties were simply groupings of like-minded intellectuals, none with memberships exceeding 400–500 people, and all insufficiently strong to make a meaningful impact upon the general public.[41]

The China Youth party had been organized by Tseng Ch'i, Li Huang, and Ho Lu-chih in Paris in 1927 in opposition to the growing organization of the CCP, and from beginning to end the party was distinguished by its advocacy of nationalism in opposition to Communism. Except for a couple of brief periods, the China Youth party had never secured a base or following of its own, although its professorial profile may have given it some influence on some university campuses. Following the outbreak of the war, it joined the twenty-four-member Advisory Council of the Supreme National Defense Conference, predecessor of the People's Political Council (Kuo-min Ts'an-cheng Hui), which was inaugurated by the Extraordinary Congress of the KMT at Wuhan in March–April 1938. Later, five members of the China Youth party were made members of the People's Political Council. Together with the National Socialist party, it continued to cooperate with the KMT throughout the war.[42]

Opposed to totalitarianism and galvanized by Japanese aggression in Manchuria, Chang Chun-mai, a professor of philosophy, founded the National Socialist party in 1931, and by the time the war started it was the largest among the minor parties, with a membership of around 500.[43] Chang repeatedly tried and failed to effect a reconciliation between the KMT and the CCP. Mao rebuffed Chang's open letter of December 1938 calling on the CCP to give up its own army, its special regional government, and its devotion to Marxism in order to enhance the unity of all anti-Japanese political parties.[44] The National Socialist party sent seven members to the first People's Political Council and, like other minor parties, was preoccupied with the question of how to resolve the dilemma of democracy—whether to legalize the CCP before or after it handed over its army to the national government.

One significant development that grew out of the People's Political Council was the formation in 1939 of the Democratic League, which throughout the war pursued its objectives of democratization of the government and nationalization of the army. (The CCP rightly claimed that the nationalization of the army depended on the KMT's guarantee that it would give up tutelage and adopt democracy.) The league played a major role in mediating between the KMT and the CCP in the latter part of the war and during the Marshall mission to China. The leadership of the league comprised the leaders of minor parties in the People's Political Council. The league enjoyed popularity among university students, particularly at Kunming where Governor Lung Yun, who was reported to be a secret member, became its staunch supporter.[45] Buoyed by American involvement in KMT-CCP relations in 1944, the league strived to chart a third road toward China's future, incorporating democracy and socialism, distinct from the authoritarianism and Communism of the KMT and the CCP respectively. But no sooner had the war come to an end than the league was overtaken by internal strife.

Puppet Regimes

Thus far only the politics of unoccupied China has been examined, but to get a more complete picture the gaze must be shifted. The entire eastern part of the country, along with all the major cities and communications, was behind enemy lines, and more than half the Chinese population fell under Japanese rule. To govern the vast, newly conquered territory and population and better utilize their resources, Japan set up a series of puppet governments, the last of which was the pseudo-KMT regime headed by Wang Ching-wei at Nanking.

By the time Japan occupied most of eastern China, it had already acquired substantial experience in ruling the Chinese populations of Taiwan and Manchuria (the three northeastern provinces of China). In both cases, Japan had little difficulty in successfully recruiting numerous Chinese collaborators or traitors to fill the ranks of the puppet governments.[46]

Puppet Governments in North China

When Peiping fell on July 28, 1937, the business community took the lead in negotiating with the enemy to set up a peace preservation committee. As elsewhere in occupied China, the political machinery in North China was set up and controlled by the Japanese special service (Tokumu kikan), which was headed by Major General Kita Seiichi from October 1937 to March 1940. He was the veritable ruler of the North China provisional government established on December 14, 1937, Wang K'o-min was the nominal head of that government until his replacement by Wang I-t'ang in June 1940. Nearly all the leaders of the puppet regime were ranking members of the former Peiyang government, such as Wang K'o-min himself, Wang I-t'ing, T'ang Erh-ho, and Ch'i Hsieh-yuan. Interestingly, despite inducements and pressure, Wu P'ei-fu, Ts'ao K'un, and Chin Yun-p'eng all refused to serve as head of state. Even Ts'ao Ju-lin, reviled as a traitor during the May Fourth Movement in 1919, refused active participation in the puppet government.[47] Accompanying the establishment of the North China puppet regime was the emergence of a people's organization called the Hsin Min

Hui (New People's Association) on the model of the Hsieh Ho Hui (Concordia Society), established throughout Manchuria with the goals of thought control, elimination of racial prejudice, realization of unity between Japan and Manchuria, and coordination of governmental affairs. Its real function, however, was to mobilize manpower and resources to support and further Japan's imperialist rule and expansion.

Shortly after the inauguration of Wang Ching-wei's Nanking puppet regime in March 1940, Wang K'o-min was compelled to resign from his positions in the North China puppet government, whose title was changed to Council of North China's Political Affairs under the tutelage of the Nanking government. The head of the council was Wang K'o-min's rival Wang I-t'ang, whose administration in North China lasted for three years until his removal by the Japanese on February 9, 1943. Disappointed with Wang's performance, the Japanese wanted to double their efforts to mobilize the manpower and resources to make North China the supply base for the "Great Pacific War." Wang was succeeded by Chu Shen, who died of jaundice after only a few months in office. Then Wang K'o-min was recalled, but he served for only a year and had to resign due to illness. Wang Yin-t'ai succeeded him and served in that office until the Japanese surrender. Most of these individuals were incarcerated for treason. Wang K'o-min died in prison while the others were executed or sentenced to prison terms.

From beginning to end, the North China puppet government, whose jurisdiction covered the four provinces of Hopei, Honan, Shansi, and Shantung, was never integrated politically or economically with the Nanking puppet government under Wang Ching-wei, but the puppet governments set up earlier in Central and South China were brought into the fold of the puppet Nanking government.

Halfhearted Puppet Government in the South

The Japanese military forces that first attacked Shanghai and then Nanking in December 1937 showed little regard for human life or the restoration of Chinese civil society, as the awful massacres they carried out in Nanking amply demonstrated. Not until March 28, 1938, did Japan inaugurate a puppet regime in Shanghai. Initially, the Japanese tried to persuade T'ang Shao-i, the first premier of the Chinese Republic, to head the so-called Reformed Government of the Republic of China, but when he refused they turned to Liang Hung-chih, who was well-versed in Chinese poetry and a confidant of Tuan Ch'i-jui in the Peiyang government. Liang assumed the presidency of the executive branch of the government.

Seeking to replicate the Hsin Min Hui of the North China puppet regime, Col. Usuda Kanzo, chief of the Japanese special service at Shanghai, transformed the Hsing-Ya (Rejuvenating Asia) Society, an amalgamation of all sorts of undesirables organized in the early stages of the war at Shanghai, into the Ta-min (Great

People) Association, with T'ao Hsi-shan as acting chairman. In November 1938, together with the Reformed Government, the Ta-Min Association moved to Nanking, where soon Liang Hung-chih himself assumed its chairmanship. The unusual emphasis accorded the Ta-Min Association reflected Premier Konoe's desire to use it as an instrument for effecting cooperation between China, Japan, and Manchukuo as part of his "New Order in East Asia," but by the end of 1940 the association was defunct as the newly inaugurated pseudo-KMT government of Wang Ching-wei tried to replace it with its own apparatuses. Prior to Wang's defection, Japan briefly encouraged union between the North China Provisional Government and the Reformed Government of the south. The two sides met at Peiping and established the Associated Council for the Government of the Republic of China in September 1938. The council accomplished nothing, however, and the two puppet governments remained separate until the Reformed Government was completely absorbed into Wang Ching-wei's national government.

Wang Ching-wei—A Reluctant Traitor

When the war broke out, the Konoe administration predicted that China could be defeated in six months. Before the fall of Nanking, Chiang Kai-shek was not unreceptive to German Ambassador Oscar Trautmann who, as a potential mediator, approached him on December 2, 1937, with terms that Chiang felt were not inconsistent with the preservation of China's essential national interests.[48] Later, however, Japan raised its demands, including particularly the recognition of Manchukuo, which was totally unacceptable to Chiang and the Chinese public. On January 16, 1938, Konoe declared that "hereafter, the imperial government will not deal with the national government."[49] Ironically, before the year was over, Konoe nullified his own statement by making a new overture. On November 3, 1938, in a radio address to the nation, Konoe announced his "New Order in East Asia," which was to be based on cooperation among Japan, China, and Manchukuo in the fields of politics, economics, and culture. Japan hoped to establish international justice in East Asia and form a common struggle against Communism. What Japan fought for was the establishment of an eternal peace in East Asia, to accomplish which Japan invited China's participation.[50]

Apparently based upon Konoe's new policy, Wang Ching-wei's emissaries, Kao Tsung-wu and Mei Ssu-p'ing, reached an agreement with Imai Takeo, chief of the China Unit of the General Staff, at Shanghai on November 20, 1938, focusing on a common struggle against communism and economic cooperation "in order to realize the common ideal for the establishment of a new order in East Asia."[51] The terms of agreement, however, much harsher than those proposed by Japan a year earlier, included the recognition of Manchukuo, the stationing of Japanese troops in Inner Mongolia, and economic exploitation of North China.[52]

Nearly three weeks after his November 3 radio address, Konoe issued another statement on November 22 revealing much of the contents of the agreement signed by Wang's emissaries and Imai on November 20, 1938. By the time Konoe's statement reached Chungking, Wang had left the city and was ensconced in Hanoi. Despite Chiang Kai-shek's strong denunciation in a lengthy statement on December 26, 1938, three days later Wang issued his famous Yen (29th) telegram from Hong Kong setting forth his proposal for peace and urging the national government and Chiang to accept Konoe's "three principles"—friendly neighbors, common defense against the Communists, and economic cooperation—as a basis for negotiations to conclude the war. Accompanying his Yen telegram was a personal letter to Chiang urging him to seize the opportunity for negotiations.[53]

Two days after the Yen telegram was made public, the Central Executive Committee of the KMT met on January 1, 1939, to expel Wang permanently from the KMT. On the other hand, Chiang sent Ku Cheng-kang, formerly Wang's man, to Hanoi with a passport and a large sum of money, and probably a personal letter as well. On February 1, Kao Tsung-wu arrived at Hanoi and together with Wang reached the decision to set up a KMT puppet government in Nanking. Kao then proceeded to Japan where, in negotiating with Japanese leaders on Wang's behalf, he made three points: (1) if Japan wished to contact Chiang, Wang would help to mediate; (2) if Japan wanted to contact any person other than Chiang, Wang would be willing to help in his capacity as an oppositionist; and (3) if Japan wanted him to come forth and assume responsibility, he would be willing to do so. On March 18, Japan's five-minister conference elected Wang to lead a government of collaboration.[54]

On March 21, 1939, a team of Chiang's special service men led by Ch'en Kung-shu attempted to assassinate Wang but failed and instead killed Wang's nephew, Tseng Chung-ming. This turn of events not only shocked and saddened Wang, but also accelerated his turn to the Japanese fold. Without delay, Japan despatched Imai and Inukai Ken to Hanoi to invite Wang to Shanghai. Wang first boarded a French ship, but he transferred to a Japanese vessel on the high seas, thereby making himself a hostage of Japan.[55]

Inauguration of the Puppet Nanking Government

Wang's first order of business was a trip to Japan in early June and a meeting with all the appropriate Japanese dignitaries. War Minister Itagaki insisted that the sovereignty of the new central government had to be limited and the substance and reality of the existing provisional and Reformed governments had to be preserved, although Wang managed to wring some concessions from Itagaki that would give his future government a semblance of the KMT national government, such as use of the Nationalist flag and of a revamped Three Principles of the People as its official orthodoxy.

With the Wang–Itagaki talks as a base, negotiations continued back in Shanghai between Wang and Col. Kagesa, chief of a special group assigned to coordinate negotiations with Wang. It had long been understood that the new Nanking government would have to recognize Manchukuo, fight Communism jointly with Japan, and accept Japanese economic exploitation of occupied China, but now Wang learned that even more serious concessions were being demanded of him. First, Japanese defense interests in Inner Mongolia would preclude Nanking's jurisdiction over that province. Second, North China would remain virtually independent of Nanking as the newly created North China Political Council would control its own political and economic matters and retain most of its tax revenues. Further, the Japanese navy would be allowed to protect its special interest in the "special area" of the Yangtze valley. Third, the withdrawal of Japanese troops from China would not be effected. Fourth, Japanese advisers would be assigned not only to the military units but to all kinds of organizations, including all levels of schools. Fifth, despite Wang's plea to Tokyo, Japan would not retreat from its total domination over the Chinese economy and finances, thus depriving the new government of any real chance of success. Moreover, China would have to compensate Japanese civilians for war damages they had suffered, though Japan itself renounced war indemnities. Finally, Japan denied Nanking the opportunity to build up an army of its own by refusing to provide funds and arms and by controlling the Chinese forces through Japanese advisers.[56]

The fruits of the negotiations between Wang and Kagesa were the "Outline of Readjustment of Sino-Japanese Relations" signed on October 30, 1939, which after minor revisions became the official Wang-Japan Agreement two months later. The agreement, based on the terms laid down by the Japanese Imperial Conference on November 30, 1938, became the "Basic Treaty of Sino-Japanese Relations" signed by Wang and Abe Nobuyuki at Nanking on November 20, 1940, when Japan formalized its relations with the Wang regime.[57]

After his return from Japan, Wang busied himself with setting up the Nanking government as a rival to Chungking. At first he seemed confident that once he raised the banner, many of his former subordinates and like-minded politicians, as well as some wavering generals such as Fourth War Zone Commander-in-Chief Chang Fa-k'uei, would respond to his call. While waiting for their response, Wang attempted to resolve the issue of the two existing puppet governments. In late June he met separately with Wang K'o-min in Peiping and Liang Hung-chih in Shanghai, but nothing came of these meetings since both men resisted Wang's plan to absorb their governments into his. Wang also held many meetings with Wu P'ei-fu, the strongman of North China in the 1920s whom Japanese military leaders were especially interested in recruiting, but Wang and Wu failed to agree. Wu's death on December 4, 1939, removed at least one of Wang's problems.[58] Finally, a summit meeting of the three Chinese puppet governments, convened at Tsingtao on January 23–24, 1940, succeeded

in clearing away the last obstacle to the creation of the Nanking central government—or the return of the national government as Wang Ching-wei preferred to
have it—which was officially inaugurated on March 20, 1940.

Problems and Achievements of Wang Ching-wei's Regime

Despite his claim to the contrary, there can be no doubt that the government
that Wang Ching-wei had worked fifteen months to establish was a full-
fledged puppet regime whose existence depended upon the Japanese and that
served the interests of Japan. First, North China, like Inner Mongolia, turned
out to be another Manchukuo except in form. It was under the total control of
the Japanese North China Army Command. With respect to the economic
exploitation of North China, the China Development Company, created in
1935 as an offshoot of the South Manchurian Railway Company, was empowered to exercise control over all industries concerned with resource development
in North China as soon as the Japanese occupied the Peiping-Tientsin area. In
April 1938 it was transformed into the North China Development Company, and
in November the Japanese provided it with 350 million yen of capital. It had
many subsidiary firms monopolizing communications, transportation, harbors,
telephone and telegraph, salt manufacturing and sale, coal, and iron and steel.

North China was well integrated into Japan's war economy. The provisional
government and later the Political Council were nothing but tools to oppress the
people and to exact from them their money, labor, and lives. Simultaneously, in
November 1938, Japan launched the Central China Development Company with
a capital of 100 million yen, which served to dominate all the major industries in
the area, particularly in Shanghai. Most of the important private enterprises
owned by Chinese either were openly seized with little compensation or became
jointly owned with the Japanese. To exploit and control occupied China in support of Japan's war efforts, a China Board was established in October
1938. This later became the Asia Development Board (Koain), which was composed of high-ranking army and navy officers. In early 1939, four Koain liaison
agencies were set up in Kalgan, Peiping, Shanghai, and Amoy to administer
political, economic, and cultural affairs in connection with the "China Incident."

While Japan exercised effective control of occupied China through advisers, it
had more direct control over the "special administrative areas" in Shanghai,
Tsingtao, and Amoy. Having already directly run Tsingtao and Amoy, the Japanese navy also had free use of Hainan Island. The rivalry between the army and
navy only increased their acrimonious demands on China and the suffering of the
Chinese people. The unrestricted issuance of military scrip in China during the
war was the equivalent of outright confiscation of the material and property of
the Chinese people.

From the outset, Wang's regime was handicapped by a shortage of revenue.
For instance, in the mid-1930s, the budget of the national government was

around Ch $1 billion (U.S. $300 million), of which Ch $425 million came from customs revenues, Ch $250 million from salt revenue, Ch $150 million from consolidated excise taxes, and the rest from miscellaneous revenues. The first-year budget of Wang's government, according to one source, was only a modest Ch $25.1 million in contrast with a prospective revenue of Ch $18 million.[59] Since May 1938, funds from the Chinese customs had been deposited in the Yokohama Specie Bank; only a fraction of the customs fees was returned to Wang's government. To facilitate the initial work of Wang's government, however, the bank floated a loan of Ch $40 million. The salt revenue was largely kept by the Japanese army, and even the opium tax was out of the control of Wang's government. The fiscal chaos was compounded by the wide circulation of *fa-pi* (legal tender) issued by the Chungking government, which showed that the people in Japanese-occupied China had more faith in Chiang Kai-shek's anti-Japanese government at Chungking than they did in Wang's puppet government at Nanking. After the Pearl Harbor Incident, customs revenues from the Chinese harbors plummeted almost to zero, while Japanese exactions on Chinese increased by leaps and bounds. Throughout its six-year existence, the Wang regime never acquired financial solvency.[60]

The fortunes of Wang's government were tied to the index of Japanese military success. Following Japan's initiative, Germany, Italy, Hungary, Spain, Rumania, Vichy France, Thailand, and Manchukuo all established diplomatic relations with the Wang regime, which in turn joined the international Anti-Communist Pact. Wang's stature rose above that of other Asian leaders when Japan optimistically launched a Greater East Asia Co-Prosperity Sphere, encouraging the Asian nations to drive Western colonialism out of Asia on the one hand while exploiting the rich economic resources of the newly occupied areas on the other. In November 1943, the Wang regime signed a treaty of alliance with Japan, which relaxed some of the insidious provisions of the Basic Treaty of 1940, such as the stationing of Japanese troops in China.[61]

When the Wang regime was first established, its jurisdiction did not extend very far beyond the Huai River, though the Lunghai railway, running along the south bank of the Yellow River, was specifically placed under the control of Nanking. Its western boundary extended to the border of Szechwan. South of the Yangtze, Nanking controlled northern Kiangsi, with the cities of Nanchang and Kiukiang. Further south, its boundaries bypassed Hunan and northern Kwangtung, where the Hankow-Canton railway was interrupted, but included southern Kwangtung and Hainan Island. On the southeast, except for coastal cities like Foochow and Amoy, Nanking controlled half of Chekiang and about one-third of Fukien. After 1944, Honan Province was added to Nanking's domain.

Even before the Nanking government was established, Wang had the idea of building an army of his own after the model of the Huang-p'u Military Academy, which had become Chiang Kai-shek's power base. Wang first established a

Central Officers' Training Corps at Shanghai and later the Central Military Academy at Nanking, which graduated two classes of one thousand students each. Aside from the officers' training program, the central task of Wang's army-building was twofold: reorganization of the puppet troops and promoting defection of KMT troops. As time progressed, bolstered by the influx of troops from former warlord armies, Nanking's puppet army swelled to nearly 600,000 men. While these troops posed little menace to Chungking—many of them actually colluded with the Nationalist armies—they did constitute a barrier to the expansion of Communist forces. Little wonder that the CCP charged the KMT and Chiang with being united with the enemy or puppet troops. Moreover, there was some truth to Communist charges that the Nanking puppet troops not only prevented the New Fourth Army from taking over the Nanking-Shanghai area but also facilitated the KMT takeover after V-J day.[62]

Wang Ching-wei had the good fortune to escape seeing the collapse of his own regime or to experience the humiliation of being incarcerated or executed as were his wife and associates. After eight months in Japan for medical treatment, he died November 9, 1944. After Wang's incapacitation, Ch'en Kung-po acted as chairman assisted by Chou Fu-hai. It is interesting to note that these two most powerful men in the puppet government had been founding members of the CCP in 1921 and had gone through a life cycle from Communist to anti-Communist to traitor. Even more puzzling was Wang himself, whose brilliant revolutionary career as an anti-Manchu had eventuated in his final years as a collaborator with the national enemy. At the very least, however, the Wang case should not be written off lightly as the tale of a traitor to China.

Conclusion

China in the 1930s was still burdened with the vestiges of warlordism, which had characterized the political scene since the centrifugal tendencies released by the death of Yuan Shih-k'ai in 1916. The immediate prewar years witnessed the extension and centralization of the national government's and of Chiang Kai-shek's power through the suppression of the Fukien Rebellion in 1933–34, the expulsion of the Communists from Kiangsi in late 1934, the defeat of the Liang-Kwang revolt in mid-1936, and the negotiated settlement of the Sian Incident in early 1937. When the war with Japan broke out in July 1937, Chiang's star shone brighter than that of any other Chinese leader in the Republican era.

Within his own camp, Chiang was mainly concerned with military and governmental affairs, leaving the Ch'en brothers to run the KMT on his behalf. With Japan's all-out invasion of Manchuria, Chiang firmly believed that the correct course for himself and China must be "internal pacification before resistance against external aggression." This remained his policy until the Sian Incident of 1936. From Mussolini and Hitler, Chiang learned how to consolidate and expand his own power while he came to rely increasingly on the Huang-p'u graduates, who were entrenched in the Central Army. The fast-growing Fu-Hsing She, guided by its parent organization the Li-Hsing She, was the hallmark of the Fascist movement in China and an important force in KMT politics even after it was formally merged into the Three People's Principles Youth Corps in 1938.

Chiang did not depend solely upon the Huang-p'u faction and the CC Clique. There was as well the Political Study group and the British-American returned students' group of H. H. Kung and T. V. Soong, which despite its nepotistic roots probably helped somewhat to liberalize and democratize Chiang's harsh regime. Although many of these factions were powerful enough to play an important role in the regime, their power and authority derived from none other than Chiang himself. Here lies the mystique of Chiang's regime, which was tinged with the traditional Chinese authoritarianism and absolutism modified by the influence of Western democracy.

Despite the progress toward political integration in the years before the war, China was still considerably fragmented. Aside from peripheral areas like Sinkiang, Tsinghai, Tibet, and Ninghsia, important provinces in the rear were not in the hands of the national government or Chiang. The Chinese Communists in north Shensi were not the only group that resisted the penetration of the KMT's or Chiang's power. Szechwan, Yunnan, and Shansi did just the same, though less successfully.

Kwangsi was the exception. Li Tsung-jen and Pai Ch'ung-hsi cooperated wholeheartedly with Chiang throughout the war in return for some degree of autonomy for Kwangsi. Yen Hsi-shan, the long-lived warlord of Shansi, played a complicated hand during the war and managed to survive without tarnishing his reputation too much to enable him to stay on good terms with Chiang after the war.

Szechwan's leading warlord, Liu Hsiang, succeeded in altering his warlord image by his enthusiastic participation in the fighting against Japan, but his premature death deprived Szechwan of a strong leader and weakened the resistance to the penetration of the national government into the province. Not until 1940 when Chang Ch'un was made governor of Szechwan did Chiang complete his control over the minor warlords of the province whose enormous natural resources and manpower enabled China to fight a protracted war as it did. The massive migration of people from the east to Szechwan accelerated the cultural exchanges and enhanced nationalism.

Yunnan, too, benefited immensely from the war, but not as much as Szechwan. Yunnan soldiers fought heroically in the war even as frictions grew between the national government at Chungking and the provincial government at Kunming, which was China's only outlet to the outside world. Try as he might, Lung Yun was unable to resist successfully the penetration of the Chungking government, but he patronized the Democratic League and encouraged the anti-Chiang sentiment that was frequently expressed at Southwest Associated University.

Elsewhere in China, from the very outset, Wang Ching-wei was pessimistic about the War of Resistance, nor was he alone in this respect. After the fall of

Wuhan in October 1938, Wang saw that the continuation of resistance might invite even greater disasters for China. Wang's despair coincided with Konoe's peace overture in November 1938, an opportunity that Wang believed should not slip by. When Wang failed to convince Chiang Kai-shek to respond to Konoe's overture, he fled from Chungking and temporarily settled in Hanoi. There he issued his own response to Konoe's peace initiative, which eventuated in the negotiations with Japan leading to the establishment of his Nanking puppet government in 1940.

Once embarked upon his course, there was no turning back despite his unhappiness with the harsh Japanese terms that guaranteed his government would be no more than a dependency of Japan. On the other hand, Wang and his domineering wife may have been content with the authority and power in their grip. Indeed, had Japan emerged victorious from the war, Wang's government would have been second to none among the countries of the Great East Asia Co-Prosperity Sphere, and Wang would have been better off than Chiang. Nonetheless, despite his impeccable record as a revolutionary youth, one cannot but conclude that Wang's later career revealed him to be an opportunist.

To the common people under Japanese occupation, Wang's puppet government rendered some service. The reinstitution of a KMT national government at Nanking, even in name alone, had given the people a sense of a return to normality and helped restore some national pride. In more realistic terms, the puppet government had mitigated some of the harshness and cruelty of Japanese military rule. As Japan expanded the war to the Pacific, it would have to rely more and more on the Chinese not only for the exploitation of Chinese resources and manpower, but also to maintain order for a secure rear. In Japanese-occupied China there was an abundance of unemployed officials, soldiers of fortune, and hack intellectuals who were ready and eager to serve the puppet government under Wang Ching-wei, a man whose name alone conveyed a sense of legitimacy.

Yet some of Wang's chief lieutenants and military commanders had connived with Chungking or Chiang through Chiang's secret service chief Tai Li in preparing for the worst. When B–29s took off from Szechwan to bomb Japan, it was a signal that the fate of the Japanese was sealed. So too was Wang's. As a standard-bearer of anti-Communism, Wang's anti-Communist government facilitated the surrender of the Nanking-Shanghai area to Chungking or Chiang, thus precluding a Communist takeover at the time. Hence Wang fulfilled at least part of the mission of helping the KMT or Chiang's government that he had set for himself upon leaving Chungking six years earlier.[63]

Notes

1. Li Yun-han, *Chung-kuo chin-tai shih* (A history of modern China) (Taipei: Three People's Bookstore, 1985), p. 515; Li Shou-k'ung, *Kuo-min ko-ming shih* (A history of national revolution) (Taipei: Central Literary Service, 1965), p. 571.

2. Li Ta-chao, "Statement on the Communists' Entry into the KMT," (1924) in *Ko-ming wen-hsien* (Revolutionary literature), ed. Lo Chia-lun (Taipei: Central Cultural Service, 1957), vol. 9.

3. M. Herman Mast and William G. Saywell, "Revolution Out of Tradition: the Political Ideology of Tai Chi-t'ao," *Journal of Asian Studies* 39, 1 (1974): 73–98; Chou I-shih, "A Random Piece on the Western Hills Conference Group," *Wen-shih tzu-liao* (Materials on literature and history) (Beijing: Chinese Literature and History Press, 1986), vol. 12.

4. Wu Tien-wei, "A Review of the Wuhan Debacle: The Kuomintang-Communist Split of 1927," *Journal of Asian Studies* 29, 1 (1969); Chiang Yung-ching, *Pao Lo-ting yu Wu-han cheng-ch'uan* (Borodin and the Wuhan regime) (Taipei: Commercial Press, 1963).

5. Fan Hsueh-sui, "The Reorganizationalists as I Know Them," *Wen-shih tzu-liao* 95 (1986): 209–30; Ch'en Kung-po, *K'u-hsiao lu: Ch'en Kung-po hui-i* (Bitter smiles: The reminiscences of Ch'en Kung-po) (Hong Kong: Hong Kong University Press, 1979), pp. 160–70.

6. James E. Sheridan, *China in Disintegration* (New York: The Free Press, 1975), pp. 185–87; Wang Yu-t'ing, "The Great Battle of the Central Plain," *Chuan-chi wen-hsueh* (Biographical literature), nos. 273–277 (1985).

7. Ch'en, *K'u-hsiao lu*, pp. 320, 357.

8. T'ao Hsi-sheng, "Cross Currents," *Chuan-chi wen-hsueh*, no. 2, (1964): 165–94; John H. Boyle, *China and Japan at War, 1937–1945: The Politics of Collaboration* (Stanford: Stanford University Press, 1972), chap. 9.

9. Kuomintang Archives Commission, *Chung-hua min-kuo chung-yao shih liao ch'u-pien* (Initial edition of important materials on the history of the Republic of China) (Taipei: KMT Archives Commission, 1981), 3:45–50; Lung Sheng-wu, "The True Historical Event concerning Wang Ching-wei's Flight Through Kunming," *Jen yu shih* (Men and events), no. 58 (March 1988): 37–41.

10. Ch'en Kuo-fu, *Ch'en Kuo-fu hsien-sheng ch'uan-chi* (Collected works of Mr. Ch'en Kuo-fu) (Taipei: Cheng-tsung Bookstore, 1952), 5:36–37.

11. T'ang Liang-hsiung, *Tai Li chuan* (Biography of Tai Li) (Taipei: Chuan-chi wen-hsueh-she, 1981), pp. 418–20. Mao Ching-hsiang's interviews with the author on April 3 and August 12, 1974. Mao was Chiang's most confidential secretary from 1925 to 1952.

12. K'ang Tse, "Origins of the Revival Society," *Wen-shih tzu-liao* 37 (1986): 134–135; Kan Kuo-hsuan, *Lan-i she, Fu-hsing she, Li-hsing she* (The Blue Shirt, Revival, and Vigorously Carrying Out societies) (Taipei: Biographical Literature Press, 1984), pp. 112–15.

13. Hsuan Chieh-hsi, "A Complete Account of the Blue Shirt Society," *Chuan-chi wen-hsueh*, no. 246 (1982): 30–32; Kan, *Lan-i she*, pp. 1–2.

14. Lloyd E. Eastman, *Seeds of Destruction: Nationalist China in War and Revolution* (Stanford: Stanford University Press, 1984), pp. 30–31; Kan, *Lan-i she*, pp. 118–19.

15. Maria Hsia Chang, *The Chinese Blue Shirt Society: Fascism and National Development* (Berkeley: University of California, Institute of East Asian Studies, 1985), pp. 25–26.

16. Roger B. Jeans, "Carsun Chang and the United Front, 1937–1938," paper presented at an international conference on "The 50th Anniversary of the 'July 7' Incident," New York, 1987; K'ang Tse, "An Account of the Establishment of the Three Principles of the People Youth Corps," *Wen-shih tzu-liao* 40 (1986): 200.

17. K'ang, "An Account of the Establishment," p. 200.

18. Ibid., pp. 203–7; Eastman, *Seeds of Destruction*, p. 93.

19. Zhou Enlai (Chou En-lai), *Selected Works of Zhou Enlai* (Beijing: Foreign Languages Press, 1981), p. 221.

20. Eastman, *Seeds of Destruction*, pp. 97–98.

21. Li Chung-shu, "Merger of Political Work Between the Three Principles of the People Youth Corps and the Youth Army," *Wen-shih tzu-liao* 96 (1986): 100–104.

22. Li Ken-yuan, "The Political Study Clique and I," *Wen-shih tzu-liao*, 3:82–105; Han Yu-ch'en, "Political Activities of the Political Study Clique," *Wen-shih tzu-liao* 48 (1986): 176–215.

23. Wang Yu-yung, "The Rise and Fall of the Political Study Clique," *Wen-shih tzu-liao* 4 (1986): 78–97.

24. Parks M. Coble, *The Shanghai Capitalists and the Nationalist Government 1927–1937* (Cambridge: Harvard University Press, 1980), pp. 47, 161.

25. Ch'en Keng-ya, "K'ung Hsiang-hs'i's Embezzlement of U.S. Bonds," *Wen-shih tzu-liao* 50 (1986): 246–53; Ning En-ch'eng, "The Source of China's Income Tax," *Chuan-chi wen-hsueh*, no. 337 (June 1990), 95–97.

26. Huang Ying-ch'ien, "A Brief Account of the Situation in Szechwan after the Death of Liu Hsiang," *Wen-shih tzu-liao* 12 (1986): 79–80; Teng Han-hsiang, "Manipulation and Struggle between Liu Hsiang and Chiang Kai-shek," *Wen-shih tzu-liao* 5 (1986): 53–71.

27. Teng Han-hsiang, "How Chiang Kai-shek Assigned Chang Ch'un to Seek Control of Szechwan," *Wen-shih tzu-liao* 5 (1986): 72–89.

28. Jen P'ei-ying, "Chiang Kai-shek's Alleged Attempt to Conquer Tibet Was Aimed at Hsi-k'ang," *Wen-shih tzu-liao* 33 (1986): 140–54.

29. Liu Wen-hui, "Historical Road to People's Camp," *Wen-shih tzu-liao* 33 (1986): 15–17.

30. Lin Nan-yuan and Sun Tai-hsing, "Biography of Lu Han," *Wen-shih tzu-liao* 98 (1986): 66–67; Lu Han, "The 60th Army in the Bloody Battle at Taierhchuang," *Wen-shih tzu-liao* 90 (1986): 46–77.

31. Tu Yu-ming, "The Story of Chiang Kai-shek's Determination to Get Rid of Lung Yun," *Wen-shih tzu-liao* 5 (1986): 36; Yunnan Committee of Political and Consultative Conference, *Historical Materials on Lung Yun* (Kunming, n.d.), pp. 69–70.

32. Lung Yun, "A Few Pieces of Reminiscences on the Period Before and After the War of Resistance," *Wen-shih tzu-liao* 17 (1986): 53–56; Lo Lung-chi, "Some Reminiscences on My Participation in Political Consultation until the Nanking Peace Negotiations," *Wen-shih tzu-liao* 20 (1986): 193.

33. Yunnan Committee of Political and Consultative Conference, *Historical Materials on Lung Yun*, p. 66.

34. Tu, "The Story of Chiang K'ai-shek's Determination," pp. 32–33; Lung, "A Few Pieces of Reminiscences," pp. 56–58.

35. Huang Ch'i-han, "The Kwangsi Clique and Its Reactionary Political Activities," *Wen-shih tzu-liao* 7 (1986): 119–29; Huang Shuo-hsiung, "The New Kwangsi Clique and Opium," *Wen-shih tzu-liao* 34 (1986): 195.

36. Li Tsung-jen, *The Memoirs of Li Tsung-jen*, ed. T. K. Tong (Boulder: Westview Press, 1979), p. 424; Mou Chia-chu, "Pai Ch'ung-hsi," *Min-kuo jen-wu hsiao chuan* (Short biographies of personages in the Republican era) (Taipei: Chuan-chi wen-hsueh, 1981), 1:31.

37. Eastman, *Seeds of Destruction*, pp. 29–30; Li Chi-shen, "A Brief Account of Mr. Li Chi-shen," *Wen-shih tzu-liao* 67 (1986): 148–51.

38. Yen Hsi-shan, *Product Certification and Distribution According to Labor* (Nanking: The Northwest Guardian, 1936), pp. 1–3; Ch'en Ch'ang-chieh, "Before and After the West Shansi Incident in 1939," *Wen-shih tzu-liao* 90 (1986): 82–90.

39. Chao Ch'eng-shou, "Narration of My Participation in Yen Hsi-shan's Secret Dealings with the Japanese," *Wen-shih tzu-liao* 54 (1986): 205–23; Nan Kuei-hsin, "Yen Hsi-shan's

Secret Dealings with the Japanese During the War of Resistance," *Wen-shih tzu-liao* 5 (1986): 121–23; Tetsuya Kataoka, *Resistance and Revolution in China: The Communists and the Second United Front* (Berkeley: University of California Press, 1974), p. 287.

40. Chao, "Narration of My Participation," pp. 234–35; Nan, "Yen Hsi-shan's Secret Dealings," pp. 124–25.

41. Chang Chih-i, *K'ang-chan chung ti cheng-tang ho p'ai-pieh* (Political parties and factions in the War of Resistance) (Chungking: Tu-shu Sheng-huo Press, 1939), pp. 54–109; Chung-yang t'ung-chan pu and Chung-yang tang-an kuan, eds., *K'ang-Jih min-tsu t'ung-i chan-hsien* (Anti-Japanese national united front) (Beijing: Archives Press, 1986), 3:108.

42. Li Huang, "The Birth of the China Youth Party," *Chuan-chi wen-hsueh*, no. 100 (September 1970): 3.

43. Chung-yang t'ung-chan pu and Chung-yang tang-an kuan, eds., *K'ang-Jih min-tsu t'ung i chan-hsien*, 3:123–24.

44. Chang Chun-mai, "An Open Letter to Mao Tse-tung," *Tsai-sheng* (Reborn), no. 10 (December 1938), as reprinted in Kuo Hua-lun, *Chung-kung shih-lun* (Analytical history of the Chinese Communist Party) (Taipei: Institute of International Relations, 1969), 3:418–20.

45. Lo, "Some Reminiscences," p. 208.

46. Wang Tzu-heng, "Japan's 'Loot, Burn, and Kill All' Policy in Puppet Manchukuo," *Wen-shih tzu-liao* 39 (1986): 61–81; Chiang Nan-tung et al., *Wei-chou kuo shih* (History of puppet Manchukuo) (Kirin: People's Press, 1980), pp. 142–43, 372–73.

47. Ts'ao Ju-lin, *I-sheng chih hui-i* (Memoirs) (Hong Kong: Ch'un-ch'iu Press, 1966), pp. 321–30.

48. KMT Archives Commission, *Chung-hua min-kuo chung-yao shih-liao*, vol. 6, part 3, pp. 79–80; Boyle, *China and Japan at War*, pp. 69–72.

49. Boyle, *China and Japan at War*, p. 80.

50. Peter Duus, *The Rise of Modern Japan* (Boston: Houghton Mifflin, 1976), p. 218; KMT Archives, *Chung-hua min-kuo*, 6:3:32.

51. T'ao Hsi-sheng, "Ten Points of Discussion on the Secret Agreement Between Wang Ching-wei and Japan," written in December 1940, as reprinted in *Chung-kuo chin-tai shih-lun: Ti erh-tz'u Chung-Jih chan-cheng* (A collection of writings on modern Chinese history—the Second Sino-Japanese War), ed. Wu Hsiang-hsiang (Taipei: Cheng-chung Bookstore, 1956), 9:214; Boyle, *China and Japan at War*, pp. 194–98.

52. Huang Mei-chen, ed. *Wang wei cheng-ch'uan tzu-liao hsuan chi* (Selected materials on Wang's puppet regime) (Shanghai: People's Press, 1984), pp. 10–16; Boyle, *China and Japan at War*, pp. 197–98.

53. KMT Archives, *Chung-hua min-kuo*, 6:3:51–52.

54. Huang, ed., *Wang wei cheng-ch'uan*, p. 15; Imai Takeo, "Confession," in ibid., pp. 17–27.

55. Ch'en Kung-shu, "A Complete Account of the Wang Case of Hanoi," *Chuan-chi wen-hsueh*, no. 242 (July 1982): 112–22; Imai, "Confession," p. 20.

56. T'ao Hsi-sheng, "Ten Critiques of the Treaty Between Japan and Wang Ching-wei," in *Chung-kuo chin-tai shih-lun*, ed. Wu Hsiang-hsiang, 9:226–50; Boyle, *China and Japan at War*, pp. 270–75.

57. Imai, "Confession," pp. 24–26; Chu Chi-hua, *Wang cheng-ch'uan ti k'ai-ch'ang yu shou-ch'ang* (The beginning and the end of Wang's regime) (Hong Kong: Ch'un-ch'iu Journal Press, 1959), 1:111–12.

58. Huang, ed., *Wang wei cheng-ch'uan*, p. 12; Chu, *Wang cheng-ch'uan*, 1:87–90.

59. Arthur Young, *China's Wartime Finances and Inflation, 1937–1945* (Cambridge: Harvard University Press, 1965), p. 5.

60. Chu, *Wang cheng-ch'uan*, 1:115.

61. Ibid., 1:120–25; KMT Archives, *Chung-hua min-kuo*, 6:4:1005–40.

62. KMT Archives, *Chung-kuo min-kuo*, 6:3:445–59.

63. Fu Ta-hsing, "Random Pieces on Wang Ching-wei's Army Building," *Wen-shih tzu-liao* 99 (1986): 171–80; Ts'ao Hsuan-ch'ing, "An Account of Wang Ching-wei's Army Building," *Wen-shih tzu-liao* 99 (1986): 181–84; Chu, *Wang cheng-ch'uan*, 2:17ff.

4

THE CHINESE COMMUNIST MOVEMENT

T'ien-wei Wu

IN THE eight years of the War of Resistance against Japan, the CCP army, a mere 40,000 men as of 1937, grew to over a million men in 1945. The population of the Communist-controlled areas increased from 1.5 million to over 100 million, and the original territory of 92,000 square kilometers expanded to 950,000 square kilometers in nineteen resistance bases. In the corresponding period, the membership of the CCP enjoyed spectacular growth from 40,000 to 2.7 million. In sum, the CCP was transformed from one among many military-political actors in Chinese politics to a major contender for national power.

What factors were responsible for the astounding success of the CCP? As early as 1939, Mao Tse-tung coined the slogan of the "three magic weapons" with which the CCP would defeat the enemy in the Chinese revolution, namely, the united front, party-building, and the armed struggle.[1] The purpose of this chapter is to explore the interrelationship among these three factors in the context of the War of Resistance.

The peaceful solution of the explosive Sian Incident in January 1937 not only hastened a rapprochement between the Soviet Union and China but also opened a new chapter in the tortuous relations between the Chinese Communist party and the Kuomintang. It was Japan's all-out invasion of China, however, that proved to be the catalyst in accelerating the formation of a second united front between the two parties and overcoming Chiang Kai-shek's firm anti-Communist stand. Chou En-lai correctly commented that "the peaceful resolution of the Sian Incident promoted nationwide armed resistance to Japan. Thus, armed resistance was brought about through pressure, and we can say the same of the negotiation and the united front."[2]

The negotiations between the KMT and the CCP, begun at Sian in February 1937 and later shifted first to Hangchow and then to Lushan, were marked by twists and turns. Chiang Kai-shek and Sung Tzu-wen (T. V. Soong) represented the Nationalists and Chou En-lai, Po Ku (Ch'in Pang-hsien), and Yeh Chien-ying the Communists. The thorny questions that defied resolution were the reorganization of the Red Army and the abolition of an independent Communist government. Chiang was adamant in refusing to yield on the issues of his complete control over the reorganized Red Army and of the semi-independent status of the renamed border government under the CCP.[3]

On July 15, shortly after the outbreak of the July 7 Lukouch'iao Incident, the CCP submitted a declaration on CCP-KMT cooperation drafted by Chou En-lai. After some minor changes made by Chiang, the KMT accepted the declaration but did not release it until September 22. The main terms offered by the CCP were similar to those offered to the KMT Third Plenum in February 1937:

> 1. Dr. Sun Yat-sen's Three Principles of the People being what China needs today, our party is ready to fight for their complete realization;
> 2. We shall give up our policy of encouraging insurrection to overthrow the KMT regime, call off the Sovietization movement and discontinue the policy of forcible confiscation of the land of the landlords;
> 3. We shall abolish the present Soviet government and call for the practice of democracy in the hope that state power will be united throughout the Country; and
> 4. The Red Army will give up its present name and designation, that it will be reorganized as part of the National Revolutionary Army and that it will be ready for orders to march to the anti-Japanese front and to its duty.[4]

The delayed release of the CCP declaration may have been due to Chiang's effort to keep the sensitive issue of KMT-CCP cooperation from coming out into the open in the hope that a modus vivendi between Nanking and Tokyo might still be worked out and war averted. Despite his speech at Lushan on July 17 in which he declared he would make no further retreats in the face of Japanese aggression, it was only after Japan opened a new front at Shanghai on August 13 that Chiang decided to fight Japan. Reluctantly, he also decided to settle the question with the CCP.

The reorganization of the Red Army into the Eighth Route Army of the National Revolutionary Army began on August 22 with the appointment of Chu Teh as its commander-in-chief and P'eng Te-huai as his deputy. The Eighth Route Army comprised three divisions: the 115th Division, with Lin Piao as commander and Nieh Jung-chen as deputy; the 120th Division, with Ho Long as commander and Hsiao K'o as deputy; and the 129th Division, commanded by Liu Po-ch'eng, with Hsu Hsiang-ch'ien as deputy.

The actual strength of the Eighth Route Army probably reached forty thousand men, double the limit authorized by the KMT. By January 1938, the remnants of the guerrilla forces left behind in Kiangsi and environs by the Long March in October 1934 came out from the mountains and were organized into the New Fourth Army. Yeh T'ing, a famous general from the Northern Expedition, was appointed commander, and Hsiang Ying, a worker prominent in the February 1923 Peking-Hankow railway strike, was Yeh's deputy. The strength of the New Fourth Army was set at twelve thousand men, and it was assigned to fight along a line from Sunchiafu to Kiangyin in Anhwei and Kiangsu provinces south of the Yangtze River.

The soviet government was reorganized as the Shen-Kan-Ning (Shensi-Kansu-Ninghsia) Border Region government with its capital at Yenan. Its chairman was Lin Po-ch'u, with Chang Kuo-t'ao his deputy, but Chang acted as chairman from the beginning until his defection to the KMT in April 1938. The boundaries of the border government area were not clearly defined at first. The KMT vaguely agreed that it would include fifteen counties (hsien), but the CCP claimed there were eighteen—a figure finally recognized by the KMT in July 1940, by which time the CCP was then claiming twenty-three counties. After 1941, Communist writers invariably referred to the Shen-Kan-Ning border government as encompassing twenty-six counties: nineteen in northern Shensi, six in Kansu, and one in Ninghsia, although some sources went as high as twenty-eight counties and one municipality (Yenan). The whole area was estimated at 92,000 square kilometers with a population of 1,420,000.[5]

The CCP convened a week-long enlarged conference of its Politburo, attended by over twenty party and military leaders, at Loch'uan, Shensi, in late August 1937 to consider the new situation created by the War of Resistance against Japan. Urgent issues that the conference needed to resolve were the aims of the war, KMT-CCP relations in the united front, and the military strategy of the Eighth Route Army. Chang Wen-t'ien, supported by Mao Tse-tung, outlined a position reminiscent of Lenin's concerning World War I. Chang proposed that the war should aim at securing the defeat of both the Japanese imperialists and Chiang Kai-shek and his government, and that the Eighth Route Army must maintain its complete independence, fight a guerrilla war with its base in the mountains, and preserve and expand its strength. This view was challenged by Chang Kuo-t'ao, who was probably supported by Chou En-lai. Mao decided to adjourn the conference for three days, and it had barely resumed when he produced a remarkable compromise document entitled "Resolution on the CCP Tasks in the Current Situation," along with the "Ten-Point Program for National Salvation" that had been prepared earlier and was adopted and issued on August 25.[6]

The resolution promised full cooperation with the KMT while criticizing the Nationalists for failing to introduce political reforms or mobilize the masses, and for not implementing the Ten-Point Program for National Salvation proposed by the CCP. This program aimed at the defeat of Japanese imperialism through a platform of national unity and total mobilization of all human and material resources.[7]

The Military Buildup

Mao Tse-tung's famous aphorism that "political power grows out of the barrel of a gun" succinctly expressed his conviction about the importance of an army to the success of a political or mass movement. Mao was no more antithetic toward the KMT nor any less nationalistic than were other leaders of the CCP, nor did he have any greater insight than they about the need to preserve the independence and expand the power of the Eighth Route Army. In fact, the military strategy of the CCP in dealing with Japan, the national enemy, and with the KMT, an ostensible friend, was the consensus of the CCP leadership that had emerged from their struggle against the KMT, particularly in the course of the protracted negotiations that had led up to the formation of the second united front.

CCP leaders were well aware that the numerical weakness of the Eighth Route Army precluded its playing a major role in the defense of North China against the Japanese. So few in number and so deficient in equipment were the Communist troops at the beginning of the war that if they engaged in positional warfare, they could have easily been wiped out by the enemy as were other KMT crack troops. There was no doubting the determination and anti-Japanese commitment of these forty thousand young men and women, but it was imperative that they not be squandered in battle against the Japanese because they represented the germ plasm of the Chinese revolution. Moreover, they also had to be on guard against KMT troops who might turn against them. The mutual suspicion that was the legacy of ten years of fighting was far from dissipated, and the fragile expressions of goodwill evoked by the formation of the united front remained to be tested in practice.

In the first place, what has been called the second united front between the KMT and the CCP was not a concept that Chiang Kai-shek accepted. Six months of negotiations between the two parties had borne little fruit simply because Chiang had insisted on a policy of dissolving the Communists and controlling the Red Army by refusing to grant the CCP legal status and the Red Army an independent command. Only when the situation in North China became critical as a result of the massive Japanese invasion did Chiang wind up negotiations and urge the Eighth Route Army to march to the front at once to repel the enemy. Even then, however, he stopped short of committing himself to making the CCP a full-fledged partner in the KMT-CCP cooperation.

Chiang's shrewd attitude toward the CCP, which at the same time revealed his insecurity, must have convinced most of the CCP leaders, above all those who negotiated with him—such as Chou En-lai, Po Ku, Chu Teh, and Yeh Chien-ying—that the CCP's choices were rather limited. Either Yenan could capitulate to Chiang or it could persist in its basic demands—sole control of the Red Army by the CCP and the preservation of the semi-independent border region government. In attaining their basic goals, the CCP leaders proved to be equally astute and resolute.

The CCP now faced the test of actually carrying out what had long been the central point of its propaganda—marching to the north to fight the Japanese. In doing so, it confronted the crucial dilemma of how to preserve and expand the Red Army without letting down the public trust that it would fight the enemy. Available CCP documents indicate that as early as July 22, 1937, in discussing the reorganized Red Army, P'eng Te-huai spelled out a view that undoubtedly prevailed among CCP leaders generally that "absolute leadership of the CCP over the Red Army must be maintained."[8] As a guiding principle, P'eng's idea was crystallized by Mao in his directive to Chou En-lai and others on September 14, 1937, in which he reiterated the point, "Not a single KMT man be allowed to enter into the Red Army."

In the same context, Chang Wen-t'ien and Mao revealed the military strategy that had been adopted, particularly in CCP relations with the KMT, namely, to "select only mountainous areas suitable for strategic defense when stationing troops; keep constantly on the alert for a surprise attack and sabotage; and do not ask for big cities for stationing troops."[9] Needless to say, despite its public announcements to the contrary, the CCP put self-preservation and expansion above fighting the Japanese. The end justified the means. Those who didn't grasp the CCP decision were regarded as poor Leninists who failed to understand the workings of dialecticism and historical materialism.

Certainly, the CCP was right to claim that the Red Army excelled in guerrilla warfare rather than in fighting a positional warfare against the enemy, but this meant that the Red Army could play only a minor role in fighting the enemy on the North China front. With its main goal that of "developing guerrilla warfare in the mountains," the Eighth Route Army began to move in batches, not all at once as demanded by the KMT, into the Wut'ai mountains in northeastern Shansi. The 115th Division was the first to move, followed by the 120th Division, while the 129th Division stayed behind to defend the Shen-Kan-Ning base area.

By mid-September, the 115th Division reached its destination in northeastern Shansi under the overall command of Yen Hsi-shan, field marshal of the Second War Zone. Later in September, all three divisions were dispatched to Shansi with one regiment from each retained in northern Shensi. The 115th Division settled in the Wut'ai mountains in the northeast, and the 120th Division in the T'aiyao mountains in the east, around which resistance bases could be established.[10]

In the last week of September, Lin Piao's 115th Division scored a major victory during the battle of P'inghsing Pass along the inner section of the Great Wall. It virtually wiped out a Japanese convoy escorted by a force of over one thousand men, and it captured a large amount of military equipment and other materials. Unquestionably, it was the first great victory in North China since the war began, but the 115th Division also suffered heavy losses of nearly a thousand men killed or wounded. While Lin Piao's victory served to boost the morale of the Chinese army considerably and deflect the allegation that the Eighth Route Army had evaded engagement with the enemy, Lin's victory could not alter the outcome of the battle of P'inghsing Pass, which ended in another Chinese defeat.[11]

Almost a month after Lin Piao's feat, the 769th Regiment of the 129th Division led by Commander Ch'en Hsi-lien and Wang Nai-kuei destroyed twenty-four Japanese warplanes in a successful attack on a makeshift Japanese airport in Tai County. This operation was mounted in support of the Chinese defense in the battle of Hsinkow, where 100,000 Chinese troops, half of them KMT troops commanded by Wei Li-huang, were engaged. Heavy casualties were incurred on both sides in the greatest battle the Chinese had undertaken in North China. On the eastern front along the Peiping-Hankow railway, however, the Japanese drive was so swift that Taiyuan was threatened from the east and soon evacuated without serious fighting. With the fall of Taiyuan, Chinese positional warfare in North China virtually ended, and a new phase of the war commenced in which the Eighth Route Army played a major role. Unlike the KMT army units in North China, which engaged in positional warfare, the Eighth Route Army moved freely among the people in areas often inaccessible to the Japanese.

In Hopeh and Shansi, a political vacuum was created as the KMT fled south-ward in disorder and as county and district governments ceased to function. Many groups with divergent backgrounds and motives emerged to contest leadership and maintain order. Among them were students and intellectuals from Peiping and Tientsin, remnants of former warlord armies, KMT stragglers, soldiers of fortune, bandits, and Communist guerrillas.

Among these groups the Communist guerrillas enjoyed certain decisive advantages, including manpower—the most important factor—as well as organization and know-how acquired through the land revolution and the civil war with the KMT. Most of all, they had the Eighth Route Army and the CCP behind them. As in the preceding decade, a Red Army man was not merely a soldier, he was entrusted with organizing the people, collecting taxes, setting up local government (or a soviet), and conducting propaganda. In the early stages of the war, these guerrilla activities were actually facilitated by the swiftness of the Japanese advance along the railway lines that fully occupied the Japanese in taking one city after another, leaving them no time nor manpower to pacify the extensive countryside behind their occupied line.

Chin-Ch'a-Chi and Other Resistance Bases

Since the middle of September 1937, Nieh Jung-chen, deputy commander of the 115th Division, had worked in the Wut'ai mountains. When the main force of the 115th Division departed that area on October 23, 1937, Nieh and about two thousand men remained at Wut'ai and set up the first guerrilla base and the Chin-Ch'a-Chi (Shansi-Chahar-Hopeh) military headquarters, which served as a model for other guerrilla bases that were to be established. The Eighth Route Army fighting behind the enemy lines apparently had the blessings of Chiang Kai-shek at that time.[12]

After the fall of Taiyuan in early November, local underground Communists, anti-Japanese railway workers, Yen Hsi-shan's dare-to-die youth detachment, and students joined forces with the newly arrived 129th Division and established the Shansi-Hopeh-Shantung-Honan base along the Taihang mountains extending to the south Hopeh plain and western Shantung north of the Yellow River. In early 1938, the base repeatedly destroyed Japanese offenses and became the center of CCP activities in North China. Ho Lung led the 120th Division in northwestern Shansi during the battles of Hsinkow and Taiyuan in October and November 1937. They established the Shansi-Suiyuan base centering around Ningwu and Shen-ch'ih counties.[13] The Shantung base was initiated by Fan Chu-hsien, a KMT prefecture director from western Shantung, who organized the local people to fight the Japanese and closely cooperated with the CCP after refusing to withdraw to the south of the Yellow River in November 1937. Later, in central, southern, and eastern Shantung, two Communist-led guerrilla forces emerged to pose a direct challenge to KMT forces in the province.

Although the CCP's main success was in North China, the Communists also established bases in the Yangtze valley and in Central China where they had eight bases in all: East Kiangsu, Central Kiangsu, South Kiangsu, Huai River North, Huai River South, Central Anhwei, East Chekiang, and Hupeh-Honan-Anhwei.

The backbone of these bases was the New Fourth Army, but some of them developed out of residual Communist influences, particularly in the Tapieh mountains. In South China there were two resistance bases: the East River base in Kwangtung, and Ch'iung-ya in Hainan Island. Other bases, which were less well-defined and much weaker, included Hunan-Hupeh-Kiangsi, Hopeh-Jehol-Liaoning, Shantung-Hopeh-Honan, Shansi-Hopeh-Honan, Central Hopeh, Hupei-Honan-Anhwei. The number of bases fluctuated. Some sources say there were sixteen, while others list as many as nineteen or twenty-two.[14]

Many factors influenced the timing and pace of base development. Lyman Van Slyke enumerates seven in particular: (1) the availability of Communist military units and political cadres; (2) the presence of local cadres; (3) mountainous remote areas and marsh lands; (4) local societies of traditional, social, and economic structure; (5) disruption of local administration at the county level; (6) the presence of Japanese forces; and (7) the presence of KMT power.[15]

Despite its widely noted successes, the CCP was far from satisfied with its work in establishing guerrilla bases and expanding the Red Army. In a telegram sent from southern Shansi to the CCP leaders on November 13, 1937, Chou En-lai proposed to "expand the Red Army so as to strengthen the decisive role of the Red Army (it is in this task that we have been least successful)." He asked Chu Teh, P'eng Te-huai, and Jen Pi-shih to order the recruitment of thirty thousand men in North China. As of this time, the Eighth Route Army had only organized ten thousand people in guerrilla units, and in fourteen counties in Shansi where guerrilla units operated, the number of guerrillas was only a little over four thousand.[16]

Chou was disappointed primarily with the New Fourth Army rather than with guerrilla warfare in North China. What he omitted saying was that at this early stage, the CCP was making every effort via guerrilla warfare to assist the KMT forces in fighting the enemy rather than in competing with KMT forces behind enemy lines. Of course, the CCP did not foresee how long the war would last, and, like the KMT, it focused on the battle of Wuhan as the critical struggle whose outcome would determine the future of the war. When Wuhan fell on October 25, 1938, the KMT forces were greatly reduced and weakened. In contrast, by the time the war was one year old, the Eighth Route Army had grown from 40,000 men to a formidable force of 250,000 men, a development that must have alarmed both the KMT and the Japanese. Hence, the KMT decided to check and compete with the CCP forces behind the enemy lines while the Japanese launched mopping-up campaigns in North China.

Competition and Friction Behind the Enemy Lines

The CCP's basic strategy in the War of Resistance changed slightly at the Sixth Plenum of the Sixth Central Committee held at Yenan in October–November 1938. It was decided that the Eighth Route and New Fourth armies should completely abandon mobile warfare, which had hitherto been employed in the most favorable circumstances, in favor of guerrilla warfare exclusively, with the goal of expanding the Red Army. While harboring no ill will toward the KMT, the CCP stressed political, economic, cultural, and military competition with the KMT and the Japanese behind the enemy lines.

Until the fall of Wuhan, KMT and CCP forces, operating at equal strength behind enemy lines, cooperated fairly well in the Japanese-occupied areas and concentrated on fighting the enemy, as did other Chinese forces, many of which were provincial or warlord armies. After the fall of Wuhan, however, the balance gradually tilted toward the CCP for obvious reasons. The national government, now ensconced in distant Chungking, was too far away to provide adequate attention and assistance to KMT-sponsored guerrilla movements except through its field marshals and provincial governments in Shantung, Honan, and Shansi. In the new phase of war, the Japanese wanted to consolidate their gains and make preparations for a protracted war, which required mopping-up campaigns to clear guerrilla forces from North China. In this critical situation, the political alignment of guerrilla forces became increasingly polarized, and the few previously neutral forces had to choose sides. The growing strength of the CCP and the flight of Wang Ching-wei compelled the KMT and Chiang Kai-shek to devise a new strategy for war and survival. The CCP was treated no longer as an ally but as a rival in the war against Japan. This entailed fighting for control of guerrilla forces behind enemy lines and suppressing underground Communist activities in the rear areas. Finally, the CCP, convinced that its own future as well as the outcome of the War of Resistance hung in the balance, resolutely engaged in building resistance bases behind the enemy lines, which could be consolidated and expanded on the principle of self-reliance.

In these circumstances, numerous cases of friction occurred between the KMT and the CCP, who were fighting for control of the guerrilla forces behind enemy lines. Each blamed the other for the violent clashes that claimed thousands of casualties. In September 1939, CCP forces in Shantung openly challenged KMT forces, even attacking the provincial government, while in Hopeh, P'eng Te-huai's troops defeated three Nationalist divisions and put an end to KMT guerrilla activities in that province.

The Hundred Regiments Battle

Meanwhile, the Eighth Route Army faced the even greater problem of Japanese operations that increasingly threatened the survival of the guerrilla base areas, particularly in the Hopeh and Shantung plains. Between 1938 and 1940, the Japanese launched at least 109 campaigns, each involving more than 1,000 troops, and 10 large campaigns of over 10,000 men.[17] The Japanese built blockade houses, walls, and ditches to prevent Communist guerrillas from receiving food and supplies from the plains. Another threat to the CCP guerrilla base areas came from the more active role played by the puppet troops following the inauguration of Wang Ching-wei's strongly anti-Communist government at Nanking on March 30, 1940.

There were other reasons pushing the CCP to take the military offensive. The Communists may have wanted to demonstrate to Chiang Kai-shek and the KMT that allegations asserting that they were only interested in expanding the Red Army and not in fighting the enemy were untrue. Staging a great offensive against the Japanese might serve to improve KMT-CCP relations and forestall rapprochement between Chungking and Nanking or between Chungking and Tokyo, about which many rumors had been circulating.

On the eve of the Hundred Regiments battle, the Eighth Route Army had grown to about 400,000 men strong, most of them constituting the 115 regiments that plunged into the three-and-a-half-month battle (August 20–December 5, 1940) that was waged in three stages. In the initial stage, over a hundred regiments from the 115th, 129th, and 120th divisions attacked Japanese targets along the Shihchiachuang-Taiyuan, Peiping-Hankow, and Tungpu (Tatung to Fenglingtu) rail lines, inflicting heavy casualties. The Japanese army was apparently caught unprepared as the shock-wave of the Communist attacks spread throughout North China. Effective Japanese resistance did not come until the latter part of September as the battle entered its second stage, during which Communist troops tried to consolidate their gains by taking many Japanese strongholds in the Taihang mountains. During the third stage (October 6– December 5), the initiative passed to the Japanese, who launched a full-scale campaign in Shansi and Hopeh. The Eighth Route Army suffered heavy losses, mainly because of the inferiority of arms and lack of supplies.

The Hundred Regiments battle was doubtless the greatest victory the CCP army had ever fought and won during the entire war. A Japanese source estimated the Japanese loss of lives at 20,645 with an additional 5,155 puppet

Chinese troops killed in battle. Enormous stocks of war matériel were seized, and over six hundred miles of railway were destroyed along with many bridges and tunnels. The Chingching coal mine, which supplied high grade coal to the An-shan Steel Works, sustained heavy damages and was rendered inoperative for six months. The CCP recovered over forty of the county seats it had lost before the battle in Shansi and Hopeh, and it consolidated its control over twenty-six of them.[18]

The engineer of the victory of the Hundred Regiments battle was P'eng Te-huai, who had acted in his capacity as secretary of the North China branch of the Military Commission without securing prior approval from the CCP Central Military Commission headed by Mao. In his autobiography, P'eng made an eloquent defense of his strategy in response to criticisms later leveled against him. "Without the Hundred Regiments battle," P'eng said, "our resistance bases in Shansi and Hopeh may have been reduced to guerrilla areas, and we would not have built a regular army of one million supported by two million militia men."[19]

In the wake of the Hundred Regiments battle, the Japanese launched the "security-strengthening movement," the core of which was the "Three-all" policy (loot all, kill all, burn all), which became standard procedure during and after the Hundred Regiments battle. For the Communists operating behind enemy lines, 1941 and 1942 were critical years during which the Red Army was reduced from 500,000 to 300,000 men, the population under Communist control was severely diminished, and the Communists held only 10 of the 437 counties in North China.[20] Out of dire necessity, the CCP launched the programs of "better troops and simpler administration" and other economic measures such as "reduction of rent and interest rates," which became parts of the *cheng-feng* (rectification) movement.

In spite of the campaigns and blockades against the Communists in North China, the Japanese war plan for 1942 aimed at defeating the KMT army, not the Eighth Route Army. As late as autumn 1942, the Japanese North China Area Army still believed that "the central issue for the solution of the China incident lies in the destruction of Chiang Kai-shek's resistance against Japan."[21] There is no denying, however, that while more than ten divisions of KMT troops in the Chungt'iao mountains in southern Shansi north of the Yellow River were easily vanquished by the Japanese, the Eighth Route Army not only survived but succeeded in forging itself into a force eventually strong enough to challenge successfully the supremacy of the KMT in China. Among many other reasons, the most important one lay in Mao's claim that "the party controls the gun." In his eyes, a Red Army man was a propagandist and organizer of the party.

Struggles and Growth of the Party

The eight years of war between China and Japan witnessed the transfiguration of the CCP and of Mao Tse-tung as its leader. By April 1945, when the CCP

Seventh Congress convened at Yenan, party membership had swelled from an estimated 40,000 at the beginning of the war in 1937 to 1.2 million. At the Seventh Congress Mao became the undisputed leader of the CCP, and his thought was elevated to the level of the Marxist classics.[22]

Mao consolidated his leadership in struggles against Chang Kuo-t'ao and against the returned students group (those who had studied in the Soviet Union) headed by Wang Ming (Ch'en Shao-yu). Mao's gradual rise to power since the Tsun-yi conference in January 1935 during the Long March was primarily due to his control of the Red Army. Before the war, Chang Kuo-t'ao was still a power to be reckoned with. Despite the fact that two-thirds of Chang's Fourth Front Army had been lost in the western campaigns in Kansu in early 1937, that army still had an edge over the First Front Army, which was Mao's support.

Alienated by the struggle and criticism sessions staged against Chang Kuo-t'ao by Mao and his collaborators, particularly Chang Wen-t'ien, the secretary-general of the CCP, some forty high-ranking officers of the Fourth Front Army planned a coup against Mao and the party leadership, but they were betrayed and arrested.[23] Riding the tide of the anti-Japanese united front, Mao and the CCP leadership reshuffled the personnel of the Fourth Front Army into the newly created Eighth Route Army, thus eliminating the identity of the former.

Until Wang Ming, accompanied by K'ang Sheng (Chao Jung), returned from Moscow on November 29, 1937, Mao as titular head of the CCP had virtually a free hand in Yenan to run CCP affairs. No other leader in the CCP hierarchy, including Chang Wen-t'ien and Chou En-lai, had a following large enough to pose a challenge to Mao. Wang Ming, however, was in quite a different category. Well-versed in Marxism-Leninism and fluent in Russian, Wang was the leader of the returned students group and author of the August 1 manifesto that ushered in the era of the second united front. Since the fall of 1931, Wang had been in Moscow where he became a prominent figure in the Comintern. Against the background of massive Soviet military aid en route to China, Wang's arrival with Stalin's instructions for the Chinese party created the impression that he was Moscow's choice for party leader, and he immediately overshadowed Mao in the CCP leadership. After the reshuffling of the party leadership in Yenan, Wang proceeded directly to Hankow, which at this time was the center of China's War of Resistance, the place where negotiations with the KMT concerning the united front had to be conducted and where Soviet aid was being sent.

The membership of the reorganized Politburo of the CCP was as follows: Mao Tse-tung, Chang Wen-t'ien, Chou En-lai, Chu Teh, Chang Kuo-t'ao, Wang Chia-hsiang, Ch'in Pang-hsien, Jen Pi-shih, Ch'en Yun, P'eng Te-huai, Hsiang Ying, Liu Shao-ch'i, K'ang Sheng, Wang Ming, Teng Fa, and Ho Ko-ch'uan.[24] With the post of secretary-general abolished, the new secretariat of the CCP had five members: Chang Wen-t'ien, Mao Tse-tung, Wang Ming, Ch'en Yun, and K'ang Sheng. A new Yangtze Bureau was established with Wang Ming as the chief.

Even a cursory examination of the reorganized party hierarchy demonstrates that Wang Ming had the upper hand over Mao. Except for Mao, all the other members of the new secretariat had been to Moscow, and Chang Wen-t'ien and Ch'in Pang-hsien had been leaders of the returned students group. The newly established Yangtze Bureau was intended to replace Yenan as the center of the Chinese Communist movement. During the Wuhan period, Wang Ming virtually ignored the leadership at Yenan and maintained direct communication with CCP regional leaders throughout China. On the other hand, Wang was at a disadvantage in not serving on the CCP's Military Committee, which Mao had dominated since the Tsun-yi Conference and which he used to build up his following by controlling personnel assignments. Wang, however, enjoyed good relations with Hsiang Ying, leader of the New Fourth Army, and with P'eng Te-huai, who was the effective commander of the Eighth Route Army in North China since Chu Teh spent the greater part of the war years in Yenan. Although P'eng Te-huai claimed that he had begun to oppose the Wang Ming line at the Sixth Plenum of the CCP Sixth Central Committee in October 1938, he admitted in his memoirs that it was not until the winter of 1943 that he had a full understanding of the mistaken character of Wang's policies.[25]

At first blush, it seems incomprehensible that P'eng Te-huai would have launched such a gigantic undertaking as the Hundred Regiments battle in the summer of 1940 without obtaining the prior approval of the Military Committee and Mao at Yenan. Such being the case, however, P'eng probably either had support from Wang Ming or felt that Mao was not the indisputable leader whose consent he needed to secure. Mao began openly to challenge the returned student group only after the New Fourth Army Incident in January 1941 and Hitler's invasion of the Soviet Union in June 1941, when he perceived the group was vulnerable domestically and internationally. The claims of Maoist writers that Mao denounced the Wang Ming line long before this are simply untrue.

The Sixth Plenum of the CCP Sixth Central Committee

At the Sixth Plenum, lasting for forty days in October–November 1938, a series of major speeches was delivered by CCP leaders including Mao, who gave the political report, followed by Wang Chia-hsiang, Chang Wen-t'ien, Chu Teh, Chou En-lai, Wang Ming, Chang Hao, Hsiang Ying, and Liu Shao-ch'i. Among these speakers, only Liu can be identified as a follower of Mao, and it appears that Mao had lost the status of *primus inter pares* among CCP leaders that he had enjoyed since the Tsun-yi Conference.[26]

The resolution of the plenum was based upon Mao's lengthy report entitled "On the New Stage." (Its subtitle was "The New Stage of the Development of the National War of Resistance against Japan and the Anti-Japanese National United Front.") Mao's report had two major objectives—to create party unity after the defection of Chang Kuo-t'ao, and to support the united front and the KMT in the War of Resistance against Japan.

To this day, Communist historians criticize Wang Ming's second "left" line, which they say was expressed in the two slogans: "Subordinate everything to the national anti-Japanese united front" and "Everything through the national anti-Japanese united front." Wang's actual words at the plenum are worth quoting:

> Both Mao [Tse-tung] and Lo [Fu, i.e., Chang Wen-t'ien] have pointed out that we must set an example, i.e., on the one hand we must uphold the principle— "resistance against Japan is above everything, everything is subordinate to resistance against Japan," "everything is for the national anti-Japanese united front, everything is through the national anti-Japanese united front," and "everything is subordinate to the interests of the war of resistance, everything is for the victory of the war of resistance."[27]

Shortly before his death in 1974, Wang Ming was able to vindicate himself. He pointed out that the twin slogans "Subordinate everything to the national anti-Japanese united front" and "Everything through the national anti-Japanese united front" were recommended by Georgy Dimitrov, the secretary-general of the Comintern. Wang merely transmitted these slogans to the CCP Politburo meeting in early December 1937. He claimed that he did not mention them again "not because I considered them wrong, but simply because there were no occasions to mention them."[28]

There is no question that what Wang Ming said is correct. The resolution adopted by the plenum said virtually the same thing concerning the need to subordinate everything to the interests of the War of Resistance and to place the national anti-Japanese united front above all else.[29] In fact, in "On the New Stage" Mao himself used sycophantic language to please Chiang Kai-shek.

The Rectification Movement

By the fall of 1941, the Chinese domestic scene and the international situation had both changed drastically. The Soviet Union terminated military aid to China following the German invasion of June 1941. Almost immediately thereafter, Moscow requested that the CCP explore the possibility of stepping up military operations against Japan to prevent it from opening up a second front against the Soviet Union.[30] This proposal would likely have found support among the Russian returned students, particularly Wang Ming. (Incidentally, the returned students were protégés of Bukharin, Pavel Mif, and A. I. Rykov, all of whom were purged by Stalin in 1938. None of them deserves the label of Stalinist that has been affixed to them.) Mao began to see that the returned students were of no use in securing Soviet aid for the CCP, and that Stalin did not care about what might happen to them in the intraparty struggle within the CCP.

In the critical years of intraparty struggle from 1935 to 1941, the so-called Mao-Lo alliance (Lo Fu, i.e., Chang Wen-t'ien) and other returned students, particularly Wang Chia-hsiang, K'ai Feng (Ho Ko-ch'uan), Yang Shang-k'un, and Chu Jui, had supported Mao in his bid for party leadership against Po Ku (Ch'in Pang-hsien), Chang Kuo-t'ao, and Wang Ming. The death of Hsiang Ying and the New Fourth Army disaster deprived Wang Ming of a possible ally and left him without military backing. Meanwhile, with the CCP military completely in his grip, Mao saw that the usefulness of his Russian-returned allies was over, and he decided that the time had come to settle the score with them. In doing so, Mao could count on overwhelming support from the old guard of the party, who looked upon the returned students as upstarts whose unwarranted rise to power had been imposed on the CCP by the Soviets.

The enormous growth of the party and the Red Army created new and difficult problems. In Yenan a large bureaucracy had developed, and students and visitors flooded the Communist capital. There was an urgent need to provide newcomers with a unified if rudimentary knowledge of Marxism-Leninism and of the history of the Chinese Communist movement, and to instruct them regarding the new economic, political, and united front policies. Most of all, the CCP had to devise ways and means for survival in the face of the KMT economic and military blockade, the assault of the puppet forces, and the onslaught of the Japanese mopping-up campaigns. Mao's first concern was his own interest, then the party, and finally the nation. By the fall of 1941, Mao clearly saw that he had to establish himself as the sole leader of the CCP before he would have the chance to compete effectively with Chiang Kai-shek for national leadership.

After winning the support of K'ang Sheng, Ch'en Yun, P'eng Chen, and Kao Kang, Mao set up several study groups for ranking cadres in the fall of 1941. Then, on February 1, 1942, using the Central Party School as a platform, Mao launched his *cheng-feng* movement in a speech entitled "Rectify the Style of Party Work," which he followed up a week later with another speech entitled "Against Stereotypes in the Party." Mao called upon the party to fight subjectivism, sectarianism, and stereotyped writing. The major purpose of the rectification, according to two of its leaders in Yenan, Li Wei-han and Hsu Hsiang-ch'ien, was to oppose dogmatism represented by Wang Ming and to liquidate the influence of his "left" thought. Empiricism was also targeted by the movement.[31]

The objects of rectification were none other than the high-ranking and veteran cadres. K'ang Sheng was put in charge of a commission to oversee the movement, and he elaborated Mao's original ideas in two lectures of his own. On April 3, 1942, the CCP Central Committee issued its "Decisions Concerning the Central Committee's Discussions and Comrade Mao Tse-tung's Reports on the Rectification of the Three Styles," outlining procedures for the unfolding *cheng-feng* movement. The staff of all government organizations as well as students were instructed to devote three months to studying the CCP documents as well as six articles by Mao, three by Stalin, and one each by Lenin, Dimitrov, Liu Shao-ch'i, Ch'en Yun, and K'ang Sheng.[32] After this would come discussion meetings, followed by the review and investigation of each individual's work, which was then to be submitted to the Central Committee for approval.

Despite his avowed policy to the contrary, Mao allowed, tolerated, and even encouraged the employment of pressure, extraction of confessions, and use of torture in the campaign. Emboldened by invitations to engage in criticism as well as self-criticism, many persons spoke out against the CCP leadership and Yenan society, among them famous writers like Ting Ling and Hsiao Chun. None went so far in their criticism as did Wang Shih-wei, a member of the Academia Sinica, who instantly was looked upon as the spokesman for the Yenan youth. Wang wrote a series of wall-poster articles, the best known of which, entitled "Wild Lily," was most offensive to CCP leaders. At the struggle meeting against him, Wang was convicted of being a former Trotskyite and was thrown in jail. Twenty years later, however, Mao accused Wang of having been a KMT special agent and disclaimed responsibility for his execution during the war by CCP security personnel.[33]

In addition to suppressing criticism, an effort was made to curb excesses in dealing with the critics themselves. In July 1943, the Central Committee adopted a nine-point "Decision of the CCP Central on the Investigation of Cadres," which was designed to accomplish this objective. Ironically, the seventh point of the decision—struggle to save those who have fallen (also known as emergency salvation)—triggered a massive hysteria that is beyond comprehension. For instance, at Resist Japan University, 602 people were ferreted out on suspicion of being KMT spies. This was 57.2 percent of cadres above the platoon level at the university. Of the 406 people in the cadre detachment at the university, 373, or 75 percent, were found to be spies or were suspected of spying. Even Yeh Chien-ying, chief-of-staff of the Red Army, was allegedly a suspect. At the height of the campaign, Chou En-lai was recalled from Chungking, as was P'eng Te-huai from the North China front, and both men were forced to confess to empiricism, which buttressed the dogmatism of Wang Ming.[34] One by one, Po Ku, Lo Fu, Yang Shang-k'un, and other leaders of the returned students group were forced to write confessions, but Wang Ming steadfastly resisted doing this to the very end.[35]

Today, Communist leaders unjustifiably blame K'ang Sheng for the excesses and atrocities committed during the rectification movement while trying to exonerate Chairman Mao. More than twenty years after *cheng-feng*, however, Mao and K'ang again collaborated in another movement—the Cultural Revolution—whose excesses and atrocities overshadowed the earlier campaign. Indeed, it was Wang Ming who rightly pointed out that there were some similarities between the rectification movement and the Cultural Revolution.[36]

On the other hand, there were also positive aspects to the rectification movement. Ideological unity was enhanced as the entire party, particularly its newest recruits, was instructed in the history of the Chinese Communist movement and imbued with some rudimentary grasp of Marxism-Leninism. In addition, party members were given a better understanding of the various CCP policies that were to be implemented in the final stage of the war. Over the period from the beginning of *cheng-feng* to the convening of the Seventh Party Congress in April 1945, the CCP was transformed from an offspring of Soviet communism to an independent Chinese Communist movement led by Mao. On the eve of the Seventh Congress, Mao wrote that the rectification movement and the production movement were the two most important links in the chain of revolution that "have already made and continue to bring about decisive effects on both the spiritual and material lives [of the party]."[37]

The Production Movement

The most difficult years for the Chinese Communists, both in their rear area, the Shen-Kan-Ning border region, and in the base areas behind enemy lines, were unquestionably 1941 and 1942, even though the Communists did manage to hang on. Mao summarized the critical situation in 1944:

> In the two years 1941–42, our party was placed in an extremely difficult position. During this stage its base areas shrank in size, the population fell to under 50,000,000, the Eighth Route Army was reduced to 300,000, the loss of cadres was very great, and our finances and economy were very heavily strained.[38]

A sharp increase in the number of nonproductive military, government, and party personnel in the Shen-Kan-Ning border area from 14,000 in 1937 to 73,000 in 1941 contrasted with the continuous decline of foreign aid, mainly from overseas Chinese, and the cut-off of KMT subsidies, which together had provided 74.7 percent of the border government's revenues in 1940. Meanwhile, the tax burden upon the peasants increased from 1.2 percent of their grain production in 1937 to 16.5 percent in 1941.[39] Though the threat of a KMT invasion of Communist North Shensi was more apparent than real, the CCP leadership took no chances, setting up a special defense command for this purpose.[40]

As the situation in the North China base areas deteriorated, a CCP directive of November 1941, entitled "Concerning Military Building in the Anti-Japanese Areas," called for decentralization as the guiding strategy. The following measures were ordered: (1) reducing the ratio of regular army to local troops, and making all the armed forces local troops in the most difficult areas; (2) replenishing manpower and ammunition losses from local troops to the maximum extent; (3) stepping up manufacture of improved hand grenades, mines, and old-style cannons, and distributing them to the people's militia; (4) adopting new military tactics such as tunnel, mine, and sparrow warfare.

The initial campaign for "better troops and simpler administration" (*ching-ping chien-cheng*) was outlined in a directive of December 4, 1941, and supplemented by a further directive of June 30, 1942. According to Li Wei-han, the initial stages of the campaign made some headway in combining offices, differentiating between political affairs and administrative work, promoting county government, reducing the number of personnel, and strengthening lower-level organizations, but the results were far from satisfactory. At a conference of economic and financial affairs cadres in March 1943, Mao set forth five goals for the campaign: excellence and simplicity, unity, efficiency, frugality, and opposition to bureaucratism.

The campaign for better troops and simpler administration was accompanied by a drive for production under the slogan of salvation through production. Everyone from Mao and Chu Teh on down, without exception, was expected to engage in raising food. At this time, the 359th Brigade at Nanniwan was touted as a model of self-reliance and self-sufficiency. Mao's well-known report "Economic and Financial Problems," delivered in December 1942, provided considerable impetus to the production campaign. As a result, many government organizations and military units became nearly self-sufficient in food. Typically, they devoted half a day to "rectification" and the other half to production. Mao stressed that the alternative to working with one's own hands to increase production was starvation and defeat.[41]

Naturally, agriculture was accorded the top priority, and it enjoyed tremendous success in the two years of the production movement. Industry, some of it involved in the cooperative movement, also made great strides. By the end of 1943, the CCP and its Red Army had developed into a force with the will and power to challenge Chiang Kai-shek and the KMT for national leadership.

KMT-CCP Relations

From the outset, KMT-CCP relations in the War of Resistance were marked by suspicion, maneuver, and manipulation. Chiang Kai-shek never ceased his policy of containing, restricting, and combating the CCP, while the CCP insisted on independence and self-determination and devoted itself to expansion. Chiang never even officially recognized the KMT-CCP cooperation or united front. The day after finally releasing the CCP manifesto of July 15, 1937, which he had sat upon for more than two months, Chiang issued a statement expressing the hope that "Now that the Chinese Communists have given up their prejudices," they would "contribute all their strength to the nation's war effort against aggression under a unified command."[42] A unified command was never created. After the fall of Nanking, Chiang changed the designation of the Eighth Route Army, a peacetime usage, to the Eighteenth Group Army, a temporary wartime unit.

Despite appearances to the contrary, it was patriotism on both sides that brought about the cooperation between the KMT and the CCP and that kept them together throughout the war. The hostile attitude and mutual mistrust that they brought to their cooperation was deeply rooted in the experience of the first "united front," which had ended in disaster for the CCP, and in the ensuing civil war, which had hardened their hatred and steeled their determination to eliminate each other. In view of their past antagonistic relations, their wartime cooperation, problematic though it may have been, was still remarkable.

The Era of Goodwill

The CCP went to war believing that if mass mobilization succeeded in bringing millions of Chinese into the anti-Japanese united front, victory was assured. Its Ten-Point Program of Resistance against Japan and National Salvation, adopted at the Lo-ch'uan conference on August 25, 1937, was quite compatible with the KMT Program of Armed Resistance and National Reconstruction adopted almost a year later by the first meeting of the newly established People's Political Council.[43]

Chiang Kai-shek himself encouraged the Eighth Route Army to advance to enemy-occupied areas and conduct guerrilla warfare for which it was famous. As early as July 16, 1937, Yeh Chien-ying submitted a note to Chiang expressing the CCP's willingness "to dispatch part of [our troops] to penetrate deep behind enemy lines and strike the enemy," while admitting that the Red Army lacked expertise in defensive warfare.[44]

Contrary to the conventional wisdom, the CCP was very slow and even vacillating in expanding its army and setting up guerrilla bases behind enemy lines. After the successful establishment of the Shansi-Chahar-Hopeh border government on January 10, 1938, the CCP began to consider the possibility of establishing resistance bases elsewhere behind enemy lines. It was not until after the fall of Wuhan, however, that this was given major emphasis. As Chou En-lai admitted later on, during the Wuhan period party leaders had downplayed guerrilla warfare in the Yangtze basin and "did not take advantage of the withdrawal of the Kuomintang to go to the countryside, mobilize the peasants, and wage widespread guerrilla warfare."[45]

The fall of Wuhan on October 25, 1938, as well as the loss of all the major cities and railways, marked the end of the first phase of the war and signaled the beginning of a period of protracted war in which guerrilla warfare would become increasingly important. At this time the CCP had neither the intention nor the ability to dominate the field of guerrilla warfare behind enemy lines. Addressing New Fourth Army cadres in March 1939, Chou En-lai revealed the strategic decision taken by the Sixth Plenum of the Central Committee to focus attention on the enemy's rear areas, and he invited all anti-Japanese forces to cooperate with the CCP in areas dominated by Communist forces.[46]

A KMT military conference in November 1938 decided to devote one-third of military resources to fighting guerrilla warfare behind enemy lines.

Many middle-ranking KMT officers were sent to a newly established guerrilla training school headed by Yeh Chien-ying. The KMT, however, never fully developed its potential for guerrilla warfare, mainly because of the constant burden of having to face the enemy in positional warfare.[47]

A more visible example of CCP-KMT wartime cooperation was the establishment of a political department, under the Military Council, headed by Ch'en Ch'eng with Chou En-lai and Third Party leader Huang Ch'i-hsiang as deputy ministers. Kuo Mo-jo, Mao Tun, and T'ien Han were among the famous Communist writers who joined the political department. During the Wuhan period, the CCP enjoyed considerable freedom of action in Wuhan itself, and possibly in other major cities. The CCP's official organ, the *Hsin-hua jih-pao* (New China daily), was published throughout the war, first at Hankow and then at Chungking (and reprinted at Kweilin and Sian until 1939), and it enjoyed a wide readership even though it was frequently censored. In general, despite KMT attempts to curb the growth of the CCP and its army, the party enjoyed considerable freedom on a national scale to conduct propaganda and engage in other activities to a degree unprecedented even during the first united front of 1924–27.

Despite its serious reservations, CCP support for the war and the KMT was real and sincere. Notwithstanding Chiang's mistrust of the CCP and Mao's misgivings about the KMT, cooperation between the two parties continued. It seems that most CCP leaders, including Mao, were optimistic about the prospects for KMT-CCP relations during the first two years of the war. With respect to the united front, Mao was no less conciliatory or ingratiating toward Chiang and the KMT than was Wang Ming. Expressing his sincere support for Chiang and the national government, Mao called upon CCP members to join the KMT and its Youth Corps in order to promote long-term cooperation between the two parties, and he pledged that the CCP would not attempt to control the activities of Communists who joined the KMT.[48]

Even before the Sixth Plenum of the CCP Sixth Central Committee was adjourned, Chou En-lai returned to Wuhan bearing a letter from Mao to Chiang requesting that Chinese Communists be allowed to join the KMT and the Youth Corps. In another letter submitted to Chiang at Chungking on January 25, 1939, Chou En-lai said:

> As our cooperation is long-term, the CCP at its Sixth Plenum specially decided that the CCP will no longer develop membership within the KMT and its troops. If the KMT should allow the CCP members to join the KMT and the Youth Corps, we would hand over the roster of the CCP members in order to fortify mutual trust. . . . The CCP has no intention whatsoever to discriminate against or overthrow the KMT. On the other hand, under your leadership, the KMT has made tremendous progress and will naturally consolidate its leadership of political power even more, so that the partial development of the CCP should not pose a threat.[49]

Chiang's reply was negative. Commenting twenty years later, Chiang said he realized the CCP was again trying to infiltrate the KMT on a large scale, and he refused to be deceived again. He justified his refusal by invoking the "painful experience" of the first united front of 1924–27, conveniently forgetting that it had not been his followers but the Communists who were driven underground or killed and whose party had been shattered. In any case, by January 1939, Chou En-lai must have known that the honeymoon between the KMT and the CCP was definitely over.

Conflict Without a Split

As the war entered a new phase of protraction and attrition, the national government, now securely ensconced in Chungking, moved to strengthen itself against its internal enemies. In January 1939, the KMT Fifth Plenum adopted the "Measure for Restricting the Activities of Alien Parties," which was later supplemented by additional measures. By the summer of 1939, the highwater mark of the KMT-CCP second united front had passed. Clashes for control of guerrilla bases behind enemy lines grew rapidly, particularly in Hopeh, Shantung, and northern Kiangsu, resulting in heavy casualties.

On the second anniversary of the July 7 Incident, the CCP Central Committee sent a long letter to the KMT identifying the problems of capitulation and internal dissension within the united front as the two main issues that the two parties faced in their relations during the next stage of the war. These problems would arise from the enemy's attempts to split the KMT-CCP united front.[50] Suggesting the need to concentrate political and military efforts behind enemy lines, the letter proclaimed the CCP's continued adherence to the policy of subordinating everything to the needs of the War of Resistance and of doing everything through the united front.[51]

The CCP's efforts to forestall the anti-Communist drive of the KMT failed. According to Mao, the first anti-Communist upsurge erupted between December 1939 and March 1940 as a result of the territorial expansion of the Shen-Kan-Ning Border Region in northern Shensi, the defection of Yen Hsi-shan's New Army to the Communists in northwestern Shansi, and the defeat of three divisions of KMT troops in southeastern Hopeh by Eighth Route Army forces.[52]

Apparently fearful of jeopardizing KMT-CCP relations, Mao made a quick retreat in a speech of March 1, 1940, in which he specified that Communist forces might fight against supposedly friendly armies only if they had just grounds, it was to their advantage, and it was done with restraint. By exercising such restraint, Mao argued, the Communists could win over middle forces and deter die-hards from launching a full-scale civil war.[53] With reference to local armed conflicts, an August 1939 directive from the CCP Central Committee said that "we will not attack unless we are attacked; if we are attacked we will certainly counterattack. In doing so, we will not give the splitters any pretext that may affect the united front on the one hand and, on the other, from the standpoint of self-defense, we will give those engaging in friction a severe blow and a good lesson for their offensive action against us."[54]

Far more serious than the many incidents that characterized the first anti-Communist upsurge was the well-publicized New Fourth Army Incident. We know now that this much touted incident was not an isolated phenomenon, nor was it purely a case of KMT-CCP conflict.

Hsiang Ying, the leader of the New Fourth Army, had been at odds with Mao since 1931. Remaining in Kiangsi after the Long Marchers set out in October 1934, Hsiang and several thousand guerrillas survived to constitute the backbone of the New Fourth Army, which was founded in January 1938. It quickly grew from 12,000 men in 1938 to 100,000, and it became Hsiang Ying's instrument for attempting to transform Yunling in southern Anhwei into the Yenan of the Communist south.

Hsiang's occasional assertiveness in implementing policies and directives other than those prescribed by the CCP Central Committee must be seen as a challenge to Mao and the CCP leadership. Rarely did Mao directly send instructions to Hsiang; nearly all directives were cosigned by Wang Chia-hsiang and sometimes by Chu Teh as well. Hsiang's quarrel with Yenan apparently reached crisis proportions in May 1940 when he thrice unsuccessfully submitted his resignation.

Although since 1940 the long-term objective of the New Fourth Army had been "northward development and development behind the enemy lines," in view of Chiang's order that the New Fourth Army must move to the north of the Yellow River, the CCP leadership's short-term solution, to say the least, was imprudent.[55] The CCP was well aware of the KMT determination and its order to clear the New Fourth Army from the area north and south of the Yangtze River as early as September 1940, and as many as twenty KMT divisions were marching eastward to menace CCP forces north of the Yangtze. The New Fourth Army in northern Kiangsu under Ch'en I precipitated the battle of Huang-ch'iao against a KMT army under Han Te-ch'in, resulting in the annihilation of two KMT divisions in early October. The CCP believed that Chiang Kai-shek would exact revenge for this, but to defer the crisis, Chiang unexpectedly had a personal talk with Chou En-lai on the fourth anniversary of his release from Sian.[56]

On October 19, 1940, two weeks after the Huang-ch'iao disaster, the Nationalist high command ordered both the Eighth Route Army and the New Fourth Army to move north of the Yellow River by the end of November. The CCP procrastinated as long as possible, responding evasively on November 8. On December 9, Chiang personally ordered that by December 31 the entire New Fourth Army must move north of the Yangtze (the greater part of the New Fourth Army had been operating north of the river since the summer of 1940), and all of the Eighth Route Army must move north of the Yellow River where it belonged. The CCP leadership decided to comply with Chiang's order.[57]

On December 29, the CCP leadership approved Hsiang Ying's and Yeh T'ing's redeployment plan according to which the New Fourth Army would move directly northward to cross the Yangtze in batches toward its final destination in eastern Anhwei. The CCP Central directive also announced that Yeh would remain with the army in its northward move while Hsiang Ying would be reassigned. The next day, however, after being warned by Chou En-lai of the peril involved in taking the direct northern route, the CCP instructed the New Fourth Army to alter its original plan and, in the interest of safety, proceed in batches through southern Kiangsu.[58]

The New Fourth Army's march south when it was supposed to be redeploying to the north of the Yangtze was apparently construed as evidence of its intention to defy Chiang's order and take refuge in the mountains. Moreover, the New Fourth Army had allowed the December 31 deadline to elapse; it began to move out only on January 3, 1941. When it reached Maolin on January 5, it was waylaid by as many as seven KMT divisions numbering over fifty thousand men. The nine thousand men of the New Fourth Army fought desperately for a week until they were overwhelmed. Five thousand men were taken prisoner, including Commander Yeh T'ing, and the rest were killed or wounded. Unbelievable as it may seem, the attack on the New Fourth Army was the decision of Ku Chu-t'ung, acting without a specific order from Chiang. As commander-in-chief of the Third War Zone, Ku would have known of Chiang's intention to eliminate the New Fourth Army at an opportune time had it continued to defy the order to move north of the Yangtze.[59]

On January 17, 1941, Chiang announced the disbandment of the New Fourth Army. In response, the CCP launched its greatest ever propaganda campaign against the KMT and Chiang since the move to Chungking. Now it was up to Chiang to beat a quick retreat. In an interview with Soviet Ambassador Panyushkin, Chiang, accusing the New Fourth Army of "defying orders for a long time," stated that his disbandment order was purely a matter of enforcing military discipline and had nothing to do with politics.[60]

Chiang ignored a twelve-point list of CCP demands that included repeal of the order to disband the New Fourth Army, cessation of attacks on CCP forces, and punishment of Ho Ying-ch'in, Ku Chu-t'ung, and others involved in the incident. In protest, the seven Communist members boycotted the opening of the People's Political Council on March 1, 1941. Chou En-lai succeeded in winning much sympathy and support from the small parties and intellectual leaders as well as from foreign diplomats in Chungking, particularly the Americans.

Despite much evidence to the contrary, the incident turned out to the advantage of the CCP.[61] Chou's confrontation tactics, coupled with his resolution of self-sacrifice, seemed to have paid off. Claiming that the Communist boycott of the PPC had put the KMT on the defensive, Chou exulted that "Chiang looked like a dog dropped in water. He was so inanimate that he gave an insipid speech to close the meeting. All Chungking, China, and the world were concerned with, and inquiring, whether the CCP delegates would be present [at the council]. It was Yenan, the CCP leadership, on which hangs the balance of [Chinese] unity."[62]

Most of the New Fourth Army's forces had already moved north of the Yangtze prior to the incident, so the losses incurred—about 10 percent of the army's total strength—were far from constituting a serious blow to the CCP's long-term strategy. The incident, however, caused so much irreparable damage to KMT-CCP relations that it is something of a miracle that an open civil conflict was averted for the balance of the war.

The so-called third anti-Communist upsurge that Mao talked about was occasioned by the publication of Chiang's *China's Destiny* in January 1943, timed to coincide with the abolition of unequal treaties by the Western powers, notably the United States and Great Britain. This highly nationalistic book blames the imperialists for most of China's problems, but it was far from being "a revealing *Mein Kampf* of China's present leader," as John S. Service described it in a report to the U.S. State Department.[63] Nor can one agree with Chou En-lai that the book is permeated with fascist ideology. What Chou probably found most objectionable is the statement in the book that "The Kuomintang is the headquarters of our national reconstruction. . . . The independence of our nation hinges upon the success of the Kuomintang Revolution. Without the Kuomintang, there would be no China."[64]

The parochial, arrogant, and conservative approach outlined in *China's Destiny* may be seen as Chiang's return to his early wartime theme of "One faith, one party, and one will." By deliberately ignoring the CCP's contributions to the national revolution and the War of Resistance against Japan, Chiang both distorted history and displayed a lack of magnanimity inappropriate to a great, charismatic leader.

The much-touted "third anti-Communist upsurge" never materialized. It was rumored that Chiang had decided to use Hu Tsung-nan's troops, which formed a cordon around the Shen-Kan-Ning border area, to launch an attack aimed at capturing the Red capital at Yenan, but under the pressure of the CCP propaganda campaign no such thing occurred. One report claims that General Stilwell, swayed by Chu Teh's appeal, threatened Chiang with the withdrawal of U.S. air forces from China if Chiang launched a civil war.[65]

The "anti-Communist upsurges" were intertwined with endless and fruitless negotiations between the KMT and the CCP that dragged on for three years until the end of the war. The talks centered on four issues: the legal status of the CCP, recognition of the border region government, increase in the number of authorized Communist troops, and the demarcation of war zones. The third round of negotiations coincided with Mao's new demands for a democratic coalition government and with the assertion of an American interest in the outcome of the talks.[66] To this end, Ambassador Patrick J. Hurley signed a five-article accord with the CCP at Yenan in November 1944, but his intervention probably did more to complicate than facilitate the fruitless KMT-CCP negotiations.[67]

At the Seventh National Congress of the CCP in April 1945, Chou En-lai, who was more responsible than anyone else for the execution of the CCP united front policy, reviewed his own successes and failures. Employing the concept of a two-line struggle against both right and left deviations, Chou concluded that:

> The problem of leadership is, therefore, the central problem of the united front. The Right deviationists waive leadership, while the "left" isolates itself, becoming a "commander without an army. . . ." I myself made quite a number of mistakes. . . . In future, if we fail to understand clearly the enemy, our own ranks, or the question of leadership, if we are unwary or blind with regard to any one of these points, it is on that point that we will make mistakes.[68]

Conclusions

The development of the Chinese Communist movement and the state of KMT-CCP relations were both greatly influenced and conditioned by the progress of the war against Japan. Both behind enemy lines and in the Shen-Kan-Ning border area, against great odds and under most difficult conditions until the end of 1942, the Chinese Communists not only survived but gained strength. By 1943, as U.S. forces counterattacked in the Pacific, it became clear that it was only a matter of time before Japan would be forced to surrender. So 1943 was as crucial to the CCP as to the KMT. Japanese and puppet troops reduced their pressure on the Communists while Chiang, beset by internal and international problems, had to seek a political solution to the Communist question. The Eighth Route Army, which had seen its strength reduced to 300,000 men in 1942 and its control eroded to a small number of county seats, rebounded in the next three years. By August 1945, Chu Teh boasted that the Red Army was one million strong, backed by a militia of 2.2 million and a population of 100 million people in nineteen liberated areas in as many provinces of China. The CCP numbered 1.2 million members.

The numerical strength of the KMT, however, was four times greater than that of the CCP in 1945: roughly an army of 3.5 million supported by a population of 350 million in a territory that embraced three-quarters of China's fertile lands. KMT membership doubled in the war years from roughly one and a half million in 1937 to over three million in 1945. The national government, headed by Chiang Kai-shek, the most powerful leader of China since the founding of the Chinese Republic, enjoyed the prestige derived from being one of the "Big Four" in the family of nations. Yet, in the end, all this was no match for the CCP.

Whatever one's political sympathies may be, one cannot deny the fact that the formation of the anti-Japanese united front prepared the way for China to face

Japan. Without the united front, China would almost certainly have returned to Chiang's old theme, "internal pacification before resistance to external aggression" (*an-nei K'ang-wai*). Yet the second united front between the KMT and the CCP was a marriage of convenience lacking in mutual loyalty and trust from the very outset. The remarkable survival of the united front throughout the war was due to a number of factors, among which patriotism, responsible for the genesis of the united front, was the most important.

It was probably beyond Chiang's worst nightmares that within a few years the CCP and the Red Army would grow so quickly and gain so much popular support that they would be in a position to challenge the KMT and his own rule as soon as Japan surrendered. Small in number as they were in overall terms, the Chinese Communists played an important role in the War of Resistance against Japan. They tied up a large enemy force in North China that otherwise would have been used to unify the occupied areas or force Chungking to its knees. The CCP position on waging the War of Resistance without capitulation stiffened Chiang's own stance. As a fighting force on the battlefield and as a propaganda force or as organizational workers in the rear, the Communists were unrivaled. Although KMT troops undoubtedly bore the brunt of Japanese attacks throughout the war and suffered much higher losses than the Red Army, the latter persevered in fighting behind enemy lines. This was a great achievement that entailed enormous sacrifices, and it should not be lightly dismissed as some partisan observers are wont to do.

The rectification movement and the "better troops and simpler administration" as well as the production campaigns enabled the CCP, an iron-disciplined Leninist party, to weather the crisis of hunger and defeat in the bitter years of 1941–42. The ideological campaign that Mao employed primarily to boost his personal fortunes also served to impart the fundamentals of Marxism-Leninism to the Communist rank-and-file. Though by no means an original thinker, Mao's theoretical writings such as "On New Democracy" and "Yenan Forum on Literature and Art" effectively served the cause of party- and army-building.

In sum, the anti-Japanese national united front made the survival, growth, and eventual triumph of the CCP in China possible. The development of the party and the army alone would not have sufficed to cope with the delicate, changing situation in the united front had Chou En-lai not skillfully and resolutely maneuvered on the spot against the KMT and Chiang while Mao cynically manned the helm at Yenan, issuing timely guidelines. The united front policy, to which Mao made significant contributions, had to be carried out by Chou En-lai, whose contributions have been undervalued. Mao's greatest accomplishment was his success in the intraparty struggle, which enabled him to establish his authority in the CCP as Stalin had done in the Soviet Union. Unlike Stalin, who made no contribution to ideology except for the idea of "socialism in one country," Mao provided the Chinese revolutionary movement with a viable, cohesive ideology that long served as the hallmark of Chinese Communism.

Notes

1. Mao Tse-tung, "Preface to *The Communist*," *Kung-ch'an-tang jen* (The Communist), no. 1 (October 4, 1939); *Selected Works of Mao Tse-tung* (hereafter cited as *SW*) (Peking: Foreign Languages Press, 1965), 2:288.

2. Zhou Enlai (Chou En-lai), *Selected Works of Zhou Enlai* (hereafter cited as *SW*) (Beijing: Foreign Languages Press, 1981), 1:219.

3. Zhou, *SW*, 1:218; K'ang Tse, "An Episode of My Participation in the KMT-CCP Negotiations for the Second Cooperation," *Wen-shih tzu-liao* (Beijing: Chinese Literature and History Press, 1986), 71:13.

4. Chiang Kai-shek, *Soviet Russia in China* (New York: Farrar, Strauss and Cudahy, 1958), p. 87; Jen-min ta-hsueh (People's University), comp., *Chung-kuo hsien-tai shih tzu-liao hui-p'ien* (A collection of source materials on contemporary Chinese history) (Hong Kong: Cultural Materials Supplies, 1951), p. 355.

5. Wang Chien-min, *Chung-kuo kung-ch'an-tang shih kao* (A draft history of the Chinese Communist party) (Taipei: Cheng-chung Bookstore, 1965), 3:218; Hsing Kuang, "Better Troops and Simpler Administration in the Shensi-Kansu-Ninghsia Border Region Government," in *Chung-kuo k'ang-Jih ken-chu-ti shih kuo-chi hsueh-shu t'ao-lun hui lun-wen chi* (Collection of papers given at the international academic conference on the history of the base areas during China's War of Resistance against Japan), ed. Nankai University (Beijing: Archives Press, 1986), p. 276; K'ung Yung-sung, "Discuss the Special Land Policy in the Shensi-Kansu-Ninghsia Border Region during the War of Resistance," in ibid., p. 379.

6. Chang Kuo-t'ao, *Wo ti hui-i* (My memoirs) (Hong Kong: Ming Pao Monthly Press, 1974), pp. 1296–99; Wei Hung-yuan, ed. *Chung-kuo hsien-tai shih kao* (A draft history of contemporary Chinese history) (Harbin: Heilungkiang People's Press, 1985), 2:26–27.

7. Mao Tse-tung, *SW*, 2:27–28; Chung-yang t'ung-chan pu and Chung-yang tang-an kuan, eds. *K'ang-Jih min-tsu t'ung-i chan-hsien* (Anti-Japanese national united front) (Beijing: Archives Press, 1986), 3:34–36.

8. Chung-yang tung-chan pu and Chung-yang tang-an kuan, eds., *K'ang-Jih min-tsu t'ung-i chan-hsien*, 3:1920.

9. Ibid., 3:37.

10. Nieh Jung-chen, *Nieh Jung-chen hui-i lu* (Memoirs of Nieh Jung-chen) (Beijing: Warriors Press, 1983), 2:350–55.

11. Chien Sheng-huang, "The Eighth Route Army and the Battle of P'ing-hsing Pass," *Kuo-shih kuan k'an* (Journal of the Academia Historica), new series, no. 2 (1987): 133–49; Ho Li, ed. *Pai t'uan ta-chan shih-liao* (Source materials on the history of the Hundred Regiments battle) (Beijing: People's Press, 1984), pp. 37–40.

12. Zhou, *SW*, 1:221; Kung Ku-chin and T'ang P'ei-chi, *Chung-kuo k'ang-chan shih kao* (A draft history of China's War of Resistance against Japan) (N.p.: Hupei People's Press, 1985), pp. 118–123; Nieh, *Hui-i lu*, 2:355.

13. Ho Lung, *Ho Lung yuan-shuai feng pei yung ts'un* (Marshal Ho Lung's great achievements live forever) (Shanghai: People's Press, 1985), pp. 93–100.

14. Yang Sheng-ch'ing, "Characteristics of the Establishment of Base Areas in the Resistance against Japan and Their Historical Significance," *Chung-kuo k'ang-Jih ken-chu-ti*, p. 37; Zhou, *SW*, 1:222.

15. Lyman P. Van Slyke, "New Light on Chinese Communist Base Areas During the Sino-Japanese War, 1937–1945," paper presented at the Conference on the History of the Republic of China, Taipei, 1981, p. 5.

16. Zhou, *SW*, p. 97.

17. Cheng Te-yung, *Chung-kuo ko-ming shih chiao-ch'eng* (A course in the history of

the Chinese revolution) (Changchun: Kirin People's Press, 1987), p. 461.

18. Ho, ed. *Pai t'uan ta-chan shih liao*, p. 468; Tetsuya Kataoka, *Resistance and Revolution in China* (Berkeley: University of California Press, 1974), p. 220.

19. P'eng Te-huai, *Wo ti tzu-shu* (An account of myself) (Beijing: People's Press, 1981), pp. 238–41.

20. Shishito Kan, "Better Troops and Simpler Administration and the Rectification Movement," in *Chung-kuo k'ang-Jih ken-chu-ti*, p. 185; Mao, *SW*, 3:168.

21. Ishijima Kiyuki, "Concerning the Development of Base Areas in the Resistance against Japan," p. 75.

22. Wang Hui-te, "Chronicle of the Chinese Communist Party," *Chung-kuo kung-ch'an-tang ch'eng-li san-shih chou nien chi* (Commemorating the thirtieth anniversary of the establishment of the Chinese Communist Party) (Canton: South China People's Press, 1951), 2:101–8; Wang Chien-ying, ed. *Chung-kuo kung-ch'an-tang tsu-chih shih tzu-liao hui pien* (A collection of materials on the organizational history of the Chinese Communist Party) (Beijing: Red Flag Press, 1983).

23. Hsu Hsiang-ch'ien, *Li-shih ti hui-ku* (Historical reminiscences) (Beijing: Liberation Army Press, 1987), 3:566–67; Chang, *Wo ti hui-i*, 3:1166; Kuo Hua-lun, *Chung-kung shih lun* (Analytical history of the Chinese Communist Party) (Taipei: Institute of International Relations, 1969), 3:179.

24. Wang, ed., *Chung-kuo kung-ch'an-tang*, p. 296.

25. P'eng, *Wo ti tzu-shu*, p. 229.

26. Wang Ming, *Mao's Betrayal* (Moscow: Progress Publishers, 1979), p. 53; Wang, ed., *Chung-kuo kung-ch'an-tang shih kao*, pp. 330–31.

27. CCP Central Secretariat, ed., *Liu ta i-lai* (Since the Sixth Congress) (Beijing: People's Press, 1980), 1:992–93.

28. Wang, *Mao's Betrayal*, p. 72.

29. Mao Tse-tung, "On the New Stage," first published in *Chieh-fang* (Liberation, Yenan), no. 57 (November 25, 1938); reprinted in Kuo, *Chung-Kung shih lun*, 3:371–78.

30. Wang, *Mao's Betrayal*, p. 38.

31. Li Wei-han, *Hui-i yu yen-chiu* (Reminiscences and studies) (Beijing: CCP Party History Press, 1986), 2:472–97.

32. Boyd Compton, trans., *Mao's China: Party Reform Documents, 1942–1944* (Seattle: University of Washington Press, 1952), pp. 6–7; Chen Yung-fa, *Making Revolution: The Communist Movement in Eastern and Central China, 1937–1945* (Berkeley: University of California Press, 1986), p. 325.

33. Mao Tse-tung, *Mao Tse-tung ssu-hsiang wan-sui* (Long live Mao Tse-tung's thought) (reprint, Taipei: Institute of International Relations, 1974), p. 421.

34. Wang, *Mao's Betrayal*, p. 138; Hsu, *Li-shih ti hui-ku*, 3:695.

35. Wang, *Mao's Betrayal*, p. 141; Li, *Hui-i yu yen-chiu*, 2:478.

36. Wang Ming, *China: Cultural Revolution or Counter-Revolutionary Coup?* (Moscow: Novosti Press Agency Publishing House, 1969), p. 46.

37. Li, *Hui-i yu yen-chiu*, p. 496.

38. Mao, *SW*, 3:168–69.

39. Li, *Hui-i yu yen-chiu*, p. 501; Hsing, "Better Troops and Simpler Administration," p. 277.

40. Hsu, *Li-shih ti hui-ku*, 3:671.

41. Ibid., p. 677.

42. Chiang, *Soviet Russia in China*, pp. 87–88.

43. Chinese Ministry of Information, *China Handbook, 1937–1945* (New York: Macmillan, 1947), pp. 79–82.

44. Chien, "The Eighth Route Army and the Battle of P'ing-hsing Pass," p. 137.

45. Zhou, *SW*, 1:220.

46. Ibid., 1:121.

47. *K'ang-Jih min-tsu t'ung-i chan-hsien*, 3:261.

48. Kuo, *Chung-kung shih lun*, 3:365–66.

49. *K'ang-Jih min-tsu t'ung-i chan-hsien*, 3:198.

50. Ibid., 3:258.

51. Ibid., 3:268.

52. Ibid., 3:245, 325–26, 329–31; P'eng, *Wo ti tzu-shu*, pp. 230–33.

53. Mao, *SW*, 2:215.

54. *K'ang-Jih min-tsu t'ung-i chan-hsien*, 3:302.

55. Ibid., 3:302.

56. Chung-yang tang-an kuan, ed., *Wan-nan shih-pien (tzu-liao hsuan-chi)* (South Anhwei Incident [selected materials]) (Beijing: CCP Central Party School Press, 1982), p. 124.

57. Ibid., p. 109; Kuo, *Chung-kung shih lun*, 4:186–90.

58. Chung-yang tang-an kuan, ed., *Wan-nan shih-pien*, pp. 124–25.

59. Ku Chu-t'ung, *Mo-san chiu shih* (Self-account of Ku Chu-t'ung) (Taipei: Bureau of Compilation and Translation of History and Politics of the Ministry of Defense, 1981), pp. 206–7; Leng Hsin, "My Part in the Sino-Japanese War (1937–1945)," *Ch'uan-chi wen-hsueh* 5, 3 (1964): 44–45.

60. Furuya Keiji, *Chiang Kai-shek: His Life and Times* (New York: St. John's University Press, 1981), pp. 677–78.

61. Gregor Benton, "The South Anhui Incident," *Journal of Asian Studies* 45, 4 (August 1986): 681–720; Chen, *Making Revolution*.

62. Chung-yang tang-an kuan, ed., *Wan-nan shih-pien*, p. 225.

63. Joseph W. Esherick, ed., *Lost Chance in China: The World War II Dispatches of John S. Service* (New York: Random House, 1974), pp. 89–92.

64. Zhou, *SW*, 1:220.

65. Liao Ko-lung, "Several Problems Concerning the War of Resistance against Japan," *Chung-kuo k'ang-Jih ken-chu-ti*, p. 22; Furuya, *Chiang Kai-shek*, pp. 764–65.

66. Mao, *SW*, 3:255ff.

67. U.S. Department of State, *United States Relations with China, 1944–49 (White Paper)* (Stanford: Stanford University Press, 1967), 1:74–75.

68. Zhou, *SW*, 1:244.

5

THE CCP'S FOREIGN POLICY OF OPPOSITION, 1937–1945

Steven M. Goldstein

THE LEADERS of the Chinese Communist party viewed the anti-Japanese War of Resistance against the backdrop of their continuing, bitter struggle for power within China and saw foreign policy as a means to strengthen their own position vis-à-vis that of their domestic political rival, the KMT. During the war, the CCP developed a foreign policy of opposition that was shaped by the exigencies of the international environment as seen through the prism of the party's domestic political needs. Party leaders developed two major, fully articulated perspectives on foreign affairs—the *united front* and the *Teheran* paradigms—that undergirded their foreign policy of opposition. Party leaders also enunciated a series of principles and prescriptions for China's foreign policy that not only provide insights into the party's domestic revolutionary strategy but also help one understand the roots of PRC foreign policy.

Soon after the outbreak of the Sino-Japanese War, Mao Tse-tung judged that the conflict provided an opportunity to advance toward socialism via the path of what he termed "new democracy," eradicating in the process both the remnants of China's ancien régime and the excessive influence of foreign powers. He viewed China as a nation whose domestic political system was not merely linked to the international environment but actually penetrated by foreign powers who functioned in effect as domestic political actors through Chinese clients who did their bidding. His conception of China as a "semifeudal" and "semicolonial" state highlighted the symbiotic relationship between internal and external forces and, thus, the inevitable interrelationship between foreign and domestic policy. Finally, Mao viewed the "liberation" of China and the triumph of the revolution as dependent upon the leadership role of the CCP. The foreign policy of opposition proceeded from these premises.

The central question that informed the CCP approach to foreign policy was this: How can a proper understanding and, where possible, manipulation of the international environment expand the influence of the party and advance the cause of the revolution? The foreign policy of opposition functioned at many different levels. At the most basic, the CCP articulated what it considered the correct foreign policy for revolutionary China in a dangerous world and acted as a pressure group to correct what it considered the KMT's misguided or dangerous policies. Foreign policy analysis was also an instrument for educating party members and the nation at large, and for attracting political influentials in China to the Communist banner.

Assuming that KMT actions were influenced to a considerable degree by the United States and Britain as well as by Japan, the party sought to understand the policies of these states in order to exert maximum influence on the KMT within the wartime united front. Finally, of course, the CCP tried to mobilize resources from abroad either in the form of material aid or by eliciting favorable public or official opinion so as to bring additional pressure to bear on the KMT government.[1]

The United Front, 1937–41

From 1937 to 1941, the CCP leadership viewed the relationship between world politics and China's revolution through the prism of its domestic united front policy whose intellectual assumptions regarding the structure of the international environment, the motivations of other actors, and alternate political strategies were brought to bear on the foreign policy questions. The CCP used the united front paradigm to formulate a foreign policy appropriate to three very different international and domestic periods: (1) from the outbreak of the Sino-Japanese War until July–August 1939; (2) from the summer of 1939 until June 1940; (3) from June 1940 until June 1941. The essence of the united front paradigm as well as how the party applied it to its foreign policy of opposition can be understood by examining its view of Soviet foreign policy, its views regarding the foreign policies of the United States and Great Britain, and its prescriptions for Chinese foreign policy.

The Soviet Union: Leaning to One Side

Two weeks after the outbreak of the Sino-Japanese War, Mao set forth the CCP's basic foreign policy line:

> Immediately conclude a military and political alliance with the Soviet Union, and closely unite with the Soviet Union, which is most reliable, most powerful and most capable of helping China to resist Japan. Enlist the sympathy of Britain, the United States and France for our resistance to Japan, and secure their help provided that it entails no loss of our territory or our sovereign rights.[2]

As this brief statement indicates, an alliance with the Soviet Union would be an intimate one apparently requiring no safeguards for China's sovereignty, whereas a relationship with the nonfascist imperialist states had to be more distant, and caution was essential. This policy derived from the view that the imperialist states were committed to the perpetuation of a semicolonial China and the preservation of the imperialist world system whereas the Soviet Union was supposedly committed to a new international order and the liberation of China. On this basis, Mao advocated that China should seek two kinds of alignments—one with the Soviet Union based on a joint commitment and a shared world view, the other with the Western powers based on transitory shared interests in opposing Japanese aggression. Throughout the 1937–41 period, the CCP viewed the Soviet Union as China's only permanent state ally in a world of shifting alignments.

In the first period, the Soviet Union was seen as China's most reliable ally amid several wavering and unreliable international supporters. The Sino-Soviet Nonaggression Treaty of 1937 was praised as a "powerful blow to the aggressors," while Soviet military aid and diplomatic support in international forums were duly noted. Throughout 1938–39, the CCP called for even closer ties between the Soviet Union and China.[3] As the incarnation of the anti-aggressive aspirations of the people of the world, the Soviet Union was the indispensable core of any true antifascist front.

In the summer of 1939, the party began at first to disengage from, then after the signing of the Molotov-Ribbentrop Pact and the outbreak of the European war, to abandon completely the policy of seeking support from the United States and Britain. On September 14, Mao developed a second conceptualization of the international environment that would guide the party during the next ten months. He flatly stated that the policy of forming a united front with the bourgeois leaders of the West was over. Mao defined the war in Europe as an "unjust" imperialist war that true revolutionaries should oppose. China's only choice was to join the "anti-war, anti-aggression front" now consisting of the Soviet Union, the colonial peoples, and the peace-loving forces in the imperialist states. The differentiations among China's allies so carefully elaborated over the previous three years were now abandoned as Mao reverted to a pre–united front view of world affairs that saw imperialist aggression and global revolution as the defining characteristics of international affairs.[4] The warring imperialist states were preparing to confront the forces of revolution on a global scale and would soon turn their aggression toward the Soviet Union.[5] Thus, at a time when official Sino-Soviet relations were strained, CCP foreign policy clearly moved against the domestic political tide, maintaining that China's *only* international alignment should be with the Soviet Union because China's survival and ultimate liberation depended upon it.[6]

In July 1940, the CCP's global assessment changed once again. Recognition of the growing contradictions between the Western imperialist states and Japan, following the appointment of the Konoe cabinet in Tokyo, led the party to argue once more for the exploitation of imperialist contradictions, and partial alignment with the United States and Britain despite the danger that these states might try to enmesh China for their own purposes.[7] Nevertheless, the centrality of the Soviet Union and of the struggle against imperialism remained. Thus, until the outbreak of the Soviet-German War in June 1941, the central theme of CCP foreign policy statements remained what it had been since the summer of 1937— temporary alignments with the imperialists might be possible, but ultimately China's fate would be decided by its alliance with the Soviet Union. In this sense, it was a "one-ally" policy.

During the early years of the war, advocacy of alignment with the Soviet Union may have been a domestic political plus for the CCP since Moscow was the major source of aid to China at this time. Although distrust of Soviet intentions was never far below the surface of political life, the party's public standing may have benefited from its close association with Moscow. Similarly, it is plausible to suggest that the relatively calm atmosphere of the united front during these years may have partly reflected Chiang Kai-shek's reluctance to risk alienating Stalin by dealing harshly with his Chinese clients.

All this changed after the fall of 1939. Relations between the Soviet Union and China worsened, and close association with Moscow probably became a political liability. The deteriorated state of relations with Moscow may have facilitated Chiang's tougher treatment of the CCP. More important, CCP defense of such controversial Soviet actions as the invasion of Poland, the Russo-Finnish War, and, finally, the neutrality treaty with Japan in April 1941 damaged the CCP's nationalist credentials in the arena of public opinion.

Notwithstanding these political costs, the CCP nurtured within its own cadres, and sought to impress upon the entire nation, a sense of the common destiny shared by the two countries. During these years, the party not only held up the Soviet experience for special study but made no attempt to disguise its membership in and firm support of the Comintern. The party sought to propagate the idea that the CCP, like the Chinese revolution itself, was part of a revolutionary front led by the Soviet Union with Stalin as its "commander." Internationalism, then, lay at the center of the foreign policy of opposition. Clearly, this element of CCP foreign policy was rooted in a genuine conviction that in a world hostile to the Chinese revolution, the USSR was China's only genuine ally.

Such a characterization of the CCP view of Soviet foreign policy must be qualified, however. As political realists, there were definite limits to the sacrifices party leaders were willing to make on behalf of internationalism. Mao and his colleagues were well aware that the Soviet Union, constrained to maneuver and seize opportunities in the international environment, might have to undertake actions that were detrimental to the interests of China's liberation war and to the CCP itself. For example, following the Soviet-Japanese Nomonhan truce in September 1939, mindful of the possibility that Soviet support to China might be disrupted, Mao emphasized the importance of *tzu-li keng-sheng* (self-reliance or regeneration through one's own strength).[8] Mao also foresaw the "Leninist possibility" of a Soviet-Japanese nonaggression pact like that between Moscow and Berlin.[9] When the USSR and Japan signed a neutrality treaty in April 1941, the CCP defended the pact as a "victory" for Soviet foreign policy that would not affect aid to China.

Another area where Soviet interests operated to the detriment of revolutionary China was the attitude Moscow took toward the policies and leaders of the CCP itself. Not only was Stalin meticulous in avoiding even the suggestion of any dealings with, let alone support to, authorities other than the central government, there is evidence that he supported elements within the party who, in opposition to Mao, argued for a deeper united front with the KMT. But Mao's response demonstrated a willingness to oppose Soviet wishes when that served the CCP's and his own best interests.

In sum, the foreign policy of opposition was reflected in two aspects of the CCP's view of the Soviet Union. Its adherence to a consistent and apparently sincere pro-Soviet position was probably the most distinctive aspect of the party's foreign policy platform. It offered a clear, and often quite unpopular, alternative to the KMT's anti-Soviet stance. Second, while the CCP was willing to pay a price for its internationalism, there were limits. The exigencies of CCP politics and Mao's perception of what was required to defeat the KMT took precedence. If the foreign policy of opposition required that the party ignore Soviet wishes, they would indeed be ignored.

Temporary Allies and Ultimate Enemies

In sharp contrast to its view of the Soviet Union, the CCP believed that the nonfascist imperialist powers—Britain, the United States, France, etc.—were fundamentally hostile to the Chinese revolution. This hostility was rooted in their common desire to protect imperialist interests. Colonial rivalries and inherent contradictions between them and Japan, however, created conditions in which certain of the imperialist powers might potentially become supporters of China's anti-Japanese struggle in a temporary international united front. The cohesive element in such a united front would be "mutual benefit" rather than principle, and the relationship would fluctuate according to the drift of international affairs.[10]

Fundamentally, it was assumed that the nonfascist imperialist states had a manipulative and instrumental attitude toward China, defined by their needs of the moment. Temporary periods of mutual interest would arise, providing an opportunity for China to cooperate with the Western powers. At other times, however, these states would pursue self-serving courses that contravened Chinese interests by trying to terminate the war short of a Chinese victory over Japan. The interaction between these two basic configurations of the relationship between China and the imperialist states provided the central dynamic to CCP foreign policy prescriptions between 1937 and 1941.

CCP leaders ascribed the Japanese invasion to Nanking's irresolution compounded by Western (primarily British) inaction, and through 1937 they feared that this pattern would continue. The ferocity of the Japanese invasion, however, and Tokyo's unwillingness to compromise, left the national government and its Western supporters with no choice but to resist during the remainder of 1937.[11] Thus, the CCP was able to argue forcefully throughout 1938 and the first half of 1939 for a domestic and international united front.

Despite deep suspicions regarding British policy and a skeptical view of the United States, the CCP seemed confident that the Western powers would not pursue a policy of appeasement in Asia, resulting in a "Far Eastern Munich."[12] By the summer of 1939, however, this faith had been shaken by Wang Ching-wei's defection and other signs of anti-Communist and capitulationist tendencies within the KMT, as well as by an armed clash between Communist and Nationalist forces at P'ing-chiang. On top of this came reports that the British had agreed to enter into talks with Japan to resolve tensions over the Japanese blockade of Tientsin. These developments convinced party leaders that the international circumstances that had made possible an international united front policy had collapsed. Britain was now following an appeasement policy toward Japan and promoting political divisions within China to facilitate surrender. The United States might similarly sacrifice Chinese interests.[13] The conclusion the party drew was that the limits of "capitalist aid" to China had been reached, and China must now rely upon its own resources and whatever international aid might be forthcoming from the Soviet Union.

This somber analysis, which preceded the Molotov-Ribbentrop Pact and the outbreak of war in Europe, is the key to understanding Mao's immediate denunciation of the war as unjust and his reassertion of a dichotomous view of international affairs. From the CCP's vantage point, the international united front had already ended earlier in the summer, and Mao believed that China's national interest demanded that it distance itself from the major Western powers by condemning the war.

This denunciation immediately raised the question of whether the party would now revive the earlier image of a totally antagonistic imperialist bloc and abandon all hope of using imperialist contradictions to its advantage. After some apparent disagreement within the party over this question, Mao's view, restated in his essay "On New Democracy" in January 1940, won out. In it he claimed that any attempt to use imperialist contradictions would be more harmful than beneficial to China at the present time.[14] In the first half of 1940, CCP analysts asserted that Britain and the United States were trying to terminate the war in China in order to reach a settlement with Japan and draw it into an anti-Soviet alliance, although they recognized that this would not be easy to accomplish. The Western powers, it was alleged, were also seeking to manipulate Chinese domestic politics to these same ends.[15]

Although the party's stance in the first half of 1940 was one of minimal involvement in international affairs, the option of eventually returning to a united front policy was not discarded. Indeed, when France fell in June 1940 and Japanese politics simultaneously veered in a pro-Axis direction, the CCP concluded that Western interests in China's struggle might now be reactivated. An inner-party document circulated on the third anniversary of the outbreak of the Sino-Japanese War suggested that the Anglo-American policy of seeking a Far Eastern Munich had failed. Chinese foreign policy was entering a new stage in which it was again possible to benefit from imperialist contradictions, "in particular the growing contradictions between Japan and the United States."[16] During the months that followed a Japanese-American confrontation seemed to be in the offing.[17] Indeed, during these months the CCP found itself in the rather paradoxical position of hoping for the expansion of a war that it condemned as "predatory and unjust." Nevertheless, the party remained cautious and still convinced of the ultimate antagonism of the Western powers.

The intensification of the war in Europe in the spring of 1941 shattered the party's confident belief that the Far East would soon become a major military theater. With the Nazis threatening to dominate the Mediterranean basin, Britain was imperiled, and an American rescue effort would require a near total commitment in the West rather than in the Far East. The signing of the Soviet-Japanese Neutrality Pact in April 1941 heightened party concerns of renewed Western attempts to conciliate Japan at China's expense. On May 25, 1941, the CCP Central Committee issued a statement saying that "A Japanese-American compromise so as to sacrifice China and to create an anti-Communist, anti-Soviet, and anti-German Far Eastern Munich—this is the new plot brewing among Japan, the United States, and China. We must expose it and oppose it."[18] Such warnings remained a staple until the German invasion of the Soviet Union.

Unlike its stance on earlier occasions, this time the party advocated using "contradictions among the imperialists" to ward off the danger of a Far Eastern Munich. In fact, Chou En-lai went even further and argued that in the event of a war between the Western states and Japan, it would be proper for the CCP to cooperate militarily with the Western imperialists.[19] Party uncertainty as to how to assess the complicated international situation was resolved by the German invasion of the Soviet Union on June 22, 1941. Once more the party was forced to redefine its position so as to reflect the existence, at long last, of a genuine international united front against fascism. The assessment that finally emerged, while rooted in the earlier period, provided the foundation for the ensuing Teheran paradigm that will be examined below.

Tzu-li Keng-sheng: The Foreign Policy of Opposition

The preceding CCP analyses of Anglo-American policy often read a bit like weather reports. Like the weather forecaster, the role of the foreign policy practitioner appears passive, seeking merely to understand the sources of change and then taking precautions against turns for the worse. Such a view, however, is only partially correct. In fact, there were ways by which the CCP believed it could influence the actions of foreign states.

One was by mobilizing support within the various popular movements that had arisen in the United States and Britain during 1937–41 to oppose Japanese aggression and aid China. The CCP, taking note of these organizations and reporting their activities in its periodicals, argued that China should mount a broad-based campaign of "people's diplomacy" with the objective of pressuring capitalist governments to support China's struggle.[20]

Additional ways by which pressure could be exerted on China's temporary allies were derived from the CCP's strategy in the domestic political arena. Within China, the pursuit of temporary political alliances was made possible by the party's maintenance of an independent organizational structure, a territorial military and economic base, and a Communist-controlled army. These elements were the core of what came to be known as a policy of *tzu-li keng-sheng*.[21] Such a policy gave the party the organizational integrity and military and economic strength either to cooperate with others, to bring pressure to bear upon them, or to pursue its own goals independently, depending upon the circumstances, without at any time forfeiting the initiative to unreliable allies.

Similarly, the CCP argued that only a nation that derived its primary strength from a mobilized and aroused population could survive in an uncertain and conflict-ridden world. If China's wartime government followed such a path, the nation would be able to compensate for its own weakness by securing supplemental foreign aid without rendering itself subject to foreign victimization. Only if the nation as a whole pursued a policy of *tzu-li keng-sheng* could it assure that China's foreign policy would remain independent and that initiative would rest in Chinese hands.[22]

The key to successful implementation of this policy was mobilization of the masses through democratization of the political structure. There was, of course, one problem. CCP leaders believed that China's ruling KMT, a party of bourgeoisie, driven by self-interest and foreign pressures to fight the Japanese, was incapable of implementing such a policy. The KMT's desire to protect its political hegemony, as well as its weak organizational links with the masses, made it both unwilling and unable to tap the abundant manpower and natural resources of China. Its domestic priorities forced it to pursue a foreign policy of dependence or *wai-lai keng-sheng*, rendering it vulnerable to foreign pressures that sought to end China's War of Resistance on terms beneficial to imperialism.

The theme of *tzu-li keng-sheng* thus served the foreign policy of opposition in important ways. It was clearly an attempt to use foreign policy as a means of loosening the KMT's grip on power and increasing the CCP's domestic political influence. By arguing that democratization and unity were essential for China's survival, the policy of *tzu-li keng-sheng* was intended to cast doubt on the KMT's nationalist credentials. The KMT's alleged dependence on the Western powers and its refusal to reform or abandon its anti-Communist policies appeared as a sign of its lack of commitment to the anti-Japanese war. Conversely, the CCP's calls for reform and its warnings about the unreliable nature of the nonfascist imperialists demonstrated its authentic nationalist credentials and probably evoked wide appeal among the informed Chinese public, which was impatient with the United States and Britain. The concept of *tzu-li keng-sheng* thus not only drew on deep cultural and nationalist emotions, but also resonated with the non-Communist democratic elements in China who were also seeking to loosen the grip of the KMT dictatorship.

The core arguments of *tzu-li keng-sheng* regarding the requirements for a successful foreign policy, and its insights into the linkages between foreign and domestic policies, were the basis for CCP policy assessments during these years. There is ample evidence that CCP perceptions of the nature of KMT domestic policy and of Anglo-American foreign policy were shaped by the assumption of linkage. In sum, foreign policy analysis was an important political tool for a party in opposition to gauge its crucial influence on the actions of its political opponent. Finally, even with regard to the Soviet Union, Mao frequently counseled the need for *tzu-li keng-sheng* as a means of overcoming the consequences of unfavorable twists in Moscow's policies. Indeed, his determination to pursue what he thought best for the Communist movement in the face of contrary Soviet advice is probably the most concrete example of the foreign policy of self-reliance.

The Rise and Fall of the Teheran Paradigm, 1941–45

The German invasion of the Soviet Union finally brought about the formation of an international united front against fascism. Paradoxically, it also precipitated CCP movement away from the united front paradigm that it had used up until then to analyze world politics, and toward the elaboration of a fundamentally different model, namely, the Teheran paradigm. To be sure, the CCP remained focused on the problem of how best to use foreign policy to expand its own power, and key assumptions of the united front perspective were integrated into its conceptualization of the wartime Grand Alliance. Moreover, the united front paradigm, which survived as an alternative to the new world view, was resuscitated by the party in late 1944 and early 1945 in response to emerging postwar tensions and the drift of U.S. policy toward China.

In the summer of 1941, the party began to reconceptualize its world view, a process that was not completed until the winter of 1943–44, by which time the Teheran paradigm had become the core intellectual construct guiding CCP foreign policy prescriptions and actions. At the center of the reassessment was the question of how to understand the relations among the three global powers—the Soviet Union, Great Britain, and the United States. Earlier, the CCP faced the challenge of formulating a foreign policy of opposition for a highly fragmented "alliance universe" where these three potential allies were themselves in a state of incipient or actual conflict. With the German invasion of the Soviet Union, the party now took as its point of departure the idea that its potential allies were moving ever closer to genuine cooperation. Since this bore significant implications for China, the central issue for the party was to formulate a foreign policy appropriate to an alliance universe characterized by growing unity.

The Development of the Grand Alliance

The party's first task was to devise a formula linking the Soviet Union's defensive war against Germany—defined as a "just war"—with the Anglo-American conflict against the Axis that had previously been viewed as an "unjust" and "imperialist" war. This was accomplished by the assertion that all wars against fascism—including Great Britain's fight—were "just" wars. On July 12, 1941, the party Secretariat issued a "Directive Concerning the Question of the Nature of the War," in which it explained to understandably puzzled comrades that:

> 1. Under present conditions, no matter whether they are imperialist states or the capitalist class, all who oppose Fascist Germany, Italy, and Japan and aid the Soviet Union and China are good, helpful, and just. All who aid Germany, Italy, and Japan and oppose the Soviet Union and China are bad, harmful, and unjust.
> 2. By these standards, Great Britain's past war against Germany, America's action in aiding the Soviet Union, Britain, and China, as well as a possible American war against Germany and Japan are not imperialist in nature, but just.[23]

Subsequent elaborations of this theme underlined Soviet participation in the war as the central factor that defined the character of the war. This idea evolved into the notion that the participation of the Soviet Union in the Grand Alliance was the only assurance that the lofty goals of the antifascist struggle would be realized.

While emphasizing positive international developments such as the Atlantic Charter and the Anglo-Soviet and U.S.-Soviet agreements, right up until Pearl Harbor the party remained openly critical of American policy in Asia, which it feared might sacrifice Chinese interests in order to come to terms with Japan.[24] Thus, the Japanese attack on Pearl Harbor, while having no impact on the CCP's overall view of global politics, for the time being laid to rest the party's distrust of the United States. In sum, during the first year of the war, CCP analysis of international affairs and of the motives of the major powers was still rooted in a deeply skeptical united front view of the Anglo-Americans as at best temporary allies.

By mid-1942 a radically different view was beginning to emerge. An early harbinger of this change came in a July 1942 *Chieh-fang jih-pao* editorial that addressed the nature of the postwar world, citing Mao Tse-tung's 1938 essay, "On Protracted War." Mao had predicted that the current war would "be close" to being "the final war of mankind" and would be followed by "perpetual peace."[25] This forecast derived from an apocalyptic vision of a general crisis of capitalism followed by the ultimate confrontation between revolutionary and counterrevolutionary forces culminating in a world free of capitalism. Now, however, readers were presented with a very different scenario in which the wartime cooperation of the Soviet Union, England, and the United States would produce what would be "without doubt a free, democratic, peaceful and glorious world."[26]

What this implied was a radically different view of wartime cooperation and its postwar consequences. According to the earlier united front paradigm, the wartime alliance, based on agreement on certain limited goals, would eventually fall apart due to the clash of fundamentally antagonistic world views. Now the CCP was suggesting that Allied unity could be more than partial and transitory. The wartime alliance could evolve into an era of "perpetual peace" based on cooperation among states with different social systems sharing the common goals of democracy, self-determination, and equality for all states.

Implicit in this changed *weltanschauung* was a very different view of the relationship between China and its allies. China could now rest assured that its allies would provide reliable assistance during the war and make no compromises with the Japanese. Moreover, Allied support for democracy and self-determination would carry over into the postwar world, enabling a liberated China to take its rightful place in a world where capitalist nations not only still existed, but actually cooperated with "revolutionary" elements to bring about progressive changes in domestic and international politics.

Over the next fifteen months, the party elaborated the notion of growing Allied unity with respect to both wartime strategy and postwar goals. Analysis focused, in particular, on the questions of unconditional surrender, the Europe First strategy, and the issue of the second front in Europe as touchstones of Allied unity. Ever on the lookout for signs of anti-Soviet behavior on the part of the Western powers, Mao identified the Soviet Union as "the leading element in the world antifascist war."[27] The socialist nature of the USSR supposedly assured its commitment to progressive goals while its presence within the alliance ensured that these goals would be those of the alliance as a whole.

At the same time, popular pressure on Western governments was required to overcome the negative influence of "isolationists" and "imperialists" and to ensure the adherence of these states to progressive and democratic objectives. Indeed, the growth of what the party called "popular power" in the Western capitalist states was precisely the force that was credited with ensuring the adherence of these states to their wartime alliance with the Soviet Union and their commitment to the realization of progressive postwar goals. The reelection of Roosevelt, depicted as a true democrat and a representative of the "enlightened and progressive bourgeoisie," was seen as a triumph of American democracy that augured well for international democratic cooperation.[28] The party also took comfort from the manifestations of wartime unity evidenced in the Moscow, Cairo, and Teheran conferences.

Above all else, the party paid close attention to the evolution of governments in liberated Europe as the prime indicator of the Allies' commitment to change and their continuing unity of purpose. It endorsed the process of democratization undertaken in Italy after Mussolini's overthrow in August 1943 and noted with approval the significant role that the Yugoslav and French Communists were playing in their countries' provisional governments.[29] Poland, on the other hand, was cited as a negative example of a country whose narrowly based, anti-Soviet government-in-exile was using the people's sacrifices to preserve its own grip on power rather than build a new democratic Poland. The CCP drew a direct analogy between the behavior of the Polish ruling circles and that of the Kuomintang leadership.[30] Party leaders hoped that China, under Allied pressure, would become a "new democracy" like France or Yugoslavia where the Communist party played a significant role rather than remain under retrograde KMT leadership with the CCP excluded from power.

In brief, during 1943 and 1944, party writings and speeches evidenced a view of the international environment very different from that which had prevailed during the first four years of the resistance war. The Chinese Communists, of course, were not alone in these views. The American Communist leader Earl Browder, for example, hailed the Stalin-Roosevelt-Churchill meeting at Teheran as a decisive one that would usher in an era of democratic governments and world peace. Unlike Browder, however, Mao and his colleagues used the mood of Teheran not to seek reconciliation with their domestic enemies, but rather to gain a decisive advantage vis-à-vis the Kuomintang in the inevitable postwar civil conflict that they saw coming. Beginning in the summer of 1943, the party tried to turn its new theory of international relations into practice by dealing directly with the United States in order to enhance the prospects for new democracy.

The Grand Alliance and a New Foreign Policy of Opposition

The preceding discussion has dwelled on the CCP's views of the nature of the Grand Alliance and its policies on a global rather than a regional level. This emphasis reflects the actual weighting and tone of the CCP press, which focused more on the global implications of the alliance than on questions narrowly relating to China. Unlike the KMT, the CCP accepted such Allied strategic priorities as the Europe First policy and devoted enormous attention to symbolic statements emanating from the Grand Alliance.

In part, this orientation may have resulted from an honest assessment of the international situation confronting China and its implications for the CCP. The

Europe First strategy, with its corollary of Allied support for the Soviet war effort, was arguably in China's best interests since no development in the Far East, with the exception of a Japanese breakthrough into India, could decisively change the course of the war as dramatically as the defeat of Germany.[31] More important, perhaps, the earlier possibility of a Western compromise with Japan at China's expense no longer seemed credible. In short, party statements from this period suggest a strong core of strategic logic at the heart of its view of international affairs.

This explanation is not sufficient, however. A similar strategic logic should presumably have informed KMT views, yet in fact their view was quite different. In the case of both the KMT and the CCP, different conceptions of the world and, most important, quite dissimilar domestic political priorities moved them to adopt the stances that they did.

Pro-Soviet internationalism—a factor most frequently pointed to by KMT propagandists—was unquestionably a factor in CCP policy. As a Marxist-Leninist party, the CCP certainly considered support of the Soviet Union as its duty, and the party continued to believe that the Soviet Union played a vital role in the achievement of the progressive goals being articulated during the war, including the establishment of a "new democratic" China. CCP emphasis on the global implications of the Grand Alliance at a time when Moscow was not yet a participant in the Far East war served to highlight the centrality of the Soviet Union to China's war effort and its future.

Still, even this is only a partial explanation. Although the record is far from clear, it is worth noting that Mao Tse-tung never allowed the CCP's professions of internationalism to interfere with the domestic political needs of the party as he himself defined them. Thus, from 1941 to 1944, Mao apparently demurred when the Soviets asked him to take military action in support of Soviet strategic interests; ignored the advice of Comintern agents sent to China; and, most important, in the course of *cheng-feng* dealt harshly with pro-Soviet elements within the party.[32] Thus, one returns to the point that as the party in opposition, the CCP had much to gain from the prevailing direction of Allied policy and China's participation in the Grand Alliance.

In the first place, one may reasonably assume that the party leadership had ambivalent feelings about the provision of Allied military aid to the Kuomintang. By 1942, substantial KMT military assets were committed to the blockade of the Communist areas. Although Communists leaders pro forma decried the low level of Allied military support to China, they were undoubtedly aware that any increase in aid might well be used to strengthen the KMT's position vis-à-vis their own party. Certainly, they had no reason to believe that any of the aid would find its way to the Communists.[33] In the absence of any serious Japanese offensive until 1944, the CCP was probably satisfied to see the KMT supplied with just enough support to keep it in the war, but not enough to step up the threat to the Communist areas.

Minimal Allied aid to the KMT government, of course, facilitated CCP expansion of its influence within China via guerrilla warfare. It also highlighted the CCP's consistent emphasis on the importance of *tzu-li keng-sheng*, which, in turn, required democratization in China, a process that would inevitably increase Communist influence. The use of *tzu-li keng-sheng* thus provides a thread of continuity from the earlier united front paradigm, but it underwent a dramatic change after the formation of the Grand Alliance.

In the united front construct, self-reliance was principally a means of weathering unfavorable changes in the international environment. In the fall of 1941, however, another use for the term emerged. Self-reliance, with its correlate of democratization, was seen as a way to secure the support and approval of the Anglo-American Allies. As one editorial put it, "The more progress we can make in our internal unity so as to become in name and in fact a democratic state, then the greater the sympathy and aid we will receive from the antifascist peoples of the world."[34] Beginning in the fall of 1941, the CCP sought to mobilize foreign opinion in its campaign to achieve a restructuring of the KMT-dominated political system and a greater role for the party itself. This strategy was made feasible by Allied commitment to a very explicit set of democratic political principles as the credo of the antifascist war, and greatly facilitated by Roosevelt's insisting on according China the formal status of a great power.

Chiang Kai-shek's growing international stature and the enhanced legitimation the KMT government received by virtue of its ties with the United States might appear as a political obstacle to the success of the CCP's plans. Yet from 1942 on, it became clear that the CCP's foreign policy of opposition was based on a strategy that involved turning the Nationalists' apparent strengths into political liabilities. Like a jujitsu wrestler, the CCP was seeking to turn its opponent's strength and momentum to its own advantage.

With respect to the domestic audience, the strategy was very simple. The CCP tirelessly invoked the universal standards of democracy proclaimed by the Allies, and solemnly subscribed to by Chiang Kai-shek himself, in order to criticize the shortcomings of the KMT government. Chiang's failure to mobilize human resources and to democratize the political system endangered the war effort and undermined China's newly won international prestige. Thus, the party sought to turn Chiang's externally generated legitimacy into an obligation to bring about the kind of political change in China that would weaken the KMT grip on power even as it strengthened the CCP's political role.

Soon after Pearl Harbor, the party began to approach representatives of the U.S. government in an attempt to secure their beneficent intervention in China's domestic political struggle. Playing to the overriding American concern in China—the desire for a militarily effective regime capable of sustaining the anti-Japanese war—party representatives spoke candidly about the KMT's sensitivity to American opinion.[35] In a November 1942 conversation with U.S. diplomats John Carter Vincent and John Stewart Service, Chou En-lai and Lin Piao, referring to China's internal disunity, argued that "foreign influence (obviously American) with the Kuomintang is the only force that may be able to improve the situation."[36] To achieve this end, the Communist representatives restated an earlier request for "some sort of recognition of the Chinese Communist army as a participant in the war against fascism . . . [and] a proportionate share of American supplies sent to China."[37] Although the policy achieved few results initially, the boldness of the approach itself is striking.

There was, however, another important dimension to this policy. Due to the weakness of Chinese public opinion, a successful struggle along these lines required external pressure from the Allies themselves. It was not enough simply to invoke Allied democratic ideals; the Allies actually had to be drawn into China's domestic political dialogue. Once again the jujitsu analogy is instructive. The party sought to use Chiang's dependence on American support to weaken, rather than strengthen, his political position. In the Teheran paradigm, such foreign intervention was viewed with approbation rather than disfavor as in the united front formula.

But why would Allied states, in particular the United States, be willing to play the CCP's game? Communist leaders counted on Washington's concern about the ability of the Nationalist government to fight effectively against Japan as well as to contribute to postwar stability in Asia. Based on Allied behavior in Europe, the CCP hoped that foreign intervention might be forthcoming to accelerate the democratic transformation of the Chinese political system in order to achieve both of the preceding objectives. Apparently taking the democratic rhetoric of the antifascist Grand Alliance at face value, CCP leaders inclined toward the view that Western intervention, under the conditions of cooperation with the Soviet Union and the movement toward global democracy, could actually favor the "forces of liberation" in China—namely, themselves.

The summer of 1943 witnessed a dramatic escalation in the CCP's campaign against the Kuomintang and against Chiang Kai-shek. In a series of biting articles, the CCP charged that, particularly since the Japanese invasion of China, the KMT had demonstrated little concern with defending the Chinese nation. Indeed, in one of the sharpest attacks on Chiang since Pearl Harbor, the CCP compared him to the "hidden traitor" of the Sung dynasty, Chin Hui, who destroyed the country while most people were concentrating on the "public traitor," Lin Yu (likened to Wang Ching-wei or P'u Yi).[38] Focusing their criticism on *China's Destiny*, the book Chiang had published in January, the Communists charged that under his leadership the KMT had jettisoned the ideology of Sun Yat-sen in favor of Hitler/Mussolini-style fascism. Chiang's praise of "feudal" Confucian culture was condemned as a betrayal of Sun's entire revolutionary career.

The CCP put forth its claim to represent the true interests of the Chinese nation and defend the values espoused by Sun Yat-sen. As Wang Chia-hsiang expressed it, "The Chinese Communist party has not only found the correct road in China's liberation war, it has found the correct road in China's entire liberation struggle. . . . The true road in the entire course of the Chinese national liberation struggle—past, present, and future—is nothing other than the thought of Mao Tse-tung."[39] Not only did the CCP lay claim to some of the most potent symbols of the Chinese Revolution, such as Sun Yat-sen and the Three People's Principles, it also invoked the democratic rhetoric of the Allies in its struggle against the KMT. The Communists warned that China could not remain exempt from the worldwide current of democratic change. By virtue of its status as one of the great powers, the CCP suggested, China was obligated to accelerate the process of democratization—a codeword in CCP parlance for ceding greater political influence to themselves.[40]

There can be no doubt that these Communist statements were aimed at eliciting foreign intervention in the form of pressure on the KMT. U.S. diplomatic records show that Chou En-lai approached the American Embassy in Chungking while other Communist officials provided information and documentation regarding the political crisis brewing in China.[41] Apparently, the Soviet Union was also approached at this time. Peter Vladimirov, a Comintern representative in Yenan, claims that at Mao's urging he radioed Moscow requesting Soviet intervention to prevent what the Communists feared was an impending attack by the KMT.[42]

The Communists must have been gratified by the positive responses from both Washington and Moscow. The United States, in the person of General Stilwell, went so far as to propose joint KMT-Communist military action, while the Soviets publicly criticized the Nationalists and expressed concern to American Embassy officials about the threat of civil war in China.[43] For the first time since the onset of war in 1937, there appeared signs of active and coordinated Soviet-American efforts to effect political change in China. These signs provided the basis for the next and most ambitious exercise of the foreign policy of opposition in the fall of 1944.

This new stage was inaugurated by U.S. Vice-President Henry Wallace's visit to China in June 1944 and the subsequent dispatch to Yenan of the U.S. Army Observer Group—dubbed the Dixie Mission because it was in "rebel" territory. This major breakthrough provided the CCP with direct contact with American officials, who could now make their own assessments of the Communists.

At this time, party leaders were inclined toward optimism because of three concurrent sets of developments. First, the Moscow, Cairo, and, most important, Teheran conferences persuaded the CCP that Allied cooperation for the realization of democratic goals was becoming a reality. Second, since the summer of 1943, China's allies had become increasingly critical of KMT policy. As American patience with the Nationalist government began to wear thin, Roosevelt reluctantly resorted to the pressure tactics that Stilwell had long advocated. Not surprisingly, friction between the Allies quickly increased.[44] Third was the changing strategic position of the China theater. From the summer of 1943 on, China began to fade as a strategic factor in the Allies' war plans for the Far

East.[45] In its public statements and in conversations with visitors to Yenan, however, the CCP leadership never acknowledged that the Allies might circumvent the presumed necessity of confronting the Japanese army on the mainland of China. In fact, the party press featured Admiral Nimitz's statements regarding the importance of a land war in China.[46] In sum, CCP leaders believed that strategic considerations stemming from the long-range need to plan for the defeat of Japan on the mainland of China and the short-range requirement of maintaining the China front in the face of possible KMT collapse were all working in favor of greater American receptivity to CCP blandishments. Therefore, the CCP embarked on what turned out to be its most significant effort to mobilize the foreign policy issue in the struggle with the KMT.

What distinguishes this effort from the earlier one is the record of private conversations that took place between CCP leaders and American representatives. The public media, however, are no less important and accurate an indicator of CCP thinking on foreign policy. These publications were directed at both the Chinese public and foreign observers. Party leaders knew that the Yenan daily newspaper *Chieh-fang jih-pao* (Liberation daily) was regularly translated and sent to Washington. Moreover, during the summer of 1944, the party established a radio station to broadcast Communist news and statements to North America.[47] There is a close correlation between the public and the private records, which suggests that the public media rather accurately reflected the leadership's strategic thinking.

With regard to China's foreign policy priorities, CCP media related the general themes of democratization to the Chinese case, arguing that a nation's international prestige depended upon whether it was in the democratic mainstream and whether it carried its share of the fight against fascism.[48] The CCP made clear its belief that the KMT failed these tests, citing in evidence the succession of military defeats suffered during the Japanese Ichigo offensive of 1944. The CCP suggested that China was being internationally humiliated by Nationalist defeats at a time when others were on the offensive.[49]

In short, utilizing the global developments since Teheran and the immediate strategic picture in the China theater, the CCP sought once again to mobilize foreign policy in its domestic campaign against the KMT. It sought to delegitimize the Nationalists in the eyes of the Chinese public and to associate its own policies with the global trend toward democratization and the growing trend toward participation in political life of Communist parties throughout the world.

The campaign to establish links with the United States ran parallel to this domestic effort and indeed was an integral part of it. In its domestic campaign the CCP frequently pointed to the growing international stature that its own policies had earned it even as the KMT was losing ground internationally.[50] Well aware of this campaign, Chiang Kai-shek complained to Vice-President Wallace that the Communists were attempting "to use American opinion to force the Kuomintang to yield to Communist demands."[51] Mao viewed the KMT as dependent upon the United States, and in his first interview with Service, openly acknowledging the party's strategy, he asserted that "The Kuomintang in its situation today must heed the United States," and "The United States can tell Chiang what he should do—in the interest of the war."[52]

The arrival of the Dixie Mission in Yenan, seen as the first instance of successful American pressure on the KMT, confirmed the CCP leadership's view that Washington's policy had changed direction.[53] Over the next five months, in a somewhat optimistic mood generated by the prospects of military as well as political cooperation with Washington, the Communists enjoyed their most direct, and highest-level, dealings with the United States to date. These discussions have been extensively scrutinized by other scholars, so the present analysis will be restricted to discussing the Dixie Mission itself. This mission represented the fruition of the Teheran paradigm, but given the failure of American policy to meet CCP expectations, it was as well one of the major reasons for its abandonment by the CCP, signaling the end of the Teheran foreign policy.

What were these expectations? In his first meeting with Service, Mao was perfectly candid: "We only ask now that American policy try to induce the Kuomintang to reform itself. That would be the first stage. It may be the only one necessary." Should this first stage not be achieved, Mao continued, it might then be necessary to talk about direct ties between the CCP and the United States. Concerned about the continued provision of American arms to the Kuomintang, Mao suggested that it would be more proper for Washington to supply all the forces fighting against Japan, including the Communists. Condoning American "interference" in support of the "true interests of the people of China," Mao expansively suggested that "Every American official meeting any Chinese official, in China or in the United States, can talk democracy. . . . Every American soldier in China should be a walking and talking advertisement for democracy. . . . We Chinese consider you Americans the ideal of democracy."[54]

Although discussions between the Communists and the Americans focused on military questions, military cooperation was the vehicle through which the CCP sought to establish a political dialogue and relationship with Washington that would ultimately undermine the close bonds between the KMT and the United States. The CCP sought to replicate the political situation that they perceived existed in France. With the approval of the Allies, China's "new democratic government" would be a united front coalition, one based on full Communist political and military participation.

In its discussions with the Americans, the party leadership argued that the Communist armies deserved support as an active anti-Japanese force that could play a major role by coordinating with the Allies in a postlanding counterattack against the Japanese.[55] The CCP leadership undoubtedly calculated that an argument based on military utility would find a sympathetic audience among American policy makers, but their real goal was the political one of getting U.S. support for the inclusion of the CCP in a united front government in China.

Mao divulged to Service that in assessing American policy, the CCP focused on three factors: whether or not American politics was reverting to isolationism, whether or not the United States was promoting democracy in the world and in China, and whether or not Washington was willing to recognize the CCP as an effective military force and "an influence for democracy."[56] Yenan believed that a genuine commitment to democratization in China would entail American intervention in support of an increased role for the Communist forces.

Notwithstanding the dismissal of Stilwell in October 1944, Roosevelt's reelection and General Patrick J. Hurley's arrival in Yenan to find a basis for a Nationalist-Communist agreement kept alive Communist hopes for a beneficent American intervention. Hurley participated in the drafting of a set of political principles that were very close to CCP demands. Moreover, in his reply to Mao's congratulatory telegram on his reelection, Roosevelt commented encouragingly that he "look[ed] forward to vigorous cooperation with all the Chinese forces."[57] The Teheran policy seemed to be bearing fruit.

This was not to be the case, however. In hindsight, it is apparent that November 1944 was the high water mark of CCP relations with the United States and of its commitment to the Teheran view. In the months that followed, the party no longer spoke confidently of a new post–World War II era as it had earlier, nor did it pursue the "American connection" with its previous enthusiasm. This was a transitional period that lasted until May 1945, a period during which the CCP leadership read contradictory signals in the international environment, some suggesting continuation of the Teheran policy and others pointing toward a return to the united front view.

The most ominous developments it discerned were in American policy in China. Mao and Chou were appalled at Hurley's cavalier abandonment of the set of political principles he had accepted in Yenan, and his subsequent endorsement of KMT policies. In a "stormy interview" in December 1944 with Colonel David Barrett, head of the Dixie Mission, Mao vilified Chiang Kai-shek, suggested that he might seek aid from England or the Soviet Union, and threatened to embarrass the United States by publishing the agreement with Hurley.[58] From that point on, relations with the United States spiraled downward. Hurley gained ever greater control over American policy, and in January 1945 he informed Yenan that there would be no U.S. military aid until the party reached a political compromise with the KMT.[59]

Incensed at opposition within the American embassy to his pro-KMT stance, and convinced that the Soviet pressure would bring the CCP into line, Hurley moved ever closer to the Nationalists. At his April 2 press conference in Washington, he insultingly compared the Chinese Communists to warlords.[60] Ten days later, President Roosevelt, whom the CCP had viewed as a key element in shaping the transition to a democratic world, was dead, and another element of uncertainty in the form of an unknown president was added to the ominous trend in American policy. Finally, the CCP, which ascribed great importance to the founding meeting of the United Nations in late April, was bitterly disappointed that the unreformed KMT regime was given "face" (Chou En-lai's term) as a host while CCP representation was limited to just one delegate.[61] This episode cast further doubt on a central tenet of the foreign policy of opposition, namely, that the United States would intervene to promote democracy in China.

The unwelcome drift of American policy was quickly placed in a more global context. During the end of 1944, CCP attention began to focus on Greece where the British were busily suppressing the left and reinstating conservative political elements. While Chu Te and Yeh Chien-ying, in discussions with John Paton Davies, "expressed open disgust with the British handling of the Greek situation," Soviet agent Vladimirov noted in his Yenan diaries that "Mao Tse-tung shows a morbid interest in the events in Greece. The executions of Greek patriots by the British interventionists set him thinking of the possibility of doing the same in China."[62] The changes that Mao discerned in global as well as regional developments contradicted the earlier expectations of Allied "intervention" to promote more progressive, democratic regimes.

However, the Yalta Conference, whose final declaration was enthusiastically hailed by the *Chieh-fang jih-pao* as "the greatest historic document of our era," renewed CCP hopes that the alliance was still in good shape. Party media focused on the agreements to create broadly representative, provisional governments in liberated Europe pending free elections. In the months that followed, the Communist press interpreted developments in liberated Europe as indications that, for the most part, "New Democracies" were taking root.[63] Closer to home, even as American strategists plotted an assault on Japan that would bypass China, CCP leaders still professed to see strategic necessity as a potential basis on which to rebuild a relationship with Washington. *Hsin-hua jih-pao* wrote that "the tidal wave of the American counteroffensive is surging toward the China coast."[64]

Such, in brief, was the ambiguous international environment as viewed from Yenan in the first quarter of 1945. It contained elements that seemed to support a continuation of the Teheran approach to foreign affairs as well as others that suggested just the opposite. Between December 1944 and May 1945, the foreign policy of opposition combined an effort to exploit elements of the Teheran view with preparations to turn away from this fading vision of a world that might never be.

Throughout early 1945, Communist demands for elections or for the formation of a provisional government were justified with reference to the Yalta standards being implemented throughout Europe. In a section deleted from later editions of Mao's report to the Seventh CCP Congress, he buttressed his call for "coalition government" or a "provisional government" with specific reference to Yalta.[65] Such argumentation was obviously intended for a foreign as well as a domestic audience. In his last conversation with Service, Mao drove the point home for the benefit of U.S. policy makers. Supporting the Allied decision to defer the final form of government in liberated European countries pending elections, Mao pointedly asked, "Why is China an exception?"[66] Mao and his colleagues seemed undecided as to whether a secular change had occurred in American foreign policy or just a temporary reversion toward conservatism. For the time being they kept their options open and attempted to circumvent Hurley and reach sympathetic elements in the American government.[67] They still hoped that in the end strategic necessity would leave Washington no choice but to rely on Communist armies, and even to provide them with arms.

This was the context for a series of decisions emanating from the Seventh Congress. As many commentators have noted, Mao's report, "On Coalition Government," and the decisions of the Congress suggest that the party was moving toward the creation of a separate regime. Mao began to speak of "direct cooperation" with the Allies, independently of the Nationalists.[68] But this does not necessarily indicate a collision course with the United States. It is very possible that the party was moving to create a regime that would earn its spurs in the anticipated, extended land war in China and eventually, with Allied sponsorship, gain inclusion in a postwar coalition government.

The European experience, of course, suggested that pressure from the Soviet Union was essential. This might explain the increased attention paid to the Soviet Union and the CCP's attempt to cultivate Moscow.[69] Among a number of possible explanations for this is that the CCP was again looking to Eastern Europe where Soviet support for wartime, Communist resistance movements resulted in their inclusion in postwar coalition governments. Growing Soviet criticism of the KMT and support for a coalition government in China must have encouraged CCP leaders.

Alternatively, the CCP may have been preparing for an outcome in Asia quite different from those suggested either by the Teheran-Yalta paradigm or the resistance movement scenario—one much more akin to the earlier united front scenario. Such preparation surfaced as early as January 1945 and became more evident in Mao's April speech to the CCP's Seventh Congress. In an unpublished section of the speech, Mao reportedly spoke in terms that, as far as I know, had not been used by CCP leaders since 1942. "Political reality and practice demonstrate," he said, "that in the international arena the Soviet Union is our single and best friend. *All the rest are so-called Allies. . . . We must be vigilant.* Some foreigners support Chiang Kai-shek; they step forward as peacemakers, like some sort of gods. If we tear off their masks, then a hideous face is revealed."[70]

Subtle resonances with the united front view permeated Mao's entire speech to the Seventh Congress. He provided a virtual checklist of indicators to test whether the power of reactionaries in the West was growing, and if the world was moving in such a way as to cast doubt on the Teheran-Yalta paradigm and reestablish the utility of a united front perspective. The list included the negotiation of a conditional Japanese surrender, the intervention of foreign troops in China to aid counterrevolution, the provision of additional aid to an unreformed

KMT government, an attempt to perpetuate colonialism in Asia, and the dissemination of anti-Soviet propaganda.[71]

In brief, by the end of April 1945, three different international scenarios were being considered for the growing CCP-KMT confrontation:

1. The Teheran-Yalta paradigm—Allied pressure yields internal democratization;

2. The European resistance paradigm—Communist participation results from wartime cooperation with one of the great powers;

3. The united front paradigm—the CCP joins with its only "true ally," the Soviet Union, in an international environment characterized by global confrontation between the forces of revolution and those of reaction.

Between Mao's April speech and the end of the war in August, Communist views on international affairs evolved away from the Teheran-Yalta paradigm and toward the united front perspective. By July, the idea that the forces of global reaction, led by the United States, were intervening in China via the medium of the KMT, in order to preserve their imperialist interests, began to dominate CCP discourse.

This dramatic shift in CCP views resulted from three developments that, when viewed through Mao's Seventh Congress prism, suggested a significant change of course in American policy toward China.[72] First, the arrest of John Service and five others on charges of having leaked classified data bespoke a struggle within the U.S. government regarding China policy and revealed a pro-KMT drift. Second, there were growing signs of American support for KMT anti-Communist activities, notably, growing cooperation between the OSS and the KMT secret police. Finally, there were revived rumors of attempts to arrange a conditional Japanese surrender as part of a broader effort to preserve some semblance of the prewar imperialist status quo in Asia, including Anglo-Americans to maintain the colonial system. Thus, American policy in the Far East seemed of a piece with a more general shift that could be understood better through the united front paradigm of world politics.

The only piece missing was, of course, overt anti-Soviet activities, but by the summer of 1945, the CCP was interpreting growing differences among the Allies as evidence of just such anti-Soviet activities. The party press depicted the emergence of a global "struggle between two lines of development" pitting progressives who wanted to maintain wartime unity while pursuing the ideal of a new democratic world against reactionaries who wanted to maintain the old prewar system while using anti-Soviet feelings to disrupt the alliance.[73] In sum, the CCP leadership saw growing evidence that Mao's "worst case" scenario envisioned at the Seventh Congress in April was in fact taking shape.

One should not, however, exaggerate the degree of the CCP's shift. The "reactionary" current was seen as only one of two lines. There were still forces seeking to continue the commitments made at Teheran, prime among them the Soviet Union. Moreover, there were also those within the American government who inclined toward more progressive policies, and who inspired hope that American policy makers might eventually come to realize that their own long-term interests lay in supporting the forces of democratic change within China.[74] So the picture was still unclear. It would take another year before the CCP leadership definitely settled upon a united front perspective of the world.

During June and July 1945, the Communists embarked upon a policy of expansion. With the war entering a critical stage and the KMT showing little inclination to meet the party's demand for political reform, Yenan's mood turned confrontational. Realizing that tensions with Washington would increase, Mao defiantly told a visitor, "Since I have been able to fight Japan with these few rusty rifles . . . I can fight the Americans too. The first step is to get rid of Hurley, then we'll see."[75] But this was little more than bravado inspired by the accelerating shifts in U.S. policy as the war against Japan moved toward conclusion.

The possibility of Soviet pressure remained, of course, but it is difficult to say whether or not the CCP saw this as a viable option. That the Soviet Union would soon be entering the war on the China mainland was clear, and this commended to the CCP a strategy of establishing a claim for postwar power via military action in cooperation with the Red Army. Yet it was by no means clear that Moscow would cooperate with the CCP and risk jeopardizing the Far Eastern gains achieved at Yalta and soon to be embodied in the Sino-Soviet Treaty of August 1945. There is evidence that the CCP was uneasy about the extent of Soviet support they could expect as the end of the war approached.[76]

The precipitous end of the war posed a particularly difficult challenge for the CCP's foreign policy of opposition since it came at a time when the party's perspective on international affairs was still undergoing a significant reassessment. Would Soviet entry into the Far East war regenerate external pressures to democratize China along the Teheran/Yalta lines that Hurley's policies had dissipated? Would Soviet troops join up with local Communist forces as they had done in Eastern Europe? Or, if the united front scenario continued to unfold, would "revolutionary China" find itself aligned with the Soviet Union in yet another dichotomized world?

Despite the occurrence, from a CCP perspective, of certain anomalous events such as the Sino-Soviet Treaty, on the whole over the next two years global and Asian developments unfolded in a familiar pattern. The growing Soviet-American tensions as well as the nature of American policy in Asia fit neatly into the assumptions of the united front paradigm. Soon the shining image of a united and democratic world that Teheran and Yalta had briefly promised would be lost in the gathering clouds of the cold war.

Notes

The author would like to acknowledge the research assistance of Joffe Lake and Donna Milrod as well as the financial support of Smith College.

1. The many levels at which the foreign policy of opposition functioned necessarily complicate the task of understanding it. CCP statements were variously directed at multiple audiences, including the Chinese public, the KMT, Communist party members, and foreign governments. This chapter is based on the following types of materials: CCP periodicals from Yenan as well as the KMT areas, party monographs and documentary collections, inner-party directives, the reportage of diplomats and journalists, and a small number of memoirs or retrospective discussions. Given the heterogeneity of these sources, one must naturally exercise care in considering the audience and context of a particular source. No major discrepancies exist, however, between the public and private postures the party adopted on international affairs since even the public materials were also intended for intraparty use, and the mass media was an important form of inner-party communication. Yet there is no doubt that the CCP's foreign policy of opposition spoke in different voices to different audiences even as it pursued a fundamental and unified set of goals.

2. Mao Tse-tung, "Policies, Measures, and Perspectives for Resisting the Japanese Invasion," *Selected Works* (hereafter cited as *SW*) (Peking: Foreign Languages Press, 1965), 2:17.

3. Hung, "Yung-hu Chung-Su hu-pu chin-fan t'iao-yueh" (Support the Sino-Soviet Nonaggression Treaty), *Chieh-fang* (Liberation) [hereafter *CF*], nos. 13, 14, 15 (September 6, 1937): 19; "Wo-men ti wai-chiao lu-hsien" (Our foreign policy line), *Hsin-hua jih-pao* (New China daily) [hereafter *HHJP*], July 19, 1938; K'o Pao-ch'uan, "Chia-ch'iang Chung-Su kuan-hsi yu chien-ch'i k'ang-chan" (Strengthen Sino-Soviet relations and hold fast to the Resistance War), *Ch'un-chung* (The masses) [hereafter *CC*], 3, 7 (July 2, 1939): 209–10. For a review of Soviet aid to China during this period, see John W. Garver, *Chinese-Soviet Relations, 1937–1945: The Diplomacy of Chinese Nationalism* (New York: Oxford University Press, 1988), chap. 2.

4. Mao Tse-tung,"Ti-erh-tz'u ti-kuo chu-i chan-cheng chiang-yen t'i-pao" (Important points in a lecture on the Second Imperialist [World] War), in *K'ang-Jih min-tsu t'ung-i chan-hsien chih-nan* (Yenan: Chieh-fang she, 1937–40), 9:18–26. For another interpretation of Mao's thinking during this period, see John Gittings, *The World and China, 1922–1972* (New York: Harper and Row, 1974), pp. 78–79. It is probably no coincidence that during 1940 the CCP republished two documents reflecting the 1928 Sixth Comintern Congress's view of a world on the verge of war and revolution, which was revised at the 1945 Seventh Congress, which promulgated the united front. See *Shao-nien kung-ch'an-tang kuo-chi k'ang-ling* (Young Communist International Platform) (Yenan, 1940); *Chih-min-ti ko-ming yun-tung* (The colonial revolutionary movement) (Yenan: Ta-chung she, 1940).

5. See, for example, Chien Chun-jui, "Lun mu-ch'ien Ou-chan ti hsing-shih chi ch'i fa-chan chih ch'ien-t'u" (The nature of the present European war and its future development), in *Lun ti-erh-tz'u shih-chieh ta-chan* (On the Second World War), by Chu Wo-mai (N.p.: Chiao-yu shu-tien, 1939), p. 23; Hsiao San, "Kung-ch'an kuo-chi erh-shih-i chou-nien" (The twenty-first anniversary of the Communist International), *CF*, no. 100 (February 29, 1949): 30–31.

6. This was most clearly articulated in Mao's "Hsin-min chu-i lun" (On New Democracy), in Mao Tse-tung, *Hsuan chi* (Selected works) (Dairen: Ta-chung she, 1946), 1:25, 36–37.

7. "Chung-yang kuan-yu mu-ch'ien hsing-shih yu tang-ti cheng-ts'e ti chueh-ting" (Decision of the Central Committee on the present situation and the party's policy), in *K'ang-chan i-lai chung-yao wen-chien hui-chi* (Collected important documents of the period since the outbreak of the war), (N.p.: n.p., 1942), p. 133.

8. "Interview with Three Correspondents from the Central News Agency, the San Tang Pao and Hsin Min Pao," Mao, *SW*, 2:270.

9. Edgar Snow, "Will Stalin Sell Out China?" *Foreign Affairs* 18, 3 (April 1940): 458.

10. [Chang] Han-fu, "Tu-li keng-sheng yu cheng-ch'u wai-yuan" (On *Tzu-li keng-sheng* and foreign aid), *CC* 3, 1 (May 21, 1939): 835–39; and Li P'ing, "Kuo-chi hsing-shih yu wo kuo k'ang-chan" (The international situation and our resistance war), *CF*, 60–61 (January 16, 1939): 17.

11. Mao noted this retrospectively in his "On Protracted War," *SW*, 2:119.

12. "Kai-chin wai cheng-ts'e yu chia-ch'iang wai-chiao huo-tung" (Make advances in foreign policy and increase foreign policy activities), *HHJP*, October 29, 1938; [P'an] Tzu-nien, "Tsui-chin ti kuo-chi hsing-shih" (The current international situation), *CC* 2, 12 (December 25, 1938): 891; Yang Sung, "Lun tsui-chin Ou-chou ti chu-shih yu wo-kuo min-tsu k'ang-chan" (The current situation in Europe and our resistance war), *CF*, 72 (May 30, 1939): 12.

13. [Chang] Han-fu, "Ying-Jih yi ch'eng-li ch'u-pu hsieh-ting" (Great Britain and Japan reach a preliminary agreement), *CC* 3, 11 (August 13, 1939): 297; Hsu P'ing, "Hsi-fang Mo-ni-hei hui-i ti yen-chung chiao-hsun" (The grave lessons of the Western Munich), *CF* 79 (August 15, 1939): 11–13; "Ying i-chiao Chin so szu t'ung-pao" (The British transfer of four countrymen in the Tientsin case), *HHJP*, August 4, 1939; and [Chang] Han-fu, "Tung-fang Mo-ni-hei ti wei-hsien keng chin-po le" (The danger of a Far Eastern Munich is even more immediate), *CC* 3, 12 (August 20, 1939): 824.

14. For example, "Tsui-chin Mei-kuo ti yuan-tung cheng-ts'e" (Current American policy in the Far East), *HHJP*, November 18, 1939; "Mei-kuo tsai yuan-tung ti ti-li" (America's position in the Far East), *HHJP*, September 9, 1939, published by the CCP in Chungking, seems to have a more open view of American policy than that presented by Mao. This impression is confirmed by Po Ku, who told Edgar Snow that during this time the Chungking office of the Communist party wired Mao to suggest that he not attack the United States. Edgar Snow, *Random Notes on Red China* (Cambridge: Harvard University Press, 1968), p. 25. For Mao's views in January 1940, see "Hsin-min chu-i lun," p. 36.

15. Chou En-lai, "Chung-kuo k'ang-chan ti shih-ch'i ho mu-ch'ien jen-wu" (The critical juncture of China's Resistance War and present tasks), *Pa-lu-chun chun-cheng tsa-chih* (Eighth Route Army military-political journal) 2, 5 (May 25, 1940): 1–7; and Mao Tse-tung, "Hsiang-ch'ih chieh-tuan chung ti hsing-shih yu jen-wu" (The situation and tasks of the stalemate stage), in *Hsiang-ch'ih chieh-tuan chung ti hsing-shih yu jen-wu* (N.p.: Chin-pu ch'u-pan-she, 1940).

16. "Chung-yang kuan-yu mu-ch'ien hsing-shih," p. 134.

17. "Nu-li ti fang-hsiang" (The direction of our efforts), *HHJP*, January 1, 1941.

18. "Chung-kuo kung-ch'an-tang chung-yang wei-yuan-wei t'ung-chih" (Notice of the Central Committee of the Chinese Communist party), *Chieh-fang jih-pao* (Liberation daily) [hereafter *CFJP*], May 25, 1941.

19. Chou En-lai, "Min-tsu chih-shang yu kuo-chia chih-shang" (The nation first, the state first), *HHJP*, June 15, 1941.

20. There are a great number of CCP discussions of this question during these years. For a sampling, see "Kuo-chi yuan-Hua yun-tung" (The international aid China movement), *HHJP*, June 13, 1938; "Chia-ch'iang kuo-min wai-chiao" (Strengthen people's diplomacy), *HHJP*, November 8, 1938; "Lun tang-ch'ien kuo-chi chu-shih" (On the present international situation), *HHJP*, February 17, 1940; and "Mei-kuo ying-tang tui Jih ch'uan-mien chih-yun" (The United States should impose a total boycott on Japan), *HHJP*, November 22, 1940.

21. See Lyman P. Van Slyke, *Enemies and Friends: The United Front in Chinese Communist History* (Stanford: Stanford University Press, 1967), p. 109; Harrison Forman, *Report from Red China* (New York: Henry Holt, 1945), pp. 36–45.

22. Two articles from different times in the years under consideration that make basically the same point are Li P'ing, "Kuo-chi hsing-shih," 22; and "Kuo-min-tang ch'u-shao shen-ma?" (What does the Kuomintang lack?), *CFJP*, June 17, 1941.

23. "Kuan-yu chan-cheng hsing-shih wen-t'i ti chih-shih" (Directive concerning the question of the nature of the war), *CFJP*, July 27, 1941.

24. See, for example, "Mei-kuo ying ch'e-ti chi-ts'ai Jih-k'ou" (The United States should completely restrain the Japanese bandits), *HHJP*, August 24, 1941; "Mei-kuo ying ch'e-ti feng-tuan ku-hsi chih min" (The United States should thoroughly close the door on indulgence), *CFJP*, August 4, 1941; and "Lo-ssu-fu ti chin-lien yu-lei ling" (Roosevelt's order prohibiting the shipment of oil products), *HHJP*, August 4, 1941; Chou En-lai, "'Chiu-i-pa' shih-nien" (The tenth anniversary of the September 18th Incident), *HHJP*, September 18, 1941; and "Kuan-yu mu-ch'ien kuo-wai cheng-chih ti chih-shih" (Directive on the current situation of foreign politics) (N.p.: n.p., November 1941). This inner-party document was obtained at the Bureau of Investigation archives in Taipei, Taiwan.

25. "Chan-hou hsin shih-chieh ti chan-wang" (The future of the new postwar world), *CFJP*, July 12, 1942.

26. Ibid.

27. In a speech on July 1, 1943. See Takeuchi Minoru, ed., *Mao Tse-tung chi* (Collected writings of Mao Tse-tung) (Tokyo: Hokubo-sha, 1970–72), 9:36.

28. "Lun Mei-kuo cheng-chu" (On the American political situation), *HHJP*, January 13, 1944; "Mei-kuo min-chu chu-i ti ta sheng-li" (The great victory of American democracy), *HHJP*, November 9, 1944. See also "Lo-ssu-fu lien-jen ti-ssu chi ts'ung-t'ung" (Roosevelt is elected to a fourth term as president), *CFJP*, November 10, 1944.

29. For example, see "Chu Nan-kuo lin-shih cheng-fu" (Hail the Yugoslav Provisional Government), *HHJP*, December 19, 1943; "Chien-yueh Pa-erh-k'an jen-min ti hsing-lieh" (An examination of the activities of the Balkan people), *HHJP*, April 2, 1944; and "Fa-kuo kuo-ch'ing" (The French national holiday), *HHJP*, July 14, 1944.

30. "Ou-chou shih-chu" (The European situation), *CFJP*, September 13, 1944.

31. Gittings, *The World and China*, pp. 88–89.

32. The best discussion of this can be found in Garver, *Chinese-Soviet Relations*, pp. 241–47.

33. See, for example, "Yuan-chu Chung-kuo chun-shih fan-kung" (Assist a Chinese military counterattack), *HHJP*, July 25, 1942; and "Lo-Ch'iu ti wu-tzu hui-i" (The fifth Roosevelt-Churchill meeting), *HHJP*, May 14, 1943.

34. "Mei-Jih t'an-p'an" (American-Japanese talks), *CFJP*, September 26, 1941.

35. U.S. Department of State, *Foreign Relations of the United States* (hereafter *FRUS*), 1942, China (Washington, DC: Government Printing Office, 1956), p. 227. These are the words of a "representative" of Chou En-lai speaking to John Davies.

36. U.S. Department of State, *FRUS*, 1943, China (Washington, DC: Government Printing Office, 1957), p. 197.

37. Ibid. This was not a new request. It had been made at the time of the Currie visit in August 1942 and had been suggested in newspaper editorials that appeared during the course of 1942–43. See, for example, Gittings, *The World and China*, p. 100, and "Yuan-chu Chung-kuo chun-shih fan-kung."

38. "Kuo-min-tang chen yuan-wei Ch'in Hui na?" (Is the Kuomintang truly willing to be Chin Hui?), *CFJP*, August 29, 1943.

39. Wang Chia-hsiang, "Chung-kuo kung-ch'an-tang yu Chung-kuo min-tsu chieh-fang ti tao-lu" (The Chinese Communist party and the road of Chinese national liberation), *CFJP*, July 8, 1943.

40. "Ch'e-ti shih-hsien Ta-hsi-yang hsien-chang" (Thoroughly carry out the Atlantic Charter), *HHJP*, August 14, 1943; and "K'ang-chan yu min-chu pu k'o fen-k'ai" (The

Resistance War and democracy cannot be separated), *CFJP*, June 14, 1943.

41. *FRUS*, 1943, China, pp. 288–89, 301–5; and Herbert Feis, *The China Tangle* (Princeton: Princeton University Press, 1954), pp. 85–86.

42. Cited in Garver, *Chinese-Soviet Relations*, p. 249.

43. See Tang Tsou, *America's Failure in China* (Chicago: University of Chicago Press, 1963), pp. 156–62; and Barbara Tuchman, *Stilwell and the American Experience in China, 1911–1945* (New York: Bantam Books, 1972), pp. 495–96. The most important of the critical Soviet articles was that by Vladimir Rogov, which appeared in *CFJP*, September 14, 1943.

44. Tsou, *America's Failure*, p. 110ff.

45. The discussion in this paragraph draws from Tsou, *America's Failure*, chaps. 3 and 4, and Tuchman, *Stilwell*, chaps. 16–18.

46. James Reardon-Anderson, *Yenan and the Great Powers* (New York: Columbia University Press, 1980), p. 27; and "Tsai min-chu yu t'uan-chieh ti chi-ch'u shang, chia-ch'iang k'ang-chan, cheng-chu tsui-hou sheng-li!" (On the basis of democracy and unity, strengthen the resistance war and obtain final victory!), *CFJP*, July 7, 1944.

47. See, for example, *The Amerasia Papers: A Clue to the Catastrophe of China* (Washington, DC: Government Printing Office, 1970), 1:737–38, 776–78.

48. "Fa-hsi-ssu chu-i shih wang-kuo chu-i" (Fascism is the ideology of national subjugation), *CFJP*, September 13, 1943; "Mei-yu kung-ch'an-tang, mei-yu Chung-kuo" (Without the Communist Party there is no China), *CFJP*, August 25, 1943.

49. "Wan-chiu mu-ch'ien wei-chu ti chung-hsin huan-chieh" (The central link in overcoming the present crisis), *HHJP*, September 22, 1944.

50. See, for example, "Meng-pang jen-shih ti cheng-yen" (The frank admonition of the Allies), *CFJP*, July 6, 1944.

51. These are Feis's words paraphrasing Chiang. See *China Tangle*, p. 148.

52. Joseph Esherick, ed., *Lost Chance in China* (New York: Random House, 1974), pp. 297, 303.

53. In his very first conversation with John S. Service, Mao noted that he "understood that Vice President Wallace had secured the Generalissimo's approval for the dispatch of our group (Dixie Mission)." Ibid., p. 290.

54. Ibid., pp. 302–3.

55. "Ts'ung hai-shang ta-tao Jih-pen, tsung lu-shang ta-tao Tung-pei" (From the sea overthrow Japan, from the land recapture the Northeast), *CFJP*, September 18, 1944; Reardon-Anderson, *Yenan and the Great Powers*, chap. 3.

56. Esherick, ed., *Lost Chance*, pp. 298–300.

57. Reardon-Anderson, *Yenan and the Great Powers*, pp. 53–55.

58. David D. Barrett, *Dixie Mission: The United States Observer Group in Yenan, 1944* (Berkeley: University of California Press, 1970), pp. 70–75.

59. Michael Schaller, *The U.S. Crusade in China, 1938–1945* (New York: Columbia University Press, 1979), pp. 203–9.

60. Reardon-Anderson, *Yenan and the Great Powers*, p. 86.

61. See Esherick, ed., *Lost Chance*, pp. 342, 379; also United States Office of War Information, *China Press Review* (hereafter *CPR*), 50 (February 24, 1945): 1.

62. *FRUS*, 1944, China, p. 754; Peter Vladimirov, *The Vladimirov Diaries* (New York: Doubleday and Company, 1975), p. 311.

63. "K'o-li-mi-ya hui-i ti ch'eng-chiu" (The accomplishments of the Crimean [Yalta] meeting), *CFJP*, February 17, 1945; Teng Ch'u-min, "Jen-min ti cheng-ch'uan" (People's political power), *CC* 10, 3–4 (March 22, 1945): 85–91; Teng Ch'u-min, "Hsin min-chu chi Fa-lan-hsi hsing" (New democratic France), *CC* 10, 5–6 (April 5, 1945): 163–68, and *CPR*, no. 41 (February 15, 1945): 1.

64. In *CPR*, no. 81 (March 27, 1945): 1.

65. Takeuchi, ed., *Mao Tse-tung chi*, 9:257–58.

66. Esherick, ed., *Lost Chance*, pp. 376–77.

67. Schaller, *U.S. Crusade*, pp. 198–201.

68. Garver, *Chinese-Soviet Relations*, p. 260.

69. Ibid., pp. 256–62.

70. Italics added. The last sentence is an obvious reference to Ambassador Hurley. These remarks are based on the notes of P. P. Vladimirov, translated in *Mao Tse-tung's Oral Report to the Seventh Congress of the CCP: Summary Notes*, trans. Steven I. Levine (Santa Monica: Rand Paper, 1978), p. 18. In January a Kuomintang source passed on to the U.S. Embassy a purported CCP doctrine that spoke of alliance with the United States in the utilitarian manner characteristic of the united front approach. See Gittings, *The World and China*, p. 108.

71. Mao, "On Coalition Government," *SW*, 3:passim.

72. Reardon-Anderson identifies these elements in his *Yenan and the Great Powers*, chap. 6. This paragraph draws heavily from his analysis.

73. See, for example, Jui Shui, "Lun Chiu-chin-shan hui-i ti i chieh-tuan ti ch'eng-chiu" (The accomplishments of the first stage of the San Francisco conference), *CC* 10, 10 (June 1, 1945): 328, 333; and Yu Hai, "Lun shih-chieh cheng-chu" (On the world situation), ibid., 10, 12: 366–71.

74. For example, such themes are present in Mao's writings during this period. It should be noted that his comments suggesting the possibility of positive changes in American policy were deleted in later editions. See, for example, Takeuchi, ed., *Mao Tse-tung chi*, 9:299–301.

75. Cited in Reardon-Anderson, *Yenan and the Great Powers*, p. 96.

76. This paragraph is based on ibid., pp. 98–101.

6

THE MILITARY DIMENSION, 1937–1941

Marvin Williamsen

WHEN gunfire exploded on the hot summer night of July 7, 1937, terrified farmers in the small village near Lukouch'iao, not far from Peiping, must have considered this just one more in the endless series of violent incidents perpetrated by bellicose Japanese soldiers. Weeks passed before it became evident that the fire-fight that night between Japanese and Chinese soldiers signaled the onset of a new and more ominous stage in the Japanese invasion of continental China.

This chapter presents a synoptic overview of military operations during the first half of a bitter eight-year struggle—1937–41—when China was fighting alone. It begins with the desultory fire-fights of the Lukouch'iao Incident in July 1937, and concludes with the amorphous strategic situation existing toward the end of 1941 when Japan's attack on Pearl Harbor transformed the nature of the war. The second part of the chapter assesses the performance of the Chinese Army by looking at the operations of one of its technical services—the Medical Service Corps—during the initial years of the war.

In judging the military performance of the Chinese Army one immediately confronts a paradox. Chinese forces lost every major confrontation on the battlefield, yet they won the war. To understand this paradox fully, the gaze must be shifted from the military to the diplomatic battlefields. Nonetheless, there is value in focusing on military factors as this chapter does.

In the industrial era, the strength and skills of competing national armies is a measure of the relative state of modernization of the nations involved. Although the military units integrated under Chiang Kai-shek's leadership into an emerging Chinese national army were more modernized than their regional opponents within China, they were inferior in organization, equipment, training, and leadership to the Japanese Army. Assessing preparedness or combat-readiness, to borrow terms from a later era in the West, requires knowledge of the potential enemy force and comparative measurement. An army is only as ready as its enemy will permit.

There is as well a human dimension to warfare that is too easily overlooked. At this remove in space and time, the lives of millions of Chinese peasant soldiers are not easily accessible to us. Yet some means must be found to grasp the human reality of the battlefields on which so many Chinese and Japanese soldiers fought, suffered, and died. This is the reason for undertaking a brief examination of Chinese medical services. U.S. military attaché reports from the war zone on the quality and conditions of medical care furnish glimpses of the anguish of soldiers and the pain of those wounded in battle. At the same time, an examination of the Medical Service Corps is a study in microcosm of the problems and inadequacies of the Chinese Army as a whole.

In sum, the first section of this chapter overviews major operations over a four-year period. The second section details attempts to ameliorate the suffering of wounded and sick troops during this same period. The chapter concludes with an assessment of the Nationalist military effort through 1941.

The Northern Theater of Operations

After the initial military skirmishes in early July 1937, military operations in the escalating Sino-Japanese War developed in two geographically separate theaters—the central and the northern. The former grew out of the combat in the vicinity of Shanghai and spread west up the Yangtze River valley. The latter grew out of the combat in the Tientsin-Peiping area and spread west and south.

By late July, major Japanese reinforcements, brought down from Mukden to Tientsin, were advancing west along the railway toward Peiping. By the end of the month, the Japanese had captured both Peiping and Tientsin. Panic-stricken Chinese units fled before the Japanese armies, offering virtually no defense of the cities or of such strategic points as the Nankow Pass through which the railroad passed to the west. By September 13, Japanese troops had captured Tatung, a key strategic intersection for rail and road transport nets running east-west from Peiping to the great northwestern territories, and north-south from Mongolia into Taiyuan, the capital of Shansi Province. In the north, Japan's undeclared war against Chinese forces was an unmitigated rout. The lone exception was a minor but morale-boosting Chinese victory at P'inghsingkuan, where units of the Communist Eighth Route Army annihilated a brigade of the Japanese Fifth Division, capturing large amounts of matériel.[1]

One of the earliest instances of barbaric Japanese treatment of Chinese civilians took place during this time at Tungchow. In reprisal for Chinese killing of a number of Japanese civilians there, the Japanese Army embarked on a rampage of rape, slaughter, and plunder lasting several days.[2] Thereafter, the horrendously brutal treatment of defenseless Chinese—so brutal that it beggars both description and understanding—became a hallmark of Japanese aggression.

By the end of September, certain characteristics of the undeclared war had emerged. With respect to strategic movement, the modernized and mechanized Japanese Army, like all other industrialized national forces, moved by rail. This was the only efficient means of transporting the huge numbers of troops and immense quantities of matériel that modern warfare necessitated. Thus, the terrain and the existing transportation nets dictated the paths of Japanese advance. The railroads provided the invading Japanese easy access to interior tactical and strategic objectives, but the road beds and their parallel road systems also served to canalize Japanese operations. Therefore, the Chinese were afforded rich opportunities to predict Japanese troop movements and carry out ambushes and harassment operations, but they seldom made use of these opportunities. The absence of a strategic defensive plan for North China indicates both the inadequacy of Chinese war preparations and the extreme difficulty of getting troops of the regional military separatists to participate in the war to a significant degree.

After securing their western flank by occupying the rail line to the west, the Japanese turned south along the three major north-south railroads: the line leading south from Mongolia via Tatung through Taiyuan to the intersection with the east-west Lunghai railroad; the Pinghan railroad running from Peiping south through Paoting, Shihchiachuang, and Chengchow to Hankow, and then continuing south of the Yangtze to Hofei, Nanchang, and points beyond; the Tsinpu railroad, the most easterly of the main tracks, from Tientsin south, paralleling the Grand Canal, then running through Tsinan, Hsuchow, and Pangpu, west to Hofei or east to Nanking and Shanghai. The major east-west rail line, the Lunghai railroad, originated at the coastal port of Lienyunkang and stretched westward through Hsuchow, Kaifeng, Chengchow, and Sian, terminating in Lanchow.

Avoiding combat, Chinese units initially fled south in front of the Japanese advance, exposing the hastily arranged defenses of Paoting, the capital of Hopei. On September 21, Japanese forces, attacking Paoting from the north, outflanked Chinese units on the west. Nearby Chinese units failed to reinforce, or in any way assist, the Chinese forces engaging the enemy.[3]

The Japanese continued south completely out of contact with Chinese combatants. On October 10, they captured the critical rail junction of Shihchiachuang, enabling them to move troops north and east by rail and to mount an offensive west along the rail line toward Taiyuan.[4] Meanwhile, after occupying Anyang in Honan Province by October 20, Japanese units on the Pinghan railroad paused to await developments in other sectors.[5]

Other Japanese formations met with similar success against incompetent and unwilling Chinese opposition. The Japanese moved south from the Tientsin area along the Tsinpu railroad in late August and early September.[6] Chinese forces failed to concentrate their limited combat power, violating the cardinal principle of mass. Moreover, the Chinese high command constantly shifted units all over the map. Field commanders often found themselves on the eve of battle suddenly positioned beside fellow commanders with whom they had never had the opportunity to establish liaison, precluding the complex cooperation necessary in battle. Rapidly advancing mobile columns of Japanese forces outmaneuvered Chinese defenders in one town after another. By early November 1937 they had eliminated any organized resistance along the Tsinpu railroad north of the Yellow River.[7]

Another dimension of the well-coordinated Japanese attack along three major axes of advance was the series of operations in the west, centered on Taiyuan. By the end of September, while roads leading south from the city filled with panicked civilians, Chinese defensive positions were established north of Taiyuan in an east-west line hinged at various towns and stretching approximately seventy kilometers.[8] The Chinese high command was adding reinforcements in the area, but it seems likely that subordinate commanders were rarely informed of such reassignments or that defense sector commanders were ever given adequate opportunity to develop coordinated plans for defensive artillery fire or maneuver.

On October 13, Japanese infantry units, supported by air bombardments and heavy artillery fire, assaulted the Chinese line. After fierce struggles, including hand-to-hand combat at many points, on October 23 the Japanese attackers broke through the Chinese lines. On this occasion, the Chinese displayed professional competence and conducted an orderly retrograde operation to prepared positions further south along the hilltops of the Blue Dragon Ridge. The Chinese fought tenaciously during the last days of October and the first part of November, trying desperately to hold onto the last high ground north of Taiyuan, but after sustaining casualties of some thirty thousand dead and wounded, Chinese units finally broke and retreated. Some units simply fled to the west; others withdrew into Taiyuan.[9]

Meanwhile, directly to the east, the Japanese had been attacking in the direction of Taiyuan from positions in the strategic rail center of Shihchiachuang. Despite initial successes, the Chinese defenders, again failing to concentrate sufficient combat power, finally broke and ran, exposing Taiyuan from the east. Powerful Japanese units now encircled Taiyuan from the north, the east, and the southeast.[10]

On November 7, with many Chinese troops fleeing the city, the Japanese demanded surrender. Local Chinese Army commanders refused, and the Japanese, raking the city with bombs, heavy artillery, and armor, finally blasted their way through the city walls.[11] A bitter, bloody, hand-to-hand battle was waged throughout the night. At morning light, Chinese troops joined panicked hordes of refugees fleeing west over the Fen River bridge. Those refugees not killed or thrown off the bridge by frightened soldiers were strafed and bombed by Japanese planes. Tens of thousands of troops, and perhaps an equal number of civilians, died in the last days of the battle for Taiyuan. After occupying the city, Japanese forces pushed rapidly south to establish defensive perimeters along all the road and rail nets. By mid-November, most of Shansi Province was securely in Japanese hands.[12]

In December 1937, the locus of operations in the northern theater shifted east to the region between the Yellow and Yangtze rivers, linked by the north-south Tsinpu railroad. Japanese forces crossed the Yangtze from the south, while infantry units, expanding into the territory between the cities of Tsingtao and

Tsinan, encountered no opposition. Chinese forces, suspecting that the governor of Shantung, General Han Fu-chu, was trying to cut a deal with the Japanese, waited to see what he would do. Han signaled his decision on December 24 when he pulled his forces south of the Wei River and destroyed the railroad bridge. This action isolated other Chinese forces in eastern Shantung who were then forced to march great distances on foot to avoid Japanese entrapment. Shantung was slipping away without a fight. General Han then abandoned his armies entirely and flew to Kaifeng where he was arrested, then later at Wuchang court-martialed and executed by the Chinese military authorities.[13] By mid-January, Japanese ground forces captured the provincial capital of Tsinan while the Japanese fleet anchored at Tsingtao and landed troops in the city. The two forces linked up and then marched south along the Tsinpu railroad.[14] Meanwhile the Japanese column at the southern end of the railroad continued its unimpeded northward advance, crossing the Huai River at the strategically important town of Pangpu on February 9, 1938, and occupying Huaiyuan on the north bank as well.[15]

During this time, the Chinese high command was concentrating large units in defensive positions along the east-west Lunghai railroad, about midway between the two Japanese armies operating at will in the northern and southern sectors of the Tsinpu railroad. Chinese units, stretched out along the Lunghai railroad west of the port of Lienyun, began digging in to face the inevitable Japanese advance. The imminent tactical danger was the fearsome prospect of an inescapable entrapment between the two powerful enemy columns advancing to effect a linkup. The key transportation center at Hsuchow, where the Tsinpu line crosses the Lunghai line, was the strategic objective of both armies.

For more than a month, the small towns and fields north and northeast of Hsuchow witnessed continuous combat. At Linyi Chinese forces fought the Japanese to a draw, but heavy casualties kept them from pursuing retreating Japanese units.[16] On March 23, the Japanese renewed the attack, subjecting the Chinese to continuous, unanswered pounding by heavy artillery. The Chinese line was forced back. It bent but did not break. The maelstrom continued unabated for one more week, littering the battlefield with the dead and dying of both armies.[17]

During the same exhausting days, at nearby Ihsien, in brutal house-to-house and street-to-street combat, the Chinese defenders fought to the death. The entire complement of the 23d Regiment, Fourth Division, 85th Corps, troops and officers alike, was wiped out.[18] In the southern sector in early February, Chinese troops fiercely counterattacked Huaiyuan, incurring several thousand casualties, but failed to dislodge the Japanese. Neither side attempted large-scale aggressive action again in this sector until two months later in May.[19]

In terms of courage, competence, and determination displayed, the famous battle of Taierhchuang, the penultimate battle of the Hsuchow campaign, is perhaps the most impressive of the few Chinese military victories during the war.

Toward the end of March 1938, the Chinese garrisoned the walled, stone-clad city of Taierhchuang, a significant military objective because of its location on the Grand Canal and along a spur railroad connecting the Lunghai railroad with the Tsinpu line, bypassing Hsuchow on the east. Taierhchuang stood athwart the Japanese line of advance down rural roads from the northeast headed toward Hsuchow.

On March 24, Chinese units, retreating in good order before better-armed Japanese, fell back on their division positions in and outside the city but continued to harass the Japanese with intermittent fire throughout the night. They repulsed a Japanese attack at dawn, but Japanese air and artillery pounded the city all day long on March 25. That night three thousand Chinese troops assaulted the Japanese, who pulled back to the northeast by six o'clock in the morning. At a cost of thousands of lives, the reinforced Chinese defenders, subjected to continuous aerial and artillery bombardment, again repulsed successive Japanese assaults over the next three days.[20]

Chinese artillery finally arrived on the scene, boosting Chinese firepower with two 155 mm and ten 75 mm tubes. On the night of March 29, the Japanese again penetrated the city, and a desperate and terrible hand-to-hand combat ensued, continuing into the next day. The opposing troops were now so tightly entangled that for once Japanese artillery was useless, and the killing was done by individual weapons, grenades, and bayonets. The Chinese still occupied half of the remaining structures of the city, which proved useful because the native stone resisted fire and projectiles.[21] Day after bloody day, hour after exhausting hour, the starving and throat-parched troops continued to claw away at each other in the small unit actions that such cramped quarters necessitated.

For once the Chinese were able to resupply their combatants in the city, while Chinese units operating in the north of the combat zone managed to beat off Japanese attempts to reinforce and resupply their side. By April 6, Japanese units ran out of ammunition, first for their field guns, then for their mortars, and finally even for their small arms. The Japanese survivors, armed only with their bayonets, slipped out of the rubble and escaped north and northeast on April 7, leaving behind them some sixteen thousand dead as well as the shattered hulks of over a hundred tanks and armored cars. The Chinese collected artillery pieces, machine guns, and quantities of individual weapons from all over the battle-field.[22] To Chinese troops who had grown accustomed to defeat, it seemed a great victory, one well worth the terrible price in casualties that was at least equal to those of the enemy.

In human terms one can easily understand why the Chinese could not summon the necessary will, determination, and logistic wherewithal to pursue and annihilate the retreating Japanese Tenth Division. But war is not a normal human condition. The principles of war are iron laws that soldiers, no matter how exhausted they may be, ignore at their peril. Just six weeks later, the meaning of that dual failure of will and logistics became evident when the Japanese returned to Taierhchuang.

It took little more than a week for the determined Japanese commanders to move more troops and more machines to the Hsuchow front. The second fire-storm was initiated to the northeast of Hsuchow at the road junction of Linyi on April 15. Chinese positions there held for only two days. At the same time, the troops of General T'ang En-po, one of the heroes of Taierhchuang, fended off Japanese assaults to the north and east until they were outflanked on April 18. T'ang gave way, pulled back, then turned and fought. For ten more days his troops fought tooth and nail, through village and field. Again the fighting was at such close quarters, and swept back and forth so rapidly, that Japanese artillery was rendered nearly useless. For ten days the two forces struggled in death's grip while both sides sent reinforcements into the battle zone.[23]

In this, their second attempt, the Japanese were not to be denied. In the second week of May, from positions west of Hsuchow, two Japanese columns raced south and severed the Lunghai railroad. This action denied the Chinese use of the rail line for further resupply of men or matériel. The performance of Chinese forces south of Hsuchow unfortunately had nothing in common with the strength and valor on display to the north of the city. From Pangpu and the Huai River valley, strong Japanese units pushed north along the rail line and also circled west. Chinese defenders broke and fled. Well to the east, north of Nanking, other Japanese units marched north, facing only token resistance, and cleared the countryside virtually all the way to the coast.[24]

Only on the northern defensive perimeter of the city did the defenders continue to stand up to the terrifying pounding of Japanese artillery and airpower, and to waves of infantry assaults. In the end, Chinese will was not enough. By mid-May the remaining Chinese forces at Hsuchow faced encirclement and total annihilation. Those few fighting generals who had stood their ground now began to have difficulty keeping their troops in line, and they gave the order for a general retreat just in time to save what remained of their armies. Their only avenue of escape was across the flat lands to the southwest. On May 19, the first Japanese fought their way into the city.[25]

The titanic five-month struggle demonstrated Japanese mastery of strategic coordination, tactical maneuver, and combined arms warfare. The Chinese performance varied from exemplary to deplorable. A handful of dedicated and patriotic Chinese commanders displayed daring, courage, and a high order of professional competence, but those few were unfortunately a small minority. The Chinese high command had proven unable to maneuver large numbers of units on the grand scale required. Higher commanders were unable to enforce discipline or otherwise control their subordinate commanders and units. When the fighting intensified, these units hastily retreated. Such performance was reminiscent of the shrewd calculations of personal survival that motivated commanders during earlier decades of the Republic and was not what one expected in a great patriotic war against a hated national aggressor. Continuously defeated, the Chinese were demonstrably unable to resist Japanese military power. Yet no matter how many victories the Japanese had won on the battlefield, there was no end in sight to the war.

While the struggle at Hsuchow unfolded, cities along the southeastern coast were being intimidated and reduced by the dual threat of aerial and naval bombardment. Amoy was occupied on May 13, and Foochow fell by the end of the month. While mopping up remnant Chinese forces in the Hsuchow area, the relentless Japanese advance continued west along the Lunghai railroad and to the southwest in pursuit of retreating and fleeing Chinese forces.[26]

Aggressive action by some local Chinese commanders at Lanfeng and in southern Shansi slowed but could not stem the Japanese advance. Starvation, in part due to flooding, was a greater threat to the Japanese than was the Chinese Army. In southern Shantung Province, for example, an isolated Japanese unit of the Twentieth Division was reduced to eating "dogs, cats, and weeds."[27] Only part of the flooding was due to natural causes. Mostly it was due to Chiang Kai-shek's decision to slow the inexorable Japanese advance by blowing a hole in the east side of the Yellow River dikes on June 12, 1938. China's Sorrow roared out over the plains inundating huge areas, destroying crops, villages, and lives, and pushing other rivers, such as the Huai, further to the east, out of their banks. But the great flood merely inconvenienced the Japanese slightly and restricted movement to the west along the Lunghai railroad toward Chengchow.[28] Japanese commanders were already preparing their next major campaign for the Central China theater.

The Central Theater of Operations

About a month after the initial combat in North China near Peiping, the Japanese attacked Shanghai, opening a second theater of operations on the China mainland. It was not until after the fall of Nanking in December 1937 that the Japanese managed to unite their two theaters of operations.

Following a series of provocative and threatening maneuvers, the Japanese positioned major units in the Shanghai metropolitan area on August 11. More than thirty Japanese warships, including five troop transports, stood in the roadstead of the Whangpoo River.[29] Lacking capital ships in their navy or adequate interdictory aircraft with trained pilots, the Chinese were powerless to protect themselves at sea. Japanese aircraft could attack from bases in the north as well as from aircraft carriers. During the vulnerable hours on August 13 when the Japanese expeditionary forces were debarking, the minuscule, poorly equipped, and inadequately trained Chinese air arm was unable to oppose the far superior Japanese Air Force, which enjoyed almost total command of the air. With a similar advantage at sea, the Japanese boasted a combined force of naval, air, and ground power that the Chinese came nowhere near matching.

The tenacity and steadfast courage of the Chinese defenders, engaged in deadly combat in the built-up areas of Shanghai, astonished foreigners who observed the fighting from the relative safety of their concessions. The Chinese resisted the frightful weight of modern firepower with only their courage, their patriotism, and their pitifully inadequate small-caliber weapons. Battles see-sawed back and forth from house to house and lane to lane. Only a few natural obstacles like the Woosung (Soochow) Creek separated the invaders from the defenders.

In the battle of Shanghai, naval transport provided the Japanese with greater mobility for penetration and grand maneuvers. An amphibious landing north and west of the Woosung preceded a late August thrust deep into Chinese territory that was checked only by General Ch'en Ch'eng's aggressive action.[30] Water-borne transport delivered repeated Japanese reinforcements in early September. Japan's complete control of the air prevented the Chinese from engaging in aerial reconnaissance or using the firepower of airborne "artillery." Japanese commanders continually added more armor and firepower to their forces. About two hundred new tanks and one hundred additional aircraft arrived on Chinese shores during the first half of September.[31]

The Chinese fought furiously even though they lacked adequate supplies of arms, ammunition, and equipment. They suffered from inadequate medical treatment and for much of the time were short of food and water, yet they still held on. Not until October 7 did the Japanese finally force a crossing of Woosung Creek. For two weeks afterward the Chinese defenders held a defensive line that stretched for eight miles. Chinese counterattacks were repulsed by the heavy firepower of Japanese naval guns. By the end of October all Chinese positions north of Woosung Creek in the vicinity of Shanghai had been lost and huge numbers of casualties sustained.[32]

On November 5, the Japanese staged their most significant amphibious operation at Hangchow Bay only thirty miles from Shanghai. The Chinese paid a huge cost for their strategic blunders, which permitted an unopposed Japanese landing and advance. Once the Japanese were ashore in force, the Shanghai-Hangchow rail line ceased to be defensible, and all Chinese units on the Shanghai front were in danger of envelopment. Attacking simultaneously along the entire length of the Shanghai front, the Japanese pounded the exhausted, nearly starving Chinese forces with artillery as well as aerial and naval bombardment.[33] The battlefield at Shanghai was fast becoming a killing ground.

There should have been an orderly, planned, retrograde operation, a movement to the rear to prepared defensive positions according to a prearranged plan rehearsed through war game maneuvers before the war began. Instead there was chaos. Chinese units seem to have been virtually blown back by the superior killing power of Japanese arms. As decimated units pulled back piecemeal, the defensive line dissolved in panic and disorder. Wounded troops were abandoned where they lay, and a number of officers deserted their hapless soldiers. Chiang Kai-shek ordered retreat only after the rout had begun, and by the time his orders reached the line units on November 8, it was too late to reestablish command and control.[34] The battle of Shanghai ended in an uncoordinated nightmare of death, confusion, and fear.

Chinese commanders attempted to establish defensive lines fifty miles to the west on a line from Fushan on the Yangtze to Soochow, and on to the Shanghai-Hangchow railroad line, but it proved impossible to do so. The disorder in Chinese formations was too great, command and control had deteriorated too badly, and Japanese pressure from the air and on the ground was continuous and deadly. Soochow was abandoned without a fight on November 19.[35] As Japanese forces relentlessly pursued their opponents, what had been characterized as a "positional" war at Shanghai became a war of rapid movement. Japanese aircraft seemed to be everywhere, reconnoitering Chinese troop movements as well as strafing and bombing. The roads west were clogged with panic-stricken refugees.

The rapidly moving Japanese advanced along three major axes. Farthest to the north, one column chased the Chinese along the right bank of the Yangtze, battering the few defensive units they encountered. A second column, directly paralleling the first, moved along the railroad, capturing Wuhsi on November 24. To the south, a third column crossed the Shanghai-Hangchow tracks on November 19, took Wuhsing five days later, and split into smaller units to attack Nanking from the south as well as to secure several other port cities.[36]

When Tanyang fell on December 3, the Japanese were within fifty miles of the capital. Over the next ten days, they subjected Nanking and its defenders to a continuous barrage of bombs, artillery shells, and naval gunfire. The two concentric rings of defensive positions had been placed so close to the city walls that the city was within range of artillery even before the defensive positions were breached.[37] On December 6, infantry assaults began from the east and the south. The defenses were breached five days later, and the Japanese smashed through what remained of the city gates in the partially destroyed walls on December 12. Only a very few Chinese units held together under control of their officers to attempt an organized breakout. These actions defied Chiang Kai-shek's standing order to die in place.

Trapped Chinese troops were treated with frightening barbarity by their conquerors. As a matter of policy all were tortured and butchered. But soldiers were hardly the only victims of the nearly incredible cruelty and the vicious, uncontrolled behavior of the Japanese troops. After recounting some, but only some, of the unspeakable horrors visited upon the residents of Nanking in two weeks of outrage, Dorn sums up the casualties: "over 20,000 civilian men of military age had been slaughtered. At least 20,000 young women and girls had been raped, murdered, and then gruesomely mutilated. Over 200,000 civilians, and possibly as many as 300,000, had been senselessly massacred."[38] Chiang had earlier shifted the Nationalist government to Chungking and his military headquarters and personal staff to Wuhan, four hundred miles upriver. The Japanese had another victory, but the fall of the nation's capital did not produce a Chinese surrender.

Nothing comparable to the heavy fighting along the Tsinpu railroad occurred on the Pinghan line between Chengchow and Wuhan in the spring of 1938. Japanese resources were stretched too thin to permit aggressive action in both places simultaneously. The Chinese may have missed an opportunity to strike on the Pinghan while the battle for Hsuchow was in progress, but Chiang Kai-shek's headquarters was deeply engaged in the Hsuchow battle, and no subordinate operated independently. Both armies began preparations for the next major campaign—the battle for Wuhan—in the summer of 1938. The Chinese concentrated their forces in defensive positions surrounding the three cities of Hankow, Wuchang, and Hanyang that together comprised Wuhan, while the Japanese concentrated west of Nanking, centered on Hofei.

The Chinese massed some 800,000 troops to defend the city that was now the Nationalist military and political headquarters. The Japanese relied on firepower and military efficiency to compensate for a huge manpower gap. At Wuhan naval guns from destroyers and gunboats supplemented the usual array of armor, artillery, and airpower. A new element on the Chinese side of the military equation was aircraft purchased from the Soviet Union and flown by Soviet pilots who were carrying out Stalin's policy of assisting China in the war against Japan.[39]

An American military historian, General Frank Dorn, who personally observed the battle of Wuhan, has harshly criticized Chiang Kai-shek's headquarters for issuing vague and tentative general orders. These orders failed to specify precise military missions and responsibilities and denied Chiang's few capable subordinate commanders the latitude for independent action in response to local conditions and opportunities. Dorn is of the opinion that at the corps and army levels of command, only seven of the more than sixty officers could be depended upon to do their duties.[40] The chain of command in the Chinese Army consisted mostly of weak links.

In early June 1938 the Japanese began to advance from positions along the Tsinpu railroad north and south of Hofei. Farther south, Japanese troops, supported by naval vessels, began maneuvering along both banks of the Yangtze. On June 12, the Japanese attacked Anking on the Yangtze. The Chinese defenders withdrew after fighting for just one day. At various distances north of the river, four parallel columns of Japanese troops headed west toward the Pinghan railroad en route to Wuhan.[41]

On June 24, the Japanese attacked Matang, somewhat beyond the midway point between Nanking and Wuhan, and perhaps the most heavily fortified defensive position along the river in Chinese hands. Chinese defenders held out against murderous Japanese bombardment until June 27. Japanese warships easily forced their way through the large defensive boom that had been stretched across the river.[42] During the first week of July, farther up the river at Hukou, the Japanese engaged the Chinese in a bitter, close-quarters combat. Chinese reinforcements, a complete corps, arrived on the scene only after the battle was over.[43] The strategically important port city of Kiukiang, connected by rail to Nanchang, Changsha, and Hangchow, was abandoned by Chinese defenders on July 26. By the end of July, the Japanese had been in the attack for over one hundred miles and were positioned to attack the tricities, approaching Hankow from the north and northeast, Wuchang and Hanyang from the south and southeast. The vast Chinese defensive force, already in position for weeks, suffered from the siege mentality that dominated everyone's thinking. Another brutal Japanese rampage of murder, rape, and destruction downriver at Kiukiang did nothing to reassure Wuhan's anxious population.[44]

In Wuhan, a city known as one of China's three "Yangtze furnaces," morale sagged during the steamy summer months. Malaria ravaged Chinese forces, especially northern troops who were unaccustomed to the disease or the humid river valley weather. Luckily for the Chinese, Japanese troops were also suffering rampant intestinal discomforture. The weather, disease, concurrent Japanese operations against the Soviet Union in Manchuria, and Chinese disinclination for aggressive action produced a lull before the coming conflagration. But whatever hopes remained among the Chinese in Wuhan that they might escape the fate of Shanghai, Taiyuan, Nanking, and Hsuchow were surely dashed when Chiang Kai-shek and the Nationalist leadership fled to Chungking in early September.[45] The fire storm approached.

On August 20, the Japanese struck south of the great river, along the shore of Lake Poyang, and against the city of Juichang further west in the direction of Wuhan. Juichang fell four days later, but the defensive positions further north and west held up for weeks under incessant hammering.[46] The Chinese exacted a heavy price in casualties for each Japanese advance. As August passed, and September turned to October, the Japanese made gradual headway through bloody, terrible combat on the ground south of Kiukiang, well to the southeast of Wuhan.[47] Eventually the two Japanese divisions operating farthest south of the Yangtze, more or less straight west from Juichang, advanced to the Wuhan-Canton railroad and cut the line at two locations some thirty to fifty miles south of Wuhan on October 28, eliminating a potential path of Chinese retreat, and further escalating the threat to Wuhan with encirclement from the south.[48]

Further north, attempting to advance in a northwesterly direction along both banks of the Yangtze, the Japanese met the same determined defense from the dog days of August, throughout September and most of October. After the fall of Juichang, the Chinese traded ground slowly, resisting every hard-fought foot of the way. The fortified positions at Ma-t'ou-chen on the south bank held out for two solid weeks. Then it took the Japanese three more weeks of hard fighting to advance the next fifteen miles upriver to the vicinity of the T'ien-chia-chen fortress on the north shore.[49] Trapped within the fortress, the Chinese defenders fought for their lives through ten horrendous days of incessant shell fire, screaming attacks, and the unending roar of their own artillery, mortars, and automatic weapons. On September 29, when the Japanese finally crashed through the shattered defenses, they slaughtered the Chinese survivors to a man.[50]

North of the river, Japanese columns surged through and around the Tapieh mountains heading straight for the Pinghan railroad and following the roads that led to Hankow. Chinese defenders slowed but could not stop their advance. By October 12, Japanese infantry reached the railroad at points well north of Hankow.[51] Other Japanese divisions, evading Chinese defensive positions and skirting the Tapieh massif on the south, approached Hankow from the eastern foothills. The Wuhan tricities were now surrounded by Japanese columns advancing from all directions but the southwest, the area between the Han River and the upriver portion of the Yangtze. Chinese units now fled for their lives toward these exits by whatever means they could manage. On October 25, vanguard Japanese units reached Wuchang on the south bank and Hankow on the north. The battle for Wuhan was over.[52]

The battle for Wuhan was the last great battle of this first phase of the Sino-Japanese war. During fifteen months of intensive fighting the Japanese had inflicted defeat after defeat upon Chinese armies. They now controlled most of the coastal provinces and the lower and central Yangtze valley in addition to much of North China. Yet they had failed to deliver a knockout blow. The Chinese armies, battered and bloodied but still unbeaten, retreated yet further into the vast interior of their country, beyond the range of the by now overextended Japanese armies. Not until well after the Sino-Japanese War had merged into the larger drama of World War II did fighting as intense as that of these first fifteen months again occur.

Medical Services on the Chinese Battlefield

When the War of Resistance began in 1937, the appearance of unity and coherence in the Chinese Army conveyed by military organization charts was belied by the continuing reality of confusion and disorder. This is not to deny that by this time, Chiang Kai-shek's Nationalist forces, which had grown in strength during a decade of internal war, had become the most formidable of the Chinese military organizations. Chiang's officers, trained at the Central Military Academy in Nanking, were an elite corps, but the great mass of his army were illiterate peasant soldiers. For these men life in the ranks was nasty, and apt to be brutish and short as well. Necessity rather than free choice made soldiers out of Chinese farmers who could expect very little in the way of rewards for their military service.

Foreign observers were impressed with the capacity of China's peasant soldiers to tolerate conditions of misery and hardship well beyond the endurance of Western troops. Indeed, life was so harsh for China's poor that the impoverished existence of the soldiers was still sometimes better than that of farmers or of urban refugees. Most soldiers seemed to have accepted their fate and asked for little more than bare subsistence. The evolution of the Chinese Medical Service Corps provides some clues as to how conditions were slowly changing in Chinese armies.

Although provision had been made as early as 1912, the first year of the Chinese Republic, for a medical department within the Ministry of War, in reality virtually nothing was done to create such an institution. A medical college also established in 1912 had evolved by 1926 into the Peking Army Medical College, many of whose graduates entered military service in one or another of the northern armies. Most Chinese armies of that era, however, lacked any sort of medical service.[53]

Seriously wounded soldiers were commonly abandoned on the battlefields by the contending "warlord" forces. There were no medical departments in most Chinese formations. Wounded troops were either carried by their comrades many miles to a medical facility, walked there themselves if they were ambulatory, or were left on the battlefield to await their painful deaths. A lucky few were transported and treated by medical missionaries.[54]

Contemporary Western investigators believed that Chinese culture did not encourage individuals to sacrifice themselves for the maimed victims of warfare. Nor was there a tradition of medical ethics that compelled medical professionals, whether serving in or outside of military organizations, to risk personal injury in combat zones in order to help unfortunate peasant soldiers. Moreover, even such basic Western medical concepts as scientific anatomy and the germ theory of disease had barely penetrated Chinese society. The horror of Chinese battlefields can be grasped by recalling that the serious combat injuries produced by the modern engines of warfare were untreated by surgery, and that most of the wounded were left to die on or near the battlefield with little or no medical attention. Conditions were hardly any better even in the army of Feng Yü-hsiang, which was widely viewed as a model of a progressive military organization.[55]

Like its "warlord" counterparts, the Nationalist government tried to enlist the help of foreign-sponsored hospitals like the Peiping Union Medical College to help with wartime casualties. But such sporadic help as was given was an inadequate substitute for the underdeveloped military medical services. Just a few months into the war, it had become painfully obvious that military medical services were wholly inadequate.[56]

Dr. R. K. S. Lim, head of the Chinese Red Cross, was commissioned to develop some way in which the Red Cross could usefully supplement the military medical agencies. By the late 1930s, the Red Cross in China worked only for the military. Lim's report, while calling for the vigorous implementation of such improvements as were feasible, concluded that a total reorganization of military medicine was impossible under wartime conditions. In assessing the backward state of military medicine, he suggested that "fundamentally the fault lies in the ignorance, and in the material and spiritual poverty of the nation." [57]

The military medicine system had not developed sufficiently to provide adequate care for sick and wounded soldiers during the first years of the war although some improvement can be noted. By the late spring of 1938, many military units were regularly employing stretcher-bearers, and there was even an adequate supply of stretchers. Yet other systemic inadequacies persisted.[58]

In the Hsuchow campaign, for example, it took from one to three days to move the wounded from the battle zone to Hsuchow itself. Two hospitals there provided superficial medical assistance, more or less on the level of first aid, including cleaning and redressing wounds, medical inspections, as well as food, shelter, and perhaps a bed. To get higher-level treatment, including surgery, the wounded had to reach Chengchow, an overnight train journey away. After a day in Hsuchow, the wounded were transported in freight cars furnished with rush matting, water, and some food, and watched over by an attendant. Trains generally had a doctor or two aboard. This represented a major improvement in the treatment of military casualties, but the four to six days it took from the battlefield to the surgeon's table was far too long a period to warrant optimism about surviving battlefield wounds. More serious as well as convalescent cases were sent even farther away from the advancing Japanese, mostly to Hankow.[59]

During the battle of Taierhchuang, more than twenty thousand Chinese casualties passed through Chengchow in the first half of April 1938, followed by another ten thousand or so by May 1. Most of those who arrived in Chengchow were wounded in the head, arms, or legs. The paucity of serious and major wounds of the chest, thorax, and abdomen among the casualties treated at Hsuchow and Chengchow suggests that most of those so injured had died either on the battlefield or en route to treatment. Foreign observers noted the stoic forbearance of the Chinese wounded and their strength of character, which permitted the toleration of intense pain for long periods with little complaint. In addition to the battlefield wounds, among the diseases that felled soldiers in this district were venereal disease, typhus, and relapsing fever.[60]

The serious problem of transportation was exacerbated by the large number of lightly wounded (or walking wounded) who, like the more serious cases, also had to be moved all the way to Chengchow to receive treatment. Aid stations and hospital facilities closer to the front would have been much more efficient, returning able-bodied troops to the battlefront much more quickly and reducing pressure on the overburdened transport and treatment facilities. Motorized ambulances would doubtless have made things much easier during those terrible months of 1938, but there were few such vehicles available. It is a bitter irony that the advanced technology of destruction had made it to Chinese battlefields, but not the technology for supporting and treating the troops.

On a visit to the 90th Military Base Hospital at Nanchang in the summer of 1938, Captain Frank Dorn and two foreign medical specialists were appalled by what they saw. None of the supposed eleven doctors on duty was doing anything, and the nurses and orderlies were virtually untrained. Wounded soldiers who had arrived in the hospital two or three days earlier had not even been washed or had their bandages changed. Dorn summed up his impressions with the withering comment that "the so-called care of the wounded in the 90th Military Base Hospital was deplorable. . . . the manifest ignorance of those in charge was not even tempered with any sign of kindness to the sick. Nurses and orderlies seem to view the men in their care with a completely callous disregard for their suffering."[61]

Along the Yangtze in early September, the situation with respect to medical services was just as bad. The problems created by the rapidity of the Japanese advance were compounded by the flooding of the river, which made transportation even more difficult than usual. Since trucks had been withdrawn in advance of the Japanese attack, wounded but ambulatory soldiers had to walk thirty-five miles back as far as Yanghsin before they could even hope for a ride. Most of the seriously wounded died where they were hit, however long it might take death to arrive. The lucky minority were picked up by stretcher-bearers who carried them ten or fifteen miles to the first collection station, where another contingent of bearers was supposed to take over. Supplies of every kind were so inadequate that the wounded might not even get their bandages replaced en route. At the first medical treatment station, some eight hundred wounded inundated the 200-bed facility and spilled over onto the floors, the corridors, the porches, and even the bare ground. The overwhelmed medical staff could do nothing but provide some food and drink to these men.[62]

Meanwhile, the incidence of disease shot up in the hot summer months. Many units were devastated by malaria and dysentery. The standard rate of dysentery infection was 10 percent, and malaria was so common that normally no attempt was even made to cure it. Soldiers reported for duty until they collapsed.[63]

One bright spot among all these horrors was the student volunteer stretcher-bearers who also provided first aid and comfort. Many of them were upper middle school students whose enthusiasm and dedication won wide praise from otherwise critical foreign observers. Another group of somewhat older volunteers, who also received high marks for their intelligence, honesty, and dependability, were the Boy Scouts or, more simply, the "scouts," most of whom were above the age of twenty and who did such things as drive trucks and ambulances. Colonel Joseph Stilwell, at that time the U.S. military attaché, believed that "If all organizations connected with the Chinese Army were half as good as the Boy Scouts, the story of the war would have been very different."[64]

In the fall of 1938, Stilwell observed medical conditions in the vicinity of Wuning. Again, the tiny minority of seriously wounded who left the battlefield alive had to make their way some sixty miles before receiving even emergency surgery. Medical supplies were scarce, as usual. Farm houses had been commandeered in lieu of hospitals. While the summer heat had brought pestilence, the encroaching cold of winter also intensified the suffering of the wounded. Lacking clean bedding, the wounded lay on straw and covered themselves, if they were lucky, with filthy quilts. Stilwell noted a suspiciously large number of minor wounds to the hands and feet which he took to be self-inflicted. They were a ticket to the safer haven of the rear areas for convalescence. Perhaps 80 percent of the troops on this front suffered from malaria and 10 percent from dysentery.[65]

Stilwell sketched the sequence of events that a typical wounded soldier could be expected to pass through. A man wounded on October 1 at Kuantahsishan would receive first aid from his regimental medical detachment. If he was ambulatory he started out on his own; if not he would be carried in two five-mile stages and arrive on October 2 at the Number 55 Receiving Station where he would be given hot water and rice gruel. There was no bedding for him to rest on and no morphine to relieve his agony. The following day he would be transported another ten miles to the Number 103 Receiving Station where the Red Cross would provide straw for a bed, food, and a change of dressing for his wound. The wounded soldier would also get his discharge certificate, or *san p'iao*, and five dollars, which would have to suffice to pay for his food, drink, and other necessities along the way. This was all the retirement "benefit" he would ever see if he was rendered unfit for further military service.[66]

With luck, he could be transported by truck to Hsinshui, some sixty miles from the front, on October 4. There a Red Cross surgical unit would operate on him if need be. It would take from three to seven days from the time he was wounded for the soldier to reach competent surgical care. The lengthy transit to treatment centers was guaranteed to produce deeper and more serious infections that required longer periods of recovery.[67]

Although notable deficiencies persisted, there can be no doubt that the system of providing medical care for wounded combatants improved greatly during the Nationalist period. Over the first four years of the long war with Japan, a process for evacuating the wounded had been created, staffed, and implemented. Conditions were substantially improved over what they had been a decade earlier. Of course, the medical service function in Chinese military organizations of this period was not at the level provided in more advanced and more affluent national military systems elsewhere.

Over the course of a decade there had been substantial changes, but the awful reality was that the changes were too little and too late to save the lives of hundreds of thousands of Chinese soldiers wounded in battle. China had too few trained medical specialists, too little medicine and equipment, inadequate motor transport and physical facilities. The extremely rapid Japanese advance generated huge numbers of casualties that inundated and overwhelmed treatment facilities wherever a large battle developed. In these circumstances, the system for evacuating the wounded and providing primary medical care was stretched beyond the breaking point.

Conclusions

This analysis of the first four years of the Sino-Japanese War points to several important conclusions. First was the great disparity in combat power between the

Chinese and Japanese armies. Only on exceptional occasions, and even then only in relatively minor engagements, was Chinese manpower able to contest seriously the superior killing power of Japan's more modernized army. Japan's expeditionary forces in China brought together a deadly array of artillery, airpower, and armored cavalry, augmented on occasion with naval guns, in a combination of firepower that the Chinese could scarcely hope to match. The example of China's military medical service hints at the colossal inadequacy of the Chinese military system to conduct modern warfare on the scale required to defeat Japan. Other specialized areas of the Chinese Army very likely exhibited similar deficiencies.

Second was the inadequacy of Chinese leadership in the realm of military command. At the level of Chiang Kai-shek's central headquarters, the most significant failings were the inability to coordinate and control huge armies over sizable distances, and the unwillingness to delegate authority and control to the subordinate commanders of the various war areas. This was only partly Chiang Kai-shek's fault. It was also a function of historical conditions and the evolutionary development of a nationalized military system. China did not yet possess a unified national military service in 1937. The historical residue of decades of rule and misrule by many regional military separatists hopelessly complicated the problem of command.

Command failure at the highest level was frequently matched by paralyzing ineptitude at the army and division levels. The nearly universal failure of commanders to discharge their responsibilities with professional competence underscores the achievements of those few who achieved success in the midst of cowardice, betrayal, and ineptitude. There were few examples of competent staff work at any level of command. The lack of imaginative and aggressive responses to Japanese maneuvers and unplanned contingencies on the battlefield condemned to death countless soldiers who were serving under inadequate officers.

Bad generalship, of course, is not a Chinese monopoly. Every war produces an abundance of inadequacy, and the interested student of comparative military history need look no further than the western front in World War I for examples. In East Asia in the 1930s, the failure of command and staff demonstrated the lack of training in the Chinese armies at large. The same phenomenon of professional inadequacy characterized the degree of medical services available to Chinese soldiers. Those most in need of humane consideration suffered from the same failures of leadership and organization. Every soldier killed or wounded lowered the level of combat experience in the Chinese Army. Few if any combat veterans survived serious wounds to return to the battlefield.

The state of the art of delivering "modern" medical services on the battlefields reinforces another frequently encountered judgment about the war. For the Chinese, the war came too soon. The Nationalist government was not yet ready for its deadly duel with the expansionist, militarist Japanese. It seems clear that the quality of medical services to combat formations had been improving over the course of a decade, but once the war began the intensity and urgency of demands precluded any new reform initiatives.

At Hsuchow, for example, medical facilities in this large city did provide at least minimal medical care, and a system had been organized and staffed to move battlefield casualties. The system was not sufficiently developed, however, to cope with the huge demands placed on it by the overwhelming power of the Japanese and the extremely rapid movement of the Japanese military juggernaut. The Chinese system had not evolved to a stage of sophistication where Mobile Army Surgical Hospitals were in place as a part of the Standard Table of Organization and Equipment. The Chinese did the next best thing under the circumstances of poverty. They attempted to evacuate casualties to the nearest cities where treatment facilities had been designated for military use. But even that preliminary, evolutionary improvement was overwhelmed by the terrible pressures of war.

In the final analysis, this judgment sums up the entire situation of the Chinese military establishment during the first four years of the war. The power of Japan's modernized military machine, and the terrible demands of warfare in the industrial age, overwhelmed the best efforts of the Chinese Army. At this point in history, China's military establishment was simply not yet ready for war on the scale that Japanese aggression imposed.

Notes

1. Chung-hua min-kuo kuo-fang pu, shih-cheng chu, *K'ang Jih chan-shih: T'ai-yuan hui-chan* (Military history of the War of Resistance: the battle of Taiyuan) (Taipei, 1962), pp. 28–29 (series hereafter cited as *KJCS*). Hsu Lung-hsuan and Chang Ming-kai do not directly credit Communist units with the victory in *History of the Sino-Japanese War, 1937–1945* (hereafter cited as HC) (Taipei, 1971), pp. 326, 350; Frank Dorn, *The Sino-Japanese War, 1937–41: From Marco Polo Bridge to Pearl Harbor* (New York, 1974), pp. 62–64.

2. Dorn, *War*, 42. Neither side's slaughter is referenced in either the *KJCS* series or in Hsu and Chang's history. Explicit accounts of Japanese atrocities in the second Sino-Japanese War are not to be found in these military histories from the Republic of China.

3. *KJCS: P'ing-han t'ieh-lu pei-tuan yen-hsien chih tso-chan* (Combat along the northern section of the Ping-Han railroad), pp. 47–49; Dorn describes the wanton brutality and destruction by Japanese troops in Paoting, *War*, pp. 108–9; Hsu and Chang note the Chinese military withdrawal, HC, p. 339.

4. *KJCS: P'ing-han t'ieh-lu*, pp. 55–59; Dorn, *War*, pp. 109–12; HC, p. 340.

5. *KJCS: P'ing-han t'ieh-lu*, p. 72; Dorn, *War*, pp. 113, 171; HC, p. 341, 352.

6. *KJCS: P'ing-han t'ieh-lu*, p. 3; Dorn, *War*, pp. 115–18.

7. *KJCS: Chin-pu t'ieh-lu pei-tuan yen-hsien chih tso-chan* (Combat along the northern section of the Chin-pu railroad), pp. 75, 85 and appropriate maps on following pages; Dorn, *War*, p. 119; HC, p. 348 and map 5.

8. *KJCS: T'ai-yuan hui-chan*, vol. 2, map 22; *Chung-Jih chan-cheng shih-lueh* (Outline history of the Sino-Japanese war) [hereafter cited as *CJCCSL*], pp. 184–85; Dorn, *War*, pp. 123–24; HC, pp. 351–54 and map 6.

9. *CJCCSL*, p. 185; Dorn lists Chinese casualties at fifty thousand in the fighting in and around Taiyuan in late October and early November, *War*, pp. 126–27.

10. *CJCCSL*, pp. 185–86; Dorn, *War*, pp. 126–27.

11. I have accepted Dorn's recounting here although I can find no reference to a specific offer of an opportunity to surrender in either *KJCS: T'ai-yuan hui-chan* or *CJCCSL*. Given Chinese experience with Japanese forces, the point may be moot. No informed Chinese soldier could reasonably expect to survive Japanese capture. Furthermore, standing orders from the ROC Military Affairs Commission threatened execution for anyone who withdrew or surrendered without explicit orders. See *KJCS: T'ai-yuan hui-chan*, p. 95. Japanese Monograph no. 178, *North China Area Operations Record*, p. 96, does include a reference to an offer to accept a surrender at Taiyuan (or "Yang chu" in the monograph) made by the Japanese 5th Division. See Dorn, *War*, p. 127.

12. No specific figures for military casualties are given in the *KJCS* accounts, and, as usual, civilian losses are not mentioned. See *T'ai-yuan hui-chan*, p. 86; *CJCCSL*, p. 94; Dorn, *War*, pp. 127–28.

13. *KJCS: Chin-pu t'ieh-lu*, pp. 75–78; *KJCS: Hsu-chou hui-chan*, pp. 7, 261; Dorn, *War*, pp. 137–38, 140–41, 145; HC, p. 393.

14. *KJCS: Chin-pu t'ieh-lu*, pp. 81, 83–84; *North China Area Operations Record*, p. 108; Dorn, *War*, pp. 142–43.

15. *KJCS: Hsu-chou hui-chan*, pp. 1, 19; *North China Area Operations Record*, p. 108; Dorn, *War*, pp. 136, 146; HC, p. 394.

16. *KJCS: Hsu-chou hui-chan*, p. 22; Dorn, *War*, pp. 149–51; HC, pp. 396–97.

17. *KJCS: Hsu-chou hui-chan*, pp. 26, 29. Although no specific casualty figures are given, casualties were considered "serious" or "heavy." Dorn suggests corpses were strewn throughout the combat zone. *War*, p. 151.

18. Dorn refers to the total destruction of the 23d Regiment. *War*, p. 152. It is clear that many large units suffered horrendous casualty rates of from 30 percent to 66 percent dead and wounded. Such units would have been rendered useless for further employment. *KJCS: Hsu-chou hui-chan*, pp. 30, 35, 76–79.

19. *KJCS: Hsu-chou hui-chan*, pp. 19–20; Dorn, *War*, p. 149.

20. *KJCS: Hsu-chou hui-chan*, pp. 26–27, 136–38, 140. Dorn quotes Colonel Stilwell's account of the action, compiled on the ground at the Hsuchow front. *War*, pp. 150–51; Japanese Monograph no. 73, *Combat in the Taierhchuang Area* (Tokyo: Military History Section, Army Forces Far East, n.d.), p. 6; HC, pp. 398–99.

21. *KJCS: Hsu-chou hui-chan*, pp. 140–45, 153–56; *North China Area Operations Record*, p. 143; Dorn, *War*, p. 154; *Combat in the Taierhchuang Area*, p. 7.

22. *KJCS: Hsu-chou hui-chan*, pp. 178, 192; Dorn, *War*, p. 157. Both Japanese reports in *Combat in the Taierhchuang Area*, pp. 8–9, and *North China Area Operations Record*, pp. 145–46, explain the withdrawal of Japanese units on the basis of command communication failures and do not portray a sequential decline in types of ammunition. The Japanese historical team listed only 2,130 dead and 8,580 wounded Japanese troops. *Combat in the Taierhchuang Area*, p. 12. See also HC, p. 400.

23. *KJCS: Hsu-chou hui-chan*, pp. 26–27, 127–29; Dorn, *War*, pp. 160–63, quoting Stilwell's report from the scene; *North China Operations Record*, pp. 158–65; *Combat in the Taierhchuang Area*, pp. 10–11; HC, pp. 402–403.

24. *KJCS: Hsu-chou hui-chan*, pp. 247–49; *Combat in the North China Area Operations Record*, pp. 166–71; Dorn, *War*, pp. 164–65; HC, p. 403.

25. *KJCS: Hsu-chou hui-chan*, pp. 2, 248–49, 286. At Hsiaohsien and elsewhere casualties were extremely heavy and included the commanding general of a line division and his deputy. Moreover, substantial weaponry and equipment were lost. *North China Area Operations Record*, p. 166; Dorn believed the deaths of the two commanders caused Chinese troops to give up on winning the desperate battle. *War*, pp. 166–67; HC, p. 405 and map 9–1.

26. *CJCCSL*, p. 459; Dorn, *War*, p. 169; HC, p. 427.

27. *North China Area Operations Record*, p. 186.

28. *KJCS: Hsu-chou hui-chan*, p. 261, *passim*, does not explicitly admit ROC responsibility for blowing the dike. That admission wasn't made in official publications until at least a decade after the *KJCS* volumes were published. See also *North China Area Operations Record*, p. 179; Dorn, *War*, p. 178; Hsu and Chang, *Sino-Japanese War*, suggest that Japanese forces were stopped by a flood of the Yellow River, p. 326.

29. *KJCS: Sung-hu hui-chan* (Battle of Shanghai), pp. 5–6; HC, p. 357; Japanese Monograph no. 179, *Central China Area Operations Record*, p. 13; Dorn, *War*, p. 69. The best analysis of Chinese strategy at Shanghai is in Chi Hsi-sheng, *Nationalist China at War: Military Defeats and Political Collapse, 1937–1945* (Ann Arbor: University of Michigan Press, 1982), pp. 40–49.

30. *KJCS: Sung-hu hui-chan*, pp. 35–37; Dorn, *War*, p. 72; *Central China Area Operations Record*, map p. 19; HC, p. 363.

31. *Central China Area Operations Record*, p. 16 lists major unit reinforcements; Dorn, *War*, p. 73; HC, pp. 366–67.

32. *KJCS: Sung-hu hui-chan*, see maps following p. 58; Dorn, *War*, pp. 72–76; HC, pp. 368–69.

33. *KJCS: Sung-hu hui-chan*, pp. 172, 178–82, 186 and battle maps following; Dorn, *War*, pp. 76–77; HC, pp. 369–70.

34. *KJCS: Sung-hu hui-chan*, pp. 187–88, 191–92; *CJCCSL*, p. 196.

35. *CJCCSL*, p. 196; *KJCS: Sung-hu hui-chan*, pp. 204, 210; *Central China Area Operations Record*, pp. 18, 21, and map, p. 19; Dorn, *War*, pp. 87–88; HC, pp. 370, 372–73.

36. For a useful overview of operations from Shanghai to Nanking, see the general map following p. 4 in *KJCS: Sung-hu hui-chan*; *CJCCSL*, pp. 196–97; *Central China Area Operations Record, p. 21;* Dorn, *War*, pp. 70, 88–89; HC, map 8.

37. Dorn, *War*, pp. 75, 88, 90–91; *KJCS: Sung-hu hui-chan*, pp. 247, 251, 260; *CJCCSL*, p. 198; *Central China Area Operations Record*, pp. 21–24; HC, pp. 376–77.

38. Dorn, *War*, p. 93; Hsu and Chang, *Sino-Japanese War*, refer to "indiscriminate killing and burning," and more than 100,000 civilian victims, p. 377; *CJCCSL* briefly mentions the "Nan-ching ta t'u-sha" (Great Nanking massacre), p. 198. See also H. J. Timperley, *Japanese Terror in China* (New York: Modern Age Books, 1938), for general testimony.

39. The ROC Ministry of National Defense publications do not explicitly recognize the Soviet aid that was so desperately needed during the war years. In his China memoir, Soviet military adviser General Kalyagin reports that more than eight hundred aircraft were supplied in a barter-trade arrangement to ROC forces. Soviet pilots flew most of the combat aircraft. Aleksandr Ya. Kalyagin, *Along Alien Roads*, trans. Steven I. Levine (New York: Columbia University, East Asian Institute, 1983), p. 46; Dorn, *War*, pp. 184, 192–93.

40. Dorn, *War*, pp. 185, 192–93. Kalyagin understood clearly something of the terrible political reality that infected the leadership of Chinese armies. See his brief description in *Along Alien Roads*, pp. 32–41. The authors of the Japanese monographs distinguished between Chiang Kai-shek's troops and "provincial" troops, indicating their profound awareness of the hopeless Chinese command conundrum. Ch'i Hsi-sheng offers the most informed and understanding interpretation in his section "Relations among Military Groups," in *Nationalist China*, pp. 83–131.

41. Smaller detachments broke away from the central columns, seized tactical objectives, and rejoined the larger mass on the march west. *KJCS: Wuhan hui-chan* (The battle of Wuhan), pp. 5, 21, 24, map following p. 56; Dorn, *War*, pp. 182, 194–95; Kalyagin, *Along Alien Roads*, p. 91; HC, p. 417.

42. *KJCS: Wuhan hui-chan*, pp. 118–19, 121–22; Dorn, *War*, pp. 195–96; Kalyagin believed inadequate combat engineering and inconsistency in command caused the loss of Matang, *Along Alien Roads*, p. 117; HC, p. 418.

43. Dorn, *War*, p. 196. *KJCS: Wuhan hui-chan* does not mention the late arrival of the 18th Corps, although the relevant battle map shows the retreating unit from the east joining the Chinese defenders. Hsu and Chang, *Sino-Japanese War*, confirm the late arrival, p. 418.

44. *KJCS: Wuhan hui-chan*, pp. 171–72. Only Dorn mentions the barbarity and destruction in and around "abandoned" Kiukiang, in *War*, pp. 197–99. Kalyagin explains Chinese abandonment in terms of panic among troops who mistook camouflage smoke for poison gas, in *Along Alien Roads*, p. 145. The panicked retreat quickly became another rout, see HC, p. 420.

45. Dorn, *War*, pp. 202–203; Ho Ying-ch'in, *Pa-nien k'ang-chan* (The eight-year War of Resistance), 2d ed. (Taipei, 1969), p. 78.

46. Dorn, *War*, pp. 19, 204; *CJCCSL*, p. 226; Kalyagin describes the inadequacy of Chinese tactics at Juichang, using the piecemeal investment of troops as his example. He also notes Chinese successful use of terrain and prepared defensive positions after the fall of Juichang. *Along Alien Roads*, p. 151. See also HC, p. 422.

47. Dorn, *War*, pp. 204–6; *CJCCSL*, p. 226; Kalyagin, *Along Alien Roads*, p. 151; HC, pp. 422–23.

48. Dorn, *War*, pp. 217–19; *CJCCSL*, p. 216.

49. Dorn, *War*, pp. 205–6; Ho, *Pa-nien k'ang-chan*, p. 78; *CJCCSL*, p. 226; HC, pp. 421–23.

50. *CJCCSL*, p. 226. Only Dorn notes the slaughter of POWs, in *War*, p. 207.

51. Dorn, *War*, pp. 182, 218–20; *CJCCSL*, pp. 226–27; Ho, *Pa-nien k'ang-chan*, p. 79; HC, pp. 424–25.

52. *CJCCSL*, pp. 226–27; Ho, *Pa-nien k'ang-chan*, pp. 79–80; Dorn describes conditions in the city and the scene at General Hata's arrival, in *War*, p. 223.

53. U.S. National Archives, Modern Military Records Sections, Military Attaché China [hereafter MAC], Report no. 5879, June 12, 1926, "Medical Services," p. 1; MAC, Report no. 8127, October 27, 1931, "Comments on Difficulties Encountered by Foreign Medical Workers in China," pp. 4, 7; MAC, Report no. 8342, July 14, 1932, "The Medical Corps of the Chinese Army," p. 1.

54. MAC, "Medical Services," pp. 1–2; MAC, "Comments on Difficulties," p. 3.

55. Ibid.

56. MAC, "Comments on Difficulties," pp. 1–7; MAC, Report no. 9743, February 28, 1939, "The Chinese Army Medical Service," p. 1.

57. MAC, "The Chinese Army Medical Service," p. 1.

58. Ibid., pp. 4–5, 19.

59. Ibid., pp. 19–20.

60. Ibid., p. 20.

61. Ibid., pp. 20–21. Included among casualties at Nanchang were victims of poison gas. Further evidence of Japanese use of gas and of the even more terrifying preparation and employment of bacteriological agents is presented in Peter Williams and David Wallace, *Unit 731: Japan's Secret Biological Warfare in World War II* (New York: Free Press, 1989). Kalyagin reported Japanese gas attacks at Juichang in August 1938, in *Along Alien Roads*, p. 151.

62. MAC, "The Chinese Army Medical Service," pp. 22–23.

63. Ibid., pp. 23–24.

64. Ibid., pp. 19, 23.

65. Ibid., p. 24.

66. Ibid., pp. 24–25.

67. Ibid., p. 25.

7

THE MILITARY DIMENSION, 1942–1945

Hsi-sheng Ch'i

FOR FIFTY-THREE long months, beginning in July 1937, China stood alone, single-handedly fighting an undeclared war against Japan. On December 9, 1941, after Japan's surprise attack on Pearl Harbor, China finally declared war against Japan. What had been for so long a war between these two countries now became part of a much wider Pacific conflict. The expansion of the conflict changed the complexion of the Sino-Japanese War in two significant ways. First, China gained several Western allies and elevated the earlier coordination with these countries into a formal alliance. This dramatically brightened China's prospects of receiving increased military assistance and boosted its combat spirits considerably in the short run. Second, military engagements in China became integrated into the broader global strategies worked out within the highest Allied military councils. The conflict in China became truly internationalized as important moves made by the major antagonists within China were usually prompted by consideration of their implications for the broader conflict.

The present chapter first provides a broad picture of the war by highlighting the major campaigns of 1942–45. It then focuses on the strictly military factors in order to explain China's performance in the war. Finally, to assess the significance of the war, it examines the conflict in the context of China's history of resistance to imperialism.

The Major Campaigns

The Third Changsha Campaign

The impact of the Pacific War on the China theater became obvious immediately in the Changsha campaign in Hunan Province. Twice before, in the fall of 1939 and again in 1941, the Japanese had contested Chinese control over Changsha. But on both occasions, the Japanese intent was to score a local victory or to disrupt the Chinese schedule of troop training. When the Chinese defenders offered fierce resistance and inflicted considerable damage on the Japanese attackers, the latter halted operations.

When the Pacific War erupted, the Japanese Army promptly began military operations against the Western colonial possessions throughout Southeast Asia. As part of this general offensive, the Japanese also launched an attack against Hong Kong from Canton. In response, the Chinese high command promptly ordered the Fourth and the Ninth war zones to send reinforcements to South China to relieve the pressure on the British defenders of Hong Kong. To counter this move, the Japanese decided to attack Changsha simultaneously to keep the Chinese preoccupied in their own area.

On December 13, 1941, the Japanese Eleventh Army formalized its plans and mobilized 120,000 men, 600 pieces of artillery, and over 200 aircraft for the operation.[1] The original objective was to mount a limited campaign of about two weeks in order to seek out and annihilate the Chinese main forces.[2] When Hong Kong fell into Japanese hands on December 25, this presumably removed the need to prosecute the Changsha campaign. Elated, however, by their smooth progress in the early phase of the campaign, the Japanese believed that they could maximize its military impact by seizing Changsha, thereby delivering a shattering blow to the Chungking government's morale.[3]

Meanwhile, the Chinese forces had also learned a lesson from the two previous encounters and decided to try something new. General Hsueh Yueh allowed the Japanese to penetrate deeply into the main battlefield before surrounding them from all sides. As a result, the Japanese fell into the Chinese trap.[4] Eventually, the Japanese left tens of thousands of bodies on the battlefield and were forced to call a general retreat.[5] Thus, the campaign became the first instance in which the Sino-Japanese War became interwoven with the broader Pacific and international conflict.

The First Burma Campaign

At the same time that the Japanese attacked Hong Kong, they also attacked and occupied Guam, Manila, and Singapore in quick succession. Thailand became a Japanese puppet overnight, enabling Japanese forces to use the western part of that country as a staging area to drive the British out of Burma. For different reasons, both Britain and China shared a common interest in defending Burma. The British wanted to protect the flank of their far more valuable colonial possession, India, while the Chinese wanted to protect their only lifeline of supplies to the outside world. Therefore, the Chinese high command reacted quickly, sending the Fifth, Sixth, and Sixty-sixth armies from Szechwan and Kwangsi toward Yunnan to be ready to undertake a campaign in Burma in cooperation with the British. On December 16, 1941, the Chinese Expeditionary Army (CEF) was formally created.

While the British wanted to hold on to Burma, they did not relish the thought of inviting the Chinese Army into their preserve. Therefore, on December 24, 1941, the British military requested that Chinese armies refrain from entering

Burma. As soon as the Japanese attacked Burma in late January 1942, however, the British quickly changed their mind and sent out an urgent appeal for Chinese troops. At this juncture, the British could muster only eight brigades for the defense of Burma. The Chinese quickly responded and appointed the newly arrived American general, Joseph Stilwell, to lead the CEF in the Burma theater. The importance that China attached to the campaign was indicated by the fact that the Fifth, Sixth, and Sixty-sixth armies, which comprised the CEF, were virtually the last of the crack fighting units from China's strategic reserves at this time.

The battle was joined in March. Although the Chinese troops fought valiantly, the odds were stacked against them. They were poorly prepared to fight in a foreign country and were not familiar with the terrain, the language, the tropical weather, or the thick jungle. The British and Burmese forces had simply melted away. The entire British Air Force in Burma was wiped out by a single Japanese strike. Coordination among Allied forces was chaotic, and the Chinese Army's own command structure was hampered by the great differences between the command styles of Chiang Kai-shek and Stilwell.[6]

By early May, the Japanese forces had advanced to both the Burma-India border and the Burma-China border. By the time military activities in Burma came to a halt in June 1942, there was no question that the CEF had been routed. While the main body of the force retreated into China's southwest, a small portion was cut off and had to evacuate into India. Of the 100,000 troops originally sent into Burma, fewer than half survived.[7]

The first Burma campaign was a terrible setback to China. Its link with the newly gained allies through the Yunnan-Burma Road was completely severed, while Japan's occupation of Burma created a new threat to China's security from the south. Probably just as important were the serious strains that crept into the alliance relationships as each of the three parties blamed the other two for the defeat in Burma.

When Chiang asked Stilwell for a critical evaluation of the reasons for the Chinese defeat in Burma, Stilwell replied that the main factors were the Chinese lack of air support; the inferiority of Chinese troops in morale, training, equipment, number of soldiers, transportation, logistics, command, and organization; their unfamiliarity with the terrain; and their inability to conduct reconnaissance properly.[8] Given his earlier doubts about the wisdom of undertaking the Burma campaign, Chiang's bitter disappointment was hardly mollified by an answer that blamed the defeat entirely on Chinese weaknesses.

Chiang had expressed his reservations about the Burma campaign as early as his first meeting with Stilwell on March 9, 1942. He was worried about the difficulty of a Chinese Army operating in a foreign country where the local population obviously wanted to throw out their British masters. He was also worried about the lack of supplies available to his army. Chiang wanted the British to give Chinese troops control over Mandalay, and to put their own troops under Stilwell's command as were the Chinese troops.[9] Chiang had reluctantly agreed to the Burma campaign only in order not to offend the United States, because Stilwell forcefully argued for it.[10]

Chiang had repeatedly warned Stilwell to exercise extreme caution in using the Chinese troops in the campaign.

> In our Burma operations we must win victory and cannot afford a defeat. Why? Once the cream of Chinese troops as represented by the Fifth and Sixth armies is defeated, it would be impossible to counterattack not only in Burma but also in the whole of China. And there would be no efficient reserves in Yunnan or in the Yangtze valley. The consequence would be very grave for China. A defeat in Burma would not only have serious repercussions upon the morale of the Chinese troops but upon the morale of the Chinese nation. Although two or three armies are involved, their success or defeat would have grave effect upon the Chinese people.[11]

In plain language, Chiang instructed Stilwell not to gamble with his crack units, and to use them in offensive operations only when it was safe to do so.[12] The disaster that subsequently befell his best units permanently marred the relationship between Chiang and Stilwell.

Chiang also developed a very strong suspicion of and resentment toward the British military. Even before Chiang sent troops into Burma, he already had misgivings about the competence of the British military in view of the latter's sorry combat record in Hong Kong, Singapore, Malaya, and Rangoon. During the campaign, Chiang was greatly angered by the unannounced retreat of British units from battle, which exposed Chinese armies to overpowering Japanese attacks. Chiang not only questioned the credibility of British promises, he also lost respect for their military leadership. In his view, "the British military had no strategic mind" and "made no careful and long-range plans."[13]

More so than the Changsha campaign, the Burma campaign was a landmark in the internationalization of the Sino-Japanese War. It was also remarkable in being the first time in the twentieth century that China had sent a sizable expeditionary army to fight outside Chinese borders. Unfortunately, the disheartening result was a crushing defeat, the complete physical isolation of China, and the beginning of estranged relations between China and its allies.

The East China Campaign

The internationalization of the war was felt elsewhere in the country. On April 18, 1942, a fleet of American bombers launched the first large-scale air attack of the war against Japanese cities, causing widespread panic in Japanese society. Taking advantage of the lull in the Burma theater, the Japanese mobilized a large force of some 140,000 men to mount an attack against major airfields in Chekiang and Kiangsi provinces in East China to prevent their future use by U.S.

airplanes in bombing raids against the Japanese homeland. The Japanese forces began their attack in mid-May and succeeded in inflicting great damage to all the major airfields in the area. Japanese troops also removed a large quantity of rolling stock from along the Chekiang-Kiangsi rail line. By the end of August, however, the Chinese had regained control over much of the territory they had lost in the previous three months. During the fighting, the Chinese lost about 40,000 dead while the Japanese Army suffered about 1,600 deaths and 28,000 wounded.[14]

The Ch'ang-te Campaign of 1943

By and large, 1943 saw a lull in the China theater because the Japanese were preoccupied with military actions in the Pacific, and the Chinese Army faced its worst logistic situation when virtually no foreign assistance flowed into the country. Nonetheless, in these difficult circumstances, the Chinese high command pressed on with the task of assembling and training an expeditionary force for yet another attempt to reopen the Burma corridor and to reestablish contact with the outside world.

The Japanese, however, also wanted to maintain pressure on the Chinese in order to destroy their main units, to deny them the time needed for recuperation, regrouping, and retraining, and to make sure that no Chinese troops could be spared for the Burma front. Therefore, the Japanese launched a series of forays in the summer followed by a larger-scale attack, employing about 100,000 men, against Ch'ang-te in Hupeh Province in early November. They captured the city but chose to withdraw in January 1944, whereupon the Chinese forces returned and restored the precampaign front.

The Second Burma Campaign, 1944

Preparations for the second Burma campaign began as soon as the first Burma fiasco had ended. The Chinese troops that straggled into India were assembled at Ramgarh where they were given American-style military training and American weapons. The troops that returned to China were regrouped, replenished with new conscripts, and also received some American training and equipment. Throughout 1942–43, the governments of China, Great Britain, and the United States conducted intense discussions on strategies, force contributions, and division of responsibilities concerning the projected campaign. The Chinese let it be known that they would not participate in the next campaign unless their troops were assured of adequate air and naval support.[15]

When Stilwell sensed during 1943 that China was wavering about the Burma campaign, he again played on Chinese suspicions of the British as a means to exert pressure on Chiang. Stilwell argued that the British would probably gladly abandon the Burma campaign and put their resources to better use in Southeast

Asia, and would probably divert to their own use U.S. Lend Lease material that was stockpiled in India but earmarked for China. Therefore, the only way China could frustrate the British design was to pursue the Burma campaign vigorously and not give the British any excuses to back out. Stilwell remained firmly convinced that if China wanted to receive U.S. supplies, "there is no alternative to the opening of the Burma-Yunnan Road."[16]

Even as late as the early spring of 1944, the Chinese government was still undecided about the Burma campaign. China's anxiety level was raised considerably by an incursion of Outer Mongolian troops into Sinkiang Province in mid-March 1944, under the cover of the Soviet air force. This development served as a fresh reminder of the potential threat to China's security along the northwestern frontier. Chiang believed that China had two top priorities. First, the front against Japan must be stabilized so that Allied aircraft might continue their direct attacks against the Japanese homeland from Chinese airfields. Second, China should undertake preparations to become a base from which an overland counterattack against Japan could be launched. As late as March 27, 1944, Chiang still tried to convince President Roosevelt in a telegram why China should not mount an attack against Burma from Yunnan.[17]

Chiang finally abandoned his objections and ordered his troops to proceed with the campaign. By the early fall of 1943, the Chinese forces stranded in India since 1942 (the New 22d and New 38th divisions) had completed their restructuring and retraining, and in late October they had begun to move from Ledo against the Japanese in northern Burma. They made good progress. By August 1944, they had recovered the strategic town of Myitkina, having decimated the renowned Japanese 18th Division in the process. Meanwhile, the Chinese Expeditionary Force in Yunnan, consisting of sixteen divisions, also began its attack in May 1944. On January 27, 1945, these two Chinese forces (from India and Yunnan) finally linked up and completely opened the Sino-India Road.

The Chinese soldiers participating in the second Burma campaign not only were better trained and equipped but had sufficient air and artillery support and modern means of transportation and communication. As a result, they were able to deliver devastating blows to the Japanese troops in one battle after another. According to Chinese reports, the Japanese suffered 48,850 dead, and 647 captured, along with the loss of a large quantity of weapons.[18] The Chinese forces not only redeemed their honor, which had been tarnished during the previous Burma campaign, but scored stunning victories over some of the best troops in the Japanese Imperial Army.

Operation Ichigo

The victory in Burma notwithstanding, other developments within the China theater made 1944 a disastrous year for the country from a military point of view. On November 25, 1943, U.S. airplanes based in Kiangsi Province in East

China attacked Hsinchu Airfield in Taiwan, marking the first time that an air attack was launched from the mainland of China against an important Japanese military target. It was a clear signal that China-based air attacks against Japan's homeland were only a question of time. Meanwhile, Japan's position in the Pacific War had deteriorated steadily since its naval defeat at the Midway Islands in 1942.[19]

These developments prompted Japanese military planners to contemplate a large-scale operation against China, and by the spring of 1944, a plan designated as "Operation Ichigo" was approved. Operation Ichigo's objectives were to seek out and destroy China's main fighting units, secure the railway connection from Peiping through Hankow to Canton, and demolish the main Chinese airfields so that they could not be used to attack Japan's homeland or interdict Japanese shipping in the western Pacific.[20]

Although the Japanese began their preparations immediately and amassed a force of over half a million men for this campaign, they also took measures to conceal their true intentions from the Chinese.[21] By not properly assessing Operation Ichigo, the Chinese probably committed their most costly intelligence error in the entire Sino-Japanese War. The error not only caused great damage to the Chinese troops that might have been avoided but also put the Nationalist government in a militarily and politically precarious situation that carried over into the postwar era.

The Japanese began their attacks in North China (at Chengchow) on April 17, 1944, by crossing the Yellow River with a large number of tanks and artillery, protected by heavy air cover.[22] On April 27, the French military delegation in Chungking passed along to the Chinese military intelligence branch a tip obtained by the French in Indochina that the Japanese were planning an ambitious operation to link up a continental corridor through the Peiping-Hankow and Hankow-Canton railways. After evaluation by the proper agencies, the Chinese high command dismissed this tip as a smoke-screen deliberately planted by the Japanese to deceive the Chinese government. The Chinese noted that the Japanese campaign in North China had been underway for more than ten days, but that only thirty thousand troops were involved, conveying the impression that this was nothing more than a localized operation. Besides, the Chinese were unable to obtain any independent confirmation of significant Japanese military activities in either Central or South China.[23]

Probably the most important reason for China's failure to prepare for the Japanese offensive was the mindset of Chinese leaders. Since 1940, the Sino-Japanese front had essentially stabilized. Chiang Kai-shek was convinced that the Japanese Army in North China would limit its mission to restoring transportation and bolstering the puppet regime in order to facilitate Japan's exploitation of Chinese resources. He also expected the Japanese in South China to adopt a basically defensive posture. Only in Central China might the Japanese Army mount significant offensives to annihilate China's remaining combat units and to disrupt the government's plan to regroup and train its troops. Noting the shortage of vessels, the Chinese high command virtually rejected out of hand the idea that the Japanese might try to seize Chungking by going up the Yangtze valley.[24]

Indeed, during the early 1940s, Japanese behavior basically confirmed the validity of this analysis. Japanese forces made several halfhearted attempts to attack Chungking but quickly abandoned them for various reasons. The Japanese never expressed much serious interest in linking up the continental railways. The Chinese were also lulled into a false sense of security by the three consecutive victories they scored near Changsha. All these developments led them to the complacent conclusion that the Japanese had run out of steam and were no longer capable of mobilizing a first-rate army to pursue an ambitious goal in China.[25]

In addition, by 1944 the Chinese perceived the most important battlefields to be in Southeast Asia and the Burma-India theater, where the Japanese suffered from numerical inferiority. It defied the Chinese sense of military rationality for Japan to ignore these theaters and invest huge resources in a theater of apparently secondary importance such as North and Central China. Since the Chinese had always highly respected Japan's ability to protect its military secrets, it stretched the limits of credulity to believe that the Japanese would allow such an ultra-secret military plan to fall into French colonialist hands. The only conclusion the Chinese could draw was that the Japanese purposely fed the misinformation to the French in the hope of diverting Chinese troops from the Burma theater. Thus, there seemed all the more reason why China must not fall into the Japanese trap.[26]

This intelligence failure cost the Chinese valuable time that could have been used to set up a comprehensive defense. Instead, assuming that the Japanese attack was only designed to gain localized advantages and not to seize more Chinese territories, the Chinese high command confidently predicted that the attack would soon run out of momentum and that the Japanese would again voluntarily withdraw. Thus, even though China had about 400,000 troops in the northern provinces, many units actually yielded their positions initially without putting up a hard fight. To their surprise, however, this time the Japanese columns pressed on relentlessly and soon threw other Chinese units into utter confusion. As a result, the entire Chinese defense collapsed in just two months.

The Japanese had barely crushed the Chinese troops in Honan when they began the second phase of Ichigo and carried the fighting into Central China. Japan amassed a contingent of ten divisions under the Eleventh Army for this phase, making it the largest concentration of Japanese troops for a single campaign since the Russo-Japanese War of 1904.[27] China had 400,000 troops in this area, but most units simply melted away under the withering Japanese assault. The only fierce resistance occurred at Henyang (in Hunan Province), which was defended by the Tenth Army for forty-seven days. When the city finally fell, the Tenth Army was completely destroyed.

In September, the fighting spread to Kwangsi Province. By now, the Chinese could only muster 120,000 men for its defense, mostly from the provincial armies, which performed badly and suffered heavy losses. Finally, at Tushan (in Kweichow Province), the Chinese government unleashed all combat troops in its possession for a last-ditch defense, including five armies from the Eighth War Zone presumably used previously only for containing the Communists.[28] Luckily, Japanese logistics had become terribly overextended, and Japanese solders were suffering from mounting casualties as well as serious dietary deficiency. Here the Japanese advance was finally halted and Operation Ichigo brought to an end.

The damage inflicted upon China by Operation Ichigo cannot be overemphasized. Altogether, about one million government troops saw combat and at least 500,000 to 600,000 were lost, including some from the government's very last strategic reserves.[29] The provinces of Honan, Hunan, and Kwangsi had been the major suppliers of food and conscripts left after Pearl Harbor. Their loss in 1944 cut deeply into the Chungking government's ability to feed the civilian population and supply conscripts to its armies.

Chinese troops paid a steep price for their victory in the Burma theater in 1944. The armies from Yunnan (the Expeditionary Force) alone suffered about sixty-five thousand casualties. In many units casualties claimed two-thirds of their normal strength.[30] Chinese forces in India suffered equally heavy losses.[31] Since these were the best units left in the Chinese Army, and the ones given U.S. equipment, their losses were exceedingly detrimental to the overall military situation of the Chungking government.

The fall of these provinces also effectively cut off China's Third, Seventh, and Ninth war zones from the Chungking government and made it possible for Japan to mop up the remnants in these war zones one by one, much as it had done in North China during 1942–43. If this should occur, then the Japanese Army could conceivably obliterate all meaningful resistance in East China and would render it extremely difficult for the Allies to land troops in East China from which to launch a counterattack against Japan.

The Military Situation in 1945

In these circumstances, the Chungking government's first priority was to drive the Japanese out of Hunan and Kwangsi so that it could reestablish contact with the other war zones as soon as possible. In the spring of 1945, the Chinese reached agreement with the United States to train and equip thirty-six divisions with American assistance. This was called the Alpha Plan. Chiang also wanted to recall several units from Burma to fight within China.[32]

Meanwhile, the Allies were making rapid progress in both the Pacific War and the war as a whole. The U.S. Navy had effectively cut Japan's supply line to Southeast Asia, which brought about a sharp decline of popular morale and a worsening of the Japanese economy. As late as February 1945, Chiang was still convinced that the United States intended to land troops in Taiwan, the Ryukyu Islands, and on China's east coast in the near future. In a telegram to his commanders on February 1, 1945, he argued that China must aggressively prosecute the war in order to elevate its status in the postwar international order. He therefore urged his commanders to make every effort to train and prepare their troops for a massive counteroffensive against the Japanese within a short period of time.[33]

In the spring of 1945, the Chinese high command had begun to formulate a plan of a general counterattack against Japan, code-named "Iceman" (*ping-jen*) and "White Tower" (*pai-t'a*). It envisaged the counterattack to begin in the fall of 1945, aimed at retaking the ports along China's southwestern coast. This would then increase the quantity of supplies to the Chinese Army and Air Force and prepare them for the final assault against Japan itself.

By June 1945, Nazi Germany was defeated and the supply line from India had reached Kunming, with a monthly delivery of sixty thousand tons of war matériel into China. In addition, the Alpha Plan was moving toward completion. These forces were issued U.S. equipment, their fire-power was much improved, and the units were back to full strength. In April, the government launched a counteroffensive and recovered Kweilin and Lichou. In July and August, Chinese troops again went into combat with the goal of recapturing Canton. At this point, the United States dropped the atomic bombs and Japan quickly surrendered.[34]

The arrival of victory caught the Chinese government completely by surprise since Chinese leaders had unquestioningly accepted the American plan of winning the war against Japan on the ground. As a result, in the summer of 1945, the Chinese government had not felt an urgent need to jockey for positions for domestic reasons but was in the process of returning its troops to the positions they had lost during Operation Ichigo. Roughly, this line ran to the west of the railway between Peiping and Kweilin.

So unprepared were the Chinese for the Japanese surrender that they had trouble arranging transportation to send their advance party to meet with the Japanese to arrange for the latter's surrender. Operating under such pressure, Chungking instructed Japanese troops as well as puppet forces and local police to stay put and maintain order while Chinese government units were hastily dispatched from the interior.

The government's task was made difficult by its troop deployment policy in the second half of the war. As loyal units were strung out over the entire unoccupied areas, with many in faraway locations inaccessible by rail, the speed of their reconcentration was greatly impeded. Their transfer to the Japanese-occupied areas was further hampered by the huge numbers of refugees who were equally eager to return home and who vied with them for the limited carrying capacity of the railroads. Whereas the government's reoccupation of South China was facilitated by the Yangtze River and its tributaries, its reoccupation of North China and Manchuria was much delayed. The government's loyal units were also widely dispersed in reestablishing control in postwar China. A portion of these loyal troops were left behind to guard the Communist border areas while the bulk of them were sent to the lower Yangtze delta, a few key cities and railway junctions in North China, and eventually to Manchuria.

This represented a partial return to the prewar pattern of distribution of military power. With very few exceptions, military groups with strong local loyalties returned to their old territories. No northern troops stayed in the south, and few southern troops were sent north. The government's own loyal units gained a number of additional outposts beyond its prewar sphere of military influence, but the medium and small cities reverted to the local units, and a sizable portion of the countryside now fell into the hands of the Communists. This distribution of military power could not help but create grave implications in the forthcoming civil war.

Explaining China's Military Conduct

A comprehensive explanation of China's military conduct in the war would have to take into account many factors, including cultural values, historical legacy, economic capabilities, political conditions, and so forth. This task is beyond the scope of the present chapter. Instead, what will be attempted here is a strictly military analysis.

Effective military performance depends on several key variables. First, there must be a sound command structure capable of making rational decisions. Second, there must be efficient means of communications to transmit decisions through the chain of command and to give the commanders constant control over their units. There must also be sufficient transportation to allow the units to execute their orders in a timely fashion. Third, there must be adequate quality and quantity of weapons and supplies commensurable with the military missions. Fourth, there must be high-quality combatants on all levels able to perform their duties competently. Finally, the entire military endeavor must be guided by clear and coherent strategic thinking.

Rationality of Command Structure

Before 1937, the Chinese armies never had a unified command structure but were under the control of diverse factions with conflicting personal or geographical loyalties as well as different organizational formats. Although a national command structure was hastily established when the war broke out, many units retained their distinct characteristics, which rendered it difficult to make rational military decisions. Issues such as appointments, deployment, training programs, discipline, and distribution of weapons were often decided on political rather than military grounds.[35]

The command structure that was devised was cumbersome and inefficient. The country was divided into about a dozen war zones, but each was too big and unwieldy under the prevailing conditions of communication and transportation and proved incapable of reacting quickly to battlefield developments. Commanders of war zones as well as of combat units (armies, divisions) were often saddled with many civilian chores and responsibilities and could not give exclusive attention to their combat tasks.[36] The longer they were stationed in an area, the easier it was for them to become embroiled in local politics, which invariably dissipated the fighting spirit of the officers and men.[37]

A key weakness of the command structure was the traditional neglect of staff work. The Chinese staff never acquired the prestige and respect that their counterparts in other countries enjoyed. Staff officers were used as secretaries to perform clerical work while commanding officers planned and guided military operations.

Probably the worst example was set by the Chinese high command itself. According to the formal chain of command, the Ministry of Military Orders (Chun-ling-pu) should issue orders to the lower-level combat unit commanders, but the Generalissimo's personal office (Wei-yuan-chang shih-ts'ung-shih) often bypassed the Chun-ling-pu to issue orders directly to combat commanders. Finally, Chiang himself habitually countermanded his own staff by telephoning detailed verbal instructions directly to combat commanders. Lower-level commanders often did not know which of the conflicting orders to obey.[38] This command style, imitated by commanders on many levels, was particularly dangerous for China because commanders were poorly equipped to know the precise conditions in the battlefield. For instance, where the better-made military maps in the European theater had a scale of 1:20,000, the typical Chinese maps had a scale in excess of 1:1,000,000 and were cluttered with cartographical errors. This often led commanders to make disastrous misjudgments.[39]

Since such instructions usually skipped over wide geographical and organizational distances, they enabled lower-level commanders to engage in evasive actions or to submit false reports.[40] Such chaotic command structure and command style inevitably produced serious detrimental effects on China's combat performance.[41]

Communications and Transportation

Communications are important because commanders need to transmit orders speedily and securely to their units and to keep them under constant control. They also need good military intelligence to apprise them of the intentions and movements of their adversary. But modern communications equipment was scarce even in the best Chinese armies. Many units relied on runners to transmit information. Others used telephone lines that could easily be tapped or cut by enemy agents. Many intelligence branches of armies and army groups did not even possess wireless transmitters to send intelligence back to the headquarters.[42] The communications equipment in use suffered frequent breakdowns.

When troops were in movement, the commanders sometimes rode horses or cars, but the communications personnel and equipment had to travel on foot, thus causing commanders to lose contact with their soldiers.[43] Typically, the Chinese battlefield was marked by chaos. Commanders often did not know where their soldiers were. Troops in transit would recklessly intrude into the positions defended by other units without proper prior identification.[44]

Communications difficulties rendered it virtually impossible for large entities such as the war zones or army groups to orchestrate military operations. But even smaller units were severely strained as well. For instance, the division was treated as a strategic unit (*chan-lueh tan-wei*) during the war, yet a division was capable of defending only a front of less than twelve miles before its commander lost touch with his units due to poor communication. The combat experience of the war demonstrated a recurrent problem: many battles were lost or their victories failed to be fully exploited because of the inability of commanders to be kept informed of battlefield conditions or to transmit timely decisions.[45]

The lack of means of transportation further compounded communications difficulties by severely impeding troop mobility or restricting their strategic and tactical options. In 1944, China had only about six thousand trucks in the entire country, half of which were out of service due to shortage of parts. This was less than what a small American city would have, or less than the transport allocated to a single U.S. army. The serious shortage of fuel further reduced the utilization of motor vehicles.[46] Lack of infrastructure such as roads and bridges added to the difficulty.

Consequently, Chinese troops had to travel on foot. The slowness of troop movement at this rate greatly reduced the radius of their combat operations. It was nearly impossible for the troops to defend fixed assets (territory, population, resources) and maintain mobility at the same time. When in trouble, Chinese commanders could not realistically expect timely relief from friendly units from a distant area.

The most graphic example of how poor transportation hurt combat performance occurred in late 1944. As the crisis of Operation Ichigo deepened, the Chinese high command dispatched the Ninety-third Army from Szechwan to reinforce the Kwangsi front. But it took the army two months on the road to reach there.[47] When the Kwangsi situation continued to deteriorate and the Japanese were dashing toward Kweichow, Chiang released one of his last crack units, the Ninety-seventh Army, from garrison duty in the capital to go to the Kweichow front. Even though this was clearly a life-or-death situation, the government had no motor vehicles to spare, and this army had to transport all its equipment and supplies on foot for twenty days before reaching the front.[48] Meanwhile, the defeated troops (including T'ang En-po's units) from Honan were also ordered to reinforce the southern front. Having meandered through

Honan, Shensi, and Szechwan for nearly half a year, these troops finally arrived at Tushan in the nick of time to halt the Japanese advance, but their delay had allowed the Japanese ample time to devastate the rest of the southwest.[49]

Weaponry and Logistics

The Chinese Army suffered a decisive handicap with respect to the amount of weapons and supplies needed to sustain itself in action against a superior adversary in a war of attrition. The shortage of firepower was an endemic problem among Chinese troops. Even the better-equipped infantry units had only rifles and some light machine guns. Chinese-made weapons were usually of inferior quality. One government survey estimated that 80 percent of the hand grenades failed to explode.[50] Gun barrels would sometimes explode unpredictably. Their primitive weapons made Chinese troops helpless against enemies entrenched behind hardened fortifications, and the weapons' unreliability only further eroded the soldiers' confidence.[51]

Artillery was in short supply in the Chinese Army. According to Ch'en Ch'eng's investigation, China in 1935 had only 457 pieces of artillery in the entire army.[52] Even though some additional pieces were imported subsequently, the attrition rate was exceedingly high. By the 1940s, the blockade of China by Japan had effectively halted importation of all major weapons systems. The army lacked not only airplanes and tanks, but even heavy machine guns and grenade launchers. Sometimes an entire army group (*pin-t'uan*) had only one mortar unit (see table 1).

The scarcity of these specialized weapons often led the Chinese to remove them from the infantry units and to form special units (such as independent artillery units) to maximize their impact. But this method was actually counterproductive because of the poor coordination between the infantry and these specialized units.[53]

The lack of modern weapons placed the Chinese entirely at the mercy of their enemies. In the air, Japan's absolute superiority enabled it to bomb and strafe military and civilian targets with impunity. On the ground, Japan's extensive and indiscriminate use of poison gas terrorized Chinese soldiers while its tanks and armored vehicles condemned Chinese infantry soldiers to a position of absolute defenselessness.[54]

The Chinese Army survived the eight years of combat by using a large assortment of weapons of different calibers and designs. A tiny portion were imported from abroad, the majority were manufactured by a motley assortment of indigenous arsenals. It was rare for a single division to have weapons of the same standards. The resultant difficulty in the supply of parts and ammunition was a nightmare for commanders and rear services alike.[55]

Logistics was an underdeveloped branch of the military services in China. Before the war, it was common practice for many armies to put a single officer

Table 1

Weapons in the Chinese Army, June 1939 and December 1943

	1939	1943
Rifles	775,520	1,000,000
Machine guns	59,663	83,000
Trench mortars	4,403	7,800
Artillery pieces	910	1,300
Number of soldiers	2,600,000	over 3,000,000

Sources: "Kuo-chun ko pu-tui jen-ma wu-ch'i t'ung-chi piao," June 1939, Second Archive; Charles F. Romanus and Riley Sunderland, *Stilwell's Command Problems* (Washington, DC: Government Printing Office, 1956), p. 4.

in charge of logistics or to farm it out to a civilian manager (usually a business-man) who would guarantee to meet the army's minimum needs but would pocket the surplus.[56] After the war broke out, the rationalization of a military logistic system became a monumental challenge that was never effectively met.

On the national level, an efficient logistics network was never adequately developed, and the huge quantities of materials required by the combat units simply far exceeded the country's administrative or physical capability. The constant flux of battlefield conditions only exacerbated the difficulty of the rear services to make rational plans. Not surprisingly, logistics remained a gaping hole in the Chinese military structure throughout the war.[57]

In the field, the lack of mobility compelled the rear services to locate their supply depots deep in the rear to prevent their being seized by the enemy. This put a severe strain on combat units. Typically, a division only had enough transport capability to meet half of its needs. Since rice had to be transported to feed the soldiers, the transportation of ammunition sometimes received a lower priority. The diversion of soldiers to serve as carriers also significantly reduced the combat strength of many units.[58]

Therefore, the typical Chinese military unit spent the bulk of its time and energy simply trying to preserve its existence. It expected to have to take care of its own needs, including food, clothing, conscripts, weapons, and transportation. Fighting consumed too much energy, so fighting was done only when absolutely necessary. When sufficiently desperate, soldiers would not hesitate to pillage the very same people they were supposed to protect. This in turn provoked numerous incidents of friction between the army and the civilian population. Probably the worst case occurred in Honan during the early phase of Operation Ichigo. When the Chinese troops retreated in defeat, more soldiers were killed by the indignant local population than by the Japanese.[59]

The outbreak of the Pacific War was supposed to bring major relief to the

Chinese Army in weapons and supplies through the Lend-Lease program. But the closing of the Burma Road quickly dashed such hopes. The airlift over the Hump was so precarious that as of mid-1942 it only brought in about one hundred tons of materials to China monthly, a tiny fraction of the five thousand tons per month that the Chinese had expected.[60]

While the airlift capacity was significantly improved in 1943–44, only Chinese units in India and the Expeditionary Force earmarked for the second Burma campaign received significant amounts of U.S. equipment and ammunition. In October 1944, Chiang wrote and complained to Roosevelt that up to June 1944 no army in the interior of China had ever received so much as a single rifle or artillery piece from the Lend-Lease program, and that during June–October 1944, when China was under the withering attack of Operation Ichigo, it only received 60 mountain guns, 320 tank guns, and 506 bazookas.[61] For the most part, Lend-Lease materials reached China in quantity only in the waning months of the war.

Quality of Combatants

Probably the most crucial factor affecting China's combat performance was the quality of its officer corps. In the twentieth century, Chinese could acquire military education from either foreign or domestic military academies. The number of Chinese who had attended foreign military academies was very small.[62] On the other hand, from 1901 until 1943, all the domestic military academies taken together had graduated a grand total of only 128,058 regular students and 102,236 irregular trainees.[63] It is safe to assume, however, that the number of professionally trained officers at the outbreak of the war was substantially less than the total of the above two categories because of the toll taken by incessant civil wars between 1916 and 1936 as well as the loss of the Manchurian Army to the Japanese in 1931.

While military education continued during the war, it suffered severely from shortage of funds, equipment, facilities, and qualified instructors. Many schools rushed their cadets through with only a six-month program. Not only was there a sharp drop of quality, but many programs had trouble attaining full enrollment. The shortage of qualified officers was particularly pronounced in the special services. For example, the military schools only produced 16,000 graduates in engineering, transportation, communication, and mechanics between 1900 and 1943.[64]

In aggregate terms, in 1935 China had a total of 200,000 military officers in active service.[65] Yet once the war began, the attrition of officers accelerated quickly. Some of the best junior-grade officers in the Chinese Army were killed during the early months of the war. Still unaccustomed to the Japanese mode of attack, they relied heavily on individual valor to stem the enemy assault, and they paid with their lives. Between July 1937 and June 1940, the Chinese Army suffered 24,806 officers dead and 42,991 officers wounded.[66] This was over a third of China's officer corps at the beginning of the war.

As the war dragged on, the expanded army needed even more officers.[67] Inevitably, people with inferior qualifications were pressed into service, and large numbers were promoted from the ranks. The shortage of qualified officers for armies stationed in North China, particularly those units with strong local backgrounds, became an exceedingly grave problem because all military academies were located south of the Yangtze River, and their graduates were usually promptly snatched away by armies stationed in these provinces.[68]

While the line officers might rely on bravery and ingenuity to compensate for their deficiency in modern military knowledge, no such possibility existed on the leadership levels. The low quality of middle- and junior-grade officers was demonstrated by the fact that in 1944, only 27 percent of the 117,579 officers classified as middle and lower officers had received some form of formal academic military training. The rest either had been promoted from the ranks or came from diverse backgrounds.[69]

The poor quality of China's senior officer corps was an even more serious problem for several reasons. First, since China faced a powerful adversary employing modern weapons, it was encumbent upon Chinese senior officers to devise effective countermeasures against the enemy's aerial bombardment, artillery barrage, poison gas attacks, tank formations, and so forth. Second, since China decided to wage conventional warfare against Japan, the senior officers needed to possess the requisite skills to plan, mobilize, train, deploy, and execute large-scale operations.

Unfortunately, a substantial portion of Chinese commanding officers were not equal to these tasks. At the Northwest Military Conference (1943), the Chinese high command made a highly critical self-analysis of China's deficiencies. It concluded that the main reason for their defeat by Japan in many engagements was the Chinese commanders' inability to understand the basic principles of modern warfare. They did not know how large military units from different services should work together. They lacked the ability to maximize their combined impact but chose to fight independently and in isolation. They lacked judgment and a sense of solidarity and would stand on the sidelines while allowing friendly units to be annihilated. Many commanders were insufficiently aggressive and wanted to evade hard combat. Commanders on various levels seldom took the trouble to seek information or to verify the information they received. Instead, they simply passed the information along to the higher level, thus causing inaccurate information to become grossly distorted along the chain of command. Finally, many commanders had no concept about safeguarding military secrets, and they frequently exposed themselves or other Chinese armies to mortal danger.[70]

Chinese commanders not only could be faulted for their lack of organizational ability, professional knowledge, and military bravery, but their personal conduct and lifestyle also left much to be desired. Many lived with their families, which caused them to lose touch with their men, impeded the main troop movement, and sapped their enthusiasm for hard fighting.[71] It was not uncommon for officers to engage in gambling or commercial activities, which hardly inspired trust or respect from their subordinates and directly contributed to the decline of morale and discipline in the ranks.[72]

China paid dearly for its lack of a professional officers corps. To be sure, there were units in the Chinese Army that were led by able officers who performed their duties admirably, such as the Chinese units in India. But wherever poorly qualified officers were in charge, training programs were neglected or not conducted properly. Campaigns were poorly conceived, planned, and executed. Combat spirit was dissipated because soldiers lacked confidence in their leaders. Discipline was lax.[73] It is axiomatic that poorly trained and poorly led troops cannot fight. When such troops do fight, they suffer defeat and unnecessary casualties and become a liability to other friendly units. China's wartime military record confirms the validity of this generalization.[74]

As China's supreme military commander, Chiang's tactical foibles had been the subject of much complaint by his contemporaries and subordinates. The thought that China's combat performance might have been significantly improved under another leader certainly aroused a considerable amount of excited speculation during the war, sometimes from highly placed people, including the Americans.

The answer to this question is by no means obvious. In fact, Chiang was probably one of the few Chinese generals of his generation to have acquired some grasp of modern military science, a healthy appreciation of Western technology, and a strong commitment to the training and discipline of soldiers. Many of his contemporaries were semiliterate in military affairs and totally ignorant of international relations.

Up to 1937, Chiang was also the winningest general in the country, albeit in the fighting of civil wars. A realistic alternative to Chiang as China's wartime leader would most likely have been another military figure. But nearly all the plausible candidates, such as Li Tsung-jen, Pai Ch'ung-hsi, Yen Hsi-shan, Feng Yü-hsiang, or Li Chi-shen, had tested their generalship against Chiang and come up short. This record makes it depressing to speculate whether any of them could have done a better job in the fight against Japan.

In the ultimate analysis, China's war effort was a function of who controlled the guns. While Chiang retained control over his loyal troops throughout the Sino-Japanese conflict, both Feng and Yen lost much of their following through defections. Even the once highly cohesive forces under Li Tsung-jen and Pai Ch'ung-hsi eroded during the latter part of the war. Under these circumstances, a leadership change during the war was a moot issue.

Strategic Options

As stated earlier, a major feature of the Sino-Japanese War after Pearl Harbor was its internationalization. China's leaders wholeheartedly accepted the strategic premise that Japan's defeat would be achieved by a large-scale counterattack to be launched from mainland China, and they subsumed all military moves under this general premise. During the interim, China had hoped to maintain a stalemate against the Japanese forces until such time as sufficient quantities of Lend-Lease materials flowed into the country, facilitating the reorganization, retraining, and reequipping of the Chinese Army for the counterattack.

The Chinese expectation of fighting a "prolonged war" (*ch'ih-chiu-chan*) often fostered a passive mindset among leading commanders who believed that their primary responsibility was to survive the war, thereby vitiating their will to attack.[75] This mindset was expressed in several tactical manifestations and produced concomitant consequences. First, on a national level, the Chinese tended to deploy their troops in a widely dispersed mode to protect all territories equally, thus posing no offensive pressure against the Japanese on any particular front. In a given area, they again demonstrated the propensity to stretch their men evenly and thinly along the entire length of the front rather than using more imaginative and flexible defense formations. As a result, once a point was breached, the Japanese could easily make a dash toward the supply depot and threaten the survival of troops along the entire front.

Another factor that aggravated this problem of dispersion was Chungking's perceived need to station loyal KMT troops in areas not for the purpose of fighting the Japanese, but to guard against domestic rivals. In this respect, General Hu Tsung-nan's force in Northwest China had provoked the sharpest complaint from the Communists and became a major irritant in Sino-American relations.

The government regarded such surveillance as necessary because disloyal or discontented local troops often became the objects of Japanese agitation and subversion, resulting in a good number of them defecting to the Wang Ching-wei government. While General Hu's force was obviously in the Northwest to blockade the Communists, the less obvious but equally important purpose was to put the Muslim armies in the Northwest under surveillance. Contrary to popular impressions, General Hu's force was neither the only one nor the best equipped one in the Chinese Army to perform this task. Other loyal units performed similar tasks, albeit with more subtlety. Nonetheless, they represented a significant diversion from the combat resources that China could ill afford during the war.

Third, when they went into action, they preferred to invest their forces incrementally rather than in large concentrations. If the Chinese had employed their troops in large masses, they might have stopped the Japanese advance during the first phase of Operation Ichigo. Instead, the troops were deployed in small numbers and were soundly beaten in a piecemeal fashion. Even in campaigns where the Chinese enjoyed absolute superiority, this mode denied them the opportunity to achieve decisive results.[76]

Finally, when they came under attack by the Japanese, they were expected to defend their positions to the death with little hope of receiving reinforcements. But since discipline was not always rigidly enforced, and since self-preservation was a paramount concern for many warlord armies, units in such untenable situations would more likely choose to run than to stay and fight to the finish. By and large, the Chinese had given up the initiative on the battlefield and were content to maintain a reactive posture vis-à-vis the invaders.

Due to the internationalization of the conflict, however, the Japanese would neither accommodate China's wish to nurse its wounds nor allow China the leisure to train its army. Therefore, the Japanese mounted attacks against different parts of China whenever it suited their own needs to do so. Operation Ichigo probably provides the best example of the connection between the China theater and the global conflict. The primary motivation for this offensive was to salvage Japan's own rapidly deteriorating situation throughout Southeast Asia irrespective of China's military policies.

China's tragedy was that it possessed neither the means to expel the Japanese singlehandedly nor the political and military influence to shape the Allies' grand strategy. In the 1940s, the gap between the official strategic doctrine and actual developments in the China theater had widened. The Changsha campaign and the East China campaign of 1942 and Operation Ichigo of 1944 were all prompted by events beyond China's borders. In 1944, the Chinese expressed great reluctance to enter the second Burma campaign, but to no avail. Even though Allied strategic thinking had begun to shift from continental counterattack to island hopping as early as 1943, the Chinese were not aware of this shift. Yet, in late 1944, Stilwell not only was ready to impose his strategic convictions upon the Chinese government but also wanted to take over the command of its troops as well. Gradually, the Sino-Japanese War had become a sideshow. Important decisions affecting China's interests were being made elsewhere, and the ability of the Chinese leaders to control their own destiny was progressively eroded.

General Assessment and Conclusion

How should one evaluate China's wartime record as a whole? China's modern history has been almost inseparable from its struggles against foreign imperialism, so it stands to reason that one must put the Sino-Japanese War into a broader historical perspective. By comparing it with two previous historical landmarks in the span of one hundred years, the true significance of this war can be appreciated more objectively.

The Opium War of 1839–41 was the first major confrontation between China and Great Britain, the most powerful imperialist country of the time. Although the war nominally lasted some twenty-six months (June 1840–August 1842), actual fighting occurred only intermittently. The British employed fewer than ten thousand troops and a fleet of twenty-five warships. The British expeditionary force started the war by attacking Canton and moved northward along the coast to make demonstrative attacks against Amoy (Fukien), Tinghai (Chekiang), and Wusung (Kiangsu). They also made a feint toward the imperial capital. The British troops never attempted to penetrate the hinterland or even to occupy large territories along the coast. Instead, they drove directly toward the nerve center of the Chinese body politic and brought the Manchu empire to its knees. The Opium War exposed the utter impotence of China, which proved quite incapable of organizing its resources to wage a war against a highly mobile enemy. China was like an oyster—once its shell was breached at a few places, the entire body became completely vulnerable, and the Manchus were forced to sue for peace on extremely humiliating terms.[77]

In 1894, China fought a war against Japan, which was then rapidly developing into the strongest land and naval power in East Asia. This war was even shorter (it lasted only nine months, from July 1894 to April 1895) and left the entire southern and eastern parts of China untouched. Japan employed two armies and a fleet of about twenty-one ships, and it adopted nearly a straight line of attack from its homeland through the Korean peninsula to Talien (Port Arthur) in Manchuria, again pointing toward the Chinese imperial capital. At this point, the Manchus hastily sought peace.[78]

These two nineteenth-century wars, although separated by more than fifty years, revealed China's extremely limited capability to organize and mobilize human and physical resources for a large-scale resistance against a modern adversary. Once the capital, the country's nerve-center, was threatened, the entire resistance crumbled and the country quickly capitulated.

Against this historical background, China's conduct during the second Sino-Japanese War must be considered a very impressive accomplishment. By the 1930s, Japan had grown from a regional power into a world power with highly efficient air, naval, and land forces. The strength of this military machine was convincingly demonstrated both by its flawless execution of the surprise attack against Pearl Harbor and by its lightning destruction of all Western forces throughout Southeast Asia. Indeed, Japan's military leaders had confidently hoped that with only fifteen divisions they could crush China in just three months.

Instead, the second Sino-Japanese War lasted ninety-seven months, longer than the sum total of all wars China had ever fought on its own soil against foreign invaders since the beginning of the nineteenth century. Compared to the previous occasions, China's ability to organize its resources was greatly improved. It conscripted some fourteen million young men into military services, and additional tens of millions of civilians into military construction projects. As more provinces fell into enemy hands, the conscripts had to come from fewer and fewer provinces. Toward the latter part of the war, Szechwan's annual contribution was close to half a million, or about one-third of the national total. Hunan was a close second, with an annual contribution of about a quarter million men.[79] Grain had to be collected to feed over six million soldiers and government employees. In meeting these needs, China's organizational and administrative capabilities were stretched to the breaking point. Inefficiency was always present, but cynicism and corruption also became prevalent in the latter years of the war. Nonetheless, the whole nation remained defiant and persevered to the bitter end.

The war entailed eight years of incessant fighting. As table 2 shows, in six of the eight years, China sent more than one hundred divisions into action. There is no doubt that the nation was exhausted during the second half of the war, as reflected by an appreciable drop in the number of divisions in combat. Yet, after 1942, the level of fighting increased again. The data further indicate that the level of participation by armies considered loyal to the Nationalist party and Chiang personally was maintained throughout the war. Four out of every ten Chinese divisions sent into a campaign belonged to the Nationalists' hard core. In fact, the Japanese often targeted them for destruction. Although the Chinese Army suffered terrible losses in 1944, it demonstrated a renewed determination in 1945 to regain the initiative in the battlefield from the enemy.

The honor of the Chinese Army was redeemed by several valiant performances. The Shanghai campaign signaled China's determination to sacrifice its most modern city with its industrial and financial assets in order to resist an invasion. The battle of Taierchuang and the three Changsha battles showed the Chinese combat spirit and their ability to deliver repeated blows to the enemy even under extremely unfavorable conditions. Finally, the second Burma campaign left no doubt that if given proper training, sufficient weapons, logistic support, and medical attention, the Chinese soldiers were on a par with the best fighting men in the world.

The war further revealed China's enormous capacity to endure pain and injury

Table 2

Numbers of Divisions in Combat by Year

Year	KMT	Others	Total	Percent KMT
1937	89	164	253	0.35
1938	80	119	199	0.40
1939	130	173	303	0.43
1940	17	42	59	0.29
1941	90	145	235	0.38
Total 1937–41	406	643	1,049	0.39
1942	34	32	66	0.52
1943	71	93	164	0.43
1944	61	78	139	0.44
1945	44	87	131	0.34
Total 1942–45	210	290	500	0.42

Source: "Chung-Jih chan-cheng lu-chun ko pu-tui ts'an-chia chan-i i-lan-piao," April 30, 1948, Second Archive.

that surprised both the enemy and the Chinese themselves. In all, twenty-one provinces fell into enemy hands. The country lost over three million soldiers in combat, and an additional eighteen million civilians as casualties of the war.[80] The war also created ninety-five million refugees. In the areas invaded by the Japanese Army, a quarter of the population was uprooted from their homes and became refugees. In the provinces where fierce battles were repeatedly fought (e.g., Hupeh, Hunan, Honan, and Shansi), over 40 percent of the population became refugees (see table 3).[81] Needless to say, this huge refugee population severely taxed the government's ability to provide relief.

The loss of properties was the most difficult to calculate. Shortly after the war, the Nationalist government formed a special investigative commission (the Wartime Losses Investigative Commission, or K'ang-chan Sun-shih Tiao-ch'a Wei-yuan-hui) to collect data on wartime property losses. Because of the enormous administrative difficulty involved, the commission was never able to issue a definitive report, but it published preliminary findings periodically as new data were made available. Its sixth interim report released in January 1946 suggested that the losses from certain, but not all, categories of properties amounted (in August 1945 Chinese dollars) to $372,348 billion.[82] More recently, the Chinese Communists estimated that wartime property losses were in excess of U.S. $100 billion dollars.[83]

China lost its capital and all the rich and developed coastal provinces to the enemy during the early months of the war. The saga of how the Chinese shifted their capital and transported what could be salvaged of their industries to the hinterland is sufficiently well-known to need no recounting here. After 1938–39, China basically waged a resistance war from the most backward areas in the country.

In the years since the end of the Sino-Japanese War, historians and political scientists have offered very diverse, often conflicting, judgments on China's performance. The controversy has been fueled both by honest scholarly differences and by partisan considerations. Among the specific points of contention are whether the Nationalist government prosecuted the war in earnest and with commitment, whether the Nationalists or the Communists made a greater contribution to the fighting, whether China would have fared better by adopting the strategies of guerrilla warfare, and whether the Nationalists adopted the best strategy under the circumstances.

One must not let these controversies divert one's attention from an incontrovertible conclusion about China's wartime performance. Confronting a mortal threat during 1937–45, under the most difficult of circumstances, the nation pulled through. Even under the Nationalist government, and plagued by multiple handicaps, China proved to be a formidable foe. It tied down over a million and a half Japanese soldiers, stood up to countless blows, and exacted an exceedingly high toll from the enemy.

For over fifty years since the Meiji Restoration, Japan's national leaders

Table 3

Wartime Refugees and Homeless People, 1937–45

Province or city	Number of refugees	Percentage of total population
Kiangsu	12,502,633	34.83
Nanking	335,634	32.90
Shanghai	531,431	13.80
Chekiang	5,185,210	23.90
Anhwei	2,688,242	12.23
Kiangsi	1,360,045	9.55
Hupeh	7,690,000	30.13
Wuhan	534,040	43.56
Hunan	13,073,209	42.73
Fukien	1,065,469	9.25
Kwangtung	4,280,266	13.76
Kwangsi	2,562,400	20.37
Hopeh	6,774,000	23.99
Peiping	400,000	15.45
Tientsin	200,000	10.00
Shantung	11,760,644	30.71
Honan	14,533,200	43.49
Shansi	4,753,842	41.06
Manchuria	4,297,100	12.12
Suiyuan	695,715	38.20
Chahar	225,673	11.08
Total	95,448,771	26.17

Source: Shan-hou-chiu-chi tsung-shu, comp., "Nan-min chi liu-li jen-min tsung-shu piao," January 1946, Second Archive.

had been obsessed with the potential of expansion on the Asian continent. At the same time, many other powers also entertained schemes of partitioning China or acquiring separate spheres of influence. China's performance in the war sent a clear message to Japan and other potential adversaries that China could become a quagmire even for the strongest possible invaders. In this sense, the single most significant accomplishment of China's war record is that it fundamentally transformed its image, rekindled national pride and confidence, and furnished a new foundation for China's national security in the postwar era.

Notes

1. Hsueh Yueh telegram, January 30, 1942, quoted in *K'ang-Jih chan-cheng cheng-mien chan-ch'ang* (Nanking: Second Archival Center ["Second Archive"], 1987), 2:1144. Hereafter cited as *K'ang-Jih chan-cheng.*
2. Jih-pen fang-wei-ting fang-wei yen-chiu-suo chan-shih-shih, *Ch'ang-sha tso-chan,* p. 141.

3. Ibid., p. 158.

4. Ibid., pp. 213–14; Kuo-min cheng-fu chun-ling-pu chan-shih-hui tang-an, "San-tz'u Chang-sha hui-chan Hsueh Yueh chih chun-shih wen-tien," Second Archive.

5. Hsueh Yueh telegram, January 30, 1941, quoted in *K'ang-Jih chan-cheng*, 2:1158–60.

6. There is an immense literature in English on the Burma campaign. There is also a rich collection of original telegrams between the Chungking government and its generals in the field, which are included in "Kuo-min-cheng-fu chun-ling-pu chan-shih-hui tang-an" at the Second Archive. Also see Tu Yu-ming, "Chung-kuo yuan-cheng-chun ju Mien tui Jih tso-chan shu-lueh, in *Wen-shih tzu-liao hsuan-chi*, 8:37.

7. Chang Hsien-wen, ed., *K'ang-Jih chan-cheng ti cheng-mien chan-ch'ang* (N.P.: Honan jen-min ch'u-pan-she, 1987), pp. 279–80.

8. Chiang Kai-shek's Confidential File, quoted in *Chung-hua min-kuo chung-yao shih-liao ch'u-pien—tui Jih k'ang-chan shih-ch'i* (Taipei: Kuo-min-tang tang-shih wei-yuan-hui, 1981), 3:325. Hereafter cited as *Important Historical Sources*.

9. Ibid., 3:225.

10. Stilwell argued that Burma was more important to China than to Britain because Britain wanted to defend Burma only to protect India while China depended on Burma to keep its lifeline with the outside world. He believed that only a Chinese commitment could keep the British forces fighting in Burma. Ibid., 3:237.

11. Ibid., 3:243–51.

12. Ibid., 3:255–58.

13. Ibid., 3:284–88.

14. *Chao-ho shih-ch'i, shi-pa (1942, 1943) nien ti Chung-kuo p'ai-ch'ien-chun*, 1:138, 170, 172, 186, 188.

15. *Important Historical Sources*, 3:357.

16. Stilwell's report to Chiang Kai-shek, November 6, 1943, quoted in ibid., 3:415–17.

17. Chiang's telegram, quoted in ibid., 3:4440–41.

18. Ibid., 3:535–48. A large number of materials also exist at the Second Archive, Nanking. See, for example, "Ko-tz'u chan-i ti-wo shang-wang sun-shih fu-hu t'ung-chi piao, 1938–1945."

19. For a fuller treatment of this connection, see Hsi-sheng Ch'i, *Nationalist China at War: Military Defeats and Political Collapse, 1937–1945* (Ann Arbor: University of Michigan Press, 1982), pp. 70–74.

20. Jih-pen fang-wei-ting, fang-wei yen-chiu-suo chan-shih-shih, *Yi-hao tso-chan chih-i, Ho-nan hui-chan*, 1:26–27.

21. In connection with preparations, the Japanese rerouted the Yellow River, expanded the airfields, diverted railroad stocks from auxiliary lines to extend the main lines along the Peiping-Hankow railway, and repaired the railway bridge across the Yellow River. In addition to the troops, they mobilized 100,000 horses, 1,500 pieces of artillery, and 15,000 motor vehicles for this campaign, yet the Chinese intelligence failed to uncover any unusual military movements by Japan in China. The Japanese also circulated the explanation that their military activities were only designed to reopen the Peiping-Hankow railway to "substitute for the difficult navigation along the Yangtze River." See military intelligence analyses by the Chun-ling-pu in "Chun-shih wei-yuan-hui sa-san-nien chih-tao pu-shu wen-tien," Second Archive.

22. Kuo-min cheng-fu chun-ling-pu chan-shih-hui tang-an, "Ti erh-shih-pa chi-t'uan-chun chung-yuan hui-chan chan-tou hsiang-pao," Second Archive.

23. "Chun-shih wei-yuan-hui sa-san-nien chih-tao pu-shu wen-tien," Second Archive.

24. Staff meeting of the Chun-ling-pu's First Bureau, June 19, 1940, in "Chun-ling-pu ti-i t'ing mu-liao hui-i," Second Archive.

25. *K'ang-Jih chan-cheng*, 2:1172–73.

26. "Chun-shih wei-yuan-hui sa-san-nien chih-tao pu-shu wen-tien," Second Archive.

27. Jih-pen fang-wei-t'ing fang-wei yen-chiu-suo chan-shih-shih, *Yi-hao tso-chan chih-erh, Hu-nan hui-chan*, 1:37.

28. Kuo-min cheng-fu chun-ling-pu chan-shih-hui tang-an, "Kui-Liu hui-chan chan-tou yao-pao," Second Archive.

29. *K'ang-Jih chan-cheng ti cheng*, p. 363.

30. Kuo-min cheng-fu chun-ling-pu chan-shih-hui tang-an, "Yuan-cheng-chun ssu-ling chang-kuan-pu so-shu ko chan-lueh pu-tui ko chan-i shang-wang kuan-pin lo-ma t'ung-chi piao," "Kuan-yu Yuan-cheng-chun shih-yung chi i-chien, February 27, 1944, chun-wei-hui ti-erh-t'ing," Second Archive.

31. *K'ang-Jih chan-cheng*, 2:1473–74.

32. Remarks by Chiang Kai-shek to Mountbatten, March 8–9, 1944, quoted in *Important Historical Sources*, 3:464–68.

33. "Chun-wei-hui i-chiu-ssu-wu nien chi-tao pu-shu wen-tien," Second Archive.

34. *Important Historical Sources*, 3:597–602.

35. For a description of the government's effort not to offend the local or warlord forces, see the Chun-ling-pu report, January 10, 1942, in "Ko-tz'u chan-i ti-wo shang-wang sun-shih fu-hu t'ung-chi piao," Second Archive. For a description of the government's preferential treatment of loyal troops, see "Yuan-cheng-chun chan-hou pien-pin chi Mei-chieh pu-ch'ung ch'in-hsing," Second Archive.

36. For the example of Ch'en Ch'eng, see "Ch'en Ch'eng ssu-jen hui-i tzu-liao (1935–1944), part 2, *Min-kuo tang-an*, no. 2 (May 1987): 19–20. Hereafter cited as "Ch'en Ch'eng."

37. "Tsung-ku-wen yen-chiang chi-yao chi chien-yi," Second Archive. Hereafter cited as "Tsung-ku-wen yen-chiang."

38. Ibid.

39. Ibid.

40. For a good illustration of this, see *K'ang-Jih chan-cheng*, 2:1179–87.

41. For a personal account and complaint about these problems by Ch'en Ch'eng, see "Ch'en Ch'eng," pp. 19–20.

42. "Nan-yu ti-ssu-tz'u hui-i chun-ling-lei t'i-an," 1944, Second Archive.

43. *K'ang-Jih chan-cheng*, 2:1339.

44. "Nan-yu ti-ssu-tz'u hui-i chun-ling-lei t'i-an," 1944, Second Archive.

45. "Liu-chou hui-i chun-cheng-tsu t'i-an sheng-ch'a piao," 1940, Second Archive.

46. "Chiang Kai-shek yu Na-erh-sun [Donald Nelson] hui-t'an chi-lu, September 19, 1944, *Min-kuo tang-an*, no. 3 (August 1987): 62.

47. *K'ang-Jih chan-cheng ti cheng*, p. 353.

48. Ibid., p. 360.

49. Ibid., pp. 361–62.

50. Tu Yung-ling, "Pa-nien k'ang-chan lai chan-lueh chan-shu chih tsung-chien-t'ao," Second Archive.

51. "Liu-chou hui-i chun-cheng-tsu t'i-an sheng-ch'a piao," 1940, Second Archive.

52. "Ch'en Ch'eng," part 1, *Min-kuo tang-an*, no. 1 (February 1987): 10.

53. "Tsung-ku-wen yen-chiang."

54. "Liu-chou hui-i chun-cheng-tsu t'i-an sheng-ch'a piao," 1940, Second Archive.

55. *K'ang-Jih chan-cheng:* "Erh-shih-pa-nien t'ung-chi kung-shih," p. 17; Arthur Young, *China and the Helping Hand* (Cambridge: Harvard University Press, 1963), pp. 22, 125.

56. "Ch'en Ch'eng," part 1, p. 10.

57. "Liu-chou hui-i chun-cheng-tsu t'i-an sheng-ch'a piao," 1940, Second Archive.

58. Ibid.

59. *K'ang-Jih chan-cheng*, 2:1253.

60. *Important Historical Sources*, p. 570.

61. Chiang's letter to Roosevelt, October 9, 1944, in ibid., pp. 531–32.

62. Up to 1937, only 2,109 Chinese had graduated from foreign military schools, of which 1,874 had graduated from Japanese military schools. See "Chun-shih wei-yuan-hui chun-hsun-pu Chung-hua min-kuo san-shih-san nien t'ung-chi nien-chien," 1945, Second Archive, p. 244.

63. According to another report, between 1912 and 1937, all military schools in China except the Huang-p'u (Whampoa) had produced merely 33,015 graduates. The three largest schools in this group included Paoting with 6,561 graduates, Tungpei with 7,520, and Yunnan with 5,593. But none of these schools was noted for the quality of its instruction. The Whampoa and Central Officers' Academy were the largest producers of officers in modern Chinese history and had much better instructional programs. Both reports are in "Chun-wei-hui chun-hsun-pu i-chiu-ssu-san nien pien-yin chih t'ung-chi hui-k'an," 1943, Second Archive.

64. Ibid.

65. "Ch'en Ch'eng," part 1, p. 10.

66. Chun-cheng-pu, comp., "Kuo-chun k'ang-chan kuan-ping shang-wang t'ung-chi piao," June 1940, Second Archive.

67. Even in a relatively quiet year like 1940, the Chinese Army was short 54,000 officers. In 1944, China had 255,856 officers in active service. They in turn commanded a total of 4,178,510 soldiers. "Ch'uan-kuo lu-chun ko-pu-tui pien-chih kuan-ping shu-liang t'ung-chi piao," Second Archive.

68. "Chun-shih wei-yuan-hui chun-hsun-pu yeh-wu pao-kao," September 1939, Second Archive.

69. "Chun-shih wei-yuan-hui chun-hsun-pu Chung-hua min-kuo san-shih-san nien t'ung-chi nien-chien," 1945, Second Archive, p. 42. See also "Liu-chou hui-i chun-cheng-tsu t'i-an sheng-ch'a piao," 1940, Second Archive.

70. "Hsi-pei chun-shih hui-i paokao shu," 1943, Second Archive.

71. Kuo-min cheng-fu chun-ling-pu kan-shih-hui tang-an, "Ti-san-ch'an-ch'u Che-Kan chan-yu tso-chan chin-nien chiao-hsun chi chien-t'ao," November 21, 1942; "Chang Chih-chung kei Ho Ying-ch'in hsin," July 3, 1942; "Wang Yao-wu chih Chiang Chieh-shih tien," May 6, 1942, all in Second Archives.

72. In General Stilwell's assessment, the company commanders were good, battalion and regiment commanders were of uneven quality, but high-ranking officers were disappointing. See *Important Historical Sources*, 3:322–23.

73. For an authoritative account, see Ch'en Ch'eng's report of his inspection of the Chinese Expeditionary Force in 1943, in "Ch'en Ch'eng," part 2, p. 32. It should be noted that this force was composed of some of the better armies in China.

74. Ibid., pp. 19–20.

75. "Tsung-ku-wen yen-chiang."

76. Tu, "Pa-nien k'ang-chan."

77. *Chung-kuo chun-shih-shih* (Peking: Chieh-fang-chun ch'u-pan-she, 1986), 4:582–88. See also Hsin-pao Chang, *Commissioner Lin and the Opium War* (Cambridge: Harvard University Press, 1964).

78. *Chung-kuo chun-shih-shih*, 4:683–92; Immanuel C. Y. Hsu, *The Rise of Modern China* (New York: Oxford University Press, 1970), pp. 404–7.

79. "K'ang-chan ch'i-chien ko-sheng cheng-mu chuang-ting t'ung-chi piao," Second Archives.

80. Sung Shih-lun, "Pu-k'o mo-mieh ti li-shih kung-hsien," *Jen-min jih-pao*, August 31, 1985.

81. Shan-hou-chiu-chi tsung-shu, comp., "Nan-min chi liu-li jen-min tsung-shu piao," January 1946, Second Archive.

82. Wartime Losses Investigation Commission, comp., "Ti-liu-tz'u ch'uan-kuo ts'ai-ts'an sun-shih t'ung-chi piao," January 28, 1946, Second Archive.

83. Sung, "Pu-k'o mo-mieh ti li-shih kung-hsien."

8

THE CHINESE WAR ECONOMY

William C. Kirby

NO ONE knows precisely the amount of the losses suffered by the Chinese economy as a result of the war of 1937–45, but there is no doubt that they were staggering. Between fifteen and twenty million Chinese perished. China's initially small industrial output shrunk even further. In agriculture, the war intensified an already serious agrarian crisis. China's currency became increasingly worthless.

Industrial losses are the ones that have been most carefully measured, and it is clear that China's emerging modern sector was substantially worse off in 1946 than it had been in 1937. In Shanghai, the prewar center of China's modern economy, the first two years of the war witnessed the destruction of over 50 percent of Chinese industries. In the Wuhsi and Nanking regions, the damage ranged from 64 to 80 percent. In 1945–46, when the Nationalist government took control of nearly 70 percent of China's total industrial capital, it found that wartime damage or losses to these publicly owned assets reached 55 percent of industrial and mining assets, 72 percent of shipping, and 96 percent of railroads. In 1946, coal production in China (including Manchuria) was less than one-third its prewar peak and one-fifth the wartime peak production. Mines had been looted, flooded, or destroyed toward the end of the war, and they suffered from deferred maintenance. Mining of antimony and tungsten, China's chief export metals and major revenue earners for prewar government industrial investment, had ceased altogether in 1944. Total economic losses to Chinese mines, industries, transportation, and communications were estimated at U.S. $1.08 billion. (All figures given are in U.S. dollars.)

Of a prewar foreign investment in China of about $3.5 billion, an estimated $800 million was lost during the first two years of the war. To this figure must be added wartime damage estimated at $30 million to industries on Taiwan, and the colossal theft of plant equipment valued at up to $900 million in Manchuria in the immediate aftermath of the war, with production losses and replacement costs estimated at $2 billion. To give specific examples: the Manchurian iron and steel industry was expected to produce only 30,000 tons of pig iron in 1947, in comparison to 2.5 million tons in the peak year under Japanese rule; of fifteen cement plants in Northeast China, only two were in working condition.[1]

Damage to the agricultural sector, which in the prewar years had accounted for about 65 percent of China's total net domestic product, is more difficult to measure but clearly was substantial. The war was fought mainly by farmers who, along with their families, were its primary casualties. Wartime conscription withdrew farmers from the fields and permitted previously unimaginable labor shortages to develop at planting and harvest time. (No one really knows how many Chinese were under arms during the war. Estimates for Nationalist-held territories alone range from 3.5 to over 6 million men at any one time. Farmers also provided the vast majority of laborers, numbering several million, who were conscripted for airfield, road, and other construction.)[2] In Szechwan, the fact that the farm labor costs rose more quickly than crop prices forced many farms to reduce the acreage sown. Conscription was not limited to human beings but included the requisition of livestock, tools, and the critical means of transporting harvests—farmers' carts. When these conditions, together with increased grain taxes to feed the swollen armies, were combined with regional natural disasters, it meant starvation, as in the terrible Honan famine of 1942–43. By 1943, rice production had declined 16 percent from the 1931–37 average in Nationalist-held provinces, which also had to feed several million refugees from Japanese-held territory. In large parts of China, crop yields remained lower in 1949 than they had been in 1937.[3]

The war was a direct cause of the postwar crises in industry and agriculture. In a similar fashion, it set the stage for the total collapse of China's currency in one of the great monetary inflations of world history. In Nationalist territory, retail prices rose more than 230 percent annually in 1942–45; in occupied East China, inflation was even more severe after 1943. In both areas, inflation was spiraling out of control by the end of the war in 1945. During and after the war, inflation made hoarding and speculation more attractive than investment in productive activity.

Beyond its economic toll, the Chinese inflation of the 1940s had devastating political consequences for the regime. Its burdens were borne disproportionately by groups whose loyalty (or, at a minimum, nonopposition) was essential to the government—the military, the bureaucracy, and the intelligentsia. As Lloyd Eastman has put it, "Like leukaemic blood, the depreciated currency of the Nationalist government flowed through the body politic, enfeebling the entire organism—the army, government, economy, and society generally."[4] The great inflation contributed as much as any other factor to the political and military malaise that so undermined the self-confidence and, ultimately, the legitimacy of Nationalist rule.

The Nationalist defeat at the hands of the Communists just four years after Japan's surrender may have been the most important economic consequence of the war. Beyond that, however, the war, and the way China's economic resources were mobilized to fight it, had a profound impact on the nature of the

Nationalist regime, the balance of forces within it, and its approach to the challenges it faced during the war and after. By analyzing the Chinese war economy, one can gain a fuller understanding of the wartime transformation of Nationalist rule and grasp the legacy of the war economy for the later People's Republic and the Republic of China on Taiwan.

This chapter focuses on the war economy of Free China —the territory controlled by the Chinese government—and of the consequences of this war economy. The full economic history of wartime China, including the economies of occupied and Communist-held territories, can only be written when much more in the way of statistical evidence and documentary sources from all wartime Chinese regimes becomes available. Still, if the war itself can fairly be described as "the most momentous event in the history of the Republican era in China,"[5] the war economy of the Chinese government is an important chapter in the history of Chinese economic organization in the twentieth century.

The Prewar War Economy, 1932–37

As was the case with all the other major belligerents in World War II, important features of China's war economy predated the war.[6] The Nationalists had come to power in 1927 committed to the planned, rapid industrialization of China, aided by large-scale Western investment, along lines set down by Sun Yat-sen. Sun's proposals assumed an era of peace and growing prosperity, both domestically and internationally, in which China would be an essential market for European and American industrial overcapacity in the aftermath of World War I.[7] But civil wars followed by global economic depression retarded economic progress in the early years of Nationalist China. By 1932, as Japan's strategic threat to China intensified, economic development policy became increasingly militarized, in anticipation of a coming war.

In military and economic policies, as well as in bureaucratic organization, China's prewar preparations during 1933–37 bore some resemblance to the war it actually fought from 1937 to 1945. Such was the disparity in military power between China and Japan that China aimed for survival, not victory, in a protracted struggle of endurance. By 1934 it was clear that North China would be sacrificed in the event of a Japanese attack, while the government would devote nearly all its resources to the defense of the Yangtze region between Shanghai and Wuhan and the south-central provinces of Kiangsi and Hunan.[8] If the Shanghai-Nanking region fell, the government would "trade space for time," retreating to Wuhan and, if necessary, beyond.[9]

Economic policy increasingly followed military imperatives after 1932, with the aim of creating the industrial capacity to fight a modern war. The greatest concentration of planning and resources was devoted to the concept of a defensible military-economic bastion in China's interior, away from the militarily vulnerable coastal regions. A series of state industrial enterprises began to be constructed in Hunan and Kiangsi, and, to a lesser degree, in Szechwan for the production of steel, heavy machinery, and electrical equipment. Government arsenals underwent significant modernization and expansion, with new construction concentrated in the same geographical area. At the same time, construction began on China's first truck and aircraft assembly plants, and a major expansion of the national rail network was undertaken to service this "new economic center."[10]

Although an ultimate aim of prewar preparation was to render China self-sufficient eventually in military-economic terms, the government needed—as it would during the war as well—significant foreign economic and technical assistance to develop its capacity for war. This took several forms. The importance of a foreign military advisers group was demonstrated by the German military mission from 1928 to 1938. This was followed during the war by Soviet and American missions. The government imported machinery and armaments as well as advisers, primarily from the nation with which it had the closest military advisory relationship at any given time. It made extensive use of foreign technical assistance in the development of its war industries, ranging from the employment of Krupp and I. G. Farben technicians in the mid-1930s to the sizable American War Production mission in the 1940s. Both before and during the war, the government paid for imported talent and material primarily through barter and credit arrangements, with Chinese repayment normally taking the form of the export of Chinese strategic materials (tungsten, antimony, tin, and molybdenum), the mining of which was controlled by government monopoly and became an essential part of China's military-economic efforts. Thus, to a certain degree, there developed a symbiotic relationship between the war economies of China and its foreign partners.[11]

To coordinate military-economic efforts, the prewar government founded an organization that would ultimately manage the wartime economy to a considerable degree. The National Defense Planning Commission (Kuo-fang She-chi Wei-yuan-hui) was formed in 1932 under the General Staff to provide civilian expertise in the planning of basic industries and economic mobilization.[12] Known after 1935 as the National Resources Commission (NRC, Tzu-yuan Wei-yuan-hui) of the National Military Council, the most powerful arm of government, it evolved into a secret ministry of industry and planning, staffed primarily by academic scientists and engineers, mostly trained abroad, whose aim it was to design the foundations of a Chinese "national defense economy" (kuo-fang ching-chi). It oversaw the industrial and mining efforts described above and, after the outbreak of war, emerged as the leading agency for planning the war economy and China's postwar economic agenda.

The domestic political implications of the growth of this body were considerable. The militarization of economic policy demanded, paradoxically, growing civilian presence in government. The economic incompetence of the early Nationalist regime, which may fairly be described as a combined military-party (Kuomintang) dictatorship with a dearth of technical talent, was widely recognized by 1932. Academic critics of the regime urged the government to make better use of specialized talent and, in the intellectual fashion of the 1930s, called for "scientific management" of the nation's economic resources both for national defense and economic development. The geologist Ting Wen-chiang was perhaps the most influential proponent of a "new model" (hsin-shih) developmental dictatorship, in which the political leadership would rely heavily on "scientific" government planners with international experience and vision, organized in a highly educated and trained bureaucracy.[13] Ting was instrumental in the founding of the National Defense Planning Commission, which was headed by his colleague Weng Wen-hao. By 1936, although the central military apparatus under Chiang Kai-shek still dominated political decision making, it had recruited for leading government positions (e.g. in the so-called cabinet of talent of December 1935) many of China's most gifted intellectuals and scientists who, like the majority of patriotic Chinese, were consumed with the scope of the Japanese threat.

In the process, the role of government gradually expanded both at the expense of the KMT, whose role in policy making had never been adequately defined, and, more important in the context of this chapter, at the expense of the private sector of China's economy. Defense industry planning during the years 1933–37 was based on the assumption that China's survival and progress as a nation depended upon the institution of state-led, import-substituting, military-related, heavy industrial development. The planned "national defense economy" was to be entirely state-owned and state-managed, as the first step toward a "controlled" (t'ung-chih) economy in which private and foreign investment would be regulated according to national priorities. Thus, although technology transfer from advanced Western nations was essential to the creation of defense industries, the foreign role would take the form of technical assistance agreements, not equity ownership. Private Chinese capital was to have no role whatsoever. Although unfinished at the time the war broke out, the new military-industrial enterprises of the prewar period (e.g., Central Steel Works, Central Machine Works, Central Electrical Manufacturing Works) marked a step in the direction of central government control over industrial and technological development, which during the late Ch'ing and early Republican periods had occurred largely under private, provincial, or foreign auspices.[14]

In the mid-1930s, then, China was preparing economically as well as militarily for war with Japan. It was understood, however, that a "danger zone," lasting perhaps to 1940, had to be traversed before Chinese military and industrial strength could pose an unacceptable risk for Japan.[15] China had barely entered this hazardous period when full-scale hostilities broke out in the summer of 1937.

The Great Migration, 1937–39

With the onset of war, the Chinese government implemented its prewar military strategy—abandoning North China, forcing the fight to the Yangtze region, and, as necessary, "trading space for time." It had never anticipated, however, trading so much space in so short a time as proved necessary in 1937–38. In a similar fashion, the economic policy of developing defense industries in the interior was followed throughout the war, but what constituted the "interior" underwent drastic revision. By the end of 1938, it was clear that the still unfinished enterprises of the "new economic center" of Hunan and Kiangsi could not be defended against Japanese air attacks. Several of the major projects already begun, such as the Central Steel Works, were abandoned in the final stages of construction. Others, such as the Central Copper Works, Central Electrical Manufacturing Works, Central Automobile Construction Works, and Central Machine Works, were completed in more modest versions in new locations in southwestern China.[16] The timing of the war undermined the financial basis of these enterprises, the imported equipment of which was being paid for largely by strategic ore exports, which were now redirected toward emergency armaments purchases.

Even before it was clear that the government's internal migration would take it as far as Szechwan, the Industrial and Mining Adjustment Administration (Kung-k'uang Tiao-cheng Ch'u) made a major effort to relocate coastal industries away from territory likely to fall to the Japanese. Priority went to government arsenals and iron and steel plants, including, eventually, the aging Hanyang works that had begun operations under the Ch'ing. Some two hundred small machine plants and one hundred textile factories comprised the next most significant categories. The total number of removed factories has been estimated as high as 639, although only 418 ever resumed production. The majority of these were privately owned, but because the government had concerned itself primarily with state enterprises, there was no consultation with their owners before the outbreak of the war, and removal therefore occurred under even more chaotic circumstances than might otherwise have been the case. The total industrial tonnage removed, about 110,000 tons, was a negligible percentage of China's existing industry, but it formed the core of Free China's new industrial base.

Equally if not more important was the human talent that accompanied the trek west—42,000 skilled and semi-skilled workers and at least an equal number of university students. It was from the latter group that Free China's industries would recruit new engineers and technicians in coming years. Although there was no shortage of problems affecting this exodus, it was a tremendous achievement under the most difficult conditions, and that it occurred at all was attributable in good measure to an outpouring of nationalistic sentiment unprecedented in modern Chinese history.[17]

All that sentiment and more would be needed to remain optimistic about the economic conditions in which the Chinese government found itself after the fall of Wuhan and Canton in the autumn of 1938. China's industrial establishments in the north, east, and south Chinese treaty ports were lost to the government. Those territories had provided the government's major sources of prewar revenue in the form of customs, salt taxes, and taxes on factory production. Revenues fell precipitously at the same time that military expenses rose dramatically. During the first two years of the war, annual revenues fell by 63 percent, while expenditures climbed 33 percent.[18] Absent a major reduction in military expenditures and the tapping of significant new revenues, this discrepancy between income and expenses would be a permanent feature of the wartime economy and, since deficits were made up by printing money, the major cause of inflation. But military expenditures, far from being reduced, continued to expand during the war. The decimation of the German-trained central forces early in the war made the military at once more expensive and less efficient, and the regime was increasingly dependent thereafter—both for the prosecution of the war and for political survival—on the maintenance of a set of imperfectly loyal regional forces. This placed an ever greater economic burden on the fourteen provinces that now comprised Free China.

From their wartime capital of Chungking, the Nationalists ruled territory that included approximately half of China's population (excluding Manchuria) and that was responsible for over 60 percent of China's rice production. Prewar industrial production in these areas was minuscule, however, and conditions for rapid economic development were poor. Communications of all sorts were weak, and transportation costs high. Electrical power capacity—4 percent of China's total—was woefully inadequate to meet the needs of the military, industrial, and civilian apparatus that had migrated with the Nationalist government. Only 4 percent of China's industrial capital was invested in Free China's fourteen provinces. They produced only 5 percent of China's factory-made cloth. Although the region held 39 percent of China's then-estimated coal reserves, these were still largely untapped and in relatively inaccessible areas. Despite production of 27 percent of China's pig iron (with reserves of 14 percent of China's iron ore), this was almost entirely "native pig" of poor quality; there was no modern iron and steel production. Isolated from China's main rail lines, the provinces had over 40 percent of the nation's "highways," which seldom deserved the name, but only 8 percent of its motorized vehicles. Even at the height of Free China's war effort in 1943, the value of its industrial production accounted for little more than 12 percent of the prewar production of China proper.[19]

For the managers of China's war economy, the relocation was a shock and a challenge. China's internationally trained planners and engineers—"downriver people" to the natives of the new bastion[20]—were thrust into conditions in many ways more primitive than those endured by a later generation of Chinese intellectuals "sent down" to the countryside during the Cultural Revolution. In the prewar period, they had planned the erection of a set of imported basic industries with foreign technical assistance. Now they were isolated from the most modern sectors of the Chinese economy and, increasingly, from China's economic partners. By October 1938, Free China was cut off from Europe and America by sea, and road links were effectively severed with the closing of routes through Indochina (1940) and Burma (1942). Thereafter, China's main source of outside technical assistance consisted of very limited U.S. supplies carried by the China National Aviation Corporation "over the Hump" of the Himalayan mountains.[21] Despite all this, the prewar goal of achieving the military-industrial capacity to conduct a modern war did not change after the great migration, although it became immensely more difficult.

State Capitalism and Wartime Industry

The Nationalist regime's response to this challenge was to increase drastically the role of the state in the economy through a greatly enhanced effort at economic mobilization and control. To raise income for military costs, taxes were raised on income, consumption, and transit. The land tax, which had been the preserve of provincial governments since 1928, was claimed in 1941 by the central government, which collected it in kind. The government created state monopolies for tobacco, matches, sugar, and salt. To all these exactions were added further "compulsory borrowings," especially of grain to feed the armies. In industry, the government moved far in the direction of state capitalism managed by an economic bureaucracy that grew much more quickly than the economy under its direction.

The role of the Industrial and Mining Adjustment Administration in relocating factories was a first step. At the same time, the overall management of economic policy was shifted to a new Ministry of Economic Affairs (MOEA), which replaced the long moribund Ministry of Industry as well as the National Reconstruction Commission and the National Economic Council, all of which ceased to exist. Charged with the "economic administration of the whole nation," the MOEA was "the largest organization dealing with economic administration that China had ever seen."[22] The National Resources Commission was transferred to the new ministry and became its core. NRC Chairman Weng Wen-hao served jointly as economics minister. Thus, for the first time a public body, the NRC, was given a broad mandate to "develop, operate, and control" the nation's basic industries, important mining enterprises, and "other enterprises as designated by the government."[23]

Under wartime economic regulations promulgated in 1938, the NRC and the MOEA were given power to nationalize preexisting industrial, mining, and electrical enterprises; to assume "direct control of enterprises or products affecting daily necessities"; to assume the management of firms that failed to "effect measures of technical or administrative reform as ordered by the government"; and to regulate the production, pricing, and export of specific products.[24] At a time of ever greater government presumptions regarding the economy, distinctions between public and private enterprises became blurred, usually to the detriment of the latter. As Weng Wen-hao argued, in an expansion of Sun Yat-sen's conception of the role of the government, the dichotomy between state (*kuo-yu*) and private (*min-yu*) enterprises was a false one, for "nationally owned industries in fact also belonged to the people."[25]

To aid in the enforcement of economic control measures, the MOEA mandated the institution of industrial and trade organizations. The logical extension of this was the National General Mobilization Act of March 29, 1942, which in theory subjected "every person and every means of production" to government economic control.[26] The government also intruded upon the private sector in other ways, as through the forced sale of its bonds to commercial establishments and wealthy individuals.[27] No amount of government management and control of Free China's private sector, however, could create the military-related production needed for the war effort. To achieve this, new state enterprises, which Chi Ch'ao-ting called the "dominating feature" of wartime economic policy, were deemed essential.[28]

This meant above all a great expansion of the activities of the government's economic bureaucracy, in particular the National Resources Commission. In 1937, the NRC had 23 industrial and mining enterprises and fewer than 2,000 staff members under its authority. As a relatively small agency that prided itself on apolitical expertise, it had recruited its engineers above all on scholarly qualifications in consultation with leading Chinese technical universities (particularly Chiao-t'ung University in Shanghai). By the end of 1938, it was involved in 63 enterprises, running 40 by itself, and 23 others in tandem either with other government units or private capital (usually relocated factories). In 1942, the NRC controlled 40 percent of Free China's industry and had become one of the largest government bureaucracies, with an increasingly sophisticated recruitment system.[29] By 1944, the NRC had 103 units in its manufacturing, mining, and electrical enterprises, including 28 that had been "annexed" from private or local public ownership. It employed over 12,000 staff members and an estimated workforce (excluding miners) of 160,000 workers. By 1943 the value of the state contribution to all industrial production (including handicraft industries) had risen from about 15 percent to 35 percent (table 1). State concerns, larger in scale and better capitalized, accounted for 50 percent of the total paid-up capital of public and private enterprises in Free China in 1941, and nearly 70 percent by the end of 1942. This figure included the arsenals of the Ordnance Office, the repair shops of the Communications Ministry, and a wide variety of other official enterprises; but three-quarters of that amount was for NRC enterprises, which produced a growing share of principal war-industrial products (table 2).[30]

What did all this activity do for the war economy? The record is mixed. The most immediate need, because it was essential to all other industrial activity, was in electric power generation. This increased seven times between 1939 and 1944, thanks primarily to the output of the twenty (out of a total of twenty-seven) public utilities owned and operated by the NRC. Even so, by 1944, the generating capacity of Free China's electric utility systems was only 49,000 kilowatts compared to 642,000 kilowatts for occupied China and at least an additional

Table 1

Free China's Industrial Production by Ownership, 1940–44

Year	Value (in million prewar Ch $)			Percentage share			Indices of growth		
	Gov-ern-ment	Private	Total	Gov-ern-ment	Private	Total	Gov-ern-ment	Private	Total
1940	14.47	81.01	95.48	15.2	84.8	100.0	100.0	100.0	100.0
1941	28.86	92.77	121.63	23.7	76.3	100.0	199.4	114.5	127.4
1942	43.14	95.35	138.49	31.2	68.8	100.0	298.1	117.7	145.0
1943	53.59	93.98	147.57	36.3	63.7	100.0	370.4	116.0	154.6
1944	49.28	87.98	137.36	35.9	64.1	100.0	340.6	108.6	143.8

Source: Yu-kwei Cheng, *Foreign Trade and Industrial Development in China* (Washington, DC: The University Press of Washington, DC, 1956), p. 110.
Note: 3.4 Ch $ = 1 U.S. $.

600,000 for Manchuria. (The foreign-owned Shanghai Power Company alone had an installed capacity of 183,000 kilowatts.) A further 37,000 kilowatts in industrial plants boosted Nationalist China's total operating capacity only up to 86,000 kilowatts.[31] This was enough, to be sure, to make use of the electrical implements (light bulbs, radios, telephones) manufactured by the NRC's relocated Central Electrical Manufacturing Works. But it is obvious that with the exception of several dimly lit cities and hundreds of small, underpowered government factories, Free China remained a dark and preindustrial region.

Equally essential for the war economy was the production of liquid fuels. This was one commodity in which Free China had substantial, albeit previously untapped, reserves. Prior to the war, all parts of China were heavily dependent upon imported gasoline, diesel fuel, and motor oil for motorized transportation. In the mid-1930s, concerned about China's strategic vulnerability in fuels, the NRC had performed exploratory drilling in Shensi and Kansu provinces. The Yumen fields in Kansu were particularly promising, and it was there that oil was struck shortly after the war began.

The NRC's Kansu Petroleum Production and Refining Administration performed innovative extractive work, without access to foreign equipment, relying in its first years only on local resources in providing Free China's only domestic source of petroleum. By 1944 it produced about twenty million gallons of crude petroleum, which was refined into roughly seven million gallons of gasoline, kerosene, and diesel fuel.[32] Available equipment and manpower restricted its success, however, and its output came nowhere near matching wartime demand, which was estimated at approximately fifty million gallons of gasoline.

In some ways, the greater achievement came in the production of alcohol,

Table 2

NRC Control of Principal Industrial Products of Free China

	1939			1944		
	Total	NRC (%)	Other (%)	Total	NRC (%)	Other (%)
Electrical power (1,000 kwh)	91,494	10.5	89.5	154,220	33.8	66.2
Coal (1,000 tons)	5,500	4.8	95.2	5,502	20.6	79.4
Iron (tons)	62,730	0	100.0	40,134	31.2	68.8
Steel (tons)	1,200	0	100.0	13,361	56.9	43.1
Toolmaker lathes (sets)	639	0	100.0	1,350	12.8	87.2
Cutting tools (sets)	1,512	0	100.0	3,327	7.8	92.2
Power machines (sets)	870	0	100.0	8,210	26.9	73.1
Generators (kva)	439	20.3	79.7	4,926	37.1	62.9
Electric motors (hp)	9,594	21.8	78.2	6,277	81.4	18.6
Transformers (kva)	6,509	0.1	99.9	11,185	42.2	57.8
Alcohol (1,000 gal.)	812	34.5	65.5	7,346	38.5	61.5
Light bulbs (1,000)	493	39.1	60.9	1,686	49.6	50.4
Gasoline (1,000 gal.)	4	100.0	0	4,048	100.0	0
Kerosene (1,000 gal.)	4	100.0	0	2,158	100.0	0
Diesel oil (1,000 gal.)	7	100.0	0	155	100.0	0
Copper (tons)	582	100.0	0	898	100.0	0
Electron tubes (1,000)	7,445	100.0	0	11,391	100.0	0

Source: Chung-kuo chin-tai kung-yeh-shih tzu-liao (Materials on the modern history of Chinese industry), ed. Chen Chen (Beijing, 1961), 3:143–44.

which, used as a gasoline substitute, provided over three-quarters of the liquid fuels used in Free China. The NRC pioneered the use in China of alcohol as a motor fuel, both in its own facilities for the production of industrial alcohol and by its encouragement of some 120 small, private plants using native wine as raw material. In this fashion it mobilized an estimated 82 percent of practical alcohol production capacity in Free China.[33] A third category of fuel production was the extraction of gasoline from vegetable oils. The NRC's Tung-li Oil Works began operation in 1940, exploiting the tung oil extracted from the tung trees in western China. By 1943, government vegetable oil refineries and private plants that followed their lead produced 642,000 gallons of synthetic gasoline from vegetable oil.[34] In sum, without this prodigious effort, the war economy would have been quite literally immobilized.

In other areas, however, the wartime production record was less impressive and reflected in part the Nationalist government's limited ability to adapt to its new environment over the long haul. In steel making, for example, it had to trade in the dream of the Krupp-supplied Central Steel Works for a "refugee industry . . . located with reference to safety rather than with reference to raw materials supplies, transportation, or other industrial factors."[35] At the peak production of 1943, a combination of relocated plants and others newly constructed—in some cases using salvaged steel plates from wrecked ships—produced about 10,000 metric tons of steel or at most 10 percent of China's pre-1931 production.[36]

In coal production, although the roughly 6 million metric tons produced in 1943 represented a doubling of 1938 production in Free China, only about 2.5 million tons was produced near consuming areas. Given transportation difficulties, little of the coal produced away from the Szechwan-Yunnan core area of Free China was used where demand was greatest. Since wartime coal production in Japanese-held territory more than doubled, the relative share Free China's mines contributed to all Chinese production (including Manchuria) actually declined slightly to about 11 percent.[37]

After expansion in the first years of the war, mining of strategically important nonferrous metals subsequently also met with difficulties. Exports of tungsten, antimony, and tin were now essential to the war effort in two ways—as the main means of repaying the Soviet military credits granted in March and July 1938, as well as the important Tungsten and Metal Loans of October 1940 and January 1941 with the United States, and as a potentially important material contribution to the war economies of China's allies. Problems of management, finance, maintenance, and transportation combined to reduce production drastically by 1943. During Japan's Ichigo offensive of 1944 security also became a problem. Tungsten ore exports declined from 16,500 tons in 1937 to 9,000 tons in 1943. Production of antimony fell from a height of about 8,500 tons in 1940 to about 600 tons in 1943. Production of tin—of particular importance to the Allied war effort since the world's most important prewar sources were in Japanese hands—declined from 17,000 tons in 1940 to about 4,000 tons in 1943.[38]

The production pattern in the mines was but one example of the boom and bust cycle that affected the entire war economy by 1944. The migration of the government and its entourage of several million was initially a stimulant to both public and private industrial development in Southwest China. The number of reassembled migrant factories and new factories erected grew each year through 1941. Their maximum industrial production was not reached until 1943. But the rate of growth in the public sector consistently outpaced that in the private sector, which began to decline after 1942.

After 1941, several factors worked against productivity growth. Access to foreign-made spare parts became extremely difficult after the closure of the Burma Road, and repair and maintenance of equipment became more difficult and expensive. Government industries tended to handle such technical challenges better, if only because they had more incentive to try. For private industry in an increasingly inflationary economy, the uncertainties of equipment, together with those of raw materials and skilled labor—both in permanent short supply in Free China—meant that manufacturing became decidedly more risky than the certain profits of hoarding and speculation. Government industries of the NRC, operated by salaried managers whose pay bore no relation to the profits of the enterprise, aimed instead to reach fixed production goals set out in a series of three-year and annual plans.[39]

The decline of the private sector had important effects on the public sector, however, severely limiting demand for products of producer industries (steel, coal, coke, machinery). Government attempts to reduce inflation also had negative consequences for public enterprises. Price controls, truly enforceable only for the products of state enterprises, meant that many products were sold below production costs in 1943–44. The slashing of government budgets as an antiinflationary measure had several further consequences: a dramatic slowdown in the rate of establishing state enterprises (the NRC established only ten, relatively small, new enterprises from 1943 to 1945); the decreasing productivity of government workers whose wages declined in real terms; and a shortage of purchasing power by "consumers" within the state sector. For example, the Ordnance Office could not afford the NRC's steel, and its arsenals operated at a fraction of their capacity. In turn, by November 1944 the iron and steel plants under NRC control were producing at less than 25 percent of capacity. Many of the same factors affected the machine industry.[40]

In the state sector, production appears to have been adversely affected also by the management of China's new economic bureaucracy, which on the whole was not particularly well-suited to wartime conditions in China's interior. The rapid growth of the NRC's responsibilities in the early years of the war followed by the industrial depression of 1943–44, together with the chronic shortage of skilled laborers, meant that most NRC enterprises were overstaffed with recently trained engineers and understaffed with individuals with practical experience. Overhead costs were made worse by the reluctance of most engineers to engage in actual production work, reflecting the social divide between the "educated" and those with less formal training. U.S. observers of the American War Production Mission to China in 1944–45 unanimously believed that recent college graduates were increasingly "cluttering up" NRC plants, which in some cases could be run just as well by intelligent and experienced foremen.[41] Although many government enterprises appeared profitable on paper, this was often the result of inflation-style accounting—original equity capital compared with profits in current prices. Even so, 28 percent of the available financial statements of NRC enterprises during the war reported a loss. The statistically most profitable government enterprises, apart from strategic ores in the boom years of the late 1930s, were in consumer industries such as textiles and paper.[42]

Even at a time of decreased productivity in all sectors, the performance of the state sector relative to the private sector could still be a source of satisfaction for government planners.[43] Despite—or in part because of—the problems facing state enterprises, the trend continued toward an increasingly "controlled economy" with an ever-larger state role. This meant that economic planning became increasingly important. The war economy provided the government with opportunities for economic planning on a scale never before attempted in China—in the production and distribution of coal, iron, petroleum, chemicals, transportation equipment, and spare parts of all kinds—not to mention the funding of such activities under inflationary conditions. A second area of even more detailed planning, since it encompassed a much larger economy, was the nature of postwar economic development for the whole of China.

Wartime Postwar Planning

As the war economy stagnated, Chinese planners turned increasingly to China's postwar agenda, which was set down in formal plans that provide evidence of the anticipated direction of Chinese development under Nationalist rule. It is clear that the extension of government controls and the growth of the state industrial sector was intended to continue at an even greater pace in peacetime, and to affect areas of the economy that had been largely outside of government control before 1937, including light industry and foreign-owned enterprises.[44] Whether one talked, as did NRC Vice-Chairman Ch'ien Ch'ang-chao, of "following the socialist road,"[45] or of an economic policy that was, as Economics Minister Weng Wen-hao put it, "close to socialism though not entirely identical,"[46] there was a broad consensus among Chinese planners on postwar economic directions.

The first major statement on postwar planning came in October 1940 by the Chinese Economic Reconstruction Society, a nonofficial group organized in October 1939, whose members represented banking, manufacturing, university, and other professional fields as well as NRC planners. According to the economist Fang Hsien-t'ing, its membership represented "probably the best informed opinion of the leaders in Free China during wartime." In setting out objectives for postwar development, the society's lengthy "Outline of Economic Reconstruction in China" foresaw that the fundamental issues of the 1930s—the need to recover and maintain national sovereignty through military strength—would remain paramount after the war. It gave highest priority to defense-related industries, which were to be developed "as quickly as possible, as state enterprises" according to a "planned economy" that would be applied by regions and would lay the foundation "for the industrialization of the nation." The "Outline" further demanded the continuation of wartime economic controls and argued that postwar foreign investment in China, although both necessary and welcome, had to be regulated to the precise needs of Chinese plans.[47]

Among government planners, naturally there were "turf" battles between government and KMT organs concerned with postwar planning, particularly as the NRC grew in strength and prestige just as the party was declining in those terms. Nevertheless, Weng Wen-hao and Ch'en Li-fu, who led the "technocratic" and "party" camps respectively, collaborated in defining postwar plans. Weng and Ch'en cochaired a series of major planning conferences to resolve intragovernmental differences. The most important such conference met for ten days in April 1943 to review an NRC draft plan for the postwar period. It included representatives of the NRC, the Arsenal and Armaments Office, the Ministry of Communications, university faculties, industry groups, as well as Kuomintang elders. From it emerged detailed schedules for the development of key industrial sectors—the metallurgical industry (iron and steel, nonferrous metals, and export minerals); fuel industry (coal and petroleum); electric and hydroelectric power enterprises; machine industry (machines and machine parts; transportation equipment, and electrical implements); chemical industry (inorganic and organic chemicals; fuels, ceramics, resinous products, explosives, dyes); communications (including railways, highways, shipping, aviation, postal service, and telecommunication); and eleven categories of light industries. The plan covered over 300 heavy industrial enterprises and 3,000 light industrial units. The cost of completion of all parts of the plan was estimated at U.S. $2 billion with manpower requirements of 270,000 staff and 2.8 million industrial workers. All this was set down in twenty volumes of conference reports, which served as the basis for setting subsequent industrial priorities.[48]

These plans were based in part on detailed studies of current state enterprises by the NRC Economics Research Institute. There was, however, imperfect knowledge of the physical state of the facilities then under Japanese or "puppet" control, a large percentage of which would be taken over by the NRC (either solely or in joint management with provincial governments). Anticipating that Chinese technical talent would already be stretched thin in the immediate postwar period, U.S. industrial and engineering consulting firms were engaged in 1944–45 to prepare to inspect industries in Manchuria, East China, and Taiwan immediately upon the war's end.[49] Their reports and recommendations, completed in 1945–46, primarily served Chinese state planners but were also seen as the first step toward Sino-foreign technical cooperation in industrial reconstruction. Several Sino-American joint ventures for the postwar period were negotiated during the war, for example, between the NRC and Westinghouse International for a major expansion of the Central Electrical Manufacturing Works.[50] In anticipation of the entire task of postwar construction, several thousand Chinese government engineers were sent to the United States for advanced technical training. Well before the end of the war, the future leaders of Chinese industry were no longer concerned with the war economy, nor were they even in China. They were in the United States, looking toward the future.[51]

The American War Production Mission to China

The Nationalist regime's growing preoccupation with postwar planning was partly based on the assumption that U.S. participation in the war assured Japan's ultimate defeat. Therefore, scarce resources, material and human, were best devoted to postwar issues, success in which was much less certain. Although Sino-American economic relations were more cordial than those in the military sphere, they too were impaired by conflicts that would endure into the postwar period. Chief among these were the degree of American assistance China could reasonably expect, the uses to which it was to be put, and the role of the Chinese state in China's economy.

During its struggle with Japan, China received military and economic assistance from several countries, principally the Soviet Union during the first years of the war, and the United States during the final four years. The importance of Sino-American economic relations transcended the war, however, for China's postwar plans required international assistance and investment on an unprecedented scale.[52] As the only power likely to emerge from the war in a position to assist postwar reconstruction, the United States was China's logical postwar economic partner. Chinese planners assumed the likelihood of long-term U.S. government credits in the postwar years that would represent a peacetime extension of U.S.-China wartime relations.

Between 1938 and the end of the war in 1945, the United States authorized a total of $1.5 billion in grants ($825 million) and credits ($690 million) to the Chinese government. From the U.S. perspective, this aid was "to assist in the war against Japan and to contribute to the stabilization of China's wartime economy."[53] This aid reached a high point with the fully unrestricted $500 million credit of 1942, a primary (and unsuccessful) aim of which was to help stabilize China's currency. In addition, over the years 1941–45, China received $846 million in Lend-Lease materials and services, $820 million of which was in the form of outright grants.

Although generous from the American point of view, Lend-Lease assistance to China was but a small fraction of that given to Great Britain or the USSR, and never more than 4 percent of total U.S. Lend-Lease aid. Moreover, the need to fly in all materials over the "Hump" for all but the last months of the war, combined with Washington's Europe First strategy, severely restricted material aid, particularly to war production. Although Lend-Lease aimed to provide important machine tools and spare parts for state industries, these arrived in very limited quantities. Lend-Lease materials received by the NRC totaled just 927 tons by March 1944.[54]

To no small degree, China also used Lend-Lease to prepare for the postwar era. It was with funds allocated under that program that, as noted above, Chinese engineers received advanced training in major U.S. industries for periods ranging from several months to several years. The first group was sent in 1942, composed of thirty-one men from all major divisions of the NRC. Its members were each given several internships over a two-year period in such organizations as Westinghouse, RCA, DuPont, Monsanto, the Tennessee Valley Authority, U.S. Bureau of Reclamation, U.S. Steel, and American Cyanamid.[55] More than one thousand Chinese engineers, scientists, and managers associated with state enterprises followed over the next four years. Over the same period, the NRC also sent four hundred of its top officials and managers for study tours of several months in U.S. industries.[56]

While the next generation of Chinese engineers underwent training in the United States, it was the precarious state of the current Chinese war economy that most concerned and alarmed the United States, and prompted President Roosevelt to send American War Production Board chief Donald M. Nelson to China in August 1944.[57] Nelson's mandate was somehow to reconcile American and Chinese objectives by increasing Chinese war-related industrial production while at the same time discussing in general terms the American economic role in the postwar period.[58] His mission, which became known as the American War Production Mission (AWPM) to China, emphasized the first task, war production, over postwar planning. Its Chinese counterparts, like the Nationalist government as a whole, did the opposite.

Nelson's emphatic suggestion to Chiang Kai-shek that China follow the U.S. example by creating a War Production Board (Chan-shih Sheng-ch'an-chu) raised a series of issues for the Nationalist regime and its economic planners. Production stoppages caused by inflation (e.g., an arsenal's inability to afford necessary raw materials) would not themselves be overcome by a War Production Board with dictatorial powers. Indeed, any government expenditure for such a new board might itself be considered inflationary. Most difficult to accept by 1944, however, was the American conception that even a major increase in the low level of Chinese armaments and industrial production could make a difference to the outcome of the Pacific War. Potentially more convincing was Nelson's argument that "in the process of economic development there can be no distinction between wartime and postwar period," that China's postwar industrial progress would benefit from the "continuous growth" of industry during the war.[59] But by the time of Nelson's visit, Chinese postwar industrial plans had been in the making for two years and did not take China's wartime industry as their foundation. Rather, they stressed the rapid rehabilitation of industries in Japanese-occupied areas, particularly Manchuria, Taiwan, and the eastern coastal cities, and relegated to secondary status the comparatively rudimentary and undersized industrial structure of Free China.[60]

All these factors affected the ultimate form of China's War Production Board. When formally created on December 6, 1944, the board was given an impressive mandate but little real power or money.[61] On paper, the board's bureaucracy was formidable, with a Secretariat and departments of Priorities, Materials, Manufacture, Military Equipment, Transportation, Procurement, and Finance. In reality, the only thing the board possessed was its letterhead stationery; its various departments consisted of individuals with full-time responsibilities in the organs the board was supposed to coordinate.[62]

Ultimately, the board's main function was to serve as the vehicle through which the technical personnel of the American War Production Mission assisted Chinese industries. In other respects it was a fiction designed to appease the Americans without actually changing Chinese policy. The mission was instructed to do whatever it could to increase Chinese war production. With no independent authority (even over Lend-Lease requests), it served essentially as a consulting industrial engineering service to leading industries of the National Resources Commission and the Arsenal and Ordnance Office.

The mission functioned effectively in the mundane but important production matters to which American and Chinese engineers applied themselves. Its forty-six advisers from November 1944 until November 1945 (approximately twenty were in service at any one time) included specialists in iron and steel, alcohol, coal and coke, textiles, ordnance, chemicals, power, petroleum, nonferrous metals, and machine tools. The advisers personally investigated all major production units in an industry group, surveyed all available resources, and then were placed at the service of chief engineers at individual Chinese installations. Thus, apart from their demonstrated ability to advise on improved industrial techniques and to assist in repairs, they could serve as go-betweens for Chinese units within an industry group. As outsiders, they could more easily undertake some of the coordinating work that was one of the aims of the War Production Board. By all accounts, these production men worked well with their Chinese counterparts, whose positions and prestige they did not threaten. In this realm of purely technical endeavor, the mission's success was measurable. Although its original goals were much higher, it certainly deserves credit for at least some of the roughly 25 percent rise in munitions and war-related raw materials production from November 1944 to the spring of 1945, particularly if one bears in mind that production was declining rapidly before November 1944.[63]

In its second function of helping to coordinate postwar plans, however, the mission further exacerbated an emerging Chinese-American conflict. As early as 1942, American policy makers evinced strong misgivings about the direction of

Chinese postwar development plans. Not only was such planning diverting talent from the current war effort, but it was feared that a "planned" or strongly regulated Chinese economy would place unwelcome restrictions on American private enterprise. In China as elsewhere, the architects of American foreign economic policy were motivated by the belief that only an open, global, free market economy could foil the erection of trading "blocs" and high tariffs that they believed had contributed to the great depression of the 1930s. This ran counter to the Chinese officials' basic conception that foreign investment in China, although welcome and necessary, had to be regulated to the precise needs of Chinese plans and should be coordinated with the appropriate foreign government. Chinese-American differences over the form and extent of Chinese regulation of foreign firms in China began to be thrashed out in great detail, to the satisfaction of neither party, in the negotiations, begun in 1943, for a Sino-American Commercial Treaty to replace the defunct extraterritorial system.[64]

If the members of the AWPM understood the extent of Washington's misgivings regarding China's postwar plans, it was not evident from their actions. Indeed, the mission seemed to favor a stronger, not weaker, role for the Chinese state in the economy. This, after all, was the whole idea of the War Production Board, and from that perspective the Chinese state had not seemed strong enough. AWPM leaders also came to endorse certain specific Chinese postwar plans, including the most ambitious of all, the vast Yangtze gorge dam and hydroelectric power project. Without the enthusiastic support of Donald Nelson, this "TVA-like" endeavor would never have become a formal joint engineering enterprise between the NRC and the Bureau of Reclamation of the U.S. Department of the Interior. Led on the U.S. side by a "billion-dollar engineer," John L. Savage, chief design engineer for the Boulder and Grand Coulee dams, the project was to culminate with the erection of the "largest dam in the world" in the Yangtze gorges, capable of producing 10 million kilowatts annually at an overall cost of U.S. $800 million, for which a fifty-year American loan would be sought. Preliminary studies began in mid-1945. Over the next three years, the NRC spent over $2 million on the project, including $500,000 for the services of the Bureau of Reclamation in China and for its training of forty NRC engineers at its Denver headquarters, and $250,000 for subsurface explorations by a subcontractor at potential dam sites near Ich'ang.[65]

The Yangtze gorge project reflects better than any other the tremendous scope of Chinese economic ambitions for the postwar period. Its demise in May 1947 "for urgent economic reasons,"[66] which included the U.S. failure to provide anticipated funding, was symptomatic of the fate of most Chinese plans in a more sober postwar world.

The War Experience and Postwar China

Nationalist China's postwar plans have received little historical notice because they were never more than partly implemented. They were based on at least four assumptions that proved incorrect: the existence of postwar stability (or, at a minimum, lack of military disruption of production); the early rehabilitation of Japanese-held industries with, at least for a transition period, Japanese personnel; reparations in the form of industrial plant and goods from Japan; and, as indicated above, substantial credits from the American government.

In any event, the ensuing Chinese civil war, which affected all areas, proved the most important disruption. In addition, the expected Nationalist economic inheritance from the occupied areas was lessened in several ways.

Although in the years before the Pacific War the industrial economy of East China had revived somewhat—particularly during the period from September 1939 to December 1941, when the outbreak of the war in Europe led to the partial protection of consumer industries by curtailing imports—the total cutoff of economic contact with the Western nations after Pearl Harbor initiated a general industrial decline, beginning with the cotton textile and silk industries. At the same time, inflation began to impede productive activity in a manner similar to that in Free China. By 1943, prices were rising faster in Shanghai than in Chungking. Although industrial production figures for occupied China after Pearl Harbor are highly unreliable, the economist Cheng Yu-kwei has estimated industrial activity in Shanghai by measuring electric power consumption. By 1943, a severe economic depression may be inferred from the fact that industrial consumption of power was only 40 percent of the 1936 figure (table 3). Cheng argues that by the end of the war, Chinese plants in Shanghai had essentially ceased production, while Japanese-owned enterprises operated at one-fourth capacity at best.[67]

To this economic inactivity must be added the positive damage done by Soviet expropriation of Manchuria's industrial plant and the wartime U.S. bombing of Taiwan-based industries. At the same time, China was unable to get any sizable industrial reparations from Japan, and the continued employment of Japanese technical personnel proved politically impossible. Last, the postwar period showed that the aims of Chinese planners determined to shape the nation's economic agenda could not easily be reconciled with the U.S. desire to maintain many of the rights enjoyed by American firms under the system of extraterritoriality. American dissatisfaction with the statist direction of Chinese planning peaked in 1946–47 and was a major reason why an additional $500 million credit originally earmarked for China was only partially forthcoming.[68]

In several important ways, however, plans that took shape during the war *were* carried out, and they had a major impact on the Nationalist regime and on China's future. Nothing more clearly indicates the postwar direction of Chinese development than the fact that, despite all difficulties, the Chinese state and its planners continued in the direction of increased economic control and expanded the state sector and the planned economy at a rapid rate. Following the nationalization of most Japanese and "puppet" enterprises—many of which had been

Table 3

Indices of Industrial Consumption of Electric Power in Shanghai Area

Year	Indices
1936	100.0
1937	82.4
1938	72.5
1939	102.9
1940	105.5
1941	80.0
1942	50.0
1943	40.0

Source: Yu-Kwei Cheng, *Foreign Trade and Industrial Development in China*, p. 122.

effectively nationalized by Japanese-controlled, quasi-governmental holding companies during the occupation—by August 1947 the NRC's industrial empire employed about 33,000 staff members and 230,000 workers (more than 500,000 if joint ventures with provincial governments are factored in), and accounted for 67.3 percent of China's total industrial capital.[69]

The enormous expansion of the role of the economic bureaucracy that began during the war could not but affect the nature of the Nationalist regime. As the party and the military became progressively enfeebled during and after the war, the growing state sector of the economy became the main government presence in many parts of the country. As noted earlier, the decline in the power and influence of the Kuomintang dated to the early 1930s. Wartime attempts to "renovate" the party and resist the "usurpation" of authority by nonparty professionals were wholly unsuccessful.[70] Major economic decisions—often bad ones, to be sure—increasingly were made by individuals whose party credentials were nominal at best. The ongoing degeneration of the military undermined a second pillar of the Nationalist regime. The economic bureaucracy, as the largest component of national civilian government, could not by itself hold political power, even though one of its leaders, Weng Wen-hao, would rise to the premiership in 1948. But it could and did become an increasingly autonomous part of the state structure. This growing separation of economic from political and military decision making is an important and understudied aspect of the late 1940s Nationalist collapse.

If one looks beyond the Chinese civil war to the legacy of the war economy for China's subsequent development under the People's Republic of China and the Republic of China on Taiwan, several points emerge. First, even the new PRC leadership understood that the Nationalist wartime and postwar accumulation of state capital had "laid the foundation" for the PRC's state monopoly.[71]

The same could be said for the eighteen state corporations on Taiwan that provided the industrial foundation of Nationalist rule in the early 1950s. Second, pre-1949 trends in the direction of central economic planning anticipated both (in theory) the PRC's early approach to centralized planning and (in action) the less coercive method of setting of objectives that has come to define "guidance planning" on Taiwan.[72]

Third, the most important legacy of the war economy was not the rudimentary industry it first promoted and then abandoned, but the human talent developed under it. The large majority of Nationalist economic and industrial planning personnel remained in government service on the mainland, with NRC men constituting much of the first staff of Communist planning organs.[73] In the case of Taiwan, economic plans made in 1945–46 assigned a talented group of middle-level NRC managers and engineers to direct state corporations and coordinate postwar economic development on the island. Many of the most prominent individuals associated with Taiwan's economic "miracle" had NRC roots from the war period, including the majority of the heads of Taiwan's state-run industries in the past four decades and eight of the fourteen post-1950 ministers of economic affairs.

The value of the wartime experience may be most evident from one case study with which this chapter concludes. As noted above, during World War II, a significant number of Chinese engineers were sponsored by the NRC under Lend-Lease funds for advanced training in major U.S. industries. They were to be industrial leaders of China's postwar development. Some, like Wang An, remained in the United States and made illustrious careers. Most, however, returned to careers in the PRC and Taiwan.

The first and most select group of young engineers was sent in 1942, composed of thirty-one men from the major NRC divisions (e.g., the Central Machine Works, Hydroelectric Power Bureau, Central Electrical Manufacturing Works, Kansu Petroleum Administration, Mining Bureau, and Economic Research Office). Its members were each given several internships over a two-year period in American business and government organizations. Although separated by assignment and professional expertise, the thirty-one had a strong sense of cohesion and common mission. The members of this "Society of 31"[74] have remained in touch (openly or secretly) with each other for most of the past forty years.

Since 1949,[75] the group as a whole has contributed to the economic activity of the United States, the PRC, and Taiwan. Three of the group took up permanent residence in the United States. Two became project engineering managers for multinational companies; one became a shipping magnate and a multimillionaire.

The rest returned to China. Twenty-one remained on the mainland. Seven became chief engineers (*tsung kung-ch'eng shih*, the highest technical position) in sizable state enterprises. Two rose to the rank of senior (*kao-chi*) engineer in similar enterprises. Seven others pursued industrial and academic research. Of these seven, four became heads of industrial research bureaus; one ran the Foreign Affairs Office of the First Machine-Building Ministry; and two became professors, one of whom was named vice-president of Tsinghua University. Six have been named members of the Chinese People's Political Consultative Conference. Most enjoyed substantial careers in technical work until the Cultural Revolution, though none would rise to ministerial rank. None escaped political persecution then, and two were "persecuted to death," examples of the perverse destruction of human talent that so impaired China's development at the height of the Maoist era.

It is perhaps fitting that it was the revived Nationalist regime on Taiwan that received the greatest return on its wartime investment. The seven Society of 31 members who found themselves on Taiwan in 1949 have enjoyed the greatest distinction. One became a successful financier. Three became president or chairman of the board of major state-run enterprises (positions of considerably greater executive authority than that of chief engineer). Two received cabinet portfolios as ministers of economic affairs; one of these would later chair the cabinet-rank Council on Economic Planning and Development, while the other rose to the second most powerful position in the state, that of premier. The prominence of such individuals carries forth a trend from the late Nationalist period on the mainland, in which essentially nonpolitical economic bureaucrats played an increasing role in government, receiving cabinet-rank positions and sometimes more. In historical terms, if NRC founder and longtime chairman Weng Wenhao was the first Chinese "technocrat" premier in 1948, then the engineer Sun Yun-hsuan (Y. S. Sun), trained in the NRC's electric power division in the 1940s, was the second (and much more successful).[76] In this regard, at least, the war economy of Nationalist China may be seen as a predecessor of the contemporary developmental state on Taiwan.

Notes

1. The above discussion is based on the following: Yu-kwei Cheng, *Foreign Trade and Industrial Development in China* (Washington, DC: The University Press of Washington, DC, 1956), pp. 114, 158; Chien Jui, "Kuo-min-tang kuan-liao tzu-pen fa-chan ti kai-shu " (Survey of the development of Kuomintang bureaucratic capital), *Chung-kuo ching-chi-shih yen-chiu* (Research in Chinese economic history) 3 (1986): 101; Steven I. Levine, *Anvil of Victory: The Communist Revolution in Manchuria, 1945–1948* (New York: Columbia University Press, 1987), p. 69; Academia Historica, Taiwan (hereafter cited as AH), National Resources Commission (hereafter cited as NRC), "Ku-wen pao-kao" (Consulting reports): Study by Pierce Management, "Urgent Necessity for Immediate Increase in Chinese Coal Production," February 10, 1947; "McKee Report on North China Steel," December 1946; A. J. Anderson, "Report of Inspection Trip to Cement Plants in North East China," August 5, 1946; *Kang-t'ieh* (Steel) (Nanking, 1947); Weng Wenhao, "Report on the National Resources Commission," May 27, 1947 (NRC New York Office Press Release), p. 3; AH, NRC, "Ku-wen pao-kao," Behre, Dolbear & Co. reports on tungsten and antimony, March 1, 1947 and March 15, 1947. For greatest detail see Ch'i Ching-te, *Chung-kuo tui Jih k'ang-chan sun-shih tiao-ch'a shih-shu* (Historical

account of China's losses during the war with Japan) (Taipei: Kuo-shih-kuan, 1987); and Han Ch'i-t'ung, *Chung-kuo tui Jih chan-shih sun-shih wen-ku-chi* (Estimated Chinese losses during hostilities with Japan) (Shanghai: Chung-hua, 1946).

2. Lloyd E. Eastman, "Nationalist China During the Sino-Japanese War 1937–1945," in *The Cambridge History of China*, ed. John K. Fairbank and Albert Feuerwerker, vol. 13, part 2 (Cambridge: Cambridge University Press, 1986), p. 569n; Lloyd E. Eastman, *Seeds of Destruction*, pp. 58–59.

3. Ramon H. Myers, "The Agrarian System," in *Cambridge History of China* 13:2:268–69; *China Handbook 1937–1944* (Chungking: Ministry of Information, 1944), p. 348; Eastman, *Seeds of Destruction*, chap. 2; Eastman, "Nationalist China," p. 565n.

4. Eastman, "Nationalist China," p. 584.

5. Ibid., p. 547.

6. See Alan S. Milward, *War, Economy and Society, 1939–1945* (Berkeley: University of California Press, 1977).

7. See Sun Yat-sen, *The International Development of China* (New York and London, 1922 [Taipei, 1953]).

8. Bundesarchiv-Militararchiv, Freiburg, W 02–44/5, pp. 209, 217, 237, minutes of meetings between Chiang Kai-shek and his military adviser-general, Hans von Seeckt, April 28, May 2, and May 4, 1934. Only 16 percent of the military budget for 1935 was to be spent north of the Yangtze. Ibid.

9. Apparently the idea of retreating as far as Szechwan was conceived as early as 1932: see Eastman, "Nationalist China," p. 553n.

10. See Second Historical Archives of China, Nanking (hereafter cited as SHA), 28(5965), "Chung kung-yeh chien-she chi-hua shuo-ming-shu" (Explanation of the plan for heavy industries) (1936). Generally, see William Kirby, "Kuomintang China's 'Great Leap Outward': The 1936 Three-Year Plan for Industrial Development," in *Essays in the History of the Chinese Republic* (Urbana: University of Illinois, Center for Asian Studies, 1983). On individual enterprises see *Tzu-yuan wei-yuan-hui chi-k'an* (hereafter cited as *TYYK*) 1, 2 (June 1939): 85–100, 158–59, 337; 1, 3 (July 1939): 163–66; 2, 1 (January 1940): 37ff; Combined Services Forces, ed., *Kuo-fang kung-yeh chi wu-ch'i fa-chan* (National defense industries and armaments development) (Taipei, n.d.); Chinese Academy of Sciences, Peking (CAS), *Tzu-yuan wei-yuan-hui chung-yang chi-ch'i-ch'ang chien-shih* (Short history of the NRC's Central Machine Works) (N.p.: NRC internal draft history, November 1940); SHA, 28(5965)3, "Kuan-yu ch'ou-she Hsiang-t'an chung-yang kang-t'ieh-ch'ang chih pang-yueh" (On the agreement to establish the Central Steel Works at Hsiangtan), June 1936.

11. This was particularly true in the case of the Sino-German relationship (see William C. Kirby, *Germany and Republican China* [Stanford: Stanford University Press, 1984]), but it was also a factor in Sino-Soviet military-economic relations after 1937. See SHA, 28(2)389 file, "Su-lien chu Hua shang-wu tai-piao-t'uan" (Soviet commercial office in China), which includes ore delivery contracts.

12. SHA, 47(4), Weng Wen-hao, "Kuo-fang she-chi wei-yuan-hui chih mu-ti chi shuo-ming" (Goals of the National Defense Planning Commission), December 1932; CAS, *Tzu-yuan wei-yuan-hui yen-ko* (Successive changes of the National Resources Commission) (Nanking, 1949), p. 1b.

13. See Charlotte Furth, *Ting Wen-chiang: Science and China's New Culture* (Cambridge: Harvard University Press, 1970), pp. 216–19.

14. On the larger relationship between the Nationalist regime and Chinese capitalists, see Parks M. Coble, *The Shanghai Capitalists and the Nationalist Government, 1927–1937* (Cambridge: Harvard University, Council on East Asian Studies, 1980), and Marie-Claire

Bergere, *The Golden Age of the Chinese Bourgeoisie 1911–1937,* trans. Janet Lloyd (Cambridge: Cambridge University Press, 1989).

15. See the assessment by the Chinese and German war ministries in *Documents on German Foreign Policy* (Washington, DC, 1955–), C, 5, no. 363, pp. 607–8, memorandum by Trautmann, June 10, 1936.

16. *TYYK* 1, 3 (July 1939): 163; 1, 2 (June 1939): 85–100; *KYTL*, 3:839, 903–4; *Kuo-fang kung-yeh chi wu-ch'i fa-chan*, p. 225.

17. Weng Wen-hao, *K'ang-chan i-lai ti ching-chi* (The economy since the [outbreak of] the War of Resistance) (Chungking, 1942), pp. 13–27; Hubert Freyn, *Free China's New Deal* (New York: Macmillan, 1943), p. 41; Chi-ming Hou, "Economic Development and Public Finance in China, 1937–1945," in *Nationalist China During the Sino-Japanese War*, ed. Paul K. T. Sih (Hicksville, NY: Exposition Press, 1977), p. 208.

18. Eastman, "Nationalist China," p. 584.

19. Hou, "Economic Development," pp. 205–8; Cheng, *Foreign Trade and Industrial Development*, p. 111; Eastman, "Nationalist China," p. 592; Harry S. Truman Library, Independence, Missouri (hereafter cited as HST, Truman Papers), "China Mission Data Report," September 1944, pp. 1, 11a.

20. Eastman, "Nationalist China," p. 565.

21. Franklin D. Roosevelt Library, Hyde Park, New York (FDR), AWPM, box 40, Maybel T. Cragg, "History of the American War Production Mission to China" (1946), p. 19; Academia Sinica, Taiwan (hereafter cited as AS), Institute of Modern History (IMH), NRC, *ts'ai* 56–1–9/0, lend-lease files, 1942–47.

22. Ch'ao-ting Chi, *Wartime Economic Development of China* (New York, 1939), chap. 3, part 8; *Ching-chi-pu kung-pao* (Gazette of the Ministry of Economic Affairs) 1, 1 (February 16, 1938); 1, 4 (April 1, 1938).

23. *Ching-chi-pu kung-pao* 1, 13 (August 16, 1938): 608.

24. Chi, *Wartime Economic Development*, chap. 3, pp. 6–8, 12–17; *TYYK* 3, 2 (August 1942); Freyn, *Free China's New Deal*, pp. 44, 250–56; Hsi-sheng Ch'i, *Nationalist China at War: Military Defeats and Political Collapse, 1937–45* (Ann Arbor: University of Michigan Press, 1982), p. 168.

25. Weng Wen-hao, *Chung-kuo ching-chi kai-k'uang* (General situation of the Chinese economy) (Chungking, 1943), p. 9.

26. The act is published in *TYYK* 3, 2 (August 1942).

27. Ch'i, *Nationalist China at War*, p. 168.

28. Chi, *Wartime Economic Development*, chap. 3, p. 17. On general principles of wartime economic control, see T'an Chen-min, *Chan-shih t'ung-chih ching-chi* (Wartime controlled economy) (Chungking, 1940); Ch'en Ho-ch'ang et al., eds. *Chung-kuo chan-shih ching-chi chih* (Gazetteer of China's wartime economy) (Chungking, 1940); Weng Wen-hao, *Kuo-min ching-chi chien-she yun-tung* (Popular economic construction movement) (Chungking, 1940); Leonard J. Ting, "War and Industry in China," *Nankai Social and Economic Quarterly* 2, 1–2 (January 1940): 63–100.

29. On wartime hiring procedures see AH, NRC, 1941–46 files entitled "Ko chiao-yu chi-kuan chieh-shao hsueh-sheng" (Introductions of students by various educational agencies); "Chung-yang chien-chiao-yu ho-tso wei-yuan-hui" (Central educational cooperative committee); "K'ao-shih-yuan k'ao-hsuan wei-yuan-hui" (Examination Committee of the Examination Yuan); "Hsuan-yung ko ta-hsueh pi-yeh hsueh-sheng lai-hui" (Selection of college graduates to enter the commission); "Tzu-chien-an" (Cases of self-recommendation).

30. AH, NRC, file, "Tzu-yuan wei-yuan-hui chien-chieh" (Brief introduction to the NRC) (1942), pp. 1–7; *China Handbook, 1937–45* (New York: Macmillan, 1947), p. 354 (compare with somewhat lower statistics in *TYKP*, vols. 3–5 [1942–44]); Hou, "Economic Development," pp. 210–11.

31. HST, Truman papers, files of Edwin A. Locke, Jr., "China Mission Data Report," September 1944, p. 14.

32. Ibid., p. 83; On conditions at Yumen, see the memoirs of Sun Yueh-chi, "Hui-i wo yu Chiang Chieh-shi chieh-ch'u erh-san-tz'u" (Recollections of two or three encounters with Chiang Kai-shek), *Wen-shih tzu-liao* (Literary and historical materials) 84 (December 1982): 113–34. See also James Reardon-Anderson, *The Study of Change: Chemistry in China, 1840–1949* (New York: Cambridge University Press, 1991), p. 297.

33. AH, NRC, "Tzu-yuan wei-yuan-hui chien-chieh," 3; FDR, AWPM, box 40, Cragg, p. 133. See also Reardon-Anderson, *The Study of Change*, p. 300.

34. Reardon-Anderson, *The Study of Change*, p. 299.

35. FDR, AWPM, Cragg, p. 97.

36. HST, Truman Papers, Locke files, "China Mission Data Report," p. 1.

37. Ibid., p. 9.

38. Ibid., pp. 87–90; CAS, *Tzu-yuan wei-yuan-hui kuo-wai mao-i shih-wu-suo pao-kao* (Reports of the NRC Foreign Trade Office), monthly and annually, 1939–42, 1946; AH, NRC, file, "Tui Su mao-i chiao-she" (Trade negotiations with the USSR) (April 1947); AH, NRC, file, "Niu-yueh kung-tso pao-kao, 1940–44" (New York Foreign Trade Office Report, 1940–44); Arthur N. Young, *China's Wartime Finance and Inflation, 1937–1945* (Cambridge: Harvard University Press, 1965), pp. 98–99, 104–5.

39. See, for example, Chinese Academy of Social Sciences, Peking (hereafter cited as CASS), NRC, 28(2)100 "Hsi-nan ko-sheng san-nien kuo-fang chien-she chi-hua ta-kang" (Summary of natonal defense construction three-year plan for the provinces of Southwest China); 28(2)5965–2, "Kuo-fang kung-yeh chan-shih san-nien chi-hua kang-yao" (Summary of the wartime national defense industrial three-year plan [for 1942–44]).

40. FDR, AWPM, box 40, Cragg, p. 97; box 36, notes of a conference with NRC representatives, September 18–19, 1944; *China Handbook, 1937–45*, p. 366.

41. See, for example, FDR, AWPM, box 6, report of Edwin K. Smith, June 1, 1945; box 7, memorandum to H. LeRoy Whitney, June 16, 1945; box 10, NRC report to Jacobsen, September 1944, p. 7ff. On the "great prestige" enjoyed by technicians and engineers in Republican China, see Y. C. Wang, *Chinese Intellectuals and the West, 1872–1949* (Chapel Hill: University of North Carolina Press, 1966), p. 470.

42. Hou, "Economic Development," pp. 209–10.

43. See, for example, Cheng, *Foreign Trade and Industrial Development*, pp. 109–10. Cheng himself was an NRC economist during the war.

44. Bibliographical sources on postwar planning include "Tzu-liao suo-yin" (Source materials index), in *Tzu-yuan wei-yuan-hui chi-k'an* (hereafter cited as *TYCK*), monthly, 1941–46; "Tzu-yuan wei-yuan-hui yueh-k'an, chi-k'an tsung mu-lu suo-yin" (General index of *TYYK* and *TYCK*), *TYCK* 5, 4 (December 1, 1945); Aimee de Potter, ed., "Postwar Reconstruction in the Far East: A Selective Bibliography," IPR conference paper, December 1942. Important non-NRC journals concerned with postwar planning include *Ching-chi chien-she chi-k'an* (Economic construction monthly) and *Hsin ching-chi* (New economy). Two of the most important public statements on postwar planning are Weng Wen-hao, *Chan-hou ching-chi chien-she* (Postwar economic construction) (Chungking, 1941); and Weng Wen-hao, *Chung-kuo ching-chi chien-she kai-lun* (General discussion of Chinese economic development) (Chungking, 1944). See also files in SHA 28(2)934; PAC, file, "Kung-yeh chien-she chi-hua hui-i" (Conference on industrial development plan); and National Archives, Department of State Intelligence Research Report, "Trends toward State Control of Industry in China," August 20, 1946.

45. AH, NRC, file, "Tzu-yuan wei-yuan-hui chien-chieh," speech by Ch'ien Ch'ang-chao of January 21, 1942. See also Ch'ien Ch'ang-chao, "Chung kung-yeh chien-she hsien-tsai chi chiang-lai" (Present and future of heavy industrial development), *TYKP* 3, 3

(September 1942): 49–54. Even T. V. Soong discussed following a Soviet model of industrialization in a BBC speech of August 8, 1943: see Yuan-li Wu, *China's Economic Policy: Planning or Free Enterprise?* (New York, 1946). See also "Su-lien kung-yeh chien-she chih yen-chin" (Evolution of Soviet industrial development) *TYKP* 3, 6 (December 1942): 43–47.

46. AH, NRC, Weng Wen-hao papers (hereafter cited as WWH), letter, Weng Wen-hao to F. Pan, March 4, 1948.

47. H. D. Fong, introduction to "Problems of Economic Reconstruction in China," IPR conference paper, 1942, pp. 1–3; K. Y. Yin, trans., "Draft Outline of Principles for Postwar Economic Reconstruction in China," in ibid., pp. 7, 16.

48. SHA, 28(2)934 "Chan-hou kung-yeh chien-she ch'u-pu shih-shih chi-hua" (Preliminary enforcement plan for postwar industrial construction). Reports of the conference are in PAC, file, "Kung-yeh chien-she chi-hua hui-i" (Conference on industrial development plan). See also *Foreign Relations of the United States (FRUS)*, 1944, China, Gauss to Secretary of State, March 15, 1944 (Washington, DC: Government Printing Office, 1967); Howard Boorman et al. eds., *Biographical Dictionary of Republican China* (New York: Columbia University Press, 1967–71), 3:411–12.

49. See SHA, 28(2)50, file, "Chu Mei tai-piao-t'uan pan-shih-ch'u san-shih-wu nien nien-tu pao-kao" (1946 annual report of the NRC office in the U.S.); AH, NRC, file, "Wai-chi chuan-chia" (Foreign experts), list of August 16, 1945; "Ko-hsiang chi-shu ho-t'ung" (Various consulting agreements), 1945–46.

50. See files in SHA, 28(18741).

51. AH, NRC, "Tzu-yuan wei-yuan-hui chien-chieh"; file, "Hsun-lien jen-yuan ko-tan tzu-liao" (Materials on the training of various units); files, "Chi-shu wei-yuan-hui hsin-han" (Correspondence of the technical committee, 1944–46); SHA, 28(18971), files, "Chu Mei chi-shu-t'uan" (Technical office in the U.S.).

52. See Wu Ching-ch'ao, "Plan for China's Industrialization," IPR conference paper, 1945, pp. 16–18; D. K. Kieu, *China's Economic Stabilization and Reconstruction* (New Brunswick: Rutgers University Press, 1948), pp. 50–52, 127–29; H. D. Fong, *Postwar Industrialization of China* (Washington, DC, 1942), pp. 64–65, 67–69.

53. HST, George M. Elsey papers, box 59: "Summary of United States Government and Military Aid Authorized for China Since 1937," State Department Memorandum dated January 1950.

54. See IMH, NRC, *ts'ai*, 56–1–9/0, lend-lease files, 1942–47.

55. AH, NRC, "Tzu-yuan wei-yuan-hui chien-chieh"; file, "Hsun-lien jen-yuan ko-tan tzu-liao"; files, "Chi-shu wei-yuan-hui hsin-han." SHA, 28(18971), files, "Chu Mei chi-shu-t'uan." See also Wang, *Chinese Intellectuals*, pp. 136–37; *TYKP*, 11, 4–5 (October–November 1946): 196–204; 14, 4 (April 1948): 77–84.

56. See references in note 55.

57. It was also a good way to get a political liability out of the country, and "China seemed about as far away as he could be sent." See Michael Schaller, *The U.S. Crusade in China, 1938–1945* (New York: Columbia University Press, 1979), p. 166.

58. See FDR, AWPM, box 40, Cragg, "History of the American War Production Mission to China," p. 1; *FRUS*, 1944, China, pp. 248–49, Roosevelt to Nelson, August 18, 1944.

59. In his conversation with Chiang Kai-shek, September 19, 1944, in *FRUS*, 1944, China, p. 269.

60. See postwar planning documents in SHA, 28(2)934; and PAC, file, "Kung-yeh chien-she chi-hua hui-i," 1943–44.

61. See law governing the board in SHA, 4(2)1133.

62. On the degree to which existing organizations were simply given an additional

name under the War Production Board, see Kuan Te-mao,"Weng Wen-hao ch'i jen yu shih" (Weng Wen-hao, the man and his work), *Chuan-chi wen-hsueh* (Biographical literature) 36, 4 (1980): 77. For lists of leading individuals on the board, see Weng Wen-hao, "Chung-ch'ing chan-shih sheng-ch'an chu," p. 72; and Tung Tsan-yao,"Weng Wen-hao yu kuo-min cheng-fu ching-chi-pu" (Weng Wen-hao and the Economics Ministry of the national government), *Kiangsu wen-shih tzu-liao* (Kiangsu literary and historical materials) (November 15, 1984), pp. 11–12.

63. FDR, AWPM, box 40, Cragg, pp. 2–69; box 6, weekly reports of the mission, 1944–45.

64. See William C. Kirby, "Planning Postwar China: China, the United States and Postwar Economic Strategies, 1941–1948," paper delivered at the Conference on Sun Yat-sen and Modern China, Kaohsiung, November 1985.

65. AH, NRC, file, "Wai-chi" (Foreign nationals), press release on J. L. Savage; Ch'ien Ch'ang-chao papers, Huang Yu-hsien to J. L. Savage, February 21, 1946; Ch'ien Ch'ang-chao to C. P. Dunn, April 19, 1946; SHA, 52(2) 1517, *passim*; HST, Truman papers, files of Edwin A. Locke, Jr., box 8, "Precis of Dr. J. L. Savage's Preliminary Report on the Yangtze Gorge Project"; NA, records of the Bureau of Reclamation of the Department of the Interior, file 090.09, "Foreign Activities, China," 1944–45.

66. AH, NRC, Ch'ien Ch'ang-chao papers, telegram, Weng Wen-hao to Yun Chen, May 16, 1947.

67. Cheng, *Foreign Trade and Industrial Development*, pp. 114–19.

68. See *FRUS*, 1946, China, pp. 1380–81, Byrnes to Stuart, July 19, 1946; AH, NRC, WWH, letter, Yu Chen to Weng Wen-hao, October 17, 1947.

69. *TYKP* 13, 4 (October 1947): 40; Chu-yuan Cheng, *China's Economic Development: Growth and Structural Change* (Boulder: Westview Press, 1982), p. 138; Hsueh Mu-ch'iao, *The Socialist Transformation of the National Economy in China* (Beijing: Foreign Languages Press, 1960), p. 20; Thomas G. Rawski, *China's Transition to Industrialism* (Ann Arbor: University of Michigan Press, 1980), p. 30.

70. See Eastman, *Seeds of Destruction*, pp. 109–13.

71. Chu-yuan Cheng, *Communist China's Economy, 1949–1962* (South Orange, NJ: Seton Hall University Press, 1963), p. 9.

72. See William Kirby, "Continuity and Change in Chinese Economic Planning on the Mainland and on Taiwan, 1943–58," paper prepared for the Annual Meeting of the Association for Asian Studies, Washington, DC, 1989.

73. See ibid. for details.

74. So named in part also because it was formed in the thirty-first year of the Republic.

75. The following is based largely on extensive interviews in the PRC and on Taiwan with living members of this group, and with the NRC officials who supervised them.

76. Interview, Y. S. Sun, Taipei, Taiwan, July 1987.

9

SCIENCE IN WARTIME CHINA

James Reardon-Anderson

THE RELATIONSHIP between science and politics in the Nationalist and Communist areas of China during the War of Resistance is important for understanding not only the nature of China's wartime resistance, but the subsequent development of science in that country as well. In both Nationalist- and Communist-ruled areas, the interests of the political leadership and of the scientific and technical community were overlapping but not completely congruent. Political and scientific-technical elites shared a commitment to apply scientific knowledge and skills to the immediate needs of production and defense. However, the government authorities wanted that commitment to be total, while the scientists, teachers, and scholars reserved a place for more basic learning. They valued research into the fundamental workings of nature and wanted education to be rooted in theoretical foundations. This the politicians considered a waste of time and resources.

The battle over science, and the limits placed on pure as opposed to applied learning, was fought within the Nationalist and Communist camps alike. The outcome of these battles, however, was somewhat different in the two cases. Political leaders in the Communist areas more thoroughly subordinated the scientific community to the utilitarian ends of the war effort than their counterparts in the Nationalist areas were able to do. These variant outcomes affected not only the immediate contest for the control of China but also the character of Chinese science for decades to come.

Science and Politics in Wartime China

One key question stood at the center of the debate over the nature and function of science in both Nationalist and Communist camps. How much of their limited resources should be devoted to the immediate and pressing needs of increasing production and strengthening defense, and how much could be spared for training students in broader, deeper knowledge or for conducting research into more fundamental, albeit nonutilitarian, problems? The answer was not a simple one for political and scientific-technical elites in both Nationalist and Communist China.

For good reasons, government leaders in both areas favored applied science. The situation throughout resistance China was desperate. Nationalist and Communist leaders alike needed all the resources they could muster to defend themselves against Japanese attack, prepare for the coming civil war, and enhance their own power and influence within their own parties. At the same time, political leaders appreciated the need to attract Chinese students, scholars, technicians, and experts of various kinds to perform the multiple tasks envisioned for them as well as to add luster to the Nationalist or Communist cause.

Scientific-technical elites and many of their students made the long, dangerous trek from Peking, Nanking, and Shanghai to Kunming, Chungking, and Yenan because they shared with the leaders of both Chinese parties a commitment to save the nation. All recognized that the needs of survival and resistance must come first. In the field of science this meant working with limited resources, focusing on utilitarian problems, and fashioning simple, useful techniques. They also recognized that they could make a contribution only by working for and within a larger political movement, Nationalist or Communist.

Few among the scientific-technical elites thought, however, that the way to save China was to devote *all* their attention to the immediate, practical, and applied side of things. Most took a larger view of the problem: namely, that knowledge of nature should be useful in the whole of China, not just that corner to which chance had driven them; and that it should be useful not only during the War of Resistance, but in helping to rebuild the country in the postwar era.

This meant that wartime education should prepare not only technicians, but also people with the broad, deep, theoretical learning needed to lead Chinese science through the next generation. Wartime research, they believed, should address not only the problems of production and defense, but also questions at the frontiers of knowledge, for without engaging in this search there would be no science at all. Finally, it should be noted that the view Chinese scientific and technical experts took of wartime science accorded with their own career aspirations, which transcended the war. These men and women had come to the Great Rear because they cared deeply about the survival of their nation, but most saw the resistance as just one stop on a longer journey that would eventually return them to cities along the coast. There they would be able to carry on their lives as successful professionals and as loyal Chinese patriots without any contradiction between these two roles. At least in their own minds, their dual commitment to China and to science was really one and the same thing.

In short, political and scientific-technical elites in both Nationalist and Communist areas shared common aspirations as well as competing goals. Both groups recognized that whatever they did would have to answer the challenge of survival, yet each had a foot outside the common circle. The politicians favored greater utilitarianism, the scientists a more balanced approach. Shared values made it possible for them to work together, but at the same time their differences made conflict inevitable. In Nationalist China the clash was muted. In Communist China, an open conflict created profound and lasting changes.

Science and Politics in Nationalist China

In Chungking, Kunming, and other cities under Nationalist rule, the nature and role of science became a matter of dispute. On one side were conservative elements of the Kuomintang who favored strong central control and the mobilization of national resources to serve the state, and on the other were liberal intellectuals who held out for a measure of autonomy, in part to support broader, deeper education and research. Differences between these two groups are evident in the debates over school curricula, the research agenda, and science policy in general.

In 1938, as China's defenses crumbled, the country's leading universities and research institutes, their faculty, staff, students, and as much of the libraries, laboratories, and other facilities as they could carry with them, followed the Nationalist retreat west. The most famous of the wartime universities, National Southwest Associated (Hsi-nan Lien-ho Ta-hsueh, commonly called Lien-ta), was set up in Kunming by students and teachers from Peking, Tsinghua, and Nankai universities, who had marched more than 1,300 miles to reach the comparative security of mountainous Yunnan. Altogether, some sixty-two colleges and universities moved inland; their combined enrollment grew from thirty thousand in 1938 to seventy thousand by the end of the war.[1] The Academia Sinica, its several research institutes, and other scientific enterprises also relocated to the west. Every commodity in these schools and institutes—books, paper and pencils, clothes, food, drugs, and other basic necessities—was in short supply. Life in the Great Rear was a constant struggle for survival. Education and research had to compete with the business of staying alive.[2]

At Lien-ta, colleges of arts, sciences, commerce, engineering, and education were pieced together from the constituent institutions. Enrollment peaked at around three thousand students, most of whom were in engineering and commerce, the fields where the prospects for employment were brightest. The faculty numbered 350. This favorable student-teacher ratio might have enabled scholars to specialize and devote more time to research. In fact, almost all their energy was consumed by the mundane tasks of living and working under perilous conditions.

Joseph Needham, the distinguished British scientist who spent the war in China, described the difficult conditions faced by scholars and students at Lien-ta, even after the worst days were behind them.

> All the departments are housed in "hutments" built of mudbrick, and roofed very simply with tiles or tin sheets, though some have curving roofs in the great tradition of Chinese architecture. Inside, the floors are beaten earth, with

a little cement, and extreme ingenuity has been used in fitting up laboratories for research and teaching under these conditions. For example, since no gas is available, all the heating has to be done with electricity. When the supply of element wire for heaters (home-made out of clay) ran out some time ago, work was at a standstill until it was found that gun lathe shavings from one of the Yunnan arsenals would do very well. When microscope slides could not be had, windowpanes broken by air raids were cut up, and the unobtainable coverslips were replaced by local mica. Many other instances could be given of Chinese ingenuity and initiative. In many cases there are no air raid shelters, and the population scatters to the hills if a raid looks like being serious. When the siren goes, all the most valuable apparatus of the Associated University is lowered into large petrol drums built into the floors of each mud-brick building, to guard against anything but a direct hit. Even in its humble buildings, the University has been bombed several times, and many of the rows of huts destroyed.[3]

The Lien-ta College of Science included departments of math, physics, chemistry, biology, and earth sciences. Enrollment was around three hundred. The faculty numbered as many as one hundred, with eight to fourteen full and associate professors in each department. The purpose of the college and design of its curricula were essentially the same as those of the constituent universities before the war, except for the addition of courses on the application of science to wartime needs. What changed, however, was the potential for implementing this program.

Laboratories and experimental facilities, specimens and reagents, library reference works and current periodicals were all in short supply. In contrast to the industrial research institutes and schools of engineering, which received the most and best of everything, the College of Science, whose purpose was primarily academic, had the lowest priority and received only the most meager supplies.[4] Imagination and self-reliance filled some gaps. Alcohol lamps replaced gas burners, well water was distilled, and some common reagents, such as hydrogen peroxide, silver nitrate, and hydrochloric and nitric acids, were made on the spot. One reporter who visited Kunming in 1939 found the "simplest household implements, pots, kettles, meat grinders, were used for chemical experiments." But precision instruments were lacking, and the selection of experiments was dictated by the availability of supplies. Under these conditions, laboratory standards and the experimental skills of the students plummeted.[5]

The example of Lien-ta illustrates the impact of the war on scientific education as the Nationalist Ministry of Education, under the direction of Ch'en Li-fu, intervened to favor the applied fields, particularly engineering, at the expense of all others, including the pure sciences. Here, as elsewhere, the College of Engineering enjoyed the largest enrollment and best facilities. During and after their school years, Lien-ta engineers worked on road construction, water conservancy, and such problems of chemical engineering as the manufacture of cokes and dyes. Meanwhile, more than fifty subjects with a direct bearing on industrial and military problems were introduced into colleges and universities throughout

Nationalist China. In all these schools, highest priority was placed on the application of knowledge to achieve useful results.[6]

Students were quick to accept this utilitarian approach. Most university students, wanting to help save the nation and discerning where the best job opportunities lay, elected to study engineering, followed by humanities and the arts, with agriculture, medicine, and natural science far down the list of preferred majors. In 1943, of the nearly six thousand candidates who took the entrance exam for National Central University, 31 percent chose engineering, 25 percent law, 12 percent each agriculture and education, 10 percent letters, and only 5 percent each medicine and science.

Some observers expressed concern that young people were being seduced into fields that promised the most immediate returns. In the view of Academia Sinica President Chu Chia-hua, this was a "dangerous phenomenon" that threatened to undermine the foundation of basic science, but his warning was to no avail. By 1944, one-quarter of all students in schools of higher learning were studying engineering, while fewer than 9 percent chose pure science—a figure below the level of 1928, when the Nationalists first began their program to expand training in the sciences.[7]

While the ministry directed funds to applied fields, and the students followed these priorities, the fate of Chinese education remained in the hands of the teachers and school administrators, who were not always faithful to Ch'en Li-fu's utilitarian approach. One report on the state of engineering education in the Nationalist areas in 1942 describes the wide gap between these programs and the society they were supposed to serve. According to this report, the typical engineering graduate invariably discovered that "what he has studied is of no use, and what is of use he has not studied," while the people who were supposed to benefit from their expert services found that the young technicians "cannot put up with the suffering, are unwilling to take responsibility and unable to deal with practical problems."[8] The author blamed this shortcoming on the character of the education itself.

China's engineering curricula had been copied from European and American models and based on advanced technologies that had nothing to do with China. Meanwhile, Chinese scholars had failed to investigate the situation in their own country. The engineering colleges had done little to promote work-study programs or internships, students were allowed to while away their summer vacations rather than gain useful hands-on experience, and university research facilities had failed to draw in people and problems from the real world. Those charged with training China's future engineers tended to look down on the challenges of applied science as being of little scholarly value, while the educational bureaucrats diverted funds from research to areas that promised more immediate rewards. The result, this study concluded, was that Chinese engineering education "falls between two stools," and, lacking clear purpose, has become "education for its own sake."[9]

The same tension between utilitarianism and the independent quest for new knowledge marked debates over the research agenda in the Nationalist areas. Some scholars followed Ch'en Li-fu's lead, shifting their attention to problems of industry, agriculture, and public health. But others continued research begun during the previous decade, in China or abroad, which addressed basic questions about the workings of nature, while bearing little connection to the practical problems of China at war. The latter tendency was most pronounced among the scientists lodged in the Academia Sinica and the leading universities.[10]

The conflict over the role of science, evident in the fields of education and research, sharpened with the passage of time. Early in the war, when the spirit of national resistance ran high, it seemed that cooperation would be forthcoming among those engaged in scientific and technical work. "Although this has been a most difficult period," wrote one Chinese chemist in 1939, "it has been a good opportunity for the unification of chemical research and chemical industry." New industries had sprung up to meet the demands of war, new methods devised, and resources found to make up for lost imports, while everyone pitched in to save the nation. "In some cases scholars have taken control of factories, research departments have been set up within scholarly organizations, and scholarly organizations have stepped in to solve problems on behalf of the factories. . . . In the present circumstances, chemical research and chemical industry have become one." At the same time, this observer foresaw the potential for conflict between the narrow agenda of Chinese industry and the broader needs of science. The question will inevitably arise, he warned, of "how to promote research on chemical industry without compromising the freedom to do [other] chemical research."[11]

As the war continued and patience on all sides wore thin, this forecast proved correct. Spokesmen for the pragmatic or statist approach argued eloquently for scientists to support the immediate needs of war. Lu Yu-tao, editor of the journal K'o-hsueh (Science), took up the government's cause by urging the scientists to come out of their "ivory towers" and join in solving the problems confronting China. Lu charged that many scientists considered their research a "sacred, lofty" affair that should not be "vulgarized" by the demands of the marketplace. In fact, he countered, much current research was excessively theoretical and served no useful purpose, while those who performed it refused to recognize their responsibility to society as a whole. The more deeply the scientists enter into their arcane specialties, he pointed out, "the heavier becomes the odor of their pedantry." Chungking calls on its scientists to do applied studies, while the scientists reply that the government should support basic research. "In the end, the two parties remain on opposite banks, shouting their war cries. They are like two cogwheels that have not been engaged."[12]

The chief force behind the movement for applied learning was the conservative wing of the Kuomintang, but early in the war, when hopes for the united front between Nationalists and Communists were high, leftists in Chungking also promoted the view that science should serve the state. Articles in the Communist-sponsored, Chungking-based journal *Ch'un-chung* (The Masses), criticized those scholars who favored the teaching of basic science while resisting utilitarian studies. Since the outbreak of the war, one author was happy to report, many scientists had come around to the defense of their country. Now, all sides should promote this trend, while those who continue to demur should be made to see the error of their ways.[13]

Although the language of these articles was blunted in deference to the united front, much of this analysis was indelibly Marxist. Yuan Han-ch'ing, an important figure in Nationalist science, who had taught chemistry at two leading universities during the 1930s and headed an institute in Lanchow during the war, argued that the progress of Chinese science depended on the prior development of China's industry and the liberation of that country from imperialist control.

> Science becomes a necessary instrument only after the development of industry. . . . Once there is the need, once there is a path, then naturally people will be willing to receive training in scientific research. . . . Our country is a semicolony oppressed by imperialism. In this social setting, the immature shoots of our science cannot see the light, receive the rain, or breathe the air. . . . If we want to promote scientific research, we must first liberate the nation and struggle for the industrialization of the society.[14]

On the other side were scholars and scientists who favored an approach rooted in pure theoretical learning. These men and women cannot be charged with lacking concern for China. They had left the relative comfort and security of homes on the coast and in some cases foregone offers of employment abroad in order to join the resistance, hardships and all, in the Great Rear. Their defense of basic education and research, which they continued to pursue against pressure from Chungking, was based on a view of what was best for China.

Much of this opposition came from Kunming, which boasted a large concentration of scholars and intellectuals, a favorable location at the terminal for flights "over the Hump," and the protection of local warlord, Lung Yun, against political interference from Chungking. Spokespersons for the Kunming intellectual community championed the right of scholars to set their own agenda. "The basic goal of the university," explained political scientist Ch'ien Tuan-sheng, "is the quest for knowledge, it is not utility. If university education is able, at the same time, to produce something useful, that is an ancillary function and not its original goal."[15]

Several of Ch'ien's colleagues extended this principle to the study of science. In 1944, Hao Ching-sheng, a popular writer on scientific and educational affairs, praised the many effective applications of science made during the war but pointed out that these successes rested on education and research from the pre-war era, without which none of the later achievements would have been possible. In the course of the next decade, Hao observed, China would need 2.5 million technical cadres, all of whom must be trained in scientific theory. During the war, the country had paid in blood to raise itself to the ranks of the Allied powers. It could remain in this company after the war, only if Chinese science kept pace with international standards. The long-term needs of the nation depended on an investment in basic education and research, a commitment Chungking refused to honor. "From the independent academies above to the research institutes of the universities below," Hao lamented, "all are in economic straits and cannot develop. This is a situation we must deplore."[16]

Many scientists voiced similar misgivings about Chungking's neglect of pure research. Hu Hsien-su, the most prominent botanist of his generation, explained that many modern advances, which "seem to arise from an almost mystical science, are in fact the result of constant research and experimentation by ordinary scientists, burrowing away in their laboratories, wracking their brains." In Hu's opinion, this activity, far from being alien to society, deserved greater understanding and more generous support.[17] Chu Chia-hua, a geologist and acting president of the Academia Sinica, criticized Chungking for placing too much emphasis on short-term results and appealed for a more balanced program of pure and applied studies. The experience of the Soviet Union, Chu argued, shows that successful applications depend on knowledge derived from basic research.[18] In 1944, the National Research Council, a body composed of China's leading scientists, charged with advising the government on scientific affairs, followed Chu's lead by calling for an emphasis on basic research, improvement of the facilities of universities and research institutes, greater efforts to extend the knowledge and fruits of Chinese science beyond the state to the people, and closer cooperation with scientists overseas.[19]

As the struggle wore on, some critics of the applied approach charged that the Nationalists were using science to strengthen their military power, while maintaining the dominance of traditional values and a dictatorial hold on society. Among those who took issue with this effort were spokespersons on the left, who had favored utilitarianism early in the war when it served the alliance between Nationalists and Communists, but who reversed their position after the collapse of the united front. One article in the Communist journal Ch'un-chung, while agreeing that science should help defend China, pointed out that the current effort failed to combine technological progress with mass mobilization or extend the benefits of science to the general public. The author pointed out that the same people who defended the "science of national defense" also favored traditional philosophy, while rejecting the role of science in remaking Chinese culture—a clear reference to the Kuomintang right. The proper role of science, he concluded, was to enrich the masses and transform their culture, not simply to strengthen the state.[20]

Opinions of this type were not limited to the left. The editors of the centrist Wen-hua hsien-feng (Cultural pioneer), who supported the movement for a "science of national defense" and other elements of the pragmatic agenda, argued that science should also contribute to the formation of a new "national culture." In their view, the earlier defeats at the hands of imperialism had demoralized the Chinese, causing them to abandon traditional learning and embrace indiscriminate Westernization, with the result that "our nation's scholarship and culture remain the tail wagged by foreign scholarship and culture." Only when China develops its own science, they concluded, can the Chinese regain their independence and pride. "If a country does not respect scholarship and culture," they said, "then it cannot advance, become independent and strong. If a people cannot absorb the world's culture, cannot invent or create, and make no contribution to the world, then they are lost."[21]

Chinese scientists, like Chinese in other walks of life, responded to the Japanese invasion by leaving the comfort of home and work places in coastal cities to join the hard scrabble of the resistance. Adaptation to life in the Great Rear forced the scientists to become more self-reliant and innovative and to recognize the need to apply their knowledge to practical ends. The Nationalist government advanced this trend by asserting greater control over all aspects of science and technology, urging men and women in these fields to serve the common cause, and allocating funds to support this purpose. But many scientists retained a sense of their professional autonomy and a commitment to learning that transcended the demands of the moment. By war's end, the conflict between science and the state in Kuomintang China remained unresolved.

Science and Politics in Communist China

The debate over science and science policy in the Communist areas of China derived from the same tension between political and scientific-technical elites. The men who led the Chinese Communist party through the War of Resistance came to power by surviving the Long March and other arduous tests. They had become adept at living off the meager fruits of China's poorest, most backward areas, and they appreciated the necessity for making do. In striking contrast, the students, scholars, intellectuals, and experts who left the cities after 1937 to join the Communists in Yenan were a very different lot. They were not as well educated or accomplished as their counterparts in the south, but they still had a knowledge of and taste for the complexities of modern life. Therefore, between party cadres, on the one hand, and scientific-technical personnel, on the other, sharply different views developed as to the role science should play in China during the war and beyond.

The influx of refugees from occupied China injected new life into the Communist movement. According to one estimate, by the end of 1940, 100,000 migrants, about half of them students, teachers, writers, and other intellectuals, arrived in the Shen-Kan-Ning Border Region. Although the flow slowed somewhat after the imposition of the Nationalist blockade in 1939, another 86,000 came between 1941 and 1944.[22] Many of these young people had studied in

China's best middle schools and universities, where they had begun to prepare for modern, urban careers. Most were drawn to Yenan less out of a commitment to Marxism than because the Communists offered a way to help rid the nation of foreign invaders. These young men and women were not revolutionaries. For most, the resistance was merely one of life's passages. They saw no conflict among the goals of liberating China from foreign domination, rebuilding the country after the war, and going on to pursue their own careers.

To attract these students and intellectuals and absorb them into the work of the border regions, the party established schools of various types. In 1942, Yenan, which visitors described as a "student city," boasted more than twenty full-time institutions to train cadres for general military, administrative, and political tasks, or for more specialized work in propaganda, ideology, labor, transportation, the arts, medicine, pharmacology, and science and technology.[23]

The new arrivals contributed valuable skills and youthful enthusiasm to the Communist cause. Many also carried liabilities that placed them in conflict with party authorities because they came from bourgeois backgrounds that failed to prepare them for the hardships of life in the countryside. They were drawn to Yenan by a spirit of nationalism, and they lacked a partisan preference for the Communist party, knowledge of Marxism, or commitment to class struggle. They thought of themselves as modern "men of talent," who had the responsibility to attack hypocrisy and abuses of power, wherever they found them. Finally, they inclined toward a liberal view of knowledge, seeing it as a free commodity, an end in itself, the object of study by free people and of exchange among men and women of all nations. They rejected the notion that knowledge was an instrument of the state.

The main arena for the study and practice of science in the Communist areas was the Natural Science Institute (Tzu-jan K'o-hsueh Yuan). NSI was founded in 1939 for the purpose of training technicians to perform the practical tasks required to increase production and strengthen defense. The initiative came from the CCP's Finance and Economics Department, whose deputy director, Li Fu-ch'un, served as the institute's first president. The school was set up in tandem with experimental factories, where students received training and new techniques were tested and refined. The whole enterprise was designed to produce useful results.[24] The Natural Science Institute was first located in hilltop caves at Tu-fu-ch'uan-k'ou, near Ch'i-li-pu, outside the south gate of Yenan. It had the border region's only science building, which included laboratories and workshops. Glass instruments and reagents were obtained through the CCP office in Chungking from agents in Hong Kong. Laboratory equipment was manufactured in the institute's own machine shop. Despite such ingenuity, facilities were in fact limited. Laboratory equipment consisted chiefly of what could be scavenged or improvised from bits of glass and metal. Paper, ink, and other materials were scarce and of poor quality. Students passed the few available textbooks from hand to hand.

One participant vividly recalled the institute's crude, but spirited operations:

> We did not have any modern scientific apparatuses or equipment, let alone spacious and well-lit classrooms. The conditions of school life were even harder. Classes were conducted and meals taken in open air. Bricks and tree stumps were our stools, and our knees served as desks. Walls were smeared with soot and used as blackboards. When the ground was leveled, a raised portion was left to serve as a platform. The students had no paper to write on, and so they did their exercises on the ground. They had no pens to write with, and so they tied nibs onto goose feathers or twigs. Both the faculty members and students slept in caves, each of which was shared by three people in the case of faculty members and by eight, ten, or more than ten people in the case of students. They all slept in earth beds that were so crowded that they found it difficult even to turn about. Some students used to say jokingly, "When we want to turn in our sleep, we have to cry "one, two, three," so that all turn together."[25]

Once the institute was established, Li Fu-ch'un, who had endowed it with his utilitarian mission, withdrew, leaving the implementation to men who took a more sectarian, professional approach to science. At the head was Li's successor, Hsu T'e-li, who took charge of all aspects of the school—planning, curriculum, politics, and logistics—and left an indelible mark on all of them, particularly the curriculum.[26] The faculty, with the exception of Hsu and one other former university professor, were young, averaging around thirty years of age, and had some experience as students in universities in China or abroad. Students were recruited during the first half of 1940 by examination from schools in Shen-Kan-Ning and from among young intellectuals who had come to Yenan from other parts of China and were assigned to the NSI by the party's Organization Department.

Enrollment in the first class of the university section began in 1940 with twenty to thirty students, all middle school graduates, and peaked at eighty in 1942. Hsu T'e-li remembered these students as "advanced intellectual youths who had come from different parts of the country," many from "rather well-off families." Although precise data on their background is lacking, they were probably similar to students at the party's Central Research Institute, where a substantial majority were men and women in their twenties, from urban intellectual backgrounds, who had never held a job or joined a political party before coming to Yenan. These young people were well-prepared for careers in urban China, perhaps after a stint of overseas study, but not for the hardship of rural life or the harsh discipline of revolution and war.[27] Under Hsu's direction, the organization and curriculum of NSI followed the pattern of higher education in China before the war. Because the educational background of most students was minimal, the first semester, in the fall of 1940, was devoted to a review of basic math and science. When Hsu T'e-li took over, at the end of 1940, the course of study was lengthened—the middle school from three and a half to five years, the university from two to three years—and the curriculum reformed to increase the teaching of basic science in the middle school and the first year of college, postponing practical application to the last two years. Most courses relied on standard university-level English-language texts, supplemented by lectures, which were generally Chinese interpretations of the same. Students whose English was deficient had to rely on lecture notes and, in general, found the experience difficult.[28]

At first, during 1940 and 1941, the apparent contradiction between Yenan's stated commitment to production and the actual practice of more autonomous, less utilitarian scholarship was accepted, or at least tolerated, by the party center. The economic crisis brought on by the Kuomintang blockade prompted CCP leaders to demand better results from their factories and schools. They also realized, however, the need to attract intellectuals and technical experts from outside the border regions and to get the most out of those already there—goals that called for a more relaxed approach.

Throughout this period, Chinese Communist propaganda organs painted a rosy picture of the reception artists and intellectuals could expect in Yenan. On May 1, 1941, the Politburo issued a directive, affirming its commitment to "encourage free research, respect intellectuals, promote the movement for scientific knowledge and literature, (and) welcome scientific and artistic personnel" from outside the border regions. These themes were widely disseminated in editorials that promised scientific and artistic workers greater freedom, support, and opportunities to serve the nation, not only by raising production, but by continuing to do creative work in their specialized fields:

> Do we, therefore, welcome scientists and artists only because we want them to reflect the border regions, make propaganda for the border regions, and help with the reconstruction of the border regions? No, we do not mean to limit scientific and artistic activities to propaganda and application alone. We place equal emphasis, or rather we should say we place even greater emphasis, on the achievements of science and art themselves. Although we find ourselves in a wartime environment . . . , we ought not postpone the work of raising up science and art until after the war.[29]

While the political atmosphere in Yenan remained generally favorable to the intellectuals, tensions began to surface in the second half of 1941. The first signs came in attacks on the Natural Science Institute from cadres in industry and mining. Spokesman for this group was Li Ch'iang, a party veteran, telecommunications expert, and leading figure in the powerful Military Industrial Bureau (Chun-shih Kung-yeh-chu), which oversaw the border region arsenal, oil fields, and other key industries. Li charged that the institute tied up too many technical personnel whose services were needed at the production front. Given the backwardness of the border regions, the practitioners argued, there was no need for education in basic science; students should skip over the theory and proceed directly to producing useful devices. These critics apparently scored some points, for one former NSI student recalls that later that year, the curriculum of the physics department, which had previously followed the academic model of universities in the Nationalist areas, began to resemble more closely a school of engineering.[30]

The leaders of the institute did not back down. Hsu T'e-li defended the school's program on the grounds that basic knowledge was a prerequisite for acquiring practical skills. If technicians specialized too early without gaining a knowledge of the underlying science, Hsu argued, they would be able to perform only routinized tasks and lack the larger vision needed to create the sort of innovations that foster long-term development. Later in the year, the second session of the Shen-Kan-Ning Border Region Consultative Council (ts'an-i hui) heard complaints from scientific and technical personnel that the promises that had attracted them to Yenan had not been fulfilled, and that the fault for this situation lay with the party center. NSI Dean of Studies Ch'u Po-ch'uan charged that the sectarian policy of "self-reliance" within each of the three "systems" (hsi-t'ung)—party, army, and government—had led to a maldistribution of resources, hampered cooperation across jurisdictional lines, and prevented solution of many technical problems. Ch'u proposed to replace the ineffective administrative systems with a unified leadership over scientific and technical matters. This posed a radical, even seditious challenge to Communist party control.[31]

By the end of 1941, those scholars who claimed a right to professional autonomy and learning for its own sake remained in control of science policy—or at least the party continued to tolerate them. The eight-point plan passed by the Consultative Council in November included most of the demands put forward by the scientists: to increase government funding for books, instruments, and research; to strengthen the NSI as a "professional school" and create a separate organ for scientific research; to organize scientific societies and publish books and articles; and to send technical personnel to other areas of China or abroad for advanced study and invite scientific personnel from outside to visit the Communist areas. In early 1942, the border region government began to discuss these recommendations with scientific circles in Yenan. Cooperation between scholars and officials seemed to be on track.[32]

The shift from professionalism to practicality was imposed on scholars and educators by external events—namely, the intensification after mid-1942 of the movement for party rectification or *cheng-feng*. Among its several goals, the rectification campaign aimed at closing the gap between Marxist theory and Chinese revolutionary practice. This meant that education, research, and other activities related to science would be judged by the Maoists according to their utility or practical results. In the charged atmosphere of *cheng-feng*, the study of theory and the quest for basic knowledge were held up for ridicule, while those who pursued such objects were scorned. Although the rectification campaign unfolded slowly and without clear purpose in early 1942, by June Mao's supporters were in full cry, and the unfortunate targets of their anger sought shelter.

In the case of the Natural Science Institute, the first attack came from within, in an article in the July 23 issue of *Liberation Daily* by the chairman of the biology department, Lo T'ien-yu. Lo charged that his comrades at the NSI had failed to place practical application ahead of abstract theory. They had clung to a "dogmatic" reliance on foreign textbooks, rather than going "up the mountain to collect specimens or into the factory to do work." From these books, students learned meaningless abstractions like the "size of the universe," "four or five dimensional space," and the "electron" and "atomic" theories, none of which served any useful purpose. "In some courses," Lo charged, students "simply recite the Classics (chanting their lecture notes) . . . , cling to their books and sit anxiously outside the doors of the factories and farms." Lo contrasted this shabby record with the shining example of his own department of biology. Here, students studied local plants used to make dyes and drugs, teaching was based on an examination of real specimens rather than textbooks, and research focused on the natural resources and practical needs of the border regions.

To set matters right, Lo proposed a complete reorganization of the NSI, replacing the existing departments with two new ones: life sciences (biology and agriculture) and physical sciences (physics, chemistry, and engineering). The former, its position and resources greatly enhanced, would continue the correct program already begun under Lo's direction. The latter, with the old departments crammed into tighter quarters, would initiate reforms along the lines of the biology example.[33]

Lo's critique was rejected by an overwhelming majority of NSI students and staff, demonstrating the breadth and depth of support within the institute for the existing academic priorities. K'ang Yu, a faculty member in Lo's own department, pointed out that in the study of nature, just as in the study of society according to Marxism, theory and application are mutually dependent. "Without the guidance of theory," he wrote, "it is not possible to grasp politics properly. Similarly, in the natural sciences, without a foundation in theoretical science, it is not possible to grasp the techniques of applied science."[34]

K'ang agreed with Lo that scholars in China should not waste scarce human and material resources on pure theoretical research. But a foundation in basic science was necessary for all successful engineers, a fact recognized even by vocational and technical schools. With such a grounding, engineers can apply themselves to many different problems, understand their basic nature, and devise creative solutions. Without it, they are only skilled technicians, limited to the rote performance of assigned tasks and unable to respond to new and unforeseen circumstances. K'ang defended the NSI curriculum as designed to lay a broad theoretical base on which practical applications could be built. He acknowledged that incorrect practices existed, but all should share the blame. The point was for each person to examine and improve his performance. There was no reason to reorganize the institute along the lines proposed by Lo T'ien-yu.[35]

Another teacher in the biology department, Li Shan, also defended the institute, albeit from a different perspective. Li argued that given the low level of development of science and technology in the Communist areas, on the one hand, and of local industry and agriculture, on the other, the two could not be brought together fruitfully at the present time. Immediate improvement of the border region economy would come through the application of available methods and local resources, not from the classroom study of science and technology. But the long-term transformation of China required a fundamental understanding of nature and the instruments for controlling it. If scholars in Yenan take only a short-term view and neglect the basic science, Li warned,

> when the day comes that we need modern science and technology to rebuild the country and have no strong and complete scientific and technological organizations and personnel, then we will lack the confidence to decide the direction of scientific and technical development and the ability to organize the strength of an even broader scientific and technical establishment in our service. It is possible that when this situation arises, the revolution will suffer a great setback.[36]

During September and October, faculty and students met regularly to discuss the issues raised by *cheng-feng* and their implications for the institute. At least two of these sessions were packed by outside participants hostile to Hsu T'e-li. On one occasion, members of the faculty were forced to admit that materials used in their courses, which had been adopted from universities in other countries or other parts of China, bore little relation to the industry and agriculture of the border regions and suffered from a "thick dogmatist coloration." Another session nearly got out of control when it was suggested that the participants move from an abstract discussion of educational policy to Lo's proposal for reorganizing the institute.[37]

The climax came on October 26, when comrades of the NSI formally rejected Lo's charges. They denied that the institute's curriculum had neglected the application of knowledge, and they reaffirmed the need to teach basic theories and methods, even though these were derived from foreign sources and had no immediate practical use. In a separate session, NSI students sided with the faculty and administration, finding that Lo's criticisms of the institute were unfounded. These meetings concluded on October 30, with the judgment that the current leadership and organization should continue essentially unchanged.[38]

Hsu T'e-li's victory turned out to be a Pyrrhic one. According to later testimony by Mao Tse-tung, in October the "Natural Sciences Institute and all the things that went with it were handed over to the government." In any case, for the scientists and educators to approve of what they themselves had been doing was beside the point, for by this time the pressure from outside the institute could no longer be resisted. On November 9, members of the industrial community, led by Li Ch'iang, renewed the attack begun the year before. The industrialists sided with Lo T'ien-yu, charging that the institute had imported useless education from outside the border regions and placed undue emphasis on preparing students for higher study and future needs, while neglecting the immediate requirements of production and war. "To run a university in this way," they asserted, "that is, by aiming high and ignoring the immediate realities, can only result in falling into the trap of dogmatism." In the end, they concluded that the basic science program should be completely gutted and the institute transformed into an industrial vocational school.[39]

At this point, Hsu might have tried to avoid attracting the attention of higher officials who could intervene in what had been an intramural debate. That he took the opposite course was a measure of his courage and undoubtedly contributed to his undoing. Hsu chose the three hundredth anniversary of the birthday of Sir Isaac Newton, on January 14, 1943, to deliver a major speech on the nature of science and its place in the border regions. Thumbing his nose at his *cheng-feng* critics, he began by admitting that on the subject of Newton, "I know only what I have read in books." What he learned from these books, moreover, was that Newton's contribution to science derived from precisely those sources that were anathema to *cheng-feng*: namely, an interest in theory, a willingness to build on the intellectual inheritance of his predecessors, and a broad view of time and space that extended beyond his immediate condition. Hsu charged his critics with taking too narrow a view of science, its past, its future, and the scope of its application in China:

> Some of our comrades are ultra-leftists, who think that all old things have passed their time and that only proletarian things are good and useful. We must understand that Soviet science has also developed out of the inheritance of the capitalist class and, therefore, the view that all things of the capitalist class are useless is incorrect.
>
> The proletariat must certainly absorb the inheritance of the past. Marxism is a synthesis of the past experience of mankind. We should transform capitalist things into proletarian things, transform foreign things into things useful to China. Newton took Greece's things and made them his own . . . .
>
> There is another slanted view that states: This thing is now of no use, so it will be of no use in the future. It is of no use to China, so it is of no use to the border regions. This view supposes that only those things that have a direct utility are needed.[40]

Despite his brave pose, Hsu must have known that he had lost the battle. The tide of *cheng-feng* was running strong, and no one could effectively resist it.

Li Fu-ch'un, the man responsible for creating the institute and assigning it the task of aiding production in the first place, delivered the final blow. Even after leaving the presidency of NSI in late 1940, Li maintained an interest in scientific affairs. Now he became concerned that the institute had failed its original purpose, which was to train technical cadres in support of economic development.

In an open letter of January 1943, Li charged that many scientific and technical experts "still remain in their schools and other organizations and have not made practical contact with the broad production and reconstruction of the border regions." He urged these technicians to mend their ways and "join the struggle for economic development." In particular, he faulted the Natural Science Institute for paying undue attention to theory, while neglecting pressing practical problems such as the expansion of arable land, the curing of livestock illnesses, and the mining and transportation of coal, Li's letter marked the end of the debate over science policy and of attempts to develop a program of basic science education in the Communist areas.[41]

Hsu T'e-li reportedly fought to defend members of the institute who were subjected to interrogation and even torture during the brutal "cadre investigations" that marked the final stages of *cheng-feng*, but by this time he had lost all influence over scientific and academic affairs. In April 1943, Yenan University, reorganized to absorb the Natural Science Institute and other specialized schools, was turned over to Chou Yang, a hard-line Maoist who could be counted on to harness intellectual resources to the needs of production and defense. For the remainder of the war, the university recruited students and teachers from among border region natives who had been active in military and productive affairs, while young people from the cities were "sent down" to live with and learn from the peasants.[42]

Mao Tse-tung's program to "unify theory and practice" had a broad, deep impact on the study and use of science, as on other fields. In the short run, Mao's vision and the strategy that flowed from it proved effective for surviving in the impoverished backwater of rural China and ultimately seizing power throughout the country. By forcing the urban intellectuals to "hunker down," to integrate themselves with the great force of the Chinese peasantry, the Communists avoided the stagnation and loss of purpose that deflated the Kuomintang, and they successfully positioned themselves for the postwar struggle for power.

In the long run, however, *cheng-feng* had many of the unhappy effects against which the scientists-critics had warned. The leveling of scholarship left the Communists with neither the personnel nor the experience to staff and direct the development of science after 1949. The notion that learning must produce immediate, useful results failed to produce a cadre of scientists with the knowledge and skills required for the task of rebuilding the nation. Perhaps most damaging, Chinese intellectuals learned that even in the apparently apolitical study of nature, the party could not be trusted to keep its word or give space to its own supporters. Decades later, Chinese politicians and Chinese scientists are still struggling to overcome this legacy.

Conclusions

The different outcomes in the conflict between political and scientific elites in the Nationalist and Communist areas illustrate the underlying differences between these two Chinese regimes. The Nationalists wanted to take charge of and to order science, along with the rest of society, but they lacked the will, the determination, and the means to do so. In the end, they settled for a stalemate, which the scholars in Kunming welcomed but at the same time boded ill for the postwar struggle that was to come.

The Communists had a larger appetite, better methods for achieving their goals, and—for better and worse—they got what they set out to achieve. Several factors explain their greater success. First, they were in a more desperate situation, more willing to try desperate means, and more willing to enforce them. Second, they faced a much smaller, weaker intellectual community, over whom the party had unquestioned dominion. Most of China's intellectual elite, in science as in other fields, took refuge in the Nationalist areas where, acting together, they were able to resist external control. The smattering of young, semi-educated scholars in Yenan had no such might. Finally, Mao Tse-tung had a vision and the will to impose it that was unmatched by leaders in Chungking. Nationalist politics involved the shoving, hauling, and balancing of competing interests. The Communists under Mao, however, proceeded by campaigns of mass mobilization that swept the board clean. This approach had the most dramatic effect on the development of Chinese Communism and on the role of science and the scientists themselves.

Notes

1. Enrollments: Ch'en Li-fu, *Chinese Education During the War (1937–1942)* (Chungking: Ministry of Education, 1942); Chinese Ministry of Information, ed., *China Handbook* (New York: Macmillan, 1937–45), p. 399.

2. *China Handbook* (1937–43), p. 369.

3. Joseph Needham, *Chinese Science* (London: Pilot Press, 1945), pp. 13–14. Other details: Ch'ing-hua ta-hsueh hsiao-shih pien-hsieh-tsu (Committee for Editing and Writing the History of Tsinghua University), ed., *Ch'ing-hua ta-hsueh hsiao-shih kao* (Draft history of Tsinghua University) (Peking: Chung-hua shu-tien, 1981), pp. 289–316.

4. *Ch'ing-hua ta-hsueh hsiao-shih kao*, pp. 336–39; W. E. Tisdale, "Report of a Visit to Scientific Institutions in China," Rockefeller Archive Center, RG 1, series 601, box 40, pp. 26–28.

5. Hubert Freyn, *Chinese Education in the War* (Shanghai: Kelly & Walsh, 1940), p. 38.

6. Lien-ta College of Engineering: *Ch'ing-hua ta-hsueh hsiao-shih kao*, pp. 358–63, 370. Fifty subjects: *China Handbook* (1937–1943), p. 384.

7. NCU entrants, 1943: Hao Ching-sheng," K'ang-chan ch'i-nien lai chih k'o-hsueh" (Science during the past seven years of the War of Resistance), in *Chung-kuo chan-shih hsueh-shu* (Chinese wartime scholarship), ed. Sun Pen-wen (Shanghai: Cheng-chung shu-chu, 1946), p. 195. Students seduced: ibid.; Chu Chi-hua, "Ch'ing-nien yu k'o-hsueh" (Youth and science), in *Chu Chi-hua hsien-sheng yen-lun-chi* (Dissertations of Dr. Chu Chi-hua), ed. Wang Yee-chun and Sun Pin (Taipei: Institute of Modern History, Academia Sinica, 1977), p. 58. Enrollments, 1928: H. G. W. Woodhead, ed., *The China Yearbook* (Shanghai: North China Daily News & Herald, 1933), p. 537. Enrollments, 1944: *China Handbook* (1937–45), p. 330. Freyn, *Chinese Education in the War*, p. 43, states

that in 1942 one-third of the students at National Central University were studying science and technology, while in 1939 the fraction was two-thirds.

8. Ssu Hao, "Mu-ch'ien Chung-kuo kung-ch'eng chiao-yu chu wen-t'i" (Various questions on present Chinese engineering education), *Hsueh-hsi sheng-huo* (Study life) 3, 2 (July 20, 1942): 92–95.

9. Ibid.

10. The most complete account of scientific research in Nationalist China during the war is Joseph and Dorothy Needham, *Science Outpost: Papers of the Sino-British Co-operation Office, 1942–46* (London: Pilot Press, 1948). For additional information on botany, see C. Y. Chang, "Botanical Work in China During the War, 1937–43," *Acta Brevia Sinensia* (Chungking: Natural Science Society of China), no. 6 (April 1944): 3–6. On astronomy: Y. C. Chang, "The Research Activity of the National Institute of Astronomy," ibid., no. 2 (March 1943): 7–8. On mathematics and other sciences: ibid., no. 3 (May 1943): 31–33. On physics: C. Y. Fan, "Advance of Physics in War-time China," ibid., no. 8 (December 1944): 3–5. On chemistry: Tseng Chao-lun, "Progress of Chemical Research in China," ibid., no. 3 (May 1943): 15–18; Chang I-tsun, "Chung-kuo ti hua-hsueh" (Chemistry in China), in *Chung-hua min-kuo k'o-hsueh chih* (Record of science in the Republic of China) (Taipei: Chung-hua wen-hua ch'u-pan shih-yeh wei-yuan-hui, 1955), pp. 9–12; and Joseph and Dorothy Needham, *Science Outpost*, pp. 80–82. On Academia Sinica: Yeh Ch'i-sun, "Work of the Academia Sinica, 1937–41," *Quarterly Bulletin of China Bibliography* 3, 1 (1943): 7–20; and *China Handbook* (1937–44), p. 263; ibid. (1937–45), p. 351. National Academy of Peiping: "Pei-p'ing yen-chiu-yuan" (The Peiping Academy) (Peking: Executive Yuan, Bureau of Information, 1948), pp. 12–13; and *China Handbook* (1937–43), p. 412; ibid. (1937–44), p. 271; ibid. (1937–45), pp. 357–59.

11. Chou Fa-ch'i, "Hua-hsueh yen-chiu yu hua-hsueh kung-yeh" (Chemical research and chemical industry), *Hua-hsueh kung-ch'eng* 4, 3–4 (December 1939): 66–67.

12. Lu Yu-tao, "Hsien-shih-hsing ti k'o-hsueh yen-chiu" (Practical scientific research), *Wen-hua hsien-feng* (Cultural pioneer) 1, 9 (October 27, 1942): 11–14; and Lu Yu-tao, "K'ang-chan ch'i-nien lai chih k'o-hsueh chieh" (The scientific community during the past seven years of the War of Resistance), in *Chung-kuo chan-shih hsueh-shu*, ed. Sun, pp. 166–80; "Odor of pedantry," in ibid., p. 180; "Opposite banks," in ibid., p. 166.

13. For leftist views, see Tzu Nien, "Fa-hui 'Wu-ssu' yun-tung so t'i-ch'ang ti k'o-hsueh ching-shen" (Develop the scientific spirit advocated by the "May Fourth" Movement), *Ch'un-chung* 2, 24/25 (May 15, 1939): 797–98; and Wu Tsao-hsi, "Erh-ch'i k'ang-chan ti k'o-hsueh yun-tung" (Scientific movement in the second stage of the War of Resistance), *Ch'un-chung* 3, 13 (August 27, 1939): 343–47.

14. Yuan Han-ch'ing, "Lun t'i-kao k'o-hsueh ti yen-chiu" (On raising up scientific research), *Hsin min-tsu* (The new nation) 1, 12 (May 15, 1938): 5–6. Yuan's wartime experience: Joseph and Dorothy Needham, *Science Outpost*, p. 136.

15. Ch'ien Tuan-sheng quotation of 1940, in unpublished manuscript by John Israel, cited in E-tu Zen Sun, "The Growth of the Academic Community, 1912–1949," in *The Cambridge History of China*, ed. John K. Fairbank (Cambridge: Cambridge University Press, 1986), 13:416.

16. Hao, "K'ang-chan ch'i-nien lai chih k'o-hsueh," pp. 189, 194–95, 198.

17. Hu Hsien-su, "K'o-hsueh yu chien-kuo" (Science and national reconstruction), *Wen-hua hsien-feng* 2, 21 (October 10, 1943): 5–6.

18. See selected speeches by Chu Chia-hua, 1943 and 1944, in *Chu Chia-hua hsien-sheng yen-lun-chi*, pp. 43–45, 58, 85–87.

19. "Chung-shih chung-yang yen-chiu-yuan p'i-i-hui chih chien-i" (Emphasizing the proposal of the National Research Council of the Academia Sinica), *Wen-hua hsien-feng* 3, 12 (March 21, 1944): 2.

20. Ting Ssu, "K'o-hsueh ching-shen, k'o-hsueh t'ai-tu" (Scientific spirit, scientific attitude), *Ch'un-chung* 9, 12 (June 1944): 498–504.

21. This view is expressed in response to the proposals of the Advisory Committee of the Academia Sinica, mentioned above: *Wen-hua hsien-feng* 3, 12 (March 21, 1944): 2. The quotation is from the companion editorial, "Hsueh-shu yu chien-kuo" (Scholarship and national reconstruction), ibid.

22. Peter Schran, *Guerrilla Economy: The Development of the Shensi-Kansu-Ninghsia Border Region, 1937–1945* (Albany: SUNY Press, 1976), p. 99.

23. Jane L. Price, *Cadres, Commanders, and Commissars: The Training of the Chinese Communist Leadership, 1920–45* (Boulder: Westview Press, 1976), pp. 137–64.

24. Establishment and goals of NSI: Hu Chi-ch'uan, "Hui-i Yen-an tzu-jan k'o-hsueh yuan ti hsueh-hsi sheng-huo" (Remembering the study life at the Yenan Natural Science Institute), in *K'ang-Jih chan-cheng shih-ch'i chieh-fang-ch'u k'o-hsueh chi-shu fa-chan shih tzu-liao* (Historical materials on the development of science and technology in the liberated areas during the War of Resistance), ed. Wu Heng (Peking: Chung-kuo hsueh-shu ch'u-pan-she, 1983–85), 1:137. This source is cited hereafter as *KJCC*. See also Ch'u Po-ch'uan and Wei Chih, "Yen-an tzu-jan k'o-hsueh yuan" (The Yenan Natural Science Institute), *KJCC*, 4:242–44; and Hua Shou-chun, "Yung tzu-jan pien-cheng-fa chih-tao k'o-hsueh chi-shu ti yen-chiu" (Use the dialectics of nature to direct scientific and technical research), in *Shen-Kan-Ning pien-ch'u tzu-jan pien-cheng-fa yen-chiu tzu-liao* (Research materials on the dialectics of nature in the Shen-Kan-Ning Border Region), ed. Shen-hsi sheng kao-teng yuan-hsiao tzu-jan pien-cheng-fa yen-chiu hui, Yenan ta-hsueh fen-hui (Shensi Provincial Higher School Dialectics of Nature Research Society, Yenan University Branch) (Sian: Shensi jen-min ch'u-pan-she, 1984), pp. 305–6. This source is cited hereafter as *PCF*.

25. Tu-fu-ch'uan-k'ou: Wu Heng and Yen P'ei-lin, "Huai-nien Hsu-lao, wo-men ti hao lao-shih" (Remembering Old Hsu, our great teacher), *KJCC*, 1:91, 137. Laboratory: Hsu Ming-hsiu, "Chien-k'u ch'uang-yeh, wei chiao-hsueh ho pien-ch'u chien-she fu wu" (The difficult enterprise, service to education and the construction of the border regions), *KJCC*, 1:132; and Hu, "Hui-i Yen-an tzu-jan k'o-hsueh yuan ti hsueh-hsi sheng-huo," *KJCC*, 1:142. Quotation: Ts'ao Ch'ing-yuan, "Inherit and Exemplify the Work Style of the Days of Yenan—An Account of an Interview Given by Veteran Comrade Hsu T'e-li to Students of the Peking Institute of Technology," *Chung-kuo ch'ing-nien* (China youth), no. 3 (February 1, 1961), in *Survey of the China Mainland Press* (cited hereafter as *SCMP*), no. 253, pp. 20–21.

26. Biography of Hsu T'e-li: Donald W. Klein and Anne B. Clark, *A Biographic Dictionary of Chinese Communism, 1921–1965* (Cambridge: Harvard University Press, 1971), 1:363–66.

27. NSI students, recruitment and enrollment: Hu, "Hui-i Yen-an tzu-jan k'o-hsueh-yuan ti hsueh-hsi sheng-huo," *KJCC*, 1:137, 140; Ch'ung Shih, "Tzu-jan k'o-hsueh ti yen-chiu kung-tso" (Natural science research work), *PCF*, p. 101; Ch'u and Wei, "Yen-an tzu-jan k'o-hsueh-yuan," *KJCC*, 4:246–48. List of twenty-four students in the first class of 1940: P'eng Erh-ning, "Yen-an tzu-jan k'o-hsueh-yuan—wo-ti mu-hsiao" (The Yenan Natural Science Institute—my alma mater), *KJCC*, 3:335. Hsu quotation: Ts'ao, *SCMP*, p. 22. CRI students: Peter Seybolt, "Terror and Conformity: Counterespionage Campaigns, Rectification, and Mass Movements, 1942–1943," *Modern China* 12, 1 (January 1986): 47–48.

28. Curriculum: Wu and Yen, "Huai-nien Hsu-lao," *KJCC*, 1:90–91; Hsu Ming-hsiu, "Chien-k'u ch'uang-yueh," *KJCC*, 1:128; Hu, "Hui-i Yen-an tzu-jan k'o-hsueh-yuan," *KJCC*, 1:137–39. Hsu's reforms: *CFJP*, September 24 and 25, 1941, p. 3.

29. Directive: "Shen-Kan-Ning pien-ch'u shih-cheng kang-ling" (Executive Program

of the Shen-Kan-Ning Border Region), *KJCC*, 1:69. Quotation: "She-lun: Huan-ying k'o-hsueh i-shu jen-ts'ai" (Editorial: Welcome scientific and artistic personnel), *CFJP*, June 10, 1941, p. 1. See also editorials in *CFJP*, June 7, 1941, p. 1; and June 12, 1941, p. 1.

30. Attack on NSI: Hu, "Hui-i Yen-an tzu-jan k'o-hsueh-yuan," *KJCC*, 1:138–39. Li Ch'iang biography: Klein and Clark, *Biographic Dictionary*, 1:478–79. Role in MIB: "Shen-Kan-Ning pien-ch'u ping-kung fa-chan chien-shih" (Brief history of the Shen-Kan-Ning Border Region arsenals), *KJCC*, 1:168; Huang Hai-lin, "Tzu-li keng-sheng hsieh-tso fu-wu—hui Shen-Kan-Ning T'u-fu ping-kung-ch'ang chi-ch'i-pu" (Self-reliance, cooperation, and service—remembering the Machine Department of the Shen-Kan-Ning T'u-fu Arsenal), *KJCC*, 2:223–24. Critics: Wu and Yen, "Huai-nien Hsu-lao," *KJCC*, 1:92. Heated debate: Hu Chi-ch'uan, "Hui-i Yen-an tzu-jan k'o-hsueh-yuan," *KJCC*, 1:138–39.

31. Hsu T'e-li: Hsu T'e-li, "Tsen-ma-yang fa-chan wo-men ti tzu-jan k'o-hsueh" (How to develop our natural sciences), *CFJP*, September 24 and 25, 1941, p. 3. Consultative Council: Wu Chien-chih, "Wo-men ti yao-ch'iu" (Our demands), *CFJP*, November 10, 1941, p. 4. Ch'u Po-ch'uan: ibid.

32. Eight-point plan: Chao I-feng, "Fa-chan pien-ch'u k'o-hsueh shih-yeh" (Develop science in the border region), *CFJP*, November 29, 1941, p. 4. Discussion: *CFJP*, January 27, 1942, p. 4.

33. Lo T'ien-yu, "Tu 'Kuan-yu Yen-an kan-pu hsueh-hsiao ti chueh-ting' " (On reading the "Resolution on the Yenan Cadre School"), *CFJP*, July 23, 1942, p. 4.

34. K'ang Yu, "Tui Lo T'ien-yu t'ung-chih 'T'an kuan-yu Yen-an kan-pu hsueh-hsiao ti chueh-ting' chih shang-ch'ueh" (Discussion of Comrade Lo T'ien-yu's "On the Resolution on the Yenan Cadre School"), *CFJP*, September 25, 1942, p. 4, reprinted in *PCF*, pp. 141–46.

35. Ibid.

36. Li Shan, "Kuan-yu fa-chan wo-men ti tzu-jan k'o-hsueh chiao-yu kung-tso ti wo-chien" (My views on developing our natural science education and work), *CFJP*, September 25, 1942, p. 4.

37. "Dogmatist coloration": "K'o-hsueh-yuan chan-k'ai t'ao-lun 'ju-ho yu shih-chi lien-hsi' " (Science Institute opens discussion of "How to link up with reality"), *CFJP*, November 11, 1942, p. 2. Out of control: "Tzu-jan k'o-hsueh-yuan chi-hsu t'ao-lun chiao-hsueh fang-chen" (Natural Science Institute continues discussion of education policy), *CFJP*, October 23, 1942, p. 2.

38. "K'o-hsueh-yuan chiao-yu fang-chen ti t'ao-lun tsung-chieh" (Summary of discussion on the educational policy of the Science Institute), *CFJP*, November 9, 1942, reprinted in *PCF*, pp. 147–51.

39. Mao: from "Economic and Financial Problems," cited in Andrew Watson, *Mao Zedong and the Political Economy of the Border Region* (Cambridge: Cambridge University Press, 1980), p. 209. November 9 article: Li Ch'iang et al., "Tzu-jan k'o-hsueh chiao-yu yu kung-yeh chien-she" (Natural science education and industrial reconstruction), *CFJP*, November 9, 1942, reprinted in *PCF*, pp. 132–36.

40. Hsu T'e-li, "Tui Niu-tun ying-yu i jen-shih" (What we should know about Newton), *CFJP*, January 14, 1943, p. 4.

41. Li's influence in NSI: Ho Ch'un-po, "Wu Yu-chang t'ung-chih" (Comrade Yu-changu Wu), *KJCC*, 2:66. Li letter: "Li Fu-ch'un t'ung-chih kei tzu-jan k'o-hsueh-hui ti i-feng hsin" (Letter from Comrade Li Fu-ch'un to the Natural Science Society), *CFJP*, January 30, 1943, p. 4.

42. Reorganization of Yenan University: Price, *Cadres, Commanders and Commissars*, pp. 159–60; Hu, "Hui-i Yen-an tzu-jan k'o-hsueh-yuan," *KJCC*, 1:139–40; Ch'u and Wei, "Yen-an tzu-jan k'o-hsueh-yuan," pp. 254–55. Price, p. 172, cites figures showing

that most students at Yenan University in 1944 were from Shensi, Shansi, and Hopeh, from small property-owner or landlord families, and were studying administrative work. Only 49 of 1,282 Yen-ta students were in the NSI. Hsu defends NSI members: Wu and Yen, "Huai-nien Hsu-lao," *KJCC*, 1:95. Chou Yang: Klein and Clark, *Biographical Dictionary*, 2:963.

10

LITERATURE AND ART OF THE WAR PERIOD

Edward Gunn

WELL BEFORE the outbreak of fighting in 1937, the Japanese military aggression of the early 1930s prompted a number of Chinese writers to address war with Japan as a central social concern. At the same time, many other writers and artists were reluctant to follow any prescription that war should occupy the place of an obligatory theme for literature and art. These attitudes were carried over into the war period itself, bringing with them an array of divergent assumptions about the role of literature and art in society and the place of such features as popular, traditional, and regional styles and modern innovations. These attitudes and assumptions, together with political beliefs and varying types of censorship in different regions, were major collective determinants of how writers and artists constructed their images and accounts of suffering and aspirations during the war.

Certainly writers and artists, like other Chinese, held the Japanese responsible for the devastation and deprivation of the war. Yet Japan's military invasion was also seen as the culmination of the threat of imperialism that had concerned Chinese intellectuals for decades. Much of the literature and art that had existed by the eve of the war was a self-conscious product of decades of nation-building that took imperialism as a central reality. Just so, much of the literature and art produced during the war period was an extension of these themes. As often as works were committed to technical mastery of the enormity of the war, literature and art in general further sought conceptual transcendence over the devastating effects of its immediacy. The war period continued to inspire as before the imaginative construction of a Chinese world in all its internal diversity and conflict.

The war period was not a decisive era in the dynamic arenas of literature and art, but a pivotal one. The artistic and literary community took major steps toward a modern esthetic, guided by models and ideas regarded as international or cosmopolitan. At the same time, however, this community lost any serious hopes for a social autonomy by which it could inform the policies of the nation, rather than be guided by government. In the mobilization needed for war, many writers and artists identified themselves with government leadership in the name of patriotic resistance and revolution, only to find themselves circumscribed and dependent upon one government or another. As a result, the war period produced a final peak of art seeking modernity and the birth of an art emphasizing distinctiveness, as the feature more valued by government. Since cultural distinctiveness was inevitably a feature of literature and art, and since the modern world affected much of the most traditional and indigenous of their forms, these generalizations need to be explored by grouping works representing trends and issues of the times.

Resistance Literature and Mobilization

With the onset of fighting in the summer of 1937, many writers and artists employed by universities and schools and publishers of books, magazines, or newspapers stayed with their employers, either remaining in the coastal cities or relocating to the interior, chiefly Chungking, Chengtu, Kweilin, or Kunming. Still another large group was employed in a range of noncombatant services by military commanders. The recent rise of professional spoken drama, together with the decline of the film industry as a result of the fighting, made available to the official and quasi-official organizers of touring companies large numbers of writers and theater artists. These touring companies roused patriotic enthusiasm in the public and helped sustain morale among the troops. With the panache displayed during the first year of the war, the playwright T'ien Han (1898–1968) distilled the metaphor of the day into a slogan for his performers[1]:

> With four-hundred million actors,
> And a front of ten-thousand *li*,
> The globe itself as an audience,
> Watches our great historical drama

Patriotic writers and artists threw together plays and films to celebrate gallantry in important engagements—Lukouch'iao, Shanghai, Taierhchuang—before audiences with access to theaters. It was the modest street theater, however, that served the largest public.

The most performed and imitated street production, "Fang-hsia ni-ti pien-tzu" (Drop your whip) had been developed in the mid-1930s for agitation propaganda by university student groups in the cities of North China. Incorporating the standard propaganda formula of the day, the skit attracted the attention of crowds with a popular entertainment act, followed by oratory on the social issues at hand. "Drop Your Whip" went a step further. First a father and teenage daughter team introduce themselves with drum, cymbals, and song as traveling entertainers, but the daughter suddenly collapses from hunger, and her desperate father threatens to lash her. At this point a young man planted in the audience steps forward to intervene on the girl's behalf, commanding the father to drop his whip. As the young man indignantly berates the father, the daughter in turn explains that they are the victims of Japanese invaders in the Northeast. With the imminent threat to the audience itself explained, the performers lead into a patriotic song such as Nieh Erh's "I-yung chun chin-hsing ch'u" (March of the Volunteer Army).[2] The appeal, flexibility, and shock technique of the play led to numerous scripts along these lines by both Nationalist and Communist propagandists early in the war.[3]

As in drama, so in fiction certain motives of wartime resistance literature were anticipated by writers depicting events in the Northeast since 1931. The most renowned novel on the resistance in the Northeast, thanks to the promotion of Lu Hsun (1881–1936), was *Pa-yueh ti hsiang-ts'un* (Village in August or Countryside in August) (1935) by the refugee patriot Hsiao Chun (1907–1988).[4] The story portrays the fusion of dispossessed peasants, bandits, and intellectuals into a partisan unit, setting aside personal motives and loyalties in favor of disciplined commitment and obedience to higher authority and a public cause. The first blockbuster novel on the resistance published during the war, *K'o-erh-ch'in ch'i ts'ao-yuan* (Korchin banner plains or Steppes of the Korchin banner) (1939), had also been written prior to the war in 1933 by a fellow refugee, Tuan-mu Hung-liang (b. 1912).[5] After tracing the history of a large landholding clan in Northeast China, the novel focuses on the young heir, who plans to lead a social transformation of his region through his powers as landlord. Eventually, however, he is made the foil to the son of victimized tenants, Huang Ta-shan, who emerges from mysterious wanderings in Siberia to lead first a rent reduction campaign and then a partisan unit fighting the Japanese. Taken together, the prewar resistance fiction suggested that it was radicalized peasants who would effectively take up the cause of both nationalism and social transformation to sweep the Japanese and the Chinese landowning class from power. Inevitably they also popularized the figure of the bandit hero.

Patriotic literature written under the conditions of the united front after 1936 also focused on transformation of attitudes, but with less emphasis on the roles of antisocial figures and radical attacks on the rural gentry. Quasi-official emphasis fell on the conversion of soldiers, Chinese civilians, and minority tribes to the collective cause of resisting the Japanese invasion. The first treatment of soldiers to meet with some enthusiasm was the short story "Ch'a pan-ch'e mai-chieh" (Half-a-load short of wheat) (1938), by Yao Hsueh-yin (b. 1910). In keeping with established themes, the eponymous hero is a peasant victimized by the Japanese, although this time the setting is Shantung. "Half-a-load short" (or "Dumb-bell"), as he is called, develops into an admirable soldier, and much of the dialogue between him and the narrator, a politically enlightened soldier, is a catechism of familiar principles of Communist-led troops.

The story succeeds because, through the innocent peasant, it is able to evoke some of the simplest yet essential elements of combat experience. The soldiers' desperate need for humor is amply depicted. They know fear, and the hero comforts himself not with patriotic slogans but with remembered snatches of familiar and utterly irrelevant tunes. In danger he is distracted not by medals or awards, but by scrounging from a village a piece of rope for the imaginary cow he would rather be tending. The story thus advances the popular thesis of the country peasant as endowed with a love for his land, resentment for its despoilers, and reserves of savvy and physical courage, all raw material for political refinement. Yet it succeeds only by evoking the less socialized aspects of its characters.[6]

The same may be said, for example, of Hung Shen's "Fei chiang-chun" (Flying heroes) (1938), a play dealing with the elite fighter pilots of the Nationalists' small but valiant air force. The central character is a reckless fly-boy who likes to party as hard as he fights, until he is unable to respond to a critical alert and discovers social responsibility.

The more ambitious their treatment of the theme of the converted soldiers, the less writers succeeded with it. Writing to steel the morale of a suffering populace, or to move the indifferent, such works could not deal with phenomena like "small-unit mentality," or the adjustment to threats by taking life a day, or an hour, at a time, the torments of guilt, psychic breakdown under sustained or recurrent adversity, or the ambivalence toward combat experience as at once degrading and transcendent. For abstract ideals, the complexities of political rivalries, opportunism, and debatable judgment among Chinese leaders that crowded upon the simple justice of China's *cassus belli* and the enormity of Japanese treatment of prisoners and noncombatants meant that no trenchant analysis of principles, on the one hand, and circumstances, on the other, could be pursued and survive either the censor or rational prudence.

Just so, early novels like Tuan-mu Hung-liang's *Ta chiang* (The great river) (1938; first book edition, 1947) develops at novel-length the theme of two professional soldiers awakening to a sense of idealism, but only through invoking the lyrical power of nature and landscape and through episodic scenes of the sacrifices made by inspired individuals from all classes of society. The characters themselves remain inarticulate, even to themselves, and the novel is as much an elegy as a frustrated ode to such soldiers. Taken to extremes, elegies served only to enhance the confusion of complex emotions felt by soldiers.

The paradoxical sense among combat veterans that they have been elevated by their experience to a special community was taken up in an elegy with the classical name "Hsieh lu" (Dew on the shallots) (1940) by Wu-ming shih ("The anonymous one"; pseudonym of Pu Ning, b. 1917). Addressing the soldiers killed in action, Wu-ming shih writes: "Only you have the right to call yourselves the true Chinese people."[7] It is said that the radio broadcast of this elegy greatly moved the wounded veterans recuperating in the military hospital outside Chungking.[8] It is testimony once again that even the most justified of wars must let slip the reins of reason.

Perhaps, then, the crush of political constraints and emotional havoc both are why so much written and published during the war about the resistance has been allowed to sink into obscurity. Of the several films on minorities, none has been publicly screened since the war.[9] The important play by the veteran writer Lao She, *Kuo-chia chih shang* (The state above all) (first book edition, 1943), which portrayed the reconciliation of a Moslem leader with the Chinese nation in its hour of peril, has never since the war engaged the enthusiasm of his most devoted readers and never been revived in performance.

The most central question addressed by resistance literature was the transformation of attitudes among the civilian Chinese population. A good early example of this in theater is the melodrama *Yeh Shanghai* (Shanghai by night) (1939) by Yu Ling, depicting the plight of refugees in the International Settlement. The one work that has won broad critical acclaim, the most studied treatment of this issue, is the novel *Shan hung* (Mountain torrent, originally titled *Duckbill fall*) (1942; rev. ed., 1946).[10] Wu Tsu-hsiang, the author, wrote in exile from his native region, as so many did, but used southern Anhwei as a setting he knew and that was caught between major units of the Chinese and Japanese armies.

At the time of the first Japanese offensive down the Yangtze River valley, the villagers of a remote hamlet are all too willing to pay their profiteering mayor to find substitutes elsewhere to meet the quota of conscripted soldiers and laborers levied by the Nationalist government. Yet innate activists, like the self-supporting peasant Chang San-kuan, are uncomfortable with their compromises, despite the increased profits they reap supplying neighboring regions devastated by fighting. Caught between fear and loathing of soldiers and of their life and the looming menace of Japanese exploitation, between his loyalty to the welfare of his family and his pride as an able-bodied fighter, Chang San-kuan finally throws in his lot with the soldiers on impulse. Even then, however, the novel continues to develop the contradictions between factions of the village and the resistance and within Chang as he learns ever more about the idealist principles and practical compromises of the conflict he has joined. To the end the novel sustains this image of a conflicted man in a divided society to make it the most thoughtful portrait of civilians caught up in the war. That the novel, by a leftist author, argues the need of rural Chinese communities for an infusion of outside leadership that the Nationalists do not provide goes without saying.

Resistance literature on the whole continued to introduce innovations from foreign literature, and commentators admiringly noted features of these works in such terms: Hsiao Chun's debt to Fadeev and socialist realism, Tuan-mu Hung-liang's to cinematic techniques, the use of first-person narration in "Half-a-load," and the adaption of a scene from *Wilhelm Meister* as the source for "Drop Your Whip." All this, not to mention the expectations held out for film and reportage literature that were never fully met. Even in poetry the sensational pieces of the first years of the war were created out of the "drum beat" verse of Mayakovsky, such as T'ien Chien's "Kei chan-tou-che" (To those who fight) (1938).[11]

In art, the continuity of techniques inspired from abroad was also dominant in posters, cartoons, and woodblock prints that could be produced quickly and inexpensively for publication. Feng Tzu-k'ai (1898–1975), a student of foreign art, had been inspired years before by the Japanese painter Takehisa Yumeji to create a style of cartoon using brush and ink, both black-and-white and color, that was expressive of childlike naïveté, a very popular addition to the Lin Yu-t'ang magazines, especially *Yu-chou feng* (Cosmic wind). Continuing to contribute cartoons and essays to this magazine during the war, Feng added scenes of atrocity and devastation to the familiar, reassuring gentleness of his customary work to evoke a sophisticated sense of irony and horror as seen in "Bombardment II" (1938) and the satire of Japanese-sponsored governments, "Puppet Show" (1940) (figures 1 and 2).[12]

Among the woodblock artists whose technique matured at the time of the war, Li Hua and Ts'ai Ti-chih represent the modern movement, inspired by artists such as Kathe Kollwitz and promoted by Lu Hsun in the 1930s. Li Hua, who had also studied in Japan in the 1920s, in prints like "Refugees—A Contrast" (figure 3) displays the modern use of dramatic perspective, ominous dark masses, and symbolic details, such as the devastated Western-style building. The same features may be noted in the print "Refugees Flocking to the Kweilin Station" (figure 4), by the younger Ts'ai Ti-chih, a self-taught artist following the example of pioneers such as Li Hua.

As it happens, the woodblock prints also focus attention on social inequities: Those who are transported comfortably from danger as contrasted with the hapless poor and weak left to walk, and those who have the advantage of connections to purchase scarce tickets on train coaches, versus those who scramble for dangerous and often fatal perches on coach roofs. In this fashion, the historical continuities of social issues and esthetics were brought into the war. The result of such unresolved issues and political divisions was a breakdown in the unity that the resistance movement was meant to forge.

Fractures

For some time portraits of traitors, collaborators with the enemy, defeatists, and profiteers permeated the resistance literature. Such a figure held up to shame provided a target for rage that was more accessible than the Japanese, whose army stripped people of their sense of control over the course of events, and it provided a common "negative example" to unify all. In no case was this more true than in the criticism leveled against Chou Tso-jen (1885–1967), younger brother of Lu Hsun and the most prominent literary figure at the outset of the war to remain under Japanese occupation in Peiping, where he eventually served as minister of education. Yet even as Chou published treasonous statements as a collaborator, he also bridled at Japanese policies and asserted himself as the scholar-critic in the traditional literati mold. Addressing the Japanese authorities charged with promoting co-prosperity for Greater East Asia, he wrote in 1942:

Figure 1. **Feng Tzu-k'ai, "Bombardment II" (1938).**

Figure 2. **Feng Tzu-k'ai, "Puppet Show" (1940).**

Figure 3. **Li Hua, "Refugees—a Contrast."**

> With a sigh I have said that the period from the Northern and Southern
> Sung down to the end of the Ming was almost by design entirely given over to
> disorders and calamities. This indeed is an extraordinary state of affairs, and
> yet turning it over in my mind, how does the present state of affairs differ from
> that of the past? Surely it is as with Louis XIV who saw clearly that the deluge
> would come after him but made no plans to provide for the future so that
> people could live—was he not the stupidest man on earth?[13]

Historical allusions such as these were very fashionable during the war period, and the point was lost on no one. Chou's remarks incited a heated denunciation from the Japanese cultural adviser Kataoka Teppei, which in turn prompted
derisive remarks from other Chinese writers under the occupation, one suggesting that Kataoka consider *seppuku* for his breach of etiquette toward an elder.[14]
Such episodes are indicative of the failure of the Japanese to generate enthusiasm
among the Chinese writers who remained in Japanese-occupied territory, and
their eventual retreat from cultural initiatives, beyond requiring occasional token
gestures of support. Under the peculiar circumstances of the occupation, Chinese
writers cooperated with each other, at least in print, to create a more "united
front" than could be sustained elsewhere in China. While the Japanese kept a
close rein on the film world, magazines and professional theaters proliferated,
ignoring or all but openly deriding the conquerors, and not altogether at the
expense of artistic or political creeds.

Writers on the left elsewhere in China, however, not constrained by enemy

Figure 4. **Ts'ai Ti-chih, "Refugees Flocking to the Kweilin Station" (1944).**

occupation, published veiled criticism of the Nationalist government from the early years of the war on. In reportage literature from the front they expressed dismay over the failures of Nationalist commanders to lead more aggressively.[15] Essayists and playwrights, such as A Ying (Ch'ien Hsing-ts'un) in *Ming-mo i-hen* (Sorrow for the fall of the Ming) (1939), implied a parallel between the Nationalists and the corrupt Ming dynasty that fell so humiliatingly to the Manchus. In the Nationalist capital at Chungking remarkable satirists like Chang T'ien-i in fiction and Ch'en Pai-ch'en in drama, especially the outrageous and never produced *Luan-shih nan-nu* (Men and women in wild times) (1939), mocked profiteers, hypocritical patriots, and cultural functionaries who busied themselves making a living off empty promotion of the resistance effort.[16]

Leftist writers found their cause célèbre in the remarks of Liang Shih-ch'iu (1902–1987), the veteran critic of the proletarian literature movement of the 1920s and 1930s. Taking up an offer to edit the literary supplement of the *Chung-yang jih-pao* (Central daily news), in December 1938 Liang published his editorial policy: In view of the plethora of "empty eight-legged essays on the War of Resistance," while he welcomed material related to the war effort, he would also not turn away meritorious material "unrelated to the War of Resistance."[17] As it happened, a best-seller at that time was a gothic romance out of Shanghai, Hsu Hsu's *Kuei-lien* (Uncanny love) (1937). The novel had been serialized just prior to the war in *Cosmic Wind* magazine, and in book form it provided a popular diversion, depicting a spirit who appears as a beautiful woman to a young man and then as a handsome man to a nurse, tending the young man after he has fallen ill from his amorous encounter. While the popular success of Hsu Hsu's novel was ignored, many writers found in Liang's editorial remarks the explicit threat and affront to their raison d'être and denounced the editorial publicly.

Liang himself went on to write a series of familiar essays in the humorous mode, collected after the war under the title *Ya-she hsiao-p'in* (Sketches of a cottager) (1947). The restricted scope of the familiar essay barred it from serious criticism, while the ambiguities of the humor offended political activists left and right. The humorous familiar essay promoted by Lin Yu-t'ang and others in the 1930s sought through irreverence to cultivate an attitude of intellectual independence from the assertions of political institutions, while not attacking them. Liang's essays follow this irreverence, as for example, in the essay "I-shang" (Clothing), which reduces the terms of political movements to remarks on attire: A respected friend is barred from a swank hotel because his dress habits are too "proletarian" (*p'u-lo*); a happy feature of Chinese clothing is that "in the seat of the pants there is *sheng-ts'un k'ung-chien*" (lebensraum); to fail to fasten the top button of a Chinese gown is to break the tenets of the New Life (*hsin sheng-huo*) movement of the Nationalists.[18]

This appeal to cultivated tolerance of adversity and the influence of humor in ameliorating social folly could not begin to deal with the bitterness and aspirations of those who saw their ambitions checked at every turn by political enemies. Particularly after Nationalist troops wiped out a Communist unit at Wan-an, Anhwei, early in 1941, the cultural civil war deepened dramatically. The Nationalist leaders, convinced that the Communists, including the many writers on government payrolls staffing cultural and propaganda organs, were seriously subverting Nationalist authority, took a series of steps beginning in February 1941. Kuo Mo-jo (1892–1978) was demoted from his key position as director of the Third Bureau of the Political Department and placed under the leadership of a loyal Nationalist playwright, Chang Tao-fan (1896–1968), in the newly formed Central Cultural Movement Commission (Chung-yang Wen-hua Yun-tung Wei-yuan-hui). From his position as director, Chang issued a statement in the Nationalist-sponsored magazine *Wen-hua hsien-feng* (Cultural vanguard) on the "literary policy we need," emphasizing an end to exaggerated attention to the dark side of wartime society.[19]

The Central Censorship Commission for Books and Periodicals (Chung-yang T'u-shu Tsa-chih Shen-ch'a Wei-yuan-hui) under the journalist P'an Kung-chan (1895–1975) stepped up its surveillance, banning plays and driving Communist magazines and newspapers out of print. In 1942 editorship of *Central Daily News* was turned over to Su Wen (Tai K'o-ch'ung, 1907–1964), who a decade before had argued against the political polarization of literature and had been savaged in print by Lu Hsun. The renowned liberal newspaper *Ta-kung pao* (L'impartial) took a very partial turn. Its literary supplement was edited by Ch'en Chi-ying, who with his young colleagues Yin Hsueh-man and Wang Lan would become stalwarts of anti-Communist literature in Taiwan a decade later. The Nationalists also sought to compete with Communist writers in the burgeoning theatrical world of professional spoken drama companies. A Nationalist-backed company in Shanghai commissioned the young playwright Yao K'o (Yao Hsin-nung) to write what became the first major commercial success for historical drama, *Ch'ing-kung yuan* (Malice in the Ch'ing court) (1941).[20] In Chungking a Nationalist-sponsored company produced *Yeh mei-kuei* (Wild Rose) (1941) by an instructor at the Central Political Academy, Ch'en Ch'uan (1905–).

Wild Rose is a "well-made" play in the traditions of nineteenth-century European theater, combining elements of domestic love, and spy drama, and featuring a former Shanghai nightclub entertainer acting out the traditional role of Chinese beauties who bring ambitious men to ruin. Although she is apparently an opportunist who has married for money the head of the puppet North China Provisional Government in Peiping, she is in reality a secret agent of the Nationalists, finally turning seditious officials on each other and presiding over their deaths before making her escape. The play was popular and, in turn, the condemnation from Communists was intense. Articles in the official CCP newspaper *Hsin-hua jih-pao* (New China daily) and the Allied press argued that the close attention paid to the mentality of the chief traitor was too sympathetic, that idealizing a character who sleeps with traitors was degrading, and that emphasis on the work of secret agents at the expense of the collective efforts of the masses actually vitiated promotion of the necessary popular commitment to the resistance.

There was indeed a tendency in Nationalist-approved literature to promote spy drama in the wake of reversals on the battlefield. The film *Jih-pen yin-mou* (Secret agent of Japan) (1940) and Hsu Hsu's novel *Feng hsiao-hsiao* (The wind sighs) (1944–45) are conspicuous examples. But the tactic of using available women as agents was a reality, and a chilling, unglamorous portrait of the Communists' use of it appears in Ting Ling's "Wo tsai hsia-ts'un ti shih-hou" (When I was in Hsia Village) (1941).[21] The attention in the play *Wild Rose* to the mentality of a traitor is, perhaps, a point esthetically in favor of what is otherwise simply a clever melodrama.[22]

Communist retaliation for the Nationalist offensive began with open accusations that the Nationalists were capitulating to the enemy in an effort to destroy the Communists. But it went on from there. Mao Tun (1896–1981) left Chungking for Hong Kong, where he published the most famous of his wartime works, *Fu-shih* (Putrefaction) (1941). The novel is presented as the diary of a former radical student turned agent for the Nationalist police to finger and help break down Communists in Chungking. With increasing insight and self-loathing, the young woman agent records her disgust with her handlers and ranking officials meant to provide moral inspiration, her final disaffection when assigned to break a former lover, and her attempts to rescue a younger woman from a fate similar to hers. In a sense, such a work was a retort to the idealization of secret agent work in *Wild Rose*, using fascination with this topic to turn the focus from retribution for traitors to persecution of patriots. That has been more than enough to satisfy many readers. The esthetic limitation of the novel, setting aside any issues of reality, is that Mao Tun could not bring himself to portray even a glimmer of intelligent dedication and commitment among his villains, however cruel and misguided, so that as the woman's handlers and as government officials they remain stereotypes instead of effective, challenging foils to the heroine's moral and psychological struggles.

Beginning in the fall of 1941 the Communists also reorganized their own theater personnel into new companies, and in April 1942 one of them, the China Theater Arts Society (Chung-hua Chu-i She, or Chung-i) in Chungking, finally surmounted censorship to stage the most honored play on the theme of Nationalist capitulation, Kuo Mo-jo's *Ch'u Yuan*. The play is one of Kuo's wartime series of historical "Warring States" plays, designed to imply political criticism by historical parallels with that era. In the context of the times, the message of *Ch'u Yuan* was clear to everyone, including Nationalist cultural functionaries who denounced its arguments.

As portrayed in the play, Ch'u Yuan serves the state of Ch'u as a statesman by arguing (correctly) in favor of an alliance with Ch'i against Ch'in. But as tutor to the king's son, he is given to stilted moralizing, and as a poet, to eccentric fascinations. The Queen of Ch'u, favoring his rival Chang I's proposal for an alliance with Ch'in, discredits Ch'u Yuan by convincing the king that he has become mentally unbalanced and tried to molest her sexually. In the eyes of King Huai, this vitiates Ch'u Yuan's advice on state security. Ch'u Yuan is imprisoned and a report is spread that he has given in to demented despair and drowned himself. The common people know better. Two of them, his teenage maid servant and a palace guard, arrange his escape, the maid drinking poisoned wine intended for Ch'u Yuan, the guard pointing the upright official north, where he will find loyal support.

The staging of Ch'u Yuan was an important political event and honored as such, to the point that any review of its skillfulness, taste, or logic is virtually beside the point. In the leftist press the announcements and laudatory remarks on its publication and performance overshadowed other cultural events, as if to provide a defiant show of support for Kuo Mo-jo himself as the leading, beleaguered cultural official, representing what was left of the united front within the Nationalist bureaucracy.[23]

Works such as *Putrefaction* and *Ch'u Yuan* signaled a loosely coordinated shift from resistance literature back to social criticism. Such a shift is highlighted in the two most famous plays by Ts'ao Yu (Wan Chia-po, b. 1910) during the war, *Shui-pien* (Metamorphosis) (1939) and *Pei-ching jen* (Peking man) (1942). *Metamorphosis* is a classic patriotic piece on the elevation of Chinese society to a new sense of integrity and dedication through undergoing the trials of the war. The play portrays a physician who overcomes corruption and faces the ultimate challenge of having to operate on her wounded son and then declare him fit for duty at the front.

For Ts'ao Yu the portrayal of a social ideal, or an idealized society, was strongly linked to an ideal familial relationship far from the one he had known as a child. Thus, when he returned in 1942 to the portrait of decaying families that made him famous before the war, it is easy to imagine that in writing *Peking Man* Ts'ao Yu penned the ultimate exorcism of his past and its significance in this last major domestic drama. Drawing heavily on Chekhov, *Peking Man* introduces the prewar situation of an extended Peiping household presided over by a morbid patriarch and peopled with effete or malicious relations, whose declining fortunes describe the collapse of the old-style gentry family in a modernizing society. The ultimate symbol of the Chinese people suffocated by this gentry culture is a mute workman who poses for an anthropologist studying the prehistoric Peking Man. The one exemplar of genuine selfless charity and filial piety, the patriarch's niece, Su Fang, provides the final indictment of the family and its gentry culture as a lost cause by leaving the household to face the challenge of society on her own. As a social critic Ts'ao Yu might have elected to portray in the family as a whole the incapacity of characters who do live up to their traditional values to deal with the challenges and needs of a newly emerging society. It is likely, however, that he was too concerned with recreating the flaws of people in his own past to put emphasis on schematic social analysis, which would have pleased Communist critics more.[24] On the other hand, it is Ts'ao Yu's emotional and political restraint that has won this play admiration among other critics.

The Decline of the Educated Elite

What Ts'ao Yu's *Peking Man* shared with the more politically focused works, what Kuo Mo-jo's Ch'u Yuan and Ts'ao Yu's Su Fang in *Peking Man* both evoked was the image of the person with moral and intellectual strengths stifled by the social or political environment. This theme was pursued relentlessly in works about the educated elite during the war. The attempted suicide of the gifted playwright Hung Shen together with his wife and ailing daughter in 1941, the defection of Ma Yin-ch'u, the economist, to the Communists, and the assassination of the scholar-poet Wen I-to in 1946 in Kunming were all real events of the period no novel or play came close to touching upon.[25] But the social significance of these events was driven home in play after play.

Sung Chih-ti's *Wu Ch'ung-ch'ing* (Chungking fog) as early as 1940 introduced the loss of idealism as well as the decline in material circumstances among university students in the wartime capital. Hsia Yen's *Fa-hsi-szu hsi-chun* (Fascist bacillus) (1942) warns against the subordination of important medical research to the priorities of fascist politics; his *Fang-ts'ao t'ien-ya* (Fragrant grass as far as the horizon) (1945) presents the frustrations of a political economist, as well as a love story. Mao Tun's *Ch'ing-ming ch'ien-hou* (Before and after the Ch'ing-ming festival) (1945) exposes the frustrations of a patriotic industrialist victimized by profiteering bureaucrats. And in Ch'en Pai-ch'en's *Sui-han t'u* (Ever-green) (1944), the victim is again a physician whose fight against tuberculosis is vitiated by political corruption and social collapse. Finally, a noted novel of the period, Li Kuang-t'ien's *Yin-li* (Attraction) (written in 1945; first book edition, 1947), recounts a school teacher's humiliations and harrowing escape from Japanese-occupied Shantung to Chengtu, where her husband has long since moved to support the resistance. Arriving in Chengtu, she learns that her husband is a fugitive from the Nationalist police for his political activism, and she finds the same censorship and restriction of rights that had driven her from Shantung. The punchline of the novel is delivered in her reaction: "So, then, after all, I have left the dark land of the occupied zone to come to the dark land of the Rear Area."[26]

To be sure, there were plays and stories that sought to reassure audiences that appreciation of the educated elite had not waned, and that material and social problems were an inevitable but temporary condition. But there was no one left with prestige enough to push convincingly for loyal dissent or to win over wavering persons to the counsels of faith and patience. Instead, the literature of the left surmounted censorship to provide the message that power was irredeemably concentrated in the hands of ruthless, corrupt officials and profiteers.

Such themes were all the more apparent in the satirical cartoons that developed steadily into a notable art form during the war. Chang Kuang-yu created an ambitious, phantasmagoric vision inspired by the classic novel *Hsi-yu chi* (Journey to the west), titled *Hsi-yu man-chi* (Illustrated journey to the west) (figures 5 and 6). Through this series of cartoons with text in captions, the protagonist Monkey moves through strange kingdoms blatantly representing Nationalist China in a state of complete moral and social bankruptcy.[27] No less ruthless was Hsiao Ting (Ting Ts'ung), whose most scandalous success was an eight-foot water-color, "Satirical Scroll," exhibited in Chengtu in 1945.[28] The expressionist figures provide emblems of the plight of the educated and the commoners, side-by-side with profiteers and officials. In an important way the swift visual message of these clever pieces was more effective as propaganda than novels and plays.

The commitment of writers to realism in drama and fiction also meant a commitment to pursuing the complexities of social and psychological variables realism is meant to address. Hence, the attempt to reduce works of that realism to single dichotomies of suffering citizens exploited by evil officials and profiteers is less successful than the expressionist cartoon with its inspired insinuations. Given that, the most representative work of Communist social criticism is the play *Sheng-kuan t'u* (How to get promoted) (1945), written in Chungking and performed at the end of the war in Shanghai. Abandoning realism for the grotesque, the playwright Ch'en Pai-ch'en produced a venomous example of

Figure 5. Chang Kuang-yü, from "The Illustrated Journey to the West" (1945).

expressionistic satire, with sets and costumes designed by Hsiao Ting (figures 7 and 8).[29] Here the writer found his ultimate form by which to parade before an audience the vision of venal officials stripped of their pretensions and routed off the stage by an indignant mob.

The collapse of the material conditions, morale, and moral force of the educated elite, together with any hopes for an autonomous intellectual community, inspired not only condemnation of the government, but also works of realism with surprising psychological and existential dimensions, as well as social implications. The advent of war with Japan moved Pa Chin (Li Fei-kan) from his famous position of anarchism to patriotic resistance propaganda, still focused on the lives of youth committed to an ideal society. Dissatisfied with much of the results in the trilogy *Huo* (Fire) (1939–43), Pa Chin set aside debate over social engineering and turned to the depiction of educated people whose lives have reached maturity and whose sufferings cannot be reduced to simple determinants. In the novel *Han yeh* (Cold nights) (1946) Pa Chin's characteristic eye for human distress in all forms concentrates on the family of a university-educated

Figure 6. **Chang Kuang-yü, from "The Illustrated Journey to the West" (1945).**

office worker dying of tuberculosis in wartime Chungking. Here the war in its final years has eroded hopes and sympathies, poverty has forced desperate choices, cholera and tuberculosis sweep lives away, while the limitations of individuals, their self-deception and self-pity, anxiety and depression, guilt and psychological deprivation all destroy relationships.

If Pa Chin is often seen as too attached to his own characters and too indignant at their plight, the work of the scholar-author Ch'ien Chung-shu is typically seen by his critics as too severe in its ironic attachment and too light in its analysis of social problems. There is agreement, at least, that his novel *Wei-ch'eng* (Fortress besieged, or The besieged city) (1946) is a tour de force of witty rhetorical invention and satire as it describes an educated elite that is itself venal and effete—in contrast to the flattering portrait provided in Communist works of the day.

The novel describes the downward spiral of the career of a young student

在「陞官圖」上海演出的服裝及裝置設計

導演：佐臨

設計者：丁聰

財政局長　工務局長　教育局長　警察局長　省長待從　知縣夫人　省長　知縣　馬秘書　秘書長　衛生局長

Figure 7. **Hsiao Ting (Ting Ts'ung), Costumes for *How to Get Promoted* by Ch'en Pai-ch'en (1945).**

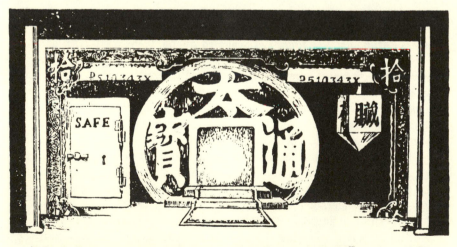

說明：台口是鈔票‧柱子是金條‧大門是金錢眼‧小門是保險箱

Figure 8. **Hsiao Ting (Ting Ts'ung), Set for *How to Get Promoted* by Ch'en Pai-ch'en (1945).**

returning from overseas on the eve of the war with a bogus diploma, on the strength of which he attempts to find security and self-respect. He is met at every turn with the clash of irreconcilable worlds: life overseas versus life in China; provincial China versus metropolitan Shanghai, tradition versus modernity, prewar conditions versus wartime conditions, single versus married life. Read chiefly as a merciless satire of manners, the rhetorical inventions also point to psychological and existential dichotomies, as the characters, like the narrative itself, resort to the rhetoric of logic or of past associations to define and assert some control over their existence. But human logic proves problematic and reasoning by analogous associations too anachronistic as guides to survival. Existence becomes a series of unintended consequences and fragmented experiences. So the events of the war that shape the narrative come to represent a fundamental human condition raised to a merciless intensity.

Regional Literature

Just as the social decline of the uprooted, withering educated elite inspired an important proliferation of literature and art, so the lot of the common people rooted in their communities was the subject of a growing regional literature. In fact, regional literature presented several continuities with prewar themes in all their diversity, representing personal or political preoccupations of the intellectuals. What made it a genre was that it focused on nonprofessionals—miners, peasants, fishermen—tied as a subculture to the economy, power structure, customs, and distinctive language of a locale always set apart from outsiders.

Wu Tsu-hsiang's *Mountain Torrent* exemplifies these features in resistance literature, as do some of the patriotic works of the writers from the Northeast. But their visions of China united were replaced soon by an emphasis on parochial interests and subcultures uninspired by a national agenda. Hsiao Hung (1911–1942), in her final and perhaps most memorable work, turned away from topical events to return to the period of her early childhood in *Hu-lan ho chuan* (Tales of Hu-lan River) (1941). From its extended opening description of the village quagmire symbolizing the conditions of Northeast China to the climactic ritual of boiling a noncompliant child bride, Hsiao Hung projects a scene of squalor, misery, and ignorance, relieved only by her attachment to an indulgent and humane grandfather. This autobiographical novel stands as a deceptively simple and engaging testament to all that drove so many bright young Chinese to hate the conditions of their homeland(s) and reject traditional culture with passionate intensity. But it is also a monument to their ambivalence. The very compassion of the grandfather, which means so much to the narrator as a child and an adult, is also helpless in the context of an ingrained communal brutality. Perhaps, then, only the overwhelming force of an outside power could ameliorate it. Or, perhaps, the very force necessary to overcome customs and practices would in its turn perpetuate such brutality, and with it the pathetic indignity of the hapless villagers. This, in fact, would become an issue that Hsiao Hung's lover, Hsiao Chun, would address a few years later when the Communists occupied the Northeast.[30]

It is tempting also to see strong autobiographical and symbolic significance in Shen Ts'ung-wen's *Ch'ang ho* (Long river) (1945), his portrait of the end of an era for the Miao people of northwestern Hunan. Heavily censored and never completed, Shen's novel presents Miao farmers and fishermen endowed with a degree of common sense, morality, and generosity superior to that of the modernizing Chinese officials and the profit-oriented mentality they bring with them. In terms of the recurrent motif in the narrative, the ripe oranges in the lush groves of a Miao grower are available free to any passerby who knows their customs; the grower's teenage daughter is also as available as the ripe fruit, to those who understand local values. But the newly installed commander of the Peace Preservation Corps unit established by the government is disingenuous in his plans for the oranges and the grower's daughter. The ironic depiction of this situation is interspersed with the introduction of a variety of characters and a careful reconstruction of recent history of the region, all suggesting the decline of a world view and the autonomy of the local culture. This is at least consistent with Shen's prewar studies of the approach of middle age and his wartime concern with the polarization of politics that was subsuming the intellectual and artistic community.[31]

Two varied strands of thought by writers committed to Marxist analysis appear among the many works depicting wartime Szechwan, represented by Sha T'ing's *T'ao chin chi* (Gold rush) (1943) and Lu Ling's *Chi-o ti Kuo Su-o* (The hungry Kuo Su-o) (1943). Neither author suggested that an awakening to nationalism or revolution was a major force in the provincial hinterland. Small-town Szechwan is dominated by merchants and their secret society connections and rivalries in *Gold Rush*, which pits them against a determined widow, the matriarch of a collapsing gentry clan, in her futile attempt to prevent them from overrunning a grave site as they hunt for gold. In the corrosion of loyalty to gentry values and the blind greed of wartime profiteers operating from their teahouses and opium dens, Sha T'ing's novel perhaps suggests the collapse of any legitimate social order.[32] Lu Ling's portrait of a mining community treats sympathetically the independent Kuo Su-o's adulterous affair, for which she is tortured to death, setting off a chain of vengeful and just actions that suggests the capacity of the individual person for heroic stature. But this is demonstrated not by any ordered, deliberate plan. Rather, the irrational conditions of society produce spontaneous reactions among individuals that alter and develop conditions that might lead them to social change.[33]

Regional literature furthered the development of modern techniques of narrative and also added stylistic range. Sha T'ing, for example, was perhaps the first author to introduce the now common verb *kao* (to do) in print, while Shen Ts'ung-wen's work continued to pioneer the use of regional Hunan speech, later taken up by other authors depicting the region after Liberation. By contrast, the many authors who traveled and sketched or painted through western China, from north to south, derived little or nothing from their exposure to these regions. Only the most fleeting technical experiments appeared, not to be revived until years later, and critics have not found much insight in the depictions of the traveling artists.[34]

The Hold of Tradition

If the regional literature of the 1940s sustained arguments that antedated the war in all their diversity, it is no less remarkable that collectively these works repeatedly resorted to the victimization of females as central to their narratives. They may be child brides, unmarried adolescents, married women of the working class, or widows of the gentry. Taken together, these works fail to do more than introduce the sympathetic or desirable attributes of these females and sympathize with their plight as victims.

In this light, the meticulous studies of manners and imaginative renderings of mentalities in the short fiction of Chang Ai-ling (Eileen Chang, b. 1921) have a particular fascination, for she takes a further interest in developing the consequences of victimization, both to the women themselves and to their society. Chang's victims survived to retaliate, not as ennobled heroines, but as self-centered or pathological figures. The most critically acclaimed work, "Chin-suo chi" (The golden cangue) (1943), introduces a young woman sold into a traditional extended household to be the wife of a hopeless cripple. There she is emotionally deprived, socially humiliated, and materially cheated. After her husband's death she lives on in deranged isolation from the clan, slowly destroying the lives of her own children in a pathological perpetuation of the cruelty that destroyed her.

Chang's most popular piece, "Ch'ing ch'eng chih lien" (Love in a fallen city) (1943), presents a young divorcee who, thrown back on the resources of her natal family, also faces the threat of humiliation and deprivation that torment the wife in "The Golden Cangue." She seizes a desperate way out by becoming the mistress of a Hong Kong businessman who, however, sets sail alone for England after setting her up in Hong Kong as a lonely figure of the demimonde. As it happens, however, the Japanese attack on Hong Kong forces the man's ship back into port, where he rejoins and eventually marries her. Chang re-creates the battle for Hong Kong, which she experienced as a university student, as though it were a monstrous projection of her protagonist's psyche, deliberately recalling with slick irony the traditional figure of the femme fatale who inspires "love that fells cities." Underlying the sympathetic treatment of the woman is a theme, not of heroism but, through a cosmic joke, of the amoral ruthlessness of a society sacrificed to a desperate woman's desire.

Through all Chang's fiction is a preoccupation with the assertion of irrational forces that shake the rationalizing order and moral norms of the Westernized, bourgeois societies of Hong Kong and Shanghai. To do this, she draws heavily on Freudian themes, but the special popularity of her work and wit was her ability to project imaginative allusions to traditional opera and fiction, poetry, and religious texts onto her portraits of cosmopolitan urban life as the social corollary to her psychological vision of the welling up of irrational drives. Chang was both fascinated and repelled by the hold of traditions, and intent on imbedding them in her work. Commenting on the films produced in China, she remarked: "It is appalling to reflect that, in the imagination of young Chinese intellectuals nurtured on a quarter century of foreign films and fiction, there is so little room for anything really Chinese."[35]

Chang's own works drew on motives and themes that had often been consigned to the most conservative response to modernization in prose literature, the popular, commercial fiction known as the "Mandarin Duck and Butterfly School." During the war this fiction continued its most imaginative innovations in the form of the fantastic adventures in the vast, never completed novels of Huan-chu-lou chu (Li Shou-min, 1902–1961). His *Shu shan chien-hsia chuan* (Swordsmen of the hills of Shu) (1932–1949) told of refugees of the Ming dynasty fleeing the Ch'ing to Szechwan, to become immortals, master magical weapons and powers, and eventually take each other on for mastery of their domain. During the war he continued with several sequels to this central tale, such as *Ch'ing-ch'eng shih-chiu hsia* (Nineteen gallants of Ch'ing ch'eng) (1943) and *Man-huang hsia-yin* (Recluse masters among the southern tribes), both of which brought his immortals into closer contact with the human world of the Chinese and the Miao. The most famous commercial writer, Chang Hen-shui (1895–1967), followed the trend in patriotic writing, although his prewar novels of love and intrigue remained in vogue. The most prolific scribbler, Feng Yu-ch'i, in novels like *Luang feng ming ch'un* (Spring song of phoenixes) (1943), treated his readers in the classic manner of erotic novels to several chapters of soft-core pornography before holding the survivors up to an awakening of more chaste ideals.

But the urban-based spoken drama also for the first time responded to the appeal of traditional features as it reached for commercial success. The two most popular productions to rely on the mystique and appeal of traditional opera itself were *Feng-hsueh yeh kuei jen* (Return on a windswept, snowy night) (Chungking, 1942), by Wu Tsu-kuang, and *Ch'iu Hai-t'ang* (Begonia or autumn quince) (Shanghai, 1942) by the novelist Ch'in Shou-ou in collaboration with a team of experienced playwrights. Both were loosely based on a social scandal involving the affair of an official's concubine with a male opera performer of female roles, which led to the ruin of the performer's career.[36]

The later war years also saw the rise of popular romance writer Hsu Hsu (1908–1980) and a younger writer following his lead, Wu-ming shih (Pu Ning). Derisively termed the "New Mandarin Duck and Butterfly School," they were in fact schooled in modern ideas and foreign literature and used these elements in their fiction. However, to the great annoyance of social activists and those committed to psychological or social realism, these writers created idealized characters with independent spirits, touched by war and revolution but ultimately detached from them, and capable of profound emotions and pristine sensitivities that their authors do not frame with any ironic detachment.

For transcendent spirit, however, nothing could match the mystique of the artist committed to the traditions of literati painting. If in society only fragmented vestiges of literati culture remained, its trappings and artifacts could still evoke in viewers an expression of the visual mastery of their inchoate psyches. No painter exemplified this homage to tradition more than Chang Ta-ch'ien (Zhang Daqian, 1899–1983), whose technical virtuosity was displayed in his extensive copies of Tun-huang religious murals as well as landscapes, figures, and flower compositions (figure 9). Chang's renderings of lotuses are numerous, and one type inspired even a poet committed to modern literature to a reflective commentary:

> **"Lotus Flowers"**
> **On Viewing a Painting by Chang Ta-ch'ien**
>
> The one, with its apparently unfailing cup,
> Holds the joy of blooming and stands
> Like a towering mountain bearing an eternity
> For which man has no words.
>
> The young leaf, in no hurry to unfold itself,
> Retains a hope in its untainted heart to loom up
> Through the haze on the water, gazing at the world
> That wears, with reluctance, an old and faded costume.
>
> But what is the real theme
> Of this performance of pain? This bent
> Lotus stem drooping its blossom
>
> Toward its root, it says nothing
> Of the ravages of storms, but of the multiple life—
> The solemn burden—it has received from the Creator.[37]

This poem by a university student, Cheng Min (b. 1924?), not only demonstrates the appeal of the tensions and balances in traditional compositions but is a testament to the inspiration even modern sensibilities drew from traditional art, whether Chang Ta-ch'ien's or that of numerous other famous colleagues.

The fusion of modern and traditional esthetics within painting itself was

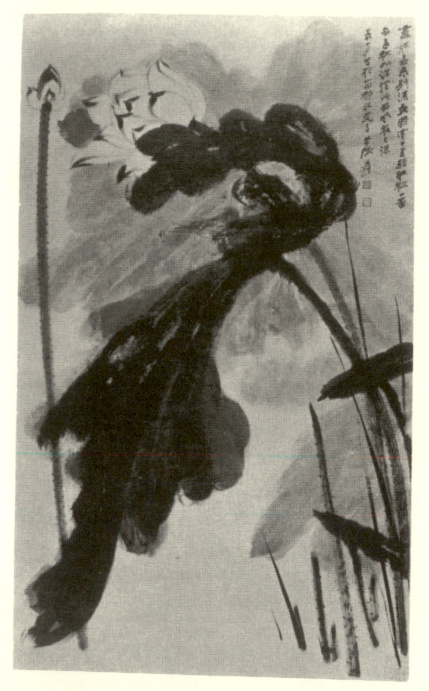

Figure 9. **Chang Ta-ch'ien, "Lotus Flowers."**

fermenting in the experiments of Hsu Pei-hung (Ju Peon, 1896–1953). During the war his most noted work was a set of controversial murals given over entirely to the use of Western techniques of mural painting to monumentalize episodes in Chinese legends. He also continued to develop his studies of horses, however, and at the end of the war he emerged with the most popular innovation to seize the public imagination. Retaining Chinese brush techniques and use of light and space, Hsu posed his horses in foreshortened perspective at the run, creating an image of tremendous vitality that answered the call for a public art of "national form" (*min-tsu hsing-shih*) (see figure 10).

The Rise of Party Literature

The issue of how to shape literature and art to the needs of mass propaganda had led to a bitter and protracted debate on the left over "national form" since the early 1930s. The chief defender of modern innovation based on foreign models was the acerbic critic Hu Feng. He was joined during the war by such representative writers as Lu Ling and Ch'en I-men, who under the pen-name S. M. published frontline war reportage during the first years of the war and later an award-winning novel on the resistance, *Nan-ching* (1942).[38] As friction deepened between the Nationalists and the Communists and within factions on the left, Ch'en I-men turned to poetry, collected under the title *Wu hsien ch'in* (The stringless lute) (1942). At its most introspective and reflective, the poetry still addresses contemporary events, as in the poem "Loneliness" (1941):

> Loneliness
> It's not the pain caused by a world
> deserted and desolate,
> It's the inability to bear the human desert made of a
> multitude of men.[39]

As independent Marxists, Hu Feng and his associates were unwilling to adopt more popular formulas for writing, and as a close associate of the late Lu Hsun, despite Communist party disapproval, Hu Feng laid claim to leadership of left-wing culture through his uncompromising criticism of works and trends. This independence and ambition could not go unchallenged by representatives of the Communist party, and Kuo Mo-jo found his vehicle to deride the Hu Feng group in the painting of Kuan Shan-yueh (b. 1912).

Kuan Shan-yueh, later one of the most celebrated artists of the People's Republic of China, was just then emerging as a promising student of the Ling-nan (Southern, or Cantonese) School. Founded earlier in the twentieth century, this group promoted freely adopting techniques from all literati and traditional prescriptions and applying them to an unlimited range of subject matter and composition. Kuan, like the strict traditionalist Chang Ta-ch'ien and other artists

Figure 10. **Hsü Pei-hung, "Running Colt II" (1946).**

of all persuasions, made virtue of the circumstances of exile in western China to travel to the hinterland. Among the resulting paintings was one that struck Kuo Mo-jo, titled "Sai-wai t'o-ling" (Camel bells north of the Great Wall) (1943) (figure 11):

> In this painting a boundless sandy waste stretches towards the horizon beneath a sullen sky. A small camel caravan plods along against the wind-whipped sand. It is not a large scroll but it truthfully depicts the desolate yet magnificent scenery north of the Great Wall and expresses the painter's own melancholy and indignant sentiments at that time.[40]

Kuo Mo-jo saw in it an opportunity both to identify the aims of the Ling-nan School with the party's search for "national forms" and to discredit the Hu Feng group by alluding to "The Stringless Lute" poems. In a colophon verse "On Kuan Shan-yueh's Painting," Kuo wrote:

> Laughable are the lutists who know no music at all,
> Yet in public try to talk about "the stringless lute." Such mad
> Chan has led astray many a good youth, and
> Has for hundreds of years ruined the art of painting.
>
> A revolution in painting must first depart from ancient elegance.
> Folk style values what is true to life and realistic.
> If the image is not realistic, it is then false,
> And the vulgar, when really driven home, is naturally
> the divine.[41]

The whole episode of literary infighting might have been simply another example of the ancient tenet that "writers scorn each other." But in Yenan discourse had taken a pivotal turn, which Kuo's verse reflects, with Mao Tse-tung's "Tsai Yen-an wen-i tso-t'an-hui shang ti chiang-hua" (Talks at the Yenan Forum on Literature and Art) (1942). As early as October 1938 Mao had telegraphed the punch of his "Talks" when he declared in Yenan:

> Being Marxists, Communists are internationalists, but we can put Marxism into practice only when it is integrated with the specific characteristics of our country and acquires a definite national form. . . . Foreign stereotypes must be abolished, there must be less singing of empty, abstract tunes, and dogmatism must be laid to rest; they must be replaced by the fresh, lively style and spirit which the common people of China love.[42]

For several years, however, such injunctions were heeded as essentially directives for those engaged in such activities as the touring propaganda theater, which had in any case already adopted popular forms across China, and not as binding on literature and art as a whole. Mao himself, it may be noted, wrote in a highly Europeanized style common to party discourse.

Figure 11. Kuan Shan-yüeh, "Camel Bells North of the Great Wall" (1943).

Then, too, the Shen-Kan-Ning region had experienced many of the same problems as the Chungking government. Writers and artists in Yenan were also largely refugees from urban culture and political authority who found employment at the new Lu Hsun Academy for the arts and in the press, and who rallied to the cause of the resistance in a variety of service roles and as war correspondents, such as Liu Pai-yu and Ting Ling (Chiang Ping-chih, 1907–1985). Just as Nationalist military reversals turned attention from combat to espionage, so Communist reversals in the field turned writing to localized guerrilla warfare. And as decisive military action waned, many writers took up the roles they knew best, social critics of the deteriorating conditions and disparities in poverty and privilege. Contacts with minorities were uncertain or openly hostile; the attitudes of many Chinese civilians uncommitted; the behavior of officials in need of reform. As Mao took strong steps to rectify failings, the writers and artists joined in with their own spontaneous criticisms of society in Yenan in 1941 and 1942, supportive of what they knew of Mao's ideals, but autonomous in their conception and execution of their work.

Mao responded to these activities with proscriptive, disciplinary, and prescriptive measures. Self-appointed critics and literary theorists, like the novelist Hsiao Chun, the poet Ai Ch'ing, and the essayist Wang Shih-wei were subjected to collective criticism by their colleagues and the most recalcitrant, Wang Shih-wei, imprisoned and eventually executed. Ting Ling, whose recent short stories "In the Hospital" and "When I Was in Hsia Village" implied a calculated inhumanity on the part of cadres, and whose essay "Thoughts on Women's Day" argued publicly that sexual discrimination against women was prevalent in Yenan, was sacked from her editorial post at *Liberation Daily*, the official party newspaper in Yenan.[43] An exhibition of woodblock prints held in Yenan in February 1942 demonstrated that artists had heeded the call of Lu Hsun to produce trenchant social criticism so well that virtually none of the satirical prints was ever subsequently circulated or published.[44]

In addition to such demonstrations of authority, Mao consulted with his political, ideological, and cultural advisers (Ch'en Po-ta, Ai Ssu-ch'i, and Chou Yang) and in May 1942 brought writers and artists together for the historic forum that would produce prescriptive policy for decades to come. As handed down to readers some months later,[45] Mao's "Talks" proved to be an exhortation to practice the principles of Soviet socialist realism, not so much by rehashing its features as by explaining why and how they should be embraced. Socialist realism is the portrayal of the revolutionary development of history through party leadership and heroic figures embodying party policy as interpretable through art and literature consistent with folk idioms. As Mao explained it, society was polarized, led either by the proletariat or the bourgeoisie. With no alternative left, the writer choosing to serve the masses must follow the leadership of the proletariat by subordinating the writer's imagination to those policies instituted for the welfare of the masses:

Intellectuals who want to integrate themselves with the masses, who want to serve the masses, must go through a process in which they and the masses come to know each other well. This process may, and certainly will, involve much pain and friction, but if you have the determination, you will be able to fulfill these requirements.[46]

By addressing the cultural community in this fashion, Mao turned the tables on the assumptions and expectations of many that their literature and art was a major means by which an autonomous cultural community would inform government. Rather, Mao suggested, their work was divorced from popular culture and mass appeal, and, with no independent base of support, they would have to follow the leadership of government if they were to live up to their ideals of service to society.

There are many ways to criticize Mao's "Talks." His assertion of the key concept of polarization is understandable in wartime, but also highly manipulative and vulnerable. His definitions of audience and "social effect" (*she-hui hsiao-kuo*) are vague, while his adoption of the reflection theory of psychology and art is narrow and unsubstantiated. His vision of the social role of writers is also very narrow, discussing them as so many "cultural officers" in a paramilitary function to win audiences over to confidence and loyalty to the party. Yet even officers, if they are to be credible, must have ideas of their own, at variance with or not governed by official policy and regulation.

The esthetic effect of "Talks" in formal terms was to uproot folk art and replace it with a distinctive set of innovations in dialogue with folk and regional idioms. In fiction, attention shifted from Fadeev as a model to the use of *k'uai-pan* (fast clapper) verse. In verse, Mayakovsky's "drum beat" style moved over to accommodate folk forms. In theater, inspiration shifted from Chekhov, Gogol, or Gorki to *yang-ko* or "rice-sprout song" music and dance. In woodblock prints, the influence of Kollwitz gave way to folk-style posters and paper cut-outs.

At the same time, however, regional speech usage was crowded with Euro-Japanese jargon used by the party and with standardized features of grammar and vocabulary. Simple forms were greatly expanded by dramatic and descriptive techniques adopted from foreign models. Characterization featured images of the workers, soldiers, and peasants themselves, where previously folk art had largely avoided them in favor of legendary, traditional figures. Where the common man had figured most prominently, as in risqué or ribald themes, eroticism was dropped or masked in more uplifting themes. And where folk oral literature had served a satirical role, releasing social and sexual tensions, it was turned toward agitation propaganda and panegyric. In all these ways, writers and artists responsive to Mao's prescriptions produced an art characterized by its distinctiveness from the modern esthetic born in 1918, as much as that esthetic had distinguished itself from tradition.

In the most celebrated examples of the new esthetic, the writers and artists addressed many of the themes current elsewhere in China, always streamlining the issues and their resolution by inserting the new functionary role of literature and art. A whole team of writers and composers, led by Ho Ching-chih and Ma K'o, collaborated to produce *Pai-mao nu* (The white-haired girl) (1944) as the first large-scale work of the "new music theater" (*hsin ko-chu*), evolved out of northern "rice-sprout song" dances. It rooted the story in local legends of a female demon, who in the play turns out to be a woman victimized by a landlord's son, seduced and abandoned by him to raise her baby in a cave, from which she raids the local temple for food left as offerings. Her supernatural mystique is finally unmasked by a Red Army officer, who restores her to society and leads the villagers in punishing the guilty members of the landlord class.

If Ho Ching-chih acknowledged that he did not produce enough authentic regional flavor,[47] Chao Shu-li (1906–1970) led the field as master of regional literature, taking his exemplary story "Li Yu-ts'ai ti pan-hua" (The rhymes of Li Yu-ts'ai or The tale of Li Yu-ts'ai's rhymes) (1943) from the classical satirical portrait of a local village situation under the heel of an exploitative headman, to a celebration of party-led village democratic action to unseat the mayor in favor of a legitimate representative. The catalyst in galvanizing the community is a local rhymester, Li Yu-ts'ai, and the narrative a showcase for his talents. In woodcuts that were widely disseminated to illustrate the Yenan spirit, tensions between troops and civilians dissolve, and party cadres see to it that private hopes are rationally accommodated, as in Ku Yuan's "Marriage Registration" (1945) (figure 12). If these works seem a modest beginning, to many they promised expansive potential for a distinctive and truly popular literature.

The Last Word

Whatever their private reservations about Mao's prescriptions and the potential of the new, committed literature, authors like Chao Shu-li and Ho Ching-chih by the end of the war were the most seminal writers on the mainland for the next two decades. Formerly productive writers on the left, such as Mao Tun and Yeh Sheng-t'ao, retired to administrative functions, overwhelmed at last by a younger generation armed with a distinctive esthetic beyond the authority of older writers to criticize. Those who challenged the new leadership and its art were stilled one after another in the years to come. A brief renaissance of fiction flourished at the end of the war as works held back or not completed during those years were published, but production dried up by 1948 with the spread of civil war and the spiral of inflation. The theater boom collapsed quickly with the restoration of the film industry and the return of the American movie in the large cities. The works of writers who emerged during the war period also played a major role in the literature of the Chinese diaspora for decades to come. Chang Ai-ling proved to be the most seminal and popular writer; Ch'ien Chung-shu the most admired by scholars; while

Figure 12. **Ku Yuan, "Marriage Registration in Village" (1945).**

Hsu Hsu and Wu-ming shih maintained appreciative audiences in Taiwan or Hong Kong.

On October 14, 1945, as refugee residents of Chungking were gradually departing to return to the east coast, they were treated in the *Hsin-min pao wan-k'an* (New people's tribune) evening edition to the poetry of Mao Tse-tung's "Snow": "Figures truly grand/Our age alone will show."[48] And so many still believed. Perhaps a few others had come across T'ien Chien's new folk-style poetry from Yenan:

> It wasn't a cart he was driving
> He was driving disaster and hate!
> It wasn't a car he was driving
> He was driving a human life!
> It wasn't a cart he was driving
> He was driving a tower of fire![49]

Figure 13. **"New Year's Print."**

Figure 14. **Liu K'ai-chü, Statue to "The Anonymous Soldier" (Chengtu).**

Figure 15. **Yen Han, "When the Enemy Comes" (1944).**

Notes

1. The verse, written in 1938, has caught the attention of several Chinese commentators, among them Ts'ao Chu-jen, *Wen-t'an wu-shih nien: hsu-chi* (Fifty years of the literary scene: A continuation) (Hong Kong, 1973), p. 101; Ssu-ma Ch'ang-feng, *Chung-kuo hsin wen-hsueh shih* (A history of the new Chinese literature) (Hong Kong, 1978), 3: 263–64.

2. The script of "Fang-hsia ni ti pien-tzu" appears in Yu Ching (Yu Ling), ed. *Ta-chung chu hsuan* (Selected plays for the masses) (Shanghai: Shanghai tsa-chih kung-ssu, 1938), 1:1–22, including song scores. Text reprinted in *Chan-wang* (Outlook) (Hong Kong), no. 232, pp. 32ff. An account of the play is found in Lan Hai, *Chung-kuo k'ang-chan wen-i shih* (A history of Chinese literature during the War of Resistance) (Shanghai, 1947; rev. ed., Tsinan, 1984), pp. 85–88. Lan Hai also cites the account of a participant in a touring theater company that performed this play: Chang Chou, *Chung-hua nu-erh* (Daughter of China) in ibid., p. 141.

3. The Nationalist playwright Hu Shao-hsuan is credited with being the first author of original scripts using innovative techniques and one of the most prolific propaganda playwrights, in Joseph Schyns et al., eds., *1500 Modern Chinese Novels and Plays* (Peiping, 1946; reprint, Hong Kong, 1966): pp. lv and 401–2.

4. English translation T'ien Chun [pseud.], *Village in August* (New York: Smith and Durrell, 1942). For a recent article on this novel, see Rudolph Wagner, "Xiao Jun's Novel *Countryside in August* and the Tradition of Proletarian Literature" in *La Litterature Chinoise au temps de la Guerre de Resistance contre le Japon* (Paris: Editions de la Fondation Singer-Polignac, 1982), pp. 57–66.

5. For special studies of Tuan-mu Hung-liang's work, see Liu I-ch'ang, *Tuan-mu Hung-liang lun* (On Tuan-mu Hung-liang) (Hong Kong: Shih-chieh, 1977), and C. T. Hsia, "*The Kor-chin Banner Plains*: A Biographical and Critical Study," in *La Litterature Chinoise*, pp. 31–56.

6. For a study of Yao Hsueh-yin's early work, see William A. Lyell, "The Early Fiction of Yao Xueyin," in *Essays in Modern Chinese Literature and Literary Criticism*, ed. Wolfgang Kubin and Rudolph Wagner (Bochum: Studienverlag Brockmeyer, 1982), pp. 39–58.

7. In *Huo-shao ti tu-men* (City gates on fire) (Shanghai, 1947), p. 78.

8. See Huang Chun-tung (Wong Chun-tong), *Hsien-tai Chung-kuo tso-chia chien-ying* (Profiles of modern Chinese writers) (Hong Kong: Yu-lien, 1972), p. 267.

9. See Jan Leyda, *Dianying: Electric Shadows* (Cambridge: The MIT Press, 1972), pp. 122ff.

10. C. T. Hsia, *A History of Modern Chinese Fiction*, 2d ed. (New Haven: Yale University Press, 1971), p. 287, provides the most reserved response to this novel, but does cite the appreciation of others. Otherwise, critics as varied as Lan Hai, *Chung-kuo k'ang-chan wen-i shih*, p. 191, and Ssu-ma Ch'ang-feng, *Chung-kuo hsin wen-hsueh shih*, 3:109–12, as well as Ts'ao, *Wen-t'an wu-shih nien*, p. 133, are approving.

11. A translation of T'ien Chien's celebrated early wartime poetry appears in Hsu Kai-yu (Hsu Chieh-yu), *Twentieth-Century Chinese Poetry: An Anthology* (Ithaca: Cornell University Press, 1963), pp. 321ff.

12. "Hung-cha" (Bombardment II) appears in Ming Ch'uan, ed., *Feng Tzu-k'ai man-hua hsuan-i* (Interpretations of Feng Tzu-k'ai's selected cartoons) (Hong Kong: Ts'un-i, 1976). "Kuei-ch'iang hsi" (Puppet show) appeared in *Ming-pao* monthly (Hong Kong), no. 123 (March 1976): 55.

13. In *Yao-t'ang tsa-wen* (Peiping, 1944), p. 15. Cited in Edward Gunn, *Unwelcome Muse: Chinese Literature in Shanghai and Peking, 1937–45 (New York: Columbia University Press, 1980), p. 162.*

14. For this episode, and a general account of literature under the Japanese occupation, see Gunn, *Unwelcome Muse*, pp. 165–67.

15. The war correspondence of S. M. (Ch'en I-men) is a prime example, published in *Ch'i-yueh* (July) magazine. See Lan, *Chung-kuo k'ang-chan wen-i shih*, pp. 135–36.

16. One of Chang T'ien-i's satirical short stories of the period, "A New Life," appears in translation in C. C. Wan, ed. *Stories of China at War* (New York: Columbia University Press, 1947). For a study of his satire during the war, see Tsau Shu-ying, "Zhang Tianyi's Satirical Wartime Stories," in *La Litterature Chinoise*, pp. 175–88. Ch'en Pai-ch'en's play "Men and Women in Wild Times" is translated (abridged) in Edward Gunn, ed. *Twentieth-Century Chinese Drama* (Bloomington: Indiana University Press, 1983), pp. 126–73.

17. *Chung-yang jih-pao*, December 1, 1938; cited in Wen T'ien-hsiang, *Kuo-t'ung-ch'u k'ang-chan wen-i yun-tung ta-shih chi* (Chronology of major events of the literary movement during the War of Resistance in the Nationalist Zone) (Chengtu: Szechwan she-hui k'o-hsueh yuan, 1985), p. 101.

18. See *Sketches of a Cottager* (Chinese-English ed.), trans. Shih Chao-ying (Taipei: Yuan-tung, 1973), pp. 77–79, 80–85.

19. "Wo-men suo hsu-yao ti wen-i cheng-ts'e," *Wen-hua hsien-feng* (Cultural vanguard) 1, 1 (September 1942): 5–16. Chang's proposals were hardly binding, and his article was submitted to criticism in later issues.

20. Translated by Jeremy Ingalls, *The Malice of Empire* (London: George Allen and Unwin, 1970).

21. Translations of this story and "Tsai i-yuan chung" (In the Hospital) (1941) appear in Joseph S. M. Lau et al., *Modern Chinese Stories and Novellas, 1919–49* (New York: Columbia University Press, 1981), pp. 266–91.

22. *Yeh mei-kuei* first appeared in *Wen-shih tsa-chih* (Literature and history magazine) (Chungking) 1, 6–8 (June 16; July 1, 16, 1941). For critical reactions, see Lan, *Chung-kuo k'ang-chan wen-i shih*, pp. 244–45; Wen, *Kuo-t'ung-ch'u k'ang-chan*, p. 195; Schyns et al., eds., *1500 Novels*, p. lvi; Ch'en Hsi-ying, in *Wen-shih tsa-chih* 2, 3 (March 15, 1942): 96–97.

23. *Ch'u Yuan* and Kuo's other wartime plays appear in *Selected Works of Guo Moruo: Five Historical Plays*, trans. Bonnie S. McDougall et al. (Peking: Foreign Languages Press, 1984). For a recent critical discussion, see Rudolph Wagner, "The Chinese Writer in His Own Mirror," in *China's Intellectuals and the State*, ed. Merle Goldman et al. (Cambridge: Harvard University, Council on East Asian Studies, 1987), esp. pp. 186–91.

24. For contemporary criticisms of *Peking Man*, see Hu Feng, "Pei-ching jen ti su-hsieh" (A sketch of *Peking Man*), and Mao Tun, "Tu Pei-ching jen" (On reading *Peking Man*), *Hsi-chu ch'un-ch'iu* (Annals of theater) (Kweilin), 2, 1 (May 25, 1942): pp. 28–31. For a later critical evaluation, see Joseph Lau, *Ts'ao Yu: The Reluctant Disciple of Chekhov and O'Neill* (Hong Kong: Hong Kong University Press, 1970), pp. 57ff.

25. Kuo Mo-jo's short story "Yueh-kuang hsia" (Under moonlight), first published in *Jen-shih chien* (The human world) (Kweilin) in October 1942, is based on the demoralizing situation that led to Hung Shen's suicide. A translation of the story appears in C. C. Wang, ed. *Stories of China at War*, pp. 152–58.

26. *Yin-li* (Shanghai: Ch'en-kuang, 1947; 1949), p. 236.

27. Excerpts from *Hsi-yu man-chi* appears in color reproduction in *Ch'ing-ming* (Shanghai) and *Mei-shu* (Fine arts), no. 6 (1957): 26–27. An appreciation of Chang's cartoons appears in the same issue of *Mei-shu*: Ma K'e, "Mei-you shih-ch'u kuang-ts'ai ti hua-to" (An unfaded bouquet), p. 35.

28. A reproduction with explanatory captions of Ting Ts'ung's "Satirical Scroll" ap-

pears in Michael Sullivan, *Chinese Art in the Twentieth Century* (Berkeley: University of California Press, 1959), appendix, plate 69.

29. The script of the play, together with illustrations of sets and costumes by Ting Ts'ung, appears in *Ch'ing-ming* (Shanghai).

30. I refer to the statements attributed to Hsiao Chun in the criticism of him by the Communist party. "Even the policies of the Manchus and the Japanese, he claimed, were not so tyrannous as those enforced by the party." Merle Goldman, *Literary Dissent in Communist China* (New York: Atheneum, 1971), p. 77, citing Yang Yen-nan, *Chung-kung tui Hu Feng ti tou-cheng* (The struggle against Hu Feng by the Chinese Communists) (Hong Kong, 1956), p. 179.

31. Shen's concern with his life as an urbanized intellectual emerged strongly shortly before the war in tales of approaching middle age, such as the satirical "Pa-chun t'u" (Eight seeds) and "Chu-fu" (The housewife), each of which was adopted as the title of a collection. Shen's social concern with the domination of literature by political institutions and functionaries was strongly registered in "Wen-hsueh yun-tung ti ch'ung tsao" (The re-creation of the literary movement), *Wen-i hsien-feng* (Literary vanguard) (Chungking) 1, 2 (October 1942), cited in Wen, *Kuo-t'ung-ch'u k'ang-chan*, pp. 202–3.

32. For a recent study of Sha T'ing's wartime work, see Wong Kam-ming, "Animals in a Teahouse: The Art of Sha Ting's Fiction," in *La Litterature Chinoise*, pp. 243–65.

33. A study of this novel appears in William Lyell, "Lu Ling's Wartime Novel: Hungry Guo Su-e," in *La Litterature Chinoise*, pp. 267–80.

34. Sullivan, *Chinese Art in the Twentieth Century*, reproduces several paintings and sketches representing the work of wartime traveling artists but largely dismisses their value.

35. "On the Screen," *The Twentieth Century* (Shanghai) 5, 4 (October 1943): 278. Cited in Gunn, *Unwelcome Muse*, p. 26.

36. See Wu Zuguang [Wu Tsu-kuang], "Le théâtre à Chongqing (1938–45)," and Delphine Baudry-Weulersse, " A propos de *Fengxue yeguiren* de Wu Zuguang," in *La Litterature Chinoise*, pp. 353–70. For *Ch'iu Hai-t'ang*, see Gunn, *Unwelcome Muse*, pp. 140–45.

37. Hsu, *Twentieth-Century Chinese Poetry*, p. 239.

38. Ch'en I-men was trained and served as an officer during the Battle of Shanghai, but biographical details are scarce, as are copies of *Nan-ching*, even though it was given an award by the large and prestigious Chinese Writers and Artists Anti-Aggression Association (Chung-hua Ch'uan-kuo Wen-i-chieh K'ang-ti Hsieh-hui), formed in 1938 and headed by Lao She. Accounts of the Hu Feng group and its clashes with others are numerous, featured in most histories of literature in the Republican era.

39. Hsu, *Twentieth-Century Chinese Poetry*, p. 416.

40. Chih Ko, "Kuan Shan-yueh's Paintings," *Chinese Literature*, no. 2 (1964): 108.

41. Hsu, *Twentieth-Century Chinese Poetry*, p. 42.

42. "Chung-kuo kung-ch'an-tang tsai min-tsu chan-cheng chung ti ti-wei" (The role of the Chinese Communist party in the national war). *Selected Readings from the Works of Mao Tse-tung* (Peking: Foreign Languages Press, 1971), p. 156; Takeuchi Minoru, ed., *Mo Takuto shu* (Collected works of Mao Tse-tung) (Tokyo: Hokubo-sha, 1970–72), 6:261.

43. For a recent study of Ting Ling during this period, see Yi-tsi Mei Feuerwerker, "The Uses of Literature: Ding Ling at Yan'an," *Essays in Modern Chinese Literature*, ed. Kubin et al., pp. 3–38.

44. See David Holm, "The Literary Rectification at Yan'an," in ibid., pp. 274–75. For the theoretical background to these events, see David Holm, "National Form and the Popularisation of Literature in Yenan," in *La Litterature Chinoise*, pp. 215–35. The pion-

eering study of the situation before and during the Yenan Forum is T. A. Hsia, "Twenty Years after the Yenan Forum," in *The Gate of Darkness* (Seattle: University of Washington Press, 1968), pp. 234–62. The most recent collection of documentary materials from Communist base areas available at the time of this study is Liu Tseng-chieh et al., ed. *K'ang-jih chan-cheng shih-ch'i Yen-an chi k'ang-Jih min-chu ken-chu-ti wen-hsueh yun-tung tzu liao* (Materials on the literary movement in Yenan and all democratic resistance bases during the War of Resistance against Japan) (Taiyuan: Shansi jen-min, 1983), 3 vols.

45. Brief quotations from the "Talks" appeared in the Chungking CCP newspaper *Hsin-hua jih-pao*, March 24, 1943 (ten months after the forum). A full text was published in the Yenan *Chieh-fang jih-pao*, October 19, 1943. In Chungking extended excerpts were published in *Hsin-hua jih-pao*, January 1, 1944. Thereafter, revised versions appeared in editions of Mao's *Selected Works*.

46. *Selected Readings*, p. 284; Takeuchi, ed., *Mo Takuto shu*, 8:148.

47. Ho Ching-chih, "Pai-mao nu ti ch'uang-tso yu yen-ch'u" (The creation and performance of *The White-haired Girl*) (1946), in *Pai-mao nu* (N.p.: Hsin-hua shu-tien, Chung-kuo jen-min wen-i ts'ung-shu, 1949), p. 201.

48. From the translation by Cyril Birch, in Hsu Kai-yu, ed. *Literature of the People's Republic of China* (Bloomington: Indiana University Press, 1980), p. 376. The early texts and publication of Mao's poems are discussed in detail in Sheng Wen-t'ing, "Mao Tse-tung 'Ch'in yuan ch'un': hsueh ti hsieh-tso yu fa-piao wen-t'i" (The question of the composition and publication of Mao Tse-tung's "Snow: To the tune of Spring in Ch'in's Garden"), *Chung-kuo hsien-tai wen-hsueh yen-chiu* (Studies in modern Chinese literature), no. 2 (1982): 41–54.

49. "Kan-ch'e chuan" (The carter's story) (1943), from the translation by Cyril Birch in Hsu, *Literature of the People's Republic of China*, p. 186.

11

WARTIME JUDICIAL REFORM IN CHINA

Hsia Tao-tai
with the assistance of Wendy Zeldin

ON JANUARY 11, 1943, China signed a treaty with Great Britain and the United States according to which those nations agreed to relinquish the right to consular jurisdiction and other special rights they enjoyed. For a hundred years, consular jurisdiction had enabled foreign powers to shield their subjects in China from Chinese legal authority and to have them tried, if necessary, under the home country's laws. It was the most degrading, disruptive, and hence most significant feature of the unequal treaties that had been imposed upon China as a result of its defeat by the British in the Opium War of 1839–42. Because of China's contribution to victory in World War II, the Allied powers agreed to relinquish extraterritorial rights. Having regained judicial sovereignty, China could fully revamp its judicial system. Even before this was achieved, however, both Nationalist- and Communist-controlled areas of China experimented with a variety of judicial reforms.

Judicial Reform in Late Ch'ing and Early Republican China

A strong resemblance exists between the Republic of China's (ROC) present judicial system and that of the civil law countries of Europe. This is due to the fact that at the end of the Ch'ing dynasty, in an attempt to convince the Western powers to relinquish the unequal treaties, the Chinese tried to emulate the European judicial model.

Another reason that motivated the Ch'ing to change its judicial system was the inadequacy of traditional Chinese law to deal with Western economic power and commercial techniques since it lacked such concepts and devices as corporations, negotiable instruments, and insurance. Moreover, Japan, which had successfully modernized its legal system and freed itself from extraterritoriality, stood as a model for China, while the Western powers provided the major incentive in the form of bilateral treaties with provisions that gave a conditional promise to relinquish extraterritorial rights if China could satisfy them with its judicial reforms.[1] To satisfy the foreign powers that its judicial system was changing, the Ch'ing government attempted to carry out reforms. It set up law schools, a modern-style legal profession, and a codification bureau charged with the task of preparing drafts of civil, criminal, and procedural codes, and it emulated the Western legal system in establishing courts and procuracies to separate judicial from executive functions.[2] China also sent students abroad to learn foreign law and officials abroad to observe foreign systems of administration of justice. All of these measures were fraught with difficulties, however, and as a result were not carried out very thoroughly. Still, a certain amount of progress was made.

With the founding of the Republic of China in 1912, Dr. Sun Yat-sen, the provisional president, pledged further revision of Chinese laws. He issued orders prohibiting torture and corporal punishment, emphasizing evidence rather than confession in establishing guilt in criminal cases, and encouraging public trials.[3] After Yuan Shih-k'ai's effort to restore imperial rule, however, these early efforts suffered a setback, and very little progress was made in judicial reform during the ensuing warlord period.

In 1926, a report by a commission sent to China by the Western powers criticized China's lack of a complete set of legal codes, scarcity of new, modern courts and prisons, improperly funded courts and prisons, and interference by the military in the administration of justice.[4] After the establishment of the Nationalist government in Nanking in 1928, certain judicial reforms were successfully carried out, such as the establishment of courts of first instance at the county level, appellate courts at the provincial level, and a court of last instance, the Supreme Court, for the entire country. In the next ten years, before the beginning of the war against Japan in 1937, Nationalist China promulgated a Civil Code (1929–31), a Code of Civil Procedure (1935), a Criminal Code (1935), a Code of Criminal Procedure (1935), as well as major commercial and administrative laws.[5]

After several unsuccessful attempts to have consular jurisdiction abolished, in December 1929, to show its determination to bring it to an end, the Nationalist government urged all government agencies concerned to make the necessary preparations for facilitating the abolition of extraterritorial rights. In May 1931, it promulgated the Implementing Regulations for Assuming Jurisdiction over Aliens in China.[6] China was determined to abolish consular jurisdiction unilaterally even if the foreign powers refused to give their consent. The law was scheduled to be implemented on January 1, 1932, but it never went into effect because of the disruptive impact of the Manchurian incident of September 18, 1931. Only toward the end of World War II were the U.S. and Great Britain willing to relinquish consular jurisdiction and sign new treaties with China.[7]

Once consular jurisdiction was abolished, new procedures were instituted for handling cases involving foreigners.[8] At the same time, the Implementation Regulations for Assuming Jurisdiction over Aliens in China were abolished and arrangements were made for foreign jurists to come to China to serve as legal advisers. Chinese jurists were also sent to the United States and England to observe the administration of justice in those two countries and to collect research materials. As a result, the U.S. State Department sent jurist Milton T. Helmick to spend three months in China in 1944. He eventually wrote a report that included six proposals for the improvement of judicial administration in China.[9] In 1945, Dean Roscoe Pound of Harvard Law School was invited by the Chinese Ministry of Justice to visit China to assess its judicial system in general and to observe how Chinese laws were actually being implemented.[10]

The discussion that follows will look first at Nationalist and then at Communist wartime judicial reforms.

Nationalist Judicial Reform

Basic Framework of Laws

A compilation of laws known as the *Liu fa ch'uan-shu* (Complete collection of the six laws), patterned after a similar Japanese collection, comprised the cornerstone of law in Republican China before, during, and after World War II and is still the basic legal text of the Republic of China on Taiwan. It actually consists of more than the six laws—the constitution, the Civil Code, the Code of Civil Procedure, the Criminal Code, the Code of Criminal Procedure, and the Commercial Code—but they are the most important. Interpretations of the law made by the Judicial Yuan and decisions rendered by the Supreme Court are used to supplement the enacted laws.[11] Several emergency laws were also enacted in the wartime period: a revised Emergency Law for Punishing Crimes Endangering the Republic (September 1937); Emergency Measures for Maintaining Security During the Extraordinary Period (July 1940); the National Mobilization Law and the Provisional Regulations Governing the Punishment of Crimes that Endanger the State (March 1942);[12] and the Regulations for Punishing Bandits (April 1944).[13]

As far as the court system of the Republic of China is concerned, in October 1932 the Court Organization Law was promulgated. It provides for courts of three instances and two trials. District courts were courts of first instance for ordinary civil and criminal cases; courts of second instance for such cases were at the provincial level. There was also a court of first instance at the provincial level for serious crimes such as sedition. A Supreme Court, the court of third instance, was established in the capital to deal with broader issues of law. The Court Organization Law provided for judicial independence as a general principle and for the judicial independence of judges in particular. It also stipulated that higher courts were not to interfere with the decision-making processes of lower courts, even though the latter are under the administrative supervision of the former.[14]

These laws and regulations formed part of the basic legal system of Nationalist China before and during World War II.[15] In the sections that follow, the attempts made by the Nationalist government to institute judicial reform and build on the rudimentary court system will be outlined. It may be noted that in general, especially in the rural areas, the laws promulgated by the government, unlike those enacted in the Chinese Communist regions, were not widely publicized.

Funding

During the warlord-dominated early years of the Republic of China, funds for running the courts, procuracies, and prisons all came from warlords' treasuries. When the Nationalist government was established, even though the funds for running the judicial organs at the central level came from the national treasury, the funds for local judicial organs were still gathered on the basis of the old system, that is, at the local level, and the provincial and county heads of government had control of them. This arrangement was plagued by the following defects.[16] Since the heads of local executive organs had complete control of these funds derived from local sources, in dispensing them the local leaders would usually not give very high priority to judicial organs. Another flaw in the system was that because the executive held the purse strings, judicial officials, to obtain funding, would have to follow the dictates of the executive. As a result, there was very little judicial independence.

Yet another problem was that judges and other judicial personnel were paid less than officials of executive organs. In addition, since certain provinces and counties in China were richer than others, judicial officials would be paid differently in different regions, and the poor areas had great difficulty in recruiting and keeping people. Finally, because the funds made available to judicial organs by the executive organs in different areas varied, so that in certain richer areas there were better prisons and more new courts established, it was necessary to have all the judicial organs in the country funded by the national treasury to achieve greater uniformity. From the late 1920s to the 1930s, proposals were made at many national conferences to have the national treasury fund judicial expenses. For example, at the National Economic Conference and the National Finance Conference held in 1928, and at the Second National Financial Conference held in 1934, there were proposals to make the central government responsible for the funding of all judicial organs in the country, but no decision on the issue was ever reached. At the National Judicial Conference of 1935, a resolution was finally adopted to have all judicial organs funded by the national treasury, but it was never carried out.

In 1939, the government finally decided to have the judicial organs in provinces not in the war zone funded by the central government first. The provinces that at that time fell into this category included Szechwan, Kweichow, Yunnan, Kwangsi, Shensi, Kansu, Ninghsia, Tsinghai, and Sikang. The only province not in the war zone that was not funded by the national treasury was Sinkiang. Thus, beginning in 1940, all the funding for new courts, prisons, and houses of detention came from the national treasury. As of 1941, moreover, all courts and prisons, no matter whether the province in which they were located was in a war zone or not, were so funded.[17]

Court and Trial Experiments

In attempting to satisfy the Western powers' demands for reform of the legal system, China often ended up borrowing too much from the West. Substantive and procedural laws modeled after those of European countries were adopted even when they were poorly suited to local conditions in China and too complicated for the contemporary Chinese context. During the war the Nationalist government sought to simplify both the civil and criminal procedural codes to speed up the judicial process. In 1942, an experimental court was established in Pishan, a small city not far from Chungking, to test the efficacy of the simplified codes. It was found that as a result of the new procedures, the time required to adjudicate cases was very much shortened. The experimental court was also used as a testing ground for a judicial assistants system. In 1944, the district court in Chungking was also turned into an experimental court because the Pishan court did not handle very many of the complicated and important cases. These two experimental courts were changed back into regular courts at the end of 1945 since they had fulfilled their purpose of proving the value of the simplified procedures.[18]

Because China is so vast and transportation, especially in inland areas, so difficult, the Nationalist government found it necessary to send judges on a circuit to make it easier for litigants to have their cases heard. Even before the war against Japan, proposals had been made to have a circuit court system adopted. For instance, at the National Judicial Conference of 1935, several different provinces and cities submitted proposals for implementation of such a system, but none was adopted.[19] During the war, the transportation problem in certain areas became even more serious, and so it became almost impossible for litigants, especially those from the war zones, to travel to the nearest district court. The problem was particularly severe for cases on appeal, since appellate courts were found only in the provincial capitals.

To remedy the situation, the Judicial Yuan promulgated laws entitled "Measures Governing Circuit Trials in the War Zones" in 1938 and "Provisional Measures Governing Civil and Criminal Procedure for Circuit Trials in the War Zones" in 1939.[20] The passage of these two laws made it possible for circuit trials to be conducted in the cities and provinces located in the war zones. Before the formal adoption of the system, the Chungking government had its ambassadors to Great Britain and the United States collect information on the circuit court system of those two countries,[21] supposedly so that China could learn from

Western experience. The extent to which the ambassadors' findings were actually used in formulating the laws, however, is debatable, since the primary aim of such an exercise was to make a good impression on the Western powers so that they would relinquish extraterritoriality. The Nationalist government implemented circuit court trials in nine provinces and the war zones. Depending upon the facility of transportation in a given area, each circuit would last from one to three months. The system was found to have popular support, not only because certain types of cases were adjudicated in less time, but also because of its educative role in making the common people more familiar with the laws.[22]

As noted above, in certain areas of China where there was no court, only a judge attached to the executive organ; there was less judicial independence; and in some provinces where there was only one appellate court in the capital city it was often difficult for litigants from inland areas to travel to the capital to attend a trial. In 1940, after the government had decided to have all judicial organs funded by the national treasury, a five-year plan was made to set up more courts of first instance, which were district courts, and courts of second instance, which were branches of the higher courts. Due to insufficient funds, the five-year plan could not be fully carried out during the war, but significant progress in the establishment of the new courts was still achieved.

Before the war there were only 302 district courts in China. Despite the funding difficulties, the number of places without a district court was reduced during the war and, even if a separate court was not established, at least more counties set up a judicial office attached to the executive office and provided a full-time judge to handle judicial functions. As a result, there was a somewhat greater separation of powers between judicial and executive functions. It may be noted that the establishment of a judicial office attached to the office of the county magistrate was designated as a transitional measure until conversion to a fully separate district court could be achieved.[23]

Other Reform Measures

Disputes regarding personal ownership rights became more acute in China due to the chaotic conditions caused by the war, and so there was a need to promote a notary public system in China. As Hsieh Kuan-sheng pointed out, if a person's private rights could be determined beforehand by means of such a system, the need to pursue litigation would be reduced.[24] In 1939, the Ministry of Judicial Administration instructed all district courts to set up a division for handling notary public matters within a specified time period. In 1942, the ministry issued another similar order. A Notary Public Law was enacted in 1943 and Detailed Rules Governing the Implementation of the Notary Public Law became effective the following year, in 1944. Because of the repeated orders from the Ministry of Judicial Administration, most of the courts carried out the plan and established notary public offices. The courts were further instructed by the ministry to launch a campaign to call people's attention to the importance of the functions performed by notary publics. During such campaigns, the courts that had a notary public office attached invited the leading personnel to give lectures and to publicize the notary public system in newspapers, theaters, and movie houses. In addition, the ministry urged such district courts to compete with each other in the publicizing campaign and presented awards to those deemed the winners.[25]

China has a long history of settling disputes through mediation. During the Ch'ing dynasty, for example, people from the same area or those in the same profession would go to a *hui-kuan* (gathering place) or *kung-suo* (association), respectively. The responsible persons in these regional or professional associations would act as mediators. In addition, the elders of a given locality would mediate neighborhood disputes. During the war, because it was difficult to have cases adjudicated by a court, the need for mediation increased. In 1943, the Ministry of Judicial Administration issued the Regulations on the Organization of Mediation Committees of Villages and Towns. Aside from mediating civil disputes, such committees were also to handle certain types of minor criminal cases. The Ministry of Judicial Administration, in orders issued in 1943 and 1945, not only instructed the courts to pay special attention to mediation, but also required them to publish figures showing how many cases were settled by the courts through mediation.[26]

Additional Nationalist wartime reforms included the improvement of the procuratorial system; the promotion of the public defender and legal aid system; the improvement of prison facilities; rehabilitation measures for prisoners, such as the requirement that convicts engage in productive labor; and the employment of convicts in certain land reclamation projects.[27] Nor were legal education and the training of judicial personnel neglected during the war. The government also made a special study of the customs of the regions inhabited by national minorities, such as Tibet, Sikang, and Ninghsia, to prepare special laws suited to their needs.

Communist Judicial Reform

After the outbreak of the Sino-Japanese War, the Chinese Communist party formed the Shensi-Kansu-Ninghsia Border Region government, which, operating within the framework of the second united front, was formally subordinate to the authority of the Nationalist government. The High Court of the border region was put in charge of both trial work and judicial administration while at the county level judicial bureaus (*ts'ai-p'an ch'u*) were established. (These became county justice bureaus [*ssu-fa ch'u*] beginning in 1943.)[28]

By 1937, the Chinese Communists controlled some eighteen base areas of varying size behind enemy lines, of which Shen-Kan-Ning was the largest and most important. From its Yenan headquarters, the Chinese Communist government issued laws and regulations that served as models for the Communist governments in all the areas under its control.[29] The "Outline for the War Against Japan and Building the Country," the general program adopted by the Communist regime, set the tone for the legal framework established in the border regions.

As part of the united front, the legal system of the border regions was also to come under the Nationalist laws and courts. The Chinese Communists adopted certain Nationalist laws, for example, those against banditry, treason, and opium,[30] and at least nominally applied others, such as the *Complete Collection of Six Laws* mentioned above and laws relating to judicial work. Since they hoped to do away with KMT law wherever possible, however, they used it on a discretionary basis, applying individual provisions that they deemed suitable.[31] More often, they issued their own laws and regulations.[32]

From 1938 to 1943, the Shen-Kan-Ning government issued a number of outlines, resolutions, decisions, and announcements of a legal nature as well as a large number of individual laws and regulations.[33] The basic policies and goals were set forth in the Outline for Administration of the Shen-Kan-Ning Border Region, a de facto constitution, which the various other border regions followed as a guide for formulating their own similar outlines and legislation.[34] The most significant and numerous of the many laws enacted by the border region governments during the war years were criminal statutes. These fell into two categories: regular criminal cases (homicide, assault and battery, theft, illegal possession of goods, serious acts violating family relationships) and special criminal cases (betrayal of the country, robbery, banditry, sabotage, destruction of camouflaged goods, use of opium and other drugs).[35]

Wartime Judicial Reforms

The view that law is subservient to politics underlay the administration of justice in the border regions. According to T'ang Yung, a cadre who wrote about judicial work, the political task was to consolidate the anti-Japanese united front; therefore, in its legislation the "anti-Japanese democratic government behind enemy lines" had to pay special attention to the interests of the various anti-Japanese classes, which were to be considered equal before the law. Furthermore, in handling concrete civil and criminal cases, judicial personnel should give precedence to the Outline for the War Against Japan and Building the Country over any laws that might be in conflict with it. "Sole concern for law without regard to politics should not be considered a correct attitude for judicial workers," T'ang wrote.[36]

All the border regions had judicial systems that shared certain common characteristics.[37] Nine such features will be illustrated below, mainly by examples drawn from the system established in the Yench'eng-Funing Border Region. The laws enacted in this region are typical of those enacted in other areas under Communist control.

Regional Exercise of Judicial Power

Judicial power was exercised by the judicial organs of the region and public security organs were only to arrest people in accordance with the law. The courts and methods of judicial procedure were based upon those instituted during the Chinese soviet period.[38] In line with united front policy, the interests of people of all classes who opposed the Japanese were to be protected. The chief targets of the courts were traitors, saboteurs, and anti-Communist elements. The courts were also to disseminate legal knowledge through their trial work and to take measures to prevent crime.[39]

Judicial organs of different levels were considered part of the government at the same level. The courts were under the unified leadership of the party and of the government of the same level and thus lacked independence.[40] At that time, heads of the prefectures under the Shen-Kan-Ning government were concurrently chiefs of the branch tribunals of the High Court (see below), and the heads of counties also served as heads of the justice bureaus. Judicial independence was condemned, and judges were warned not to assert independence from the party.[41] Beginning in 1940, a trial committee (*ts'ai-p'an wei-yuan-hui*), consisting of the head of the county government, the secretary of the county party committee, and the county judge, was established in each county. It was to discuss and decide on important cases to ensure that party policy was reflected.[42]

To outline the tasks of the courts, each region enacted a series of organic laws. The Yench'eng-Funing Border Region formulated an "Outline for Judicial Work in the Yench'eng-Funing Border Region" in 1942. Its General Principles state that the outline was based on the Outline for the War Against Japan and Building the Country, with a view to the practice of clean government and eradication of judicial ills.[43] The region was authorized to issue its own individual laws and regulations even though national laws and regulations were stated to be the basis for judicial work. The outline noted that "a court shall be established in the region as its supreme judicial organ." The Regulations Governing the Organization of the Court stipulated that it "is to be considered a component of the administrative government." The president and vice-president of the court, as well as court-appointed procurators, would receive guidance and orders from the government administration. The Court Organization Regulations further provided that "the interpretations of laws and regulations shall be carried out by the court."

Procedures for arrest and detention were covered generally in the outlines of the various regions and specifically under separate pieces of legislation. The Outline of Government of the Shen-Kan-Ning Border Region, for example, provided a number of procedural guarantees with respect to arrest, detention, interrogation, and investigation. Corporal punishment and forced confessions were prohibited.[44] For ordinary crimes committed in the border region, the policy of reform of the convict was always to be followed. At first, the most severe penalty was five years' imprisonment. Later, in 1943, it was changed and raised to a maximum of ten years' imprisonment.[45]

The Trial System

For all practical purposes, there was a two-tier court system in the border regions, consisting of either county justice bureaus[46] or local courts (the courts of first instance at the county level) and the regional High Court (the court of second and final instance). This system was spelled out in Article 4 of the Provisional Measures Governing the Trial of Judicial Cases in the Yench'eng-Funing Border Region. In theory, as part of the united front agreement, there was actually a system of three instances and three trials, the court of third instance being the Nationalist Supreme Court, whose jurisdiction the High Court was nominally under.[47] In fact, however, the court of third instance was the border region government's judicial committee.[48] In 1944, the three instances and three trials were reduced to two instances and two trials in Shen-Kan-Ning to expedite the judicial process in trials involving traitors and "reactionary elements."[49]

The legal literature of the border regions emphasized that oral confessions should not be accepted as evidence without supporting evidence. Corporal punishment was prohibited, and forced confessions were forbidden.

During the period of the war against Japan, all the border region governments enacted laws providing for a people's assessors system.[50] Except for cases involving counterrevolutionary activity, the people's assessor system was to be implemented in trying all civil and criminal cases. People's assessors were to be selected by mass groups such as trade unions, peasants' associations, women's associations, and youth leagues. For certain cases, people were also invited on an ad hoc basis to serve as assessors. Assessors enjoyed the same rights as professional judges.

Among the three basic means of selecting people's assessors—through special invitation of the trial organ, election by certain groups, and appointment by a government organ, military unit, or other group—the third method was most common during the war.[51] For instance, in cases that involved labor discipline, trade unions were to select representative workers to serve as assessors; for marriage cases, the women's association; in cases involving peasants, the peasants' association.

The Yench'eng-Funing Border Region government enacted the Regulations Governing People's Assessors in fifteen articles.[52] People's representatives could serve as assessors in major civil and criminal trials but were not to take part in the investigation of a case. Besides having no involvement in the case under trial, assessors were selected on the basis of their reputation for fairness and their lack of a court record since the establishment of the "anti-Japanese democratic government." The presiding judge was charged with ensuring that judicial procedure was followed. The judge, who was responsible for questioning, could grant permission to assessors to ask questions of their own. Upon the conclusion of the trial, the assessors consulted together and submitted their nonbinding views to the presiding judge for reference purposes.

In principle, open trials were to be held and defendants were entitled to counsel. The masses were allowed to listen and to express their views.[53] Although the circumstances of wartime interfered with providing lawyers as legal advocates, litigants could have relatives or people with knowledge of the law serve as their defenders or agents.[54] Litigants in minority regions had the right to use their own minority language during the trial. In the border region courts, a litigant was entitled to lodge an appeal.[55] A system of review of sentences of capital punishment and life imprisonment was instituted.

According to Ma Hsi-wu, civil procedure under the Nationalist government was cumbersome and favored the rich. Therefore, in Shen-Kan-Ning and other border regions the Communist governments tried to simplify judicial procedures. Ma advocated free preparation of legal documents for litigants and said that the system of two instances and two trials gave people the opportunity to appeal a case without letting it drag on forever.[56] Verdicts were to be written in a simple, vernacular style, in contrast to the high-flown language used by the old courts.[57] In general, legal formalities were minimized and legal fees waived.

The method of conducting trials according to the mass line by means of circuit trials (hsun-hui shen-li, also referred to as on-the-spot trials, chiu-ti p'an-an), known as the Ma Hsi-wu method, was developed during this period, at first in Shen-Kan-Ning and then in the other border regions. Use of this type of trial became a principle of the current PRC Code of Civil Procedure.

Circuit trials refer to mobile tribunals of a people's court that, either periodically or without fixed frequency, conduct trials in the circuit within that court's jurisdiction. The trial is to be held either in the locale where a civil case occurred or in the place where the litigants are located, to facilitate attendance by the masses.[58]

Ma Hsi-wu, a CCP member who held several posts in the Shen-Kan-Ning government, became known for his work in the legal field even though he apparently had no legal training.[59] Ma's method entailed obtaining evidence directly from the local people and writing verdicts in simple language. Ma believed that the border region governments should hold informal trials, according to the mass line, that did not make litigants fearful. He advocated three methods: trial on the spot, circuit trials, and show trials. Trial on the spot meant that judges should go to the villages and rely on the masses from the investigation stage to the trial stage. A circuit trial entailed a judge of the Higher Court or its branch tribunals taking a case to the place where it actually happened, to facilitate participation by the people involved or because it was complex. Show trials (kung-shen chih), held before the masses to educate and to act as a deterrent to crime, were conducted in one of three ways: (1) holding the trial before the masses; (2) announcing the trial decision at a mass rally; (3) having representatives from the masses participate in a public trial.[60] Note that this is different from holding a trial in public, at which people sit in the audience.

T'ang Yung, a contemporary of Ma Hsi-wu who also worked in a border region, viewed the circuit trial system as especially suitable for the shifting environment behind enemy lines. He noted that in the zones of guerrilla warfare, not only was the circuit trial the principal way of conducting trials, but guerrilla-style circuit trials should be conducted to cope with the combat situation. Since judicial cadres in the guerrilla zones might have to engage in combat, they should be armed. The guerrillas' work method in such zones was to handle problems directly and speedily. Unlike the situation in the base areas, there was no judicial organ in the guerrilla zones beyond the trial itself.[61]

After the founding of the PRC, the government synthesized past experience in conducting circuit and on-the-spot trials and incorporated the results into the Civil Procedural Code of the PRC for Trial Implementation.[62]

The mediation system as a means of settling disputes was prevalent in the border regions and was given more emphasis during the period of the war against Japan. In 1943, the Shen-Kan-Ning government issued a directive regarding the promotion of mediation work, and its High Court also issued mediation measures that helped reduce the amount of litigation.[63] Ma Hsi-wu claimed that the Chinese Communists' mediation work was aimed at enhancing mutual cooperation among the people, enhancing production, teaching people how to observe the law, and reducing litigation. The cases mediated were to be limited to general civil disputes and minor criminal cases; relatively serious criminal cases could not be handled by mediation.

In his government work report, the chairman of the Shen-Kan-Ning government encouraged people to settle disputes peacefully outside of court and advised that town and village governments select as mediators people from the masses who had good reputations, such as labor heroes and gentry with a sense of justice.[64] Mediation could be conducted in two ways: (1) mediation of a case by the trial organ, and (2) mediation by the people. From 1942 to 1944, in the entire Shen-Kan-Ning Border Region, the number of civil and criminal cases handled by means of mediation increased year after year.[65] Moreover, some villages were designated as model mediation villages, and some people were designated as model mediators.[66]

Ma Hsi-wu admitted that there were abuses of the system. Sometimes the parties to a dispute were forced against their will to go through the mediation process because those in charge wrongly believed that mediation had to take place before litigation of all civil cases. Ma stressed that mediation must be voluntary, that it should not be compulsory, and that it was not a necessary precondition for litigation. The customs and habits of the area were also to be taken into account in conducting mediation.[67] In the border regions during the war, judicial cadres were to follow the mass line and to be selected on the basis of their ideology rather than on their knowledge of earlier (Nationalist) laws.

Those trained in the old way were to be reformed so that they would have the "correct" (mass) approach.[68] Judicial cadres, especially leaders and judges, were to be loyal to the revolutionary Three Principles of the People and willing to be close to the masses, and their ideological as well as professional education was to be strengthened to make them "good judicial officers of the new democracy."[69]

Among the qualifications of judicial cadres, according to the Shen-Kan-Ning High Court in May 1941, were loyalty to the revolution, a sense of justice, the ability to analyze problems and distinguish right from wrong, endurance, a sense of responsibility, and the ability to understand the provisions of law and the work report.[70] A legal education was not required of those involved in judicial work. To train judicial cadres, short-term training classes were developed. For example, from 1939 to 1940, three such classes offered in Shen-Kan-Ning trained almost one hundred judicial cadres from worker and peasant backgrounds. Afterward, from 1942 to 1946, a school of law and a department of the judiciary (the name implies that the classes were for short-term training) were set up in Yenan University to train judicial cadres.[71] The quality of judicial cadres was wanting, however. As one cadre involved in judicial work in the Yench'eng-Funing Border Region wrote, "In handling complex cases, these judicial cadres, be it in deriving legal principles or in finding the facts, are obviously not competent enough and leave much to be desired."[72]

With respect to judicial independence, as was noted above, during the war against Japan there was no separation of powers in the border regions, and party leadership was to be followed. Later, however, in April 1946, to strengthen the postwar revolutionary legal system, the governing principles of the Shen-Kan-Ning Border Region provided that "the judicial organs of all levels shall exercise their functions and powers independently, they shall only follow the law and not be interfered with," and "Other than the judicial organs and public security organs, which enjoy their appropriate functions and powers, no other organizations or groups can make arrests or conduct trials."[73] Thus, during the war, it was considered important and necessary to have strict party leadership, but the fact that immediately after the war laws were passed in the border regions giving the courts a certain independence implies that there had been some miscarriages of justice.

Criminal legislation in the border regions was especially aimed at carrying out the party's policy of eradicating traitors.[74] The policy was based on several considerations. The anti-Japanese base areas were usually surrounded by the enemy, and in certain border regions enemy territory and Communist territory overlapped, so that the enemy, and also the KMT, constantly dispatched special agents to Communist-held areas to engage in subversive activities. Cadres in the base areas were especially well-equipped to deal with special agents, given their combat experience from the numerous battles, their thorough indoctrination in party doctrine, and the strong CCP military presence. Under the united front policy, as long as a person opposed the Japanese, regardless of class background, he or she was welcome in the border region. Thus, the focus was on limiting the activities of spies and special agents and making a special effort to win over those who were neutral or those who were inclined to join the enemy camp.[75]

In his "Annual Report" on the Shen-Kan-Ning Border Region, Chairman Lin Tsu-han devoted a whole section to the liquidation of traitors and special agents.[76] Article 7 of the "Outline for Administration of the Shen-Kan-Ning Border Region" provided that "enemies, traitors, and all other saboteurs, except for those who refuse to repent, should be treated leniently after they are arrested so that they will have a chance to reform."[77] The party Central Committee formulated the policy that the leaders of bad elements were to be severely punished, whereas those who were forced to join the group would be dealt with lightly, and those who helped to expose the bad elements would be rewarded.[78]

Prisons

In Shen-Kan-Ning, a Detention Center Department under the High Court was in charge of prisons connected with the High Court and had supervisory authority over prison facilities at lower levels.[79] The county justice bureaus (*ssu-fa ch'u*) "might or might not run a detention center and/or a prison depending upon the *hsien*'s size, location, and length of time under Communist control." Despite the attempt to legislate procedural protections during the pretrial period, such regulations were only "model targets," so that suspects might nonetheless be imprisoned for a long time, first in a special detention center or else a local prison before coming to trial. Prison policies during the war against Japan focused on release programs, chiefly through parole and broadened criteria for eligibility for release (given food and labor shortages, the government needed to try to keep people productive and self-sufficient); leniency, productivity, education, and thought reform.[80]

According to a report on judicial work of the Shansi-Chahar-Hopei Border Region, in dealing with prisoners, corporal punishment was to be avoided. Reform of the person, especially his or her thinking, was to be emphasized since some prisoners even after being released did not know what crime they were guilty of.[81] Prisoners who were released and sent to rural areas to work under supervision were not to be treated just like ordinary persons, as was sometimes the case. They were to be given indoctrination and education and were to make others aware that they were prisoners to deter crime. On the other hand, the practice in some areas of overworking released convicts was to be corrected. The report also emphasized that there should be a system for managing the released convicts, to oversee how many there were, what work they performed, and how they were treated, evaluated, and educated, as well as some connection between those involved in trial work and those in charge of prison work. It advocated curbing the tendency to treat prisoners leniently and the tendency to mistreat prisoners to seek revenge. Prisoners were to be encouraged to develop "self-rule," to make them think that they were the prison guards. Production and education were to be combined. The report advised having prison cadres set an example by working together with the convicts so that the latter would not view labor as a kind of punishment. Educating the prisoners would help them become good citizens after their release.

Thus, during the war against Japan, the Chinese Communists introduced several reforms in judicial work in the areas under their control. Among these were the people's assessors system, simplified judicial procedures, heavy reliance on mediation, emphasis on circuit trials, and attention to publicizing the laws among the people. In name, they followed the laws of the Nationalist government; in practice, invoking special circumstances, they developed and implemented their own laws. Especially in the early years, they were mindful of serving the people because they needed popular support. The laws, some of which were borrowed from the Soviet Union, were for the most part vague, giving the authorities flexibility but thereby restricting the rights of citizens. After the inauguration of the PRC government in 1949, the new regime more or less continued the practices that had been adopted in the border regions.

There were similar problems in the judicial systems of the various areas under Communist control. There were not enough trained people, a problem that persists in the PRC even today. During the war years, judicial independence was frowned upon if not prohibited, another feature of the judicial system that has remained largely the same. Separation of powers was also not incorporated into the system of administration of the various regions.

Conclusion

Consular jurisdiction (extraterritoriality) served as the initial impetus behind judicial reform in modern China. To be free of its yoke, China adopted Western-style codes of law. Chiang Kai-shek was justified in blaming consular jurisdiction for China's difficulty in attaining rule by law. He noted that its abolition would force the Chinese people to take responsibility for their own problems and no longer attribute them to the foreign presence. The legal reforms carried out during the war against Japan definitely contributed to the attainment of victory, even though, compared to the scale of reform carried out during the decade before the war, they were much more limited. Understandably, priority could not be given to judicial reform during wartime. As Dean Pound remarked, however, that the government was able to keep the wheels of justice rolling despite the difficulties it faced was certainly remarkable.[82] Those who helped carry out the reforms, moreover, are largely unsung heroes. Inflation, for example, was an extremely serious problem, and government employees, including judges and other judicial personnel, suffered greatly because of it.[83] In evaluating wartime judicial reform, therefore, the adverse conditions caused by inflation and other factors must also be taken into consideration. While the greatest advances in judicial reform occurred before the war, the fact that continued progress was made during the war, despite appalling conditions, is indeed impressive.

The Republic of China on Taiwan still follows the basic judicial system established before the war against Japan. The People's Republic follows the system that the Communists introduced in the border regions during the war. Certain legal principles, such as due process, judicial independence, and presumption of innocence, are recognized by the Nationalists, whereas the Communists have continued to repudiate them. During the last decade, while some progress was made in the development of the legal system, these principles were never accepted in the PRC. Neither the Republic of China on Taiwan nor the People's Republic of China can be considered governments that observe the rule of law. It appears, however, that the former is more likely to become such a government than the latter.

Notes

1. See Hungdah Chiu, "Legal Development in the Republic of China, 1949–1981," in *China: Seventy Years after the Hsin-hai Revolution*, ed. Hungdah Chiu with Shao-ch'uan Leng (Charlottesville: University of Virginia Press, 1984), p. 289.

2. F. T. Cheng, "A Sketch of the History, Philosophy, and Reform of Chinese Law," in *Studies in the Law of the Far East and Southeast Asia* (Washington, DC: Washington Foreign Law Society, 1956), pp. 29–45.

3. Chiu, "Legal Development," p. 287.

4. Chan Heng-chu, *Chung-kuo chin-tai fa-chih shih* (China's recent legal history) (Taipei: Commercial Press, 1973), p. 101.

5. For a list of the more important laws promulgated during this prewar period, see Committee on the History of Important Events of the Judicial Yuan, comp., *Ssu-fa-yuan shih-shih chi-yao* (History of important events of the Judicial Yuan) (Taipei: Judicial Yuan, 1982), pp. 324–25. [Hereafter cited as *History*].

6. Hsieh Kuan-sheng, *Chan-shih ssu-fa chi-yao* (Important judicial events during the war) (Taipei: Secretariat of the Judicial Yuan, 1971), p. 65.

7. *History*, p. 336.

8. Hsieh, *Chan-shih ssu-fa chi-yao*, p. 59. These included the following: (1) If a foreigner were the defendant in the case, and if the judicial organ handling the case, be it civil or criminal, were located in a place that was not the seat of a district court (not every city had a district court at the time), then prior to the stage of oral argument the defendant might ask a higher-level court to transfer the case to the nearest district court for adjudication. (2) Reciprocal treatment of foreign lawyers. That is, a foreign national would be allowed to practice law in China provided that Chinese citizens were allowed to practice law in the country of which that foreign national was a citizen. (3) Priority to building new prisons in areas that were likely to handle more cases involving foreigners. (4) Courts in cities where there were more likely to be more foreigners were to create posts for interpreters and submit monthly statistics in regard to the number of cases involving foreigners. (5) The government was to make plans for training judges and other judicial personnel to handle cases involving foreigners and for translating China's major codes into foreign languages.

9. *History*, pp. 337–41.

10. Ibid., pp. 314–46.

11. Hsiao Yung-ch'ing, *Chung-kuo fa-chih shih chien-pien* (A brief legal history of China) (Peking: Shansi People's Press, 1982), p. 291. The five chapters comprising the Civil Code were enacted during the period May–December 1929; the Code of Civil Procedure over the course of 1929–35; the Criminal Code and the Code of Criminal Procedure in 1935.

12. Associated with these two are the Provisional Regulations Governing Punishment of the Crime of Endangering National Mobilization, according to which those who violate any statutes relating to national mobilization are to be tried by a military, not a civilian, court. Ibid.

13. Ibid. Communists and leftists found these laws particularly objectionable. They viewed them as having been enacted primarily to suppress opposition groups. Also, according to Hsiao Yung-ch'ing, "the provisions of these emergency laws are more sweeping and vague than the provisions of the regular Criminal Code, and it is easier for miscarriages of justice to occur for those accused of violating them." Ibid.

14. Ibid.

15. For a description of the Nationalist government's judicial system, see, for example, "Chinese Judicial System," *China Handbook 1937–1944* (Chungking: Chinese Ministry of Information, November 1944), pp. 177–202. A "List of Outstanding Existing Civil and Criminal Laws" appears on pp. 189–95 and a "List of High Courts, Branch Courts and District Courts" as of July 1944 appears on pp. 195–98. Chinese Communist laws, courts, and so on are not mentioned.

16. Chan, *Chung-kuo chin-tai fa-chih shih*, p. 356.

17. Hsieh, *Chan-shih ssu-fa chi-yao*, p. 399.

18. Ibid., pp. 7–8.

19. *History*, p. 538.

20. For the texts of the two laws, see Hsieh, *Chan-shih ssu-fa chi-yao*, pp. 37–38 and 38–41, respectively.

21. Ibid., p. 37.

22. The Communist Chinese also claimed credit for implementing circuit trials. See Teaching and Research Office of Civil and Criminal Law of the Central Political-Legal Cadre School, "Certain Experience With Circuit Tribunals," *Cheng-fa yen-chiu* 42 (1954), and Ma Hsi-wu, "People's Judicial Work in the Shensi-Kansu-Ninghsia Border Region During the Stage of the New Democratic Revolution," *Cheng-fa yen-chiu* 11 (1955).

23. Hsieh, *Chan-shih ssu-fa chi-yao*, p. 3.

24. Ibid., p. 213.

25. See Chan, *Chung-kuo chin-tai fa-chih shih*, pp. 302–3. For the orders and other documents concerning notary publics issued by the Ministry of Judicial Administration during the period, see Hsieh, *Chan-shih ssu-fa chi-yao*, pp. 215–27.

26. Chan, *Chung-kuo chin-tai fa-chih shih*, pp. 199–201.

27. For more detailed information, see Hsieh, *Chan-shih ssu-fa chi-yao*.

28. Ma, "People's Judicial Work," p. 2.

29. Chang Hsi-po, "Laws and Regulations of the Revolutionary Bases During the New Democratic Revolutionary Period," *Chung-kuo ta pai-k'o ch'uan-shu: Fa-hsueh* (Encyclopedia Sinica: Law) (Beijing: Encyclopedia Press, 1984), p. 646.

30. Shao-chuan Leng, *Justice in Communist China: A Survey of the Judicial System of the Chinese People's Republic* (Dobbs Ferry, NY: Oceana Publications, 1967), p. 11. Chapter 1 of the book is a good overview of the pre-1949 development of the PRC's system of justice.

31. Hsiao, *Chung-kuo fa-chih shih*, pp. 422–23.

32. Leng, *Justice in Communist China.*

33. Ma, "People's Judicial Work," p. 8.

34. Chang, "Laws and Regulations," p. 646.

35. Hsiao, *Chung-kuo fa-chih shih*, p. 423.

36. T'ang Yung, "Judicial Work of the Anti-Japanese Democratic Government," in *Yen-Fu ch'u ssu-fa kung-tso ta kang* (Outline for judicial work of the Yench'eng-Funing [Border] Region), comp. Administrative Office of the Yench'eng-Funing Border Region, vol. 28, 9a–9b, of *Ssu-fa hsing-cheng pu tiao-ch'a chu suo ts'ang Chung-kung fa-lu wen-chien* (Chinese Communist legal documents held by the Investigation Bureau of the Judicial Administration Department), 28 vols. (hereafter cited as *CCLD*).

37. Chang, "Laws and Regulations," pp. 646–47.

38. Hsiao, *Chung-kuo fa-chih shih*, p. 447.

39. Ma, "People's Judicial Work," p. 8.

40. Hsiao, *Chung-kuo fa-chih shih*, p. 448. According to Hsiao, in 1943 when it was discovered that certain judicial organs were tending to work independently, the Shen-Kan-Ning government committee immediately directed: "Since political power in the border region belongs to the people, separation between the executive arm and the judiciary has no meaning. Judicial work must be carried out under the unified leadership of the government at various levels." Ibid.

41. Ibid.

42. Ma, "People's Judicial Work," p. 8.

43. Article 1, "Outline for Judicial Work in the Yench'eng-Funing Border Region," *CCLD*, 28:14a. Note that the title of this document corresponds to the title of volume 28.

44. These measures regarding trial work in the Shen-Kan-Ning Border Region are described in Ma, "People's Judicial Work," pp. 9–10.

45. Ibid., p. 9.

46. Shen-Kan-Ning, for example, had twenty-nine justice bureaus and only one local court at the county level. Leng, *Justice in Communist China*, p. 12.

47. Ibid., pp. 12–13. Shen-Kan-Ning had three branch High Courts. According to Hsiao Yung-ch'ing, the branch tribunals were established "in order to make it easier for the masses to file lawsuits as well as to strengthen the judicial organs at the county level." Hsiao, *Chung-kuo fa-chih shih*, p. 448.

48. Leng, *Justice in Communist China*, pp. 12–13.

49. Ibid.

50. Chang Tzu-p'ei and T'ao Mao, "China's People's Assessors System" (subsection of "The Jury System"), *Chung-kuo ta-pai-k'o*, p. 451.

51. Ma, "People's Judicial Work," p. 12.

52. *CCLD*, 28:15a, 18a.

53. Ma, "People's Judicial Work," p. 12. This was to be done to educate the masses.

54. Ibid.

55. Cf. articles 24–26, chapter 6, "Procedures for Appeal," of the "Provisional Measures Governing the Trial of Judicial Cases in the Yench'eng-Funing Region," *CCLD*, 28:20b–21a.

56. Ma, "People's Judicial Work," p. 10.

57. See, for example, "Annual Report of the Shensi-Kansu-Ninghsia Border Region Government for the Year 1943" (Delivered by Chairman Lin Tsu-han at the Fourth Meeting of the Border Region Government on January 6, 1944), in George Stuart Gelder, *The Chinese Communists* (Westport, CT: Hyperion Press, 1946; reprint 1975), p. 138.

58. Hsu P'ing and Ch'ai Fa-pang, "Circuit and On-the-Spot Trials," *Chung-kuo ta-pai-k'o*, pp. 684–85.

59. For background information on Ma, see Donald W. Klein and Anne B. Clark, *Biographic Dictionary of Chinese Communism, 1921–1965* (Cambridge: Harvard University Press, 1971), 2:666–68.

60. Ma, "People's Judicial Work," pp. 11–12.

61. T'ang, "Judicial Work of the Anti-Japanese Democratic Government," *CCLD*, 28:10b–11a.

62. *The Laws of the People's Republic of China (1979–1982)* (Beijing: Foreign Languages Press, 1982), 1:261.

63. Ma, "People's Judicial Work," p. 13.

64. Gelder, *The Chinese Communists*, p. 137; Shansi-Chahar-Hopei Border Region High Court, comp., *Ssu-fa kung-tso hsueh-hsi ts'ai-liao* (Material on studying judicial work), December 15, 1945, compilation no. 1, *CCLD*, 10.

65. Ma, "People's Judicial Work," p. 13. According to Ma, in 1942, civil cases settled as a result of mediation constituted less than 18 percent of all civil cases tried. In 1943, this increased to 40 percent; in 1944, to 48 percent. For minor criminal cases, in 1942, the cases settled as a result of mediation constituted 0.4 percent. In 1943, this increased to 5.6 percent; in 1944, to 12 percent.

66. Ibid.

67. Ibid.

68. See, for example, "Thoroughly Reform Judicial Work by Taking the Mass Line," *CCLD*, 2:32B.

69. Cf. Gelder, *The Chinese Communists*, p. 139, and *CCLD*, 10:3b.

70. Ma, "People's Judicial Work," p. 8.

71. Ibid. Ma notes, however, that because of the demands of work and the conditions of war, most of the students who took part in these training classes were transferred to other places before finishing.

72. Liu Pin, "The Viewpoint of Law and the Spirit of Implementation of Law," *CCLD*, 28:5b.

73. Hsiao, *Chung-kuo fa-chih shih*, pp. 448–49.

74. Ibid., p. 423.

75. Ibid., pp. 423–24. Hsiao notes that while the danger from enemy agents was emphasized, it was not to be exaggerated. While maintaining security, the people's rights were not to be neglected. Hence Mao's dictum, "If there is a counterrevolutionary, he must be liquidated; if there is a mistake, it must be rectified," which was later adopted as official policy after the founding of the PRC. Ibid.

76. Gelder, *The Chinese Communists*, pp. 133–35.

77. Hsiao, *Chung-kuo fa-chih shih*, p. 425.

78. Ma, "People's Judicial Work," p. 9. Hsiao Yung-ch'ing states that in the Shansi-Chahar-Hopei region, 71.36 percent of the cases handled in 1938 were special criminal cases involving traitors, which increased to 80.49 percent in 1939 and to 89.75 percent in 1940. It only dipped to 79.56 percent during the period from June 1941 to August 1942. From 1938 to August 1942, there were 6,172 cases in that region that involved traitors. Hsiao, *Chung-kuo fa-chih shih*, p. 423.

79. Patricia Griffin, "Prison Management in the Kiangsi and Yenan Periods," *The China Quarterly*, no. 58 (April–June 1974): 317.

80. Ibid.

81. "Several Points on Reviewing Prison Work," *CCLD*, 10:63b–64a.

82. Ts'ao Wen-yuan, ed., *The Law in China as Seen by Roscoe Pound* (Taipei: China Culture Publishing Company, 1953), p. 8.

83. Wu Hsueh-i, *Chan-shih min-shih li-fa* (Wartime civil legislation) (Chungking: Commercial Press, 1944), p. 1.

12

THE WAR AND AFTER: WORLD POLITICS IN HISTORICAL CONTEXT

James C. Hsiung

THE Sino-Japanese War of 1937–45 was undoubtedly one of the most important turning points in the history of modern China and of the world as well. From the war, the Nationalist government headed by Chiang Kai-shek emerged victorious, but in such a gravely weakened condition that it was soon defeated by the Chinese Communist party in the ensuing civil conflict. With respect to Japan, the aggressor power, defeat in the Sino-Japanese War helped turn it away from the dead end of military expansionism onto the path of liberal democracy and postwar prosperity. Finally, the war played an important role in the world's process of decolonization, which contributed to the construction of the contemporary international order.

The preceding chapters in this book have examined the impact of the war on China's politics, international relations, economy, legal system, literature, culture, and science. The present chapter summarizes the major conclusions of the volume as a whole and then discusses the broader significance of the war in an international historical context.

At the time the war began, China, politically and militarily fragmented among various contending forces, was not yet ready to confront Japan, its smaller neighbor that had attained the status of a world-class power. Chiang Kai-shek had long been unwilling to risk a premature war with Japan because he knew that such a war could only benefit the Chinese Communists at the expense of his Kuomintang government. However, the upsurge of Chinese nationalist passions in the aftermath of the Sian Incident, and the continuing provocations by the Imperial Japanese Army in North and Northeast China, left Chiang with no choice but to respond without further delay.

In the course of the war, China's fighting men were beset by many problems, including poor logistics and lack of matériel. The uneven quality of the officers corps was only partially offset by the gallantry and even brilliance of a small number of commanding generals. By the time the war was over, under the avalanche of superior Japanese military might, China had lost some four million soldiers and an additional eighteen million civilians. Over 40 percent of the vast

Chinese population had become refugees. Total wartime property losses were estimated to run in excess of U.S. $100 billion.[1] The damage the war caused to China's economy as a whole was truly staggering, as William Kirby demonstrates.

On the other hand, the fortunes of the CCP were greatly bolstered during the course of the war. At the time of the Japanese surrender in August 1945, the Communists' Red Army had swelled to 1.3 million soldiers, supplemented by a militia of 2.2 million men and supported by a population of 100 million contained within nineteen so-called liberated areas in sixteen provinces stretching over an area of one million square miles. The CCP itself boasted a membership of 1.2 million. The CCP was now in a strong position to challenge Chiang's government forces, which, though numerically still far superior, were drastically weakened by the brutality of the eight-year war against the Japanese.

History took an ironic twist. Tokyo had initiated the war in the name of anticommunism. Japan's aggression in Manchuria (China's Northeast region) in 1931 and the subsequent military buildup in North China were said to be prompted by Japan's need to defend itself against the menace of Bolshevik Russia and communism.[2] Yet the course of the war so nurtured and enhanced the power of the Chinese Communist forces that it took them just four years after V-J Day to conquer the entire mainland of China, enabling Mao Tse-tung to proclaim the birth of the People's Republic on October 1, 1949. It is evident in hindsight that Chiang Kai-shek was fully justified in refusing to embark prematurely upon a full-scale war. Thus, to the extent that the Communist victory in China was a spin-off from the Sino-Japanese War, the conflict in that sense represented an ironic turning point in history.

Inevitably, a counterfactual historical "what if" question arises. What if the war had not come in 1937? Robert Bedeski shows that despite the continuing political turmoil following the collapse of the Ch'ing empire in 1911, a serious state-building effort had already begun under Chiang Kai-shek's Nanking government. In June 1931, six years before the war commenced, a provisional constitution had been promulgated at Chiang's insistence, over the objections of KMT veterans like Hu Han-min. As William Kirby notes, the KMT government since it came to power in 1927 was committed to rapid industrialization of China, aided by large-scale Western investment. But by 1932, Japan's strategic threat to China caused a premature diversion of resources to preparation for a coming war. And the war itself brought ruin to the Chinese economy, aborting the industrialization program. Despite the exigencies of the war, which contributed to a severe circumscription of intraparty democracy, the state-building efforts continued beyond 1937. A good example of these efforts was the legal reform carried out during the wartime period that Tao-tai Hsia discusses.

At the time they won the civil war, as Bedeski argues, the Communists did not have to set the full agenda of state-building because that had already been accomplished by the Nationalists. If there had been no Sino-Japanese War to abort Chiang's constitutional reforms and thwart the process of state-building, China would most likely have continued to develop steadily into a modern constitutional state under the the KMT. Other contending political forces, including the CCP, would have had little chance of effectively challenging the KMT's legitimacy. In other words, there probably would have been no Communist rule after 1949.

To push the point about historical irony just a bit further, perhaps this is one reason why Japanese today refuse to apply the term "aggression" to their conduct and why, unlike many Germans who regret Hitler's crimes in Europe, they harbor so little remorse about the war in China. After all, if one applies a twisted sort of logic here, Japan's "excursion into and out of China" helped to place the CCP leaders on the throne in 1949. Mao Tse-tung himself quite openly admitted this in 1964, when he brushed off the attempted apologies of a group of Japanese socialists who were visiting Peking and acknowledged that the Sino-Japanese War had been his path to power. In this light, a modern-day Japanese cynic might well ask, "What sort of aggression could there have been?"

The wartime American "Dixie Mission" was sold on the myth—which it helped to perpetuate—that Chiang Kai-shek, while ever eager to fight the Communists, did not deign to fight the Japanese. By now even the CCP has changed its position on this point. The chapters by Williamsen and Ch'i substantiate the CCP's revised (post-1985) stance that KMT government forces indeed fought all the major positional battles against the Japanese, while the Communist guerrilla units took on the invader "behind enemy lines."[3]

On the other hand, the chapters by Wu, Goldstein, Gunn, and Reardon-Anderson convincingly demonstrate the importance of CCP activity during the War of Resistance outside of its widely recognized guerrilla warfare. The CCP functioned as an effective ruler of the Shen-Kan-Ning Border Region and the other areas under its control as well as an active participant in the wartime literary, cultural, and scientific arenas. A legal-judicial system, as Hsia and Zeldin chronicle, was developed in the Communist region, which became the precursor of the PRC's legal regime and judicial system after 1949. The Communists even had their own "foreign policy of opposition," as Goldstein calls it, which suggests their unremitting jostling for power with the KMT in the arena of China's wartime foreign relations.

This volume also sheds new light on certain long-disputed questions concerning wartime China. One example may be singled out here because of its many implications for a proper understanding of the war and, in particular, of China's conduct of warfare and of foreign relations.

The question is whether Chiang Kai-shek committed his best troops to action or whether he held them in reserve for essentially political reasons. Many superficial observers incorrectly assumed that Chiang would first commit his relatively nonessential troops, those considered either peripheral (the so-called *tsa-pai-erh* units) or those less than loyal to him personally. But this was not so.

In fact, from the beginning of the war Chiang employed his very best troops, and they suffered the most severe casualties throughout the fighting. Ch'i's data show that the level of participation by armies considered loyal to the KMT and to Chiang personally was maintained throughout the duration of the war. Four out of every ten Chinese divisions sent into battle belonged to the Nationalists' hard-core forces.

With the advantage of hindsight, it is not difficult to understand why. In the first place, as Garver suggests, Chiang had decided to enter the war in the conviction that Japan had to be defeated militarily before it would accept China as an independent, co-equal sovereign entity. Thus, Chiang had to commit his best resources to that end, at a minimum to deny Japan an easy victory.

Second, Chiang knew from the outset that both Britain and the United States would intervene to defend their considerable interests in China only if they were convinced that China was going under. Therefore, Chiang had to commit his best resources to demonstrate that this was a major war, menacing the vital interests of the powers. Britain and the United States would intervene, he surmised, to prevent Japan from becoming too strong through engulfing China. Japanese Foreign Minister Hirota's desire to decouple China from the West and the efforts of militarist leaders like Ishihara to promote a Pan-Asianism linking China with Japan against the West were deeply troubling to the Western powers.[4] Therefore, by resisting Japan's attempt to become a hegemon on the model of Napoleonic France or Hitlerite Germany, China was in effect acting on behalf of the powers.

These factors simultaneously explain four important phenomena of the war: (1) Chiang's motive in committing his best fighting forces from the very start of the war; (2) his tenacity and resolve to fight on even during the darkest hours in 1940; (3) the rationale behind his "war of attrition" strategy, trading space for time, until the war would eventually be internationalized by some catalytic event such as Pearl Harbor; and (4) his success in upgrading China's international standing—because China put up a good fight against Japan, the United States, at President Roosevelt's insistence, was willing to reward it with an early termination of the "unequal treaties."[5] I have called attention to this complex point to urge that in order better to understand politics in historical context, we abjure a piecemeal, ad hoc approach and instead endeavor to fit together the various pieces of the puzzle, including micromotives and macrobehavior.[6] The following section attempts such an approach with respect to the international consequences of the Sino-Japanese War.

System-Induced Behavior

The prevailing rules of world politics, as first conceived in the nineteenth century, provide the best guide to the behavior of the Japanese militarists whose reckless adventurism in North China spawned the war, to the conduct of China's wartime foreign policy, and to the response of the powers. The way in which the war ended and the nature of the postwar settlements also demonstrated the adherence of the Allies to this same tradition. Nevertheless, the war proved to be a turning point in yet one more sense—that is, providing a transition from the "old" (nineteenth-century–type) international politics to the "new" (late twentieth-century) international politics, as I shall now attempt to explain.

Certain elements in the international system prevailing at the time help to explain the origin of the war as well as the conduct of the principals. Although the League of Nations embodied the notion of "collective security," which gave its name to the interwar era, in fact so ineffectual was the League that in the 1920s and 1930s the behavior of nations did not change in any significant way. The rules of the classical "balance-of-power" system, carried over from the pre-1914 era, continued to govern international relations and the behavior of nations.

The beginning of the period saw the partial withdrawal of the Western powers from East Asia to Europe following World War I and the Bolshevik Revolution in Russia. The Japanese replaced the Germans in their previous sphere of influence and, in general, filled the vacuum left by the departing Europeans. The Great Depression of the 1930s further diverted the Western powers' attention away from East Asia. The situation in East Asia at this time was formally defined by several international agreements, including the Washington Conference agreements (1921–22), the Kellogg-Briand Pact (1928), and the London Disarmament Treaty (1930), which promised peace but provided no mechanism for the enforcement of collective security. These treaties replaced the earlier bilateral agreements defining spheres of influence. Nevertheless, the prevailing international environment contributed to the audacity of the Japanese Kwantung army in North and Northeast China and, what is more, to the rise of military dominance over the civilian government in Tokyo, which culminated in open aggression.[7]

President Woodrow Wilson had first conceived of the League as the embodiment of an alternative approach to peace to that of the balance-of-power system, which, in his view, had failed to prevent the outbreak of World War I. The League was to be the institutionalized agent of the world community, wielding the "preponderant" power needed to cope with any potential aggressor who could not be dealt with effectively by the balancing mechanism in the balance-of-power system.[8] Since the League lacked the teeth that it was supposed to have, however, due in part to the absence of the United States, the brute power politics of the pre-1914 world reasserted itself rather quickly.

Japanese inroads into China were anticipated by the first two Hobbesian rules of the game (the conduct of nations) manifested in the classical (post-1815) balance-of-power system, as formulated by Morton Kaplan. These are: "(1) Act to increase capabilities but negotiate rather than fight; and (2) Fight rather than pass up an opportunity to increase capabilities."[9] Responding to the reduced presence of the European powers in Asia, Japan seized the "opportunity to increase capabilities' at China's expense. When chastised by the League's Lytton Commission report for military aggression in Manchuria (China's Northeast provinces), Japan withdrew from the League in 1933, demonstrating that its military license in China would admit of no international restraint.[10]

But Japan ran afoul of other rules of conduct in a balance-of-power system, which call for eschewing "predominance" or quest of empire, so as not to threaten other essential actors and provoke their counteraction. Playing by the rules, for example, Germany imposed heavy penalties upon France after the war of 1870 but refrained from incorporating France as part of Germany or making it a German colony.[11] From the Mukden Incident of 1931 to the Marco Polo Bridge (Lukouch'iao) Incident of 1937, Japan brutally sought to annex China incrementally under the Amau (Amo) doctrine.[12]

The militarist drive to seek regional "predominance" was the culmination of Japan's successful modernization, which began in 1868. Japanese leaders feared the consequences for Japan of the rise of Chiang Kai-shek's Nanking government. In December 1928, the Manchurian warlord, Marshal Chang Hsueh-liang, announced his allegiance to Chiang's Nanking government, foreshadowing the end of warlordism that Japan used to its advantage. Japan wanted to subordinate China before Chinese nationalism became more powerful, but in its naked pursuit of empire-building, militarist Japan threatened the interests of major Western powers such as Britain and the United States. Even without the catalyst of Pearl Harbor, the rules of the balance-of-power game would have prompted intervention by an essential actor like the United States. The purpose of such intervention, according to these rules, would be to "constrain" Japan's empire-building or, in Kaplan's language, behavior manifesting "supranational organizing principles."[13]

Among the tell-tale signs of what was forthcoming was President Franklin D. Roosevelt's "Quarantine Speech" in late 1937, in which he warned against the general deterioration of international law and the threat to the United States of the spread of war and disorder.[14] This warning clearly went beyond the policy of nonrecognition of Japan's fruits of aggression in Manchuria, announced by Secretary of State Stimson in 1932. In early 1941, through the Hull-Nomura meetings, the United States demanded that Japan accept four principles, including that of noninterference in another country's (China's) internal affairs, and a pledge not to disturb the status quo in the Pacific other than by peaceful means. After the Japanese occupation of Indochina, on July 26, 1941, more than four months before Pearl Harbor, Roosevelt issued an executive order that froze all Japanese assets in the United States.[15]

Pearl Harbor was thus just the last straw for the United States, prompting Washington to act in order to constrain Japan in the latter's bid to become a hegemonic power. Following Germany's attack on Poland, on September 1, 1939, triggering the European phase of World War II, Britain and the other European powers were preoccupied in the European theater. As the principal remaining Western power in China and the Far East, it fell upon the United States, therefore, to constrain Japan's pursuit of the goal of "predominance."

With this in mind, one can better appreciate Chiang's confidence, upon taking on Japan in July 1937, that his country would not be left to stand alone in its resistance, and that it would soon be joined by other great powers fighting on China's side. He believed this precisely because Japan was out to conquer China in search of a "New Order in East Asia," which would drive Western influence from the Far East. Although it took considerably longer than he had anticipated for Western assistance to be forthcoming, eventually his calculation turned out to be correct.

Another manifestation of the workings of the balance-of-power system is worth mentioning at this juncture. The lenient way in which Japan was treated after its surrender in 1945, including permission to continue as an equal international actor and the bestowal of what appear to be various "free rides," was consistent with the last of Kaplan's rules for world politics in a balance-of-power system—namely, that a defeated or constrained essential actor (such as Japan) be allowed to "re-enter the system" as an acceptable "role partner."[16] Like defeated France at the Congress of Vienna in 1815, Japan was allowed to re-enter the councils of world politics shortly after its defeat. The bipolar conflict that soon set in between the United States and the Soviet Union merely emphasized the need to accord generous treatment to Japan in order to keep that country safely and happily in the U.S. camp.

The Aftermath

The remaining reasons for the generous treatment that the victorious wartime Allies accorded the defeated powers—Germany as well as Japan—were the lessons learned from the bitter experience of the aftermath of World War I. At that time, exorbitant penalties in the form of huge reparations had been forced upon Germany along with disarmament and the demilitarization of the Rhineland. These conditions, imposed at the behest of Britain and France, came back to haunt them during the Great Depression when desperate lower- and middle-class Germans voted Hitler's Nazi party into power, paving the way to World War II.

In working out the German and Japanese peace settlements at the end of World War II, the wartime Allies sought to avoid repeating these mistakes. They decided to forgo all penalties apart from dividing Germany and requiring Japan to disgorge Taiwan (taken from China after the Sino-Japanese War of 1894–95), give up Korea, which had been made a Japanese colony in 1910, and yield certain other territories it had acquired. Under American leadership, a liberal international economic order was set in place, which rested largely on the Bretton Woods and General Agreement on Tariffs and Trade regimes. Inherent in this American effort to establish a postwar international economic order was a liberal philosophy of peace based on the idea of free trade, which is anti-protectionist and antimercantile in nature. Two cardinal tenets characterized this position: (1) that free trade substantially reduces the number of targets to which force might legitimately be applied in the pursuit of state interests; and (2) that free trade increases the vulnerability of actors (because of increased interdependence), therefore making them disinclined to entertain the risks of resorting to force.[17]

Under this liberal economic order, former wartime allies whose economies had been devastated by the war had to be assisted to get back on their feet again (hence the Marshall Plan). The defeated enemy states of Germany and Japan likewise had to be helped to rehabilitate themselves expeditiously and to rejoin the world community and the global economic structure as full-fledged economic partners. Indeed, in such an international environment, Japan and Germany were able to recover their economic strength in virtually no time. Through hard work and ingenuity as well as government-business partnership and evasive protectionism, Japan was able to emerge as an economic superpower by the mid-1980s.[18]

One additional important development should be noted in the aftermath of the Sino-Japanese War as part of the Pacific conflict, namely, the disappearance of the vestiges of Western colonialism in East and Southeast Asia. This development entailed far broader implications for contemporary world politics.

In starting the war with China, Japan was not necessarily seeking to change the existing international system as a whole. Nonetheless, Japanese actions bore the seeds of a "hegemonic war" and the dire consequences of such a war. In the literature of international politics, a "hegemonic war" is defined as one which, through the actions of a state seeking "territorial, political, and economic expansion," has the potential of redefining the power distribution and values in the world system.[19] Japan's war in China and the Asia-Pacific region was just such a war.

Notwithstanding Japan's eventual defeat, the surge of Japanese military expansion produced sweeping changes in the future balance of power in the world system, not just in the Asia-Pacific region. The swift and devastating advance of Japanese military might after December 1941 routed the Western colonial powers from their imperial domains and shattered their pretense of authority in China. At its peak, Japan's power extended from the northern reaches of Manchuria (Northeast China), northeastward to the Aleutian Islands, and downward through much of China proper into Southeast Asia. From there it stretched west to the borders of India and east and south to the Pacific, approaching Australia, Midway, and Hawaii. When they retreated in the face of direct American military pressure, the Japanese left a vast political vacuum.

In areas where the Japanese, however briefly, displaced the Westerners, the exodus of Westerners and the rise of indigenous nationalism combined to prepare the ground for what was to become a tidal wave of independence and "self-determination" that soon spread from Asia to other continents in the post-1945 era.[20] Over sixty former Western colonies became independent. If the second half of the twentieth century is the age of decolonization, then the Pacific War, which Japan started by its invasion of China, and which later spread to Southeast Asia, was indeed a "hegemonic war" that engendered systemic changes of revolutionary proportions. In this sense, too, the Sino-Japanese War proved to be a turning point in modern history, notwithstanding Japan's defeat. It can be seen in hindsight that Japan left more of an impact on world politics—changing its very fabric on a global scale—than did Germany from its role in World War II.

Conclusion

Reflecting upon the Pacific War more than four decades after its end, one is drawn to the conclusion that Japan's phenomenal rise to the status of an unchallengeable economic superpower dwarfs all other post-1945 developments. By 1985, Japan's erstwhile client-sponsor relationship with the United States was transformed into a chronic U.S. financial dependency on Japan. Since 1985, when the United States became a net debtor nation for the first time since 1914—and, for that matter, the world's largest debtor—it has had to borrow $100–$120 billion a year, much of it from Japan. At this same rate of borrowing the United States will have acquired debts of over $1.5 trillion by the year 2000. To be able to repay these debts, it will have to show an annual trade surplus of $150–$200 billion—a formidable if not impossible task. Until that time comes, Japan is actually subsidizing U.S. hegemony to no end.[21]

Who could possibly have anticipated this happening at the time of Japan's defeat in 1945?[22] Commenting on Chiang Kai-shek's winning the Sino-Japanese War but losing to the Chinese Communists, whose fortunes were inordinately helped by the same war, John Garver says, "In a sense, Chiang failed by winning." This characterization may also apply to the United States in its relationship with Japan over the several decades since Pearl Harbor. In looking to the twenty-first century, when economic security will increasingly rival military security for first place among nations, the United States will feel the increasing burden of this lesson of "failing by winning."[23]

Meanwhile, China seems fatally encumbered with the Communist rule that the Sino-Japanese War bequeathed it. If its Communist economy does not improve soon enough to break its dependence on Japanese financing and high-tech, China is likely to continue to live in Japan's shadow as a de facto economic satellite.[24] What Japan was unable to achieve by military might earlier in the century—access to China's vast market, raw materials, and cheap labor—it has been able to achieve by economic means in the second half of the century. Looking back in hindsight, over four decades later, it is as though China had not won the war in 1945 after all.

In this connection, a certain degree of cynicism is perhaps appropriate. As noted above, the nature of international politics has changed in the post-1945 world by the introduction, under U.S. leadership, of a liberal global economic structure of interdependence. In this structure, the ready access to foreign markets, in terms of trade and investment, has made wars functionally obsolete. Whereas "predominance" had to be achieved by military might before, it can now be achieved through economic means. Thus, the power over trade and finance today is equivalent to military power before. Activities promoting a state's predominance in international trade and finance can, therefore, be considered the functional equivalent of military pursuits called "war" in the traditional sense.[25] The military phase of the Sino-Japanese War (and the Pacific War) ended in 1945, but a cynic might say that the war has merely been transformed into a contest using economic rather than military means. In this economic extension of the war, both China and the United States, among others, seem to be losing-badly.

This cynical view may be exaggerated, but it serves to make plain a lesson that can be learned from the experience of the Sino-Japanese War (and, for that matter, the Pacific War) over four decades earlier. The plain lesson is this: While in earlier times a military victory or defeat was clearly identifiable, it is no longer easy to pinpoint victory or defeat in an age in which nations are struggling for economic (as opposed to military) security and supremacy. In these circumstances, neither victory nor defeat has the same transparency as before. Nor can we prove a case of, for lack of a better term, "economic aggression" in the same way that we can establish a case of aggression by military might, notwithstanding all the difficulties associated with defining the latter. By all indications, this trend is only going to deepen as the world enters the twenty-first century.

Notes

1. These figures, as well as those in the following paragraph, were verified in person in 1989 during the author's meeting with archival experts at the Nanking Second Archival Center, whose holdings of archival materials on the War of Resistance are considered unsurpassed in China today.

2. See Shimada Toshihiko's dispassionate account in James W. Morley, ed. *The China Quagmire* (New York: Columbia University Press, 1983), pp. 3–232. In 1936, less than a year before the Sino-Japanese War started, Japan signed the Anti-Comintern Pact with Germany. When defending itself against the charge of aggression in Manchuria, Japan told the League of Nations that its military actions were prompted by legitimate security concerns arising from the prospects of the "Bolshevization" of China's Manchuria and Mongolia regions. See Japan Foreign Office, *Relations of Japan with Manchuria and Mongolia* (Tokyo, 1932), Document B, rev. ed., pp. 26–27, cited in O. Edmund Clubb, *Twentieth Century China*, 2d ed. (New York: Columbia University Press, 1972), p. 171.

3. See preface, note 1.

4. Li Yun-han, "The Origins of the War: Background of the Lukouchiao Incident, July

7, 1937," in *Nationalist China During the Sino-Japanese War, 1937–1945*, ed. Paul K. T. Sih (Hicksville, NY: Exposition Press, 1977), p. 10; and Akira Iriye's comments, p. 36.

5. William Tung, *China and the Foreign Powers* (Dobbs Ferry, NY: Oceana, 1970), pp. 271ff. Churchill remained very skeptical about Roosevelt's position that China should be considered one of the great powers.

6. This last phrase is borrowed from the title of a book by Thomas Schelling, *Micromotives and Macrobehavior* (New York: W. W. Norton, 1978).

7. Cf. Morley, ed. *The China Quagmire*, pp. 3–288.

8. Ray S. Baker, *Woodrow Wilson and the World Settlement* (Garden City, NY: Doubleday, 1922), 1:165; and Inis T. Claude, *Swords into Plowshares*, 4th ed. (New York: Random House, 1971), pp. 41–56.

9. Morton A. Kaplan, *System and Process in International Politics* (New York: John Wiley, 1957), p. 23.

10. See Christopher Thorne, *The Limits of Foreign Policy: The West, the League, and the Far Eastern Crisis of 1931–1933* (New York: Capricorn Books, 1973).

11. Kaplan, *System and Process*, p. 28.

12. For the "Amau Statement," April 17, 1934, see U.S. Department of State, *Foreign Relations of the United States: Japan, 1931–1941* (Washington, DC: Government Printing Office, 1943), 1:224–25.

13. Kaplan, *System and Process*, p. 23. For Japan's larger designs to divide the world with the German Nazis and the Italian fascists, see Hosoya Chihiro, "The Tripartite Pact, 1939–1940," in *Deterrent Diplomacy: Japan, Germany, and the USSR, 1935–1940*, ed. James W. Morley (New York: Columbia University Press, 1976), pp. 179–258.

14. Ruhl Bartlett, ed. *The Record of American Diplomacy: Documents and Readings in the History of American Foreign Relations*, 4th ed. (New York: Alfred Knopf, 1964), pp. 577–80.

15. For a recent analysis, see Waldo Heinrichs, *Threshold of War: Franklin D. Roosevelt and American Entry into World War II* (New York: Oxford University Press, 1988).

16. Kaplan, *System and Process*, p. 23.

17. Klaus Knorr, *Power and Wealth* (London: Macmillan, 1973), p. 196; and Robert Keohane and Joseph Nye, *Power and Interdependence* (Boston: Little, Brown, 1977), pp. 28ff.

18. Chalmers Johnson, *MITI and the Japanese Miracle* (Stanford: Stanford University Press, 1982); Frank Gibney, *Miracle by Design* (New York: Times Books, 1982). See also Robert Gilpin, *Political Economy of International Relations* (Princeton: Princeton University Press, 1987), p. 214; Richard J. Krickus, *The Superpowers in Crisis* (New York: Pergamon-Brassey, 1987), pp. 204–7.

19. Robert Gilpin, *War and Change in World Politics* (London: Cambridge University Press, 1981), pp. 10–15; Robert Jervis, "From Balance to Concert," *World Politics* 38, 1 (October 1985): 61.

20. Donald F. Lach and Edmund S. Wehrle, *International Politics in East Asia since World War II* (New York: Praeger, 1975), chap. 1; also James W. Morley, ed. *Fateful Choice: Advance into Southeast Asia, 1939–1941* (New York: Columbia University Press, 1980).

21. Gilpin, *Political Economy*, pp. 336–40; Jeffrey Garten, "Trading Blocs and the Evolving World Economy," *Current History* (January 1989): 54.

22. Cf. Stephen D. Cohen, *Uneasy Partnership* (Cambridge, MA: Ballinger, 1985).

23. I have dealt with this point in my chapter, "Balance of Power in the Twenty-first Century: Challenge for the U.S.," in *From Pacific Region toward Pacific Community*, ed. Bernard Joei (Taipei, 1989), pp. 33–46.

24. On Japan's importance to China's modernization program, see Hong N. Kim,

"Sino-Japanese Relations," *Current History* (April 1988): 153ff; also Allen S. Whiting, *China Eyes Japan* (Berkeley: University of California Press, 1989), pp. 93–128.

25. On the likelihood that economic power will eclipse military power, see Paul Kennedy, *The Rise and Fall of the Great Powers* (New York: Random House, 1987), p. 446; Edmund Dell, *Politics of Economic Interdependence* (New York: St. Martin's Press, 1987), pp. 14–51.

BIBLIOGRAPHY

Western Language

Bedeski, Robert E. *State-Building in Modern China: The Kuomintang in the Prewar Period*. Berkeley: University of California, Institute of East Asian Studies, 1981.

Boyle, John H. *China and Japan at War, 1937–1945: The Politics of Collaboration*. Stanford: Stanford University Press, 1972.

Butler, W. E., ed. *The Legal System of the Chinese Soviet Republic, 1931–1934*. Dobbs Ferry, NY: Transnational Publishers, 1983.

Chang, Carsun. *Third Force in China*. New York: Bookman Associates, 1952.

Chang, Maria Hsia. *The Chinese Blue Shirt Society: Fascism and National Development*. Berkeley: University of California, Institute of East Asian Studies, 1985.

Chen Yung-fa. *Making Revolution: The Communist Movement in Eastern and Central China, 1937–1945*. Berkeley: University of California Press, 1986.

Cheng Tien-fong. *A History of Sino-Russian Relations*. Washington, DC: Public Affairs Press, 1957.

Ch'i Hsi-sheng. *Nationalist China at War: Military Defeats and Political Collapse, 1937–45*. Ann Arbor: University of Michigan Press, 1982.

Chiang Kai-shek. *China's Destiny*, trans.Chung-hui Wang. New York: Macmillan, 1947.

———. *Soviet Russia in China*. New York: Farrar, Strauss and Cudahy, 1958.

Chinese Ministry of Information. *China Handbook 1937–1944*. Chungking, 1944.

Chiu, Hungdah, and Shao-chuan Leng, eds. *China: Seventy Years after the Hsin-hai Revolution*. Charlottesville: University Press of Virginia, 1984.

Coble, Parks M. *The Shanghai Capitalists and the Nationalist Government, 1927–1937*. Cambridge: Harvard University, Council on East Asian Studies, 1980.

Duara, Prasenjit. *Culture, Power, and the State: Rural North China, 1900–1942*. Stanford: Stanford University Press, 1988.

Eastman, Lloyd E. *Seeds of Destruction: Nationalist China in War and Revolution*. Stanford: Stanford University Press, 1984.

Esherick, Joseph W., ed. *Lost Chance in China: The World War II Dispatches of John S. Service*. New York: Random House, 1974.

Fairbank, John K., and Albert Feuerwerker, eds. *The Cambridge History of China, vol. 13, Republican China, 1912–1949, part 2*. Cambridge: Cambridge University Press, 1986.

Fishel, Wesley R. *The End of Extraterritoriality in China*. Berkeley: University of California Press, 1974.

Furuya, Keiji. *Chiang Kai-shek: His Life and Times*, trans. Chun-ming Chang. New York: St. John's University Press, 1981.

Garver, John W. *Chinese-Soviet Relations, 1937–1945: The Diplomacy of Chinese Nationalism*. New York: Oxford University Press, 1988.

Gelder, George Stuart. *The Chinese Communists*. Westport, CT: Hyperion Press, 1946; reprint, 1975.

Gunn, Edward. *Twentieth-Century Chinese Drama: An Anthology*. Bloomington: Indiana University Press, 1983.

———. *Unwelcome Muse: Chinese Literature in Shanghai and Peking, 1937–45*. New York: Columbia University Press, 1980.

Hsia, Chih-tsing. *A History of Modern Chinese Fiction*, 2d ed. New Haven: Yale University Press, 1971.

Hsu Kai-yu [Hsu Chieh-yu]. *Literature of the People's Republic of China*. Bloomington: Indiana University Press, 1980.

———. *Twentieth-Century Chinese Poetry: An Anthology*. Ithaca: Cornell University Press, 1963.

Jordan, Donald. "The Place of Chinese Disunity in Japanese Army Strategy." *The China Quarterly*, no. 109 (March 1987): 42–63.

Kataoka, Tetsuya. *Resistance and Revolution in China*. Berkeley: University of California Press, 1974.

King, Wunsz. *China and the League of Nations, the Sino-Japanese Controversy*. New York: St. John's University Press, 1965.

Kirby, William C. *Germany and Republican China*. Stanford: Stanford University Press, 1984.

Kubin, Wolfgang, and Rudolph Wagner, eds. *Essays in Modern Chinese Literature and Literary Criticism*. Bochum: Studienverlag Brockmeyer, 1982.

La Litterature Chinoise au temps de la Guerre de Resistance contre le Japon (Chinese literature during the War of Resistance against Japan). Paris: Editions de la Fondation Singer-Polignac, 1982.

Lary, Diana. *Region and Nation: The Kwangsi Clique in Chinese Politics 1925–1937*. London: Cambridge University Press, 1974.

Lauer, Thomas Leroy. "German Attempts at Mediation of the Sino-Japanese War, 1937–1938." Ph.D. dissertation, Stanford University, 1973.

Leng, Shao-chuan. *Justice in Communist China: A Survey of the Judicial System of the Chinese People's Republic*. Dobbs Ferry, NY: Oceana Publications, 1967.

Leyda, Jan. *Dianying: Electric Shadows*. Cambridge: MIT Press, 1972.

Mao Tse-tung. *Selected Works of Mao Tse-tung*, 4 vols. Peking: Foreign Languages Press, 1965.

Passerin d'Entreves, Alexander. *The Notion of the State*. London: Oxford University Press, 1967.

Pye, Lucian. *Warlord Politics: Conflict and Coalition in the Modernization of China*. New York: Praeger, 1971.

Rosinger, Lawrence K. *China's Wartime Politics, 1937–1944*. Princeton: Princeton University Press, 1944.

Schaller, Michael. *The U.S. Crusade in China, 1938–1945*. New York: Columbia University Press, 1979.

Schyns, Joseph, et al., eds. *1500 Modern Chinese Novels and Plays*. Peiping, 1946; reprint, Hong Kong, 1966.

Selden, Mark. *The Yenan Way in Revolutionary China*. Cambridge: Harvard University Press, 1971.

Sheridan, James E. *China in Disintegration: The Republican Era in Chinese History, 1912–1949*. New York: The Free Press, 1975.

Sih, Paul K.T., ed. *Nationalist China during the Sino-Japanese War, 1937–1945*. Hicksville, NY: Exposition Press, 1977.

Sullivan, Michael. *Chinese Art in the Twentieth Century*. Berkeley: University of California Press, 1959.

Thorne, Christopher. *Allies of a Kind: The U.S., Britain, and the War against Japan, 1941–1945*. New York: Oxford University Press, 1978.

Tien Hung-mao. *Government and Politics in Kuomintang China, 1927–1937*. Stanford: Stanford University Press, 1972.

Ts'ao Wen-yen, ed. *The Law in China as Seen by Roscoe Pound*. Taipei: China Culture Publishing Foundation, 1953.

Tsien Tsai. *China and the Nine Power Conference at Brussels in 1937*. New York: St. John's University Press, 1964.

Tsou Tang. *America's Failure in China, 1941–1950*. Chicago: University of Chicago Press, 1963.

Tuchman, Barbara. *Stilwell and the American Experience in China, 1911–1945*. New York: Bantam, 1972.

Tung, William. *The Political Institutions of Modern China*. The Hague: M. Nijhoff, 1964.

——. *V. K. Wellington Koo and China's Wartime Diplomacy*. New York: St. John's University Press, 1977.

Wang Ming. *Mao's Betrayal*. Moscow: Progress Publishers, 1979.

Whiting, Allen S., and Sheng Shih-ts'ai. *Sinkiang: Pawn or Pivot?* East Lansing: Michigan State University Press, 1958.

Wylie, Raymond F. *The Emergence of Maoism: Mao Tse-tung, Ch'en Po-ta, and the Search for Chinese Theory, 1935–1945*. Stanford: Stanford University Press, 1980.

Zhou Enlai [Chou En-lai]. *Selected Works of Zhou Enlai*, vol. 1. Beijing: Foreign Languages Press, 1981.

Chinese and Japanese Language

Chan Heng-chu. *Chung-kuo chin-tai fa-chih shih* (China's recent legal history). Taipei: Commercial Press, 1973.

Chang Kuo-t'ao. *Wo ti hui-i* (My memoirs). 3 vols. Hong Kong: Ming Pao Monthly Press, 1974.

Chiang Chung-cheng. *Chung-kuo chih ming-yun* (China's destiny). Chungking: Cheng-Chung shu-chu, 1943.

Chiang Nan-tung et al., eds. *Wei-chou kuo shih* (History of the puppet Manchukuo). Kirin: People's Press, 1980.

Chiang ts'ung-t'ung mi-lu (The secret diaries of President Chiang). 14 vols. Taipei: Chung-yang jih-pao ch'u-pan-she, 1979.

Chou Keng-sheng. *Pu p'ing-teng t'iao-yueh shih chiang* (Ten lectures on the unequal treaties). Shanghai: Pacific Press, 1928?

Chung-hua min-kuo chung-yao shih-liao chu-pien—tui Jih k'ang-chan shih-ch'i, ti san pien, chan-shih wai-chiao (Preliminary compilation of important historical materials of the Republic of China, the period of the War of Resistance against Japan, vol. 3, wartime diplomacy). 3 vols. Taipei: Kuo-min-tang tang-shih wei-yuan-hui, 1981. These are Chiang Kai-shek's archives.

Chung-kung T'ung-chan Pu and Chung-yang Tang-an Kuan, eds. *K'ang-Jih min-tsu t'ung-i chan-hsien* (Anti-Japanese national united front. 3 vols. Beijing: Archives Press, 1986.

Chung-kuo ta pai-k'o ch'uan-shu: fa-hsueh (Encyclopedia sinica: law). Beijing & Shanghai: Encyclopedia Press, 1984.

Chung-kuo wai-chiao-shih tzu-liao hsuan-pien, ti san tzu, (1937–1945) (Selection of materials on China's diplomatic history, vol. 3, 1937–1945). Beijing: Wai-chiao hsueh-yuan, 1958.

Ho Ying-ch'in. *Jih-pen ch'in-Hua pa-nien k'ang-chan* (Japan's aggression against China and the eight-year War of Resistance). Taipei: Committee of Compilation for the 95th Anniversary of General Ho Ying-ch'in, 1984.

Hsiao Yung-ch'ing. *Chung-kuo fa-chih shih chien-pien* (A brief legal history of China). 2 vols. Beijing: Shansi People's Press, 1982.

Hsieh Kuan-sheng. *Chan-shih ssu-fa chi-yao* (Important judicial events during the war). Taipei: Secretariat of the Judicial Yuan, 1971.

Hsu Cho-yun et al., eds. *K'ang-chan sheng-li ti tai-chia* (The price of victory in the War of Resistance). Taipei: Lien-ho pao she, 1986.

Hsu Hsiang-ch'ien. *Li-shih ti hui-ku* (Reminiscences of history). 3 vols. Beijing: Liberation Army Press, 1987.

Hu Shih. *Hu Shih jen chu Mei da-shih chi-chien wang-lai tien-kao* (Hu Shih's cable correspondence during his period as ambassador to the United States). Beijing: Chung-kuo she-hui k'o-hsueh-yuan chin-tai-shih yen-chiu-so, 1978.

Huang Chun-tung [Wong Chun-tong]. *Hsien-tai Chung-kuo tso-chia chien-ying* (Profiles of modern Chinese writers). Hong Kong: Yu-lien, 1972.

Huang Mei-chen, ed. *Wang wei cheng-ch'uan tzu-liao hsuan-chi* (Selected materials on Wang's puppet regime). Shanghai: People's Press, 1984.

Hung Shen. *K'ang-chan shih-nien-lai Chung-kuo hua-chu yun-tung yu chiao-yu* (The Chinese drama movement and education over the past ten years during the War of Resistance). Shanghai? 1947?

Inoue Kiyoshi and Eto Shinkichi, eds. *Ni-chu senso to Ni-Chu kankai* (Sino-Japanese War and Sino-Japanese relations). Tokyo: Hara shobo, 1988.

Kan Kuo-hsuan. *Lan-i she, Fu-hsing she, Li-hsing she* (Blueshirt, Revival, and Vigorously Carrying-Out societies). Taipei: Biographical Literature Press, 1984.

Kuo Hua-lun. *Chung-kung shih lun* (Analytical history of the Chinese Communist party). 4 vols. Taipei: Institute of International Relations, 1969–71.

Lan Hai. *Chung-kuo k'ang-chan wen-i shih* (A history of Chinese literature during the War of Resistance). Shanghai, 1947; rev. ed., Tsinan, 1984.

Liu Tseng-chieh et al. *K'ang-Jih chan-cheng shih-ch'i Yen-an chi ho k'ang-Jih min-chu ken-chu-ti wen-hsueh yun-tung tzu-liao* (Materials on the literary movement in Yenan and all democratic resistance bases during the War of Resistance to Japan). 3 vols. Tai-yuan, 1983.

Mao Tse-tung. *Mo Takuto shu* (Collected works of Mao Tse-tung: Variorum edition), ed. Takeuchi Minoru. Tokyo: Hokubo-sha, 1970–72.

Ming Ch'uan, ed. *Feng Tzu-k'ai man-hua hsuan-i* (Interpretations of Feng Tzu-k'ai's selected cartoons). Hong Kong: Ts'un-i, 1976.

Nankai University, ed. *Chung-kuo k'ang-Jih ken-chu-ti shih kuo-chi hsueh-shu t'ao-lun hui lun-wen chi* (A collection of papers given at the international academic conference on the history of China's anti-Japanese resistance bases). Beijing: Archives Press, 1986.

Nieh Jung-chen. *Nieh Jung-chen hui-i lu* (Memoirs of Nieh Jung-chen). 3 vols. Beijing: Warriors Press, 1983.

P'eng Te-huai. *Wo ti tzu-shu* (An account of myself). Beijing: People's Press, 1981.

Shensi Sheng Kao-teng Yuan-hsiao Tzu-jan Pien-cheng-fa Yen-chiu-hui, Yen-an Ta-hsueh Fen Hui, ed. *Shen-Kan-Ning pien-ch'u tzu-jan pien-cheng-fa yen-chiu tzu-liao* (Research materials on the dialectics of nature in the Shen-Kan-Ning border region). Sian: Shensi jen-min ch'u-pan-she, 1984.

Ssu-fa yuan shih shih chi-yao (History of important events of the Judicial Yuan). 2 vols. Taipei: Judicial Yuan, 1982.

Ssu-ma Ch'ang-feng. *Chung-kuo hsin wen-hsueh shih* (A history of new Chinese literature). 3 vols. Hong Kong, 1978.

Sung Kuang-shu. *Lung Yun chuan* (Biography of Lung Yun). Chengtu: Szechwan Nationalities Press, n.d.

Ts'ao Chu-jen. *Wen-t'an wu-shih nien: hsu-chi* (Fifty years of the literary scene: A continuation). Hong Kong, 1973.

Wang Chi-pao. *Min-kuo ssu-fa chih* (The judicial record of the Republic). Taipei: Cheng Chung Press, 1954.

Wang Jen-yuan, comp. *Tung-yuan k'an-luan shih-ch'i ssu-fa hsing-cheng chi-yao* (A sketch of important affairs of judicial administration during the period of mobilization and suppression of rebellion). Taipei: Ministry of Judicial Administration, 1972.

Wen T'ien-hsing. *Kuo-t'ung ch'u k'ang-chan wen-i yun-tung ta-shih chi* (Chronology of major events of the literary movement during the War of Resistance in the Nationalist zone). Chengtu: Szechwan she-hui k'o-hsueh yuan, 1985.

Wu Heng, ed. *K'ang-Jih chan-cheng shih-ch'i chieh-fang ch'u k'o-hsueh chi-shu fa-chan shih tzu-liao*, (Historical materials on the development of science and technology in the liberated areas during the War of Resistance). 5 vols. Peking: Chung-kuo hsueh-shu ch'u-pan-she, 1983–85.

Wu Hsiang-hsiang. *Min-kuo cheng-chih jen-wu* (Political personalities of the Republic of China). 2 vols. Taipei: Biographical Literature Press, 1963, 1969.

Wu Hsueh-i. *Chan-shih min-shih li-fa* (Wartime civil legislation). Chungking: Commercial Press, 1944.

CHRONOLOGY

1931

September 18   September 18 Incident—Japan invades China's Northeast

1937

July 7   Lukouch'iao Incident—Outbreak of the Sino-Japanese War

July 15   CCP declaration on cooperation with KMT

July 28   Fall of Peiping

August   Sino-Soviet Mutual Nonaggression Treaty

September   Battle of P'inghsing Pass

November   Brussels Conference on the Sino-Japanese Conflict

November   Fall of Shanghai and Taiyuan

December   Rape of Nanking

1938

January   Death of Szechwan warlord Liu Hsiang

January 16   Prime Minister Konoe says Japan will no longer deal with Chiang Kai-shek

March–April   Extraordinary KMT Congress confers title of *tsung-ts' ai* on Chiang Kai-shek

March–April   Battle of Taierhchuang

April	CCP leader Chang Kuo-t'ao defects to KMT
June	Chinese government diverts Yellow River
July	Convocation of People's Political Council
September	Munich Conference
October 25	Fall of Wuhan
October	Japan seizes Canton
October– November	Sixth Plenum of Sixth CCP Central Committee
November	KMT leader Wang Ching-wei defects to Japan
November	Chinese wartime capital established at Chungking
December	U.S. Export-Import Bank $25 million loan to China

1939

February	Japanese seize Hainan Island
March 21	Failed KMT attempt to assassinate Wang Ching-wei
August	Soviet-German Nonaggression Pact

1940

January	Mao Tse-tung's essay "On New Democracy"
March 20	Wang Ching-wei's puppet government established in Nanking
July	Great Britain closes the Burma Road
August– December	Hundred Regiments Battle

1941

| January 5 | New Fourth Army Incident |

April	Soviet-Japanese Neutrality Treaty
December 7	Japanese attack Pearl Harbor
December 9	China declares war against Japan

1942

February 1	CCP launches *cheng-feng* (rectification) movement
March–June	First Burma campaign
May	Mao Tse-tung's "Talks at the Yenan Forum on Literature and Art"

1943

January 11	United States and Great Britain relinquish extraterritoriality in China
January	Publication of Chiang Kai-shek's *China's Destiny*
November	Cairo Conference—China joins the Big Five powers

1944

April–September	Operation Ichigo—Japan's last major military offensive in China
May–January 1945	Chinese victory in second Burma campaign
July	U.S. Army Observer Group ("Dixie Mission") in Yenan
November 9	Death of Wang Ching-wei in Japan

1945

April–June	Seventh Congress of the CCP
August 14	Sino-Soviet Treaty of Friendship and Alliance
September 2	Japan formally surrenders

WADE-GILES—PINYIN CONVERSION TABLE OF PERSONAL NAMES

Wade Giles / Pinyin

A Ying (Ch'ien Hsing-ts'un) / A Ying (Qian Xingcun)
Ai Ch'ing / Ai Qing
Ai Ssu-ch'i / Ai Siqi
Chang Ai-ling (Eileen Chang) / Zhang Ailing
Chang, Chun-mai (Carsun) / Zhang Junmai
Chang Ch'un / Zhang Qun
Chang Ch'ung / Zhang Chong
Chang Fa-k'uei / Zhang Fakui
Chang Hao / Zhang Hao
Chang Hsueh-liang / Zhang Xueliang
Chang Kia-ngau / Zhang Jiaao
Chang Kuang-yu / Zhang Guangyu
Chang Kuo-t'ao / Zhang Guotao
Chang Po-ling / Zhang Boling
Chang Tao-fan / Zhang Daofan
Chang Wen-t'ien (Lo Fu) / Zhang Wentian (Lo Fu)
Chao Fu-san / Zhao Fusan
Chao Shu-li / Zhao Shuli
Ch'en Ch'eng / Chen Cheng
Ch'en Ch'i-mei / Chen Qimei
Ch'en Chi-tang / Chen Jidang
Ch'en Chi-ying / Chen Jiying
Ch'en Ch'uan / Chen Quan
Ch'en Hsi-lien / Chen Xilian
Ch'en I / Chen Yi
Ch'en I-men / Chen Yimen
Ch'en Kuang-fu / Chen Guangfu
Ch'en Kung-po / Chen Gongbo
Ch'en Kung-shu / Chen Gongshu

Ch'en Kuo-fu / Chen Guofu
Ch'en Li-fu / Chen Lifu
Ch'en Ming-shu / Chen Mingshu
Ch'en Pai-ch'en / Chen Baichen
Ch'en Pi-chun / Chen Bijun
Ch'en Po-ta / Chen Boda
Ch'en Yun / Chen Yun
Cheng Chieh-min / Zheng Jiemin
Cheng Min / Zheng Min
Ch'eng Tien-fong / Cheng Tianfang
Cheng Yu-kwei / Zheng Yougui
Ch'i Hsieh-yuan / Qi Xieyuan
Chi Shen / Ji Shen
Chiang Kai-shek / Jiang Jieshi
Chiang T'ing-fu / Jiang Tingfu
Ch'ien Chung-shu / Qian Zhongshu
Ch'in Shou-ou / Qin Shouou
Chin Yung-p'eng / Jin Yongpeng
Ch'iu K'ai-chi / Qiu Kaiji
Chou En-lai / Zhou Enlai
Chou Fu / Zhou Fu
Chou Fu-hai / Chou Fuhai
Chou Tso-jen / Zhou Zuoren
Chou Yang / Zhou Yang
Chu Chi-ch'ing / Zhu Jiqing
Chu Chia-hua / Zhu Jiahua
Chu Chiu-hua / Zhu Jiuhua
Chu Jui / Zhu Rui
Ch'u Po-ch'uan / Chu Boquan
Chu Shih-ming / Zhu Shiming
Chu Teh / Zhu De
Feng Tzu-k'ai / Feng Zikai
Feng Yu-ch'i / Feng Yuqi
Feng Yü-hsiang / Feng Yuxiang
Fu Ping-chang / Fu Bingzhang
Han Fu-chu / Han Fuzhu
Han Te-ch'in / Han Deqin
Hao Ching-sheng / Hao Jingsheng
Ho Ching-chih / He Jingzhi
Ho Chung-huan / He Zhonghuan
Ho Ko-ch'uan (Kai Feng) / He Gequan
Ho Lien / He Lian
Ho Lu-chih / He Luzhi

Ho Lung/ He Long
Ho Yao-tsu / He Yaozu
Ho Ying-ch'in / He Yingqin
Hsia Yen / Xia Yan
Hsiang Ying /Xiang Ying
Hsiao Chun / Xiao Jun
Hsiao Hung / Xiao Hong
Hsiao K'o / Xiao Ke
Hsiao Li-tze / Xiao Lize
Hsiao Ting (Ting Ts'ung) / Xiao Ding (Ding Cong)
Hsiao Tsan-yu / Xiao Zanyu
Hsiung Shih-hui / Xiong Shihui
Hsu En-ch'eng / Xu Encheng
Hsu Hsiang-ch'ien / Xu Xiangqian
Hsu Hsu / Xu Xu
Hsu Pei-hung (Ju Peon) / Xu Beihong
Hsu T'e-li / Xu Teli
Hsuan Chieh-hsi / Xuan Jiexi
Hsueh Yao / Xue Yao
Hu Feng / Hu Feng
Hu Han-min / Hu Hanmin
Hu Hsien-su / Hu Xiansu
Hu Shih / Hu Shi
Hu Tsung-nan / Hu Zongnan
Huan-chu-lou chu (Li Shou-min) / Huanzhulou zhu (Li Shoumin)
Huang Ch'i-hsiang / Huang Qixiang
Hung Shen / Hong Shen
Jen Pi-shih / Ren Bishi
K'ang Sheng (Chao Jung) / Kang Sheng (Zhao Rong)
K'ang Tse / Kang Ze
K'ang Yu /Kang You
Kao Ping-fang / Gao Bingfang
Kao Tsung-wu / Gao Zongwu
Koo, V. K. Wellington / Gu Weijun
Ku Cheng-kang / Gu Zhenggang
Ku Chu-t'ung / Gu Zhutong
Ku Meng-yu / Gu Mengyu
Ku Yuan / Gu Yuan
Kuan Li-cheng / Guan Lizheng
Kuan Shan-yueh / Guan Shanyue
Kuei Yung-ch'ing / Gui Yongqing
Kung, H. H. / Kong Xiangxi
Kuo Mo-jo / Guo Moro

Lao She / Lao She
Li Chi-shen / Li Jishen
Li Ch'iang / Li Qiang
Li Fu-ch'un / Li Fuchun
Li Hua / Li Hua
Li Huang / Li Huang
Li K'o-nung / Li Kenong
Li Kuang-t'ien / Li Guangtian
Li Shan / Li Shan
Li Tsung-jen / Li Zongren
Li Wei-han / Li Weihan
Liang Hung-chih / Liang Hongzhi
Liang Shang-chun / Liang Shangjun
Liang Shih-ch'iu / Liang Shiqiu
Liang Shu-ming / Liang Shuming
Lin Piao / Lin Biao
Lin Po-ch'u / Lin Boqu
Lin Tsu-han / Lin Zuhan
Lin Yu-t'ang / Lin Yutang
Liu Chien-ch'un / Liu Jianchun
Liu Hsiang / Liu Xiang
Liu Pai-yu / Liu Baiyu
Liu Po-ch'eng / Liu Bocheng
Liu Shao-ch'i / Liu Shaoqi
Liu Wen-hui / Liu Wenhui
Lo T'ien-yu / Luo Tianyou
Lu Han / Lu Han
Lu Hsun / Lu Xun
Lu Ling / Lu Ling
Lu Yu-tao / Lu Yudao
Lung Yun / Long Yun
Ma Hsi-wu / Ma Xiwu
Ma K'o / Ma Ke
Ma Yin-ch'u / Ma Yinchu
Mao Tse-tung / Mao Zedong
Mao Tun / Mao Dun
Mei Ssu-p'ing / Mei Siping
Nieh Erh / Nie Er
Nieh Jung-chen / Nie Rongzhen
Pa Chin (Li Fei-kan) / Ba Jin (Li Feigan)
Pai Ch'ung-hsi / Bai Chongxi
P'an Kung-chan / Pan Gongzhan
P'an Wen-hua / Pan Wenhua

P'eng Chen / Peng Zhen
P'eng Te-huai / Peng Dehuai
Po I-po / Bo Yibo
Po Ku (Ch'in Pang-hsien) / Bo Gu (Qin Bangxian)
Pu Ning (Wu-ming shih) / Bu Ning (Wuming shi)
Sha T'ing / Sha Ting
Shen Hung-chieh / Shen Hongjie
Shen Ts'ung-wen / Shen Congwen
Soong Ch'ing-ling / Song Qingling
Soong Mei-ling / Song Meiling
Soong, T. V. / Song Ziwen
Su Ti-min / Su Dimin
Su Wen (Tai K'o-ch'ung) / Su Wen (Dai Kechong)
Sun Fo / Sun Fo
Sun Yat-sen (Sun Chung-shan) / Sun Zhongshan
Sun Yun-hsuan (Y. S. Sun) / Sun Yunxuan
Sung Chih-ti / Song Zhidi
Tai Chi-t'ao / Dai Jitao
Tai Li / Dai Li
T'ang En-po / Tang Enbo
T'ang Erh-ho / Tang Erhe
T'ang Hsi-shan / Tang Xishan
T'ang Shao-i / Tang Shaoyi
T'ang Shih-tsun / Tang Shicun
T'ang Yung / Tang Yong
T'ao Hsi-sheng / Tao Xisheng
T'eng Chieh / Teng Jie
Teng Fa / Deng Fa
Teng Wen-i / Deng Wenyi
T'ien Chien / Tian Jian
T'ien Han / Tian Han
Ting Ling (Chiang Ping-chih) / Ding Ling (Jiang Bingzhi)
Ting Wen-chiang / Ding Wenjiang
Ts'ai Ti-chih / Cai Dizhi
Ts'ao Ju-lin / Cao Rulin
Ts'ao K'un / Cao Kun
Ts'ao Yu (Wan Chia-po) / Cao Yu (Wan Jiabo)
Tseng Ch'i / Zeng Qi
Tseng Chung-ming / Zeng Zhongming
Tso Shun-sheng / Zuo Shunsheng
Tu Yu-ming / Tu Yuming
Tuan Ch'i-jui / Duan Qirui
Tuan-mu Hung-liang / Duanmu Hongliang

Tung Tao-ning / Dong Daoning
Wang Cheng-t'ing / Wang Zhengting
Wang Chia-hsiang / Wang Jiaxiang
Wang Ching-wei / Wang Jingwei
Wang Ch'ung-hui / Wang Chonghui
Wang Fa-ch'in / Wang Faqin
Wang I-t'ang / Wang Yitang
Wang I-t'ing / Wang Yiting
Wang K'o-min / Wang Kemin
Wang Lan / Wang Lan
Wang Leh-p'ing / Wang Leping
Wang Ming (Ch'en Shao-yu) / Wang Ming (Chen Shaoyu)
Wang Nai-kuei / Wang Naigui
Wang Shih-wei / Wang Shiwei
Wang Yin-t'ai / Wang Yintai
Wei Li-huang / Wei Lihuang
Wei Tao-ming / Wei Daoming
Weng Wen-hao / Weng Wenhao
Wu I-fang / Wu Yifang
Wu Kai-hsien / Wu Gaixian
Wu P'ei-fu / Wu Peifu
Wu Ting-ch'ang / Wu Dingchang
Wu Tsu-hsiang / Wu Zuxiang
Wu Tsu-kuang / Wu Zuguang
Yang Chieh / Yang Jie
Yang Shang-k'un / Yang Shangkun
Yang Yung-t'ai / Yang Yongtai
Yao Hsueh-yin / Yao Xueyin
Yao K'o (Yao Hsin-nung) / Yao Ke (Yao Xinnong)
Yeh Chien-ying / Ye Jianying
Yeh Hsiu-feng / Ye Xiufeng
Yeh Sheng-t'ao / Ye Shengtao
Yeh T'ing / Ye Ting
Yen Hsi-shan / Yan Xishan
Yin Hsueh-man / Yin Xueman
Yu Han-mou / Yu Hanmou
Yu Ling / You Ling
Yuan Han-ch'ing / Yuan Hanqing
Yuan Shih-k'ai / Yuan Shikai

INDEX